MODERNISM, AESTHETICS AND ANTHROPOLOGY

John Hoffmann argues that a combination of aesthetics and anthropology allowed modernist writers to challenge social hierarchies they associated with the nineteenth century. He shows how Enlightenment philosophers synthesized the two discourses and how modernists working in the early twentieth century then took up this synthesis to dispute categories of social difference that had been naturalized, and thus legitimized, by pre-evolutionary and Darwinian anthropological theories. The book brings a range of new insights to major topics in modernist studies, revealing neglected continental sources for Irish anti-colonialism, the aesthetic contours of Zionism in the era of Mandatory Palestine and the influence of German idealism on critiques of racism following World War I. Working over a long historical *durée*, Hoffmann surveys the ways aesthetics has been used, and misused, to construct and contest social hierarchies grounded in anthropological distinctions.

JOHN HOFFMANN is Visiting Assistant Professor of Literature and the Humanities at Chapman University.

MODERNISM, AESTHETICS AND ANTHROPOLOGY

JOHN HOFFMANN

Chapman University

CAMBRIDGE
UNIVERSITY PRESS

Shaftesbury Road, Cambridge CB2 8EA, United Kingdom

One Liberty Plaza, 20th Floor, New York, NY 10006, USA

477 Williamstown Road, Port Melbourne, VIC 3207, Australia

314–321, 3rd Floor, Plot 3, Splendor Forum, Jasola District Centre, New Delhi – 110025, India

103 Penang Road, #05–06/07, Visioncrest Commercial, Singapore 238467

Cambridge University Press is part of Cambridge University Press & Assessment, a department of the University of Cambridge.

We share the University's mission to contribute to society through the pursuit of education, learning and research at the highest international levels of excellence.

www.cambridge.org
Information on this title: www.cambridge.org/9781009474474

DOI: 10.1017/9781009474498

When citing this work, please include a reference to the DOI 10.1017/9781009474498

First published 2025

A catalogue record for this publication is available from the British Library

A Cataloging-in-Publication data record for this book is available from the Library of Congress

ISBN 978-1-009-47447-4 Hardback

Contents

Acknowledgments

This book owes its existence to conversations with colleagues and friends over what is now, looking back, a long stretch of my life. During my time in the English department at Johns Hopkins University, Mark Thompson was an invaluable supporter who nurtured this project in its earliest stages. Mary Favret provided endless wisdom, and her keen eye for the whole brought order to my argument when it was still messy and inchoate. At various points, I also benefited from the insights of Anne Eakin-Moss, Eckart Förster, Peter Jelavich, Pat Kain, Katrin Pahl and Eric Sundquist. I hope I can continue to learn from the lessons these scholars have taught me. For their kindness and care, I feel immense gratitude to my Baltimore friends Robert Carson, Kate Eaton, Pat Giamario, Roger Maioli, Ro Nicolosi and Marina Nikhinson.

During my years in Germany, my colleagues at the Institute for Media Studies in Marburg welcomed me into the fold of the German academy, and finding my place in Germany was made easier by Marianna Fumarola, Friedhelm Schöck and members of Marburg's local Italian conversation group. Over a summer in Santa Fe, Kenneth Wolfe kept my paradigms sharp with lively games of Ancient Greek Scrabble and was kind enough to discuss my translations of Aristotle. More recently, Katharine Gillespie and Michael Valdez Moses have become close friends and inspiring interlocutors. Their uncompromising intellectual integrity does not diminish their sense of humor. I am glad for both.

An early version of Chapter 1 appeared as "Kant's Aesthetic Categories: Race in the *Critique of Judgment*" in *Diacritics* 44.2 (2016), 54–81. Portions of Chapter 6 were published in *New Literary History* 51.3 (2020), 587–614 under the title "The *Volk* against Fascism: Socialist Realism and the Aesthetics of Expressionism." For grants that allowed me to undertake research for parts of this book, I would like to acknowledge the Leonard and Helen R. Stulman Program in Jewish Studies at

Johns Hopkins, the Max Kade Center for Modern German Thought and the Denis family, who sponsored a fellowship for research at the Sheridan Libraries Special Collections.

My greatest debt is to Douglas Mao, a man whose brilliance is matched only by his generosity.

Introduction

Having accepted an editorship at *Science* after research trips to Baffinland and the Pacific Northwest, the young Franz Boas, not yet the eminence he would become, penned an essay laying out the theoretical conclusions he had drawn following his time in the field. Though ostensibly concerned with geography – Boas had trained as a geographer – the essay addresses methodological problems that would later shape the discipline of cultural anthropology, which coalesced under Boas's leadership in the early decades of the twentieth century.[1] The argument of "The Study of Geography" rests on a central gambit: a categorical distinction between two approaches to scientific inquiry: *aesthetic* and *affective*. On the one hand, aesthetic observers privilege a clear and distinct ordering of elements in a system governed by laws; on the other, affective investigators attend to the unique character of particular specimens. Thus where aesthetic science seeks to dispel obscurity and confusion by furnishing coherent arrangements of objects, affective inquiry illuminates the nature of individuals conceived as complex wholes in themselves.

A scientist pursuing aesthetic ends, while committed to organizing phenomena, does not collect masses of data into arbitrary groupings like a child gathering sand on the beach. A particular kind of order is implied in these arrangements. Fashioning an ordered structure fulfills "our aesthetical desire to bring the confusion of forms and species into a system," Boas asserts.[2] So forms and species are the constituent parts of nature conceived as a law-governed totality. From this it follows that individuals cannot be considered in isolation. Any particular case is only "a specimen of the class" that counts as the true categorial unit of an aesthetic arrangement. Therefore when an aesthetic scientist beholds natural phenomena, "he sees only the beautiful order of the world" – a world that is beautiful *because* it is ordered, and more precisely, ordered in terms of forms and species.[3]

What constitutes a form and how those forms contribute to species distinctions will be topics of considerable importance in this book, which takes a long view on the aesthetic and affective orientations by situating them with respect to their sources in eighteenth-century anthropology. For as idiosyncratic as Boas's conception of an aesthetic science may seem – few scientists would likely describe their work as part of an aesthetic enterprise – it is not an unprecedented model for the scientific method. Arguing along the same lines, Immanuel Kant maintained that a "discernible order" inheres in the "heterogeneity of natural forms," which manifest their "lawful unity" in a distinct arrangement of species: "a subordination of species and kinds" into a taxonomical hierarchy.[4] Hence the order of the natural world that Kant envisions in *The Critique of the Power of Judgment*, surely the most influential treatise in the history of aesthetics, consists in "a connection of things according to their species," where those species are subordinated to higher-order taxa within a hierarchical structure.[5] To be sure, Kant was not the first philosopher to claim that nature was an ordered whole; nor was he the only naturalist to classify organisms. He did, however, give a uniquely rigorous exposition of those positions by conjoining aesthetics and natural philosophy in the third *Critique* – a book that famously pairs a theory of beauty in its first half with a theory of nature in its second. Boas, for his part, was well versed in this Kantian aesthetics of nature. During his time as a student in Heidelberg, he had eagerly attended the aesthetics lectures held by Kuno Fischer, one of the most prominent Kantians of the day; and in "The Study of Geography," Boas acknowledges Kant for his contributions to natural philosophy.[6]

Forms and species, hierarchies and wholes – these are the conceptual underpinnings of a Kantian-Boasian aesthetics of nature. Thus the pleasure a scientist takes in apprehending the natural world in all its intricate, hierarchical connections is analogous to the satisfaction derived from contemplating a well-made work of art. The practical stakes of this theory of nature become evident once we recognize that during the eighteenth century, natural philosophers increasingly began referring to classificatory distinctions within the human species as "races." This development, whose repercussions are still being felt by members of those putative classes, is implied by the logic of taxonomy. If a single genus contains multiple species, then a particular species, it stands to reason, may contain different races – an inference that involves descending the taxonomical ladder from genus to species to subspecies and then delineating classes at a lower ordinal level. At least that was how Kant viewed the matter.[7] And while it is true that Kantian anthropology was disputed by contemporaries, it was only in the twentieth century, not least through the efforts of Boas, that the old taxonomical hierarchy was discredited and replaced by other theoretical arrangements for organizing individual humans into anthropological wholes.

This excursus illustrates the two main claims that will be made in the present book: first, that Enlightenment philosophers synthesized aesthetics and anthropology in an effort to envision well-ordered totalities, both natural and social, whose relevance for our current moment has lost none of its force; and second, that writers in the first half of the twentieth century took up this synthesis in order to challenge schemata of social differences that had been naturalized, and thus legitimized, by earlier anthropological theories. Substantiating these claims will require making arguments that run along parallel trajectories, leading from the high Enlightenment to the crisis of humanist values associated with World War II – from the racialized aesthetics of Kant, credited alongside Johann Gottfried Herder with the "birth of anthropology," to twentieth-century critics of the race concept such as W. E. B. Du Bois and Ruth Benedict; from Romantic theories of the nation to anticolonial nationalists such as W. B. Yeats; from eighteenth-century notions of the *Volk* to fascist appropriations of popular culture and the left populism of German Marxists.[8] Taken together, these parts of the argument advance the larger thesis that aesthetics has been a necessary ideological component for constructing as well as contesting social hierarchies grounded in anthropological distinctions.

* * *

Even though Boas will recede into something of a minor character in the story this book intends to tell, the distinction he drew between aesthetic and affective orientations serves as a useful heuristic device for introducing the principal arguments. To begin with, an aesthetics of nature that arrays individuals in coherent, law-governed wholes aligns its claims along theoretical axes different than those of recent defenses of aesthetics, which have sought to rehabilitate the discipline after decades of withering critique. The most persistent charge leveled against aesthetic theory has been that it obfuscates class- or status-based preferences by positing universal canons of taste.[9] On this account, aesthetic preferences reflect definite constellations of economic or political power, which furnish the real means for critics to understand evaluations of art and beauty. Hence claims to disinterested judgment, though they pretend to objectivity, are shown to conceal and thereby reinforce the very particular interests of certain social groups at the expense of others. While aesthetics was hardly the only branch of human inquiry to be subjected to this kind of ideology critique, it did make an exceptionally large target. Traditionally, theories of aesthetic experience have been concerned with concepts like taste and beauty, which strike many as being inescapably subjective if not altogether personal. Those theories would therefore seem especially susceptible to admitting ideological biases that would compromise their claims to generality.

Instead of questioning the premises or conclusions of ideology critique, recent apologists for aesthetics have more often tried to turn the tables on their critics, insisting that other aesthetic concepts such as autonomy or play entail a progressive, even radical politics that points the way to a fairer, freer or more equitable society.[10] This new and avowedly politicized remit for aesthetic theory, whereby the discourse subverts rather than consolidates social distinctions, has transformed the concept of judgment into an analytical tool for addressing the operations of contemporary capitalism and the character of postmodern society. To take one influential example, Sianne Ngai has argued that an aesthetic spectator, when presented with a work of art, experiences a feeling of pleasure that in turn licenses a judgment of taste: *that painting is beautiful*, for instance. By elucidating the structures of feeling underlying those judgments and studying the ways they are communicated in public discourse, Ngai suggests, critics may offer insights into a postmodern commodity culture where the market reduces all individual differences to matters of personal taste.[11] But if Ngai thinks that scrutinizing aesthetic judgments may explain the cultural implications of capitalism, then Michael Clune has made a more polemical case, arguing that judgments of taste provide a way of escaping the logic of the marketplace. In staking a claim about the actual merit of an artwork, not its ability to afford pleasure to a judging subject, critics repudiate an evaluative calculus that conceives of choices as equal expressions of personal preference. For Clune, this repudiation conduces to an aesthetic education that opens up spheres of value irreducible to the egalitarian norms of the market.[12]

Whether aesthetics explains, rejects or, to broach a third possibility, contributes to an "aestheticization of politics" that only compounds the problems of modern capitalism, a Kantian-Boasian aesthetics construes judgment in terms more general than these politicized theories of taste. According to the Kantian model, judgment is a cognitive procedure that mediates between a particular phenomenon and a general rule, law or principle. So, for example, if our hypothetical aesthetic scientist were to come across an organism in the field and wished to place it in a taxonomical category, a judgment would have to link particular and general: *that individual organism belongs to this general species*. Likewise, assigning a unique human to a subspecies will necessitate making a judgment: *that person belongs to this race*. What is more, and this is the truly decisive point, if those individual categories are to combine into a taxonomical hierarchy, then ascending from a single species to superordin-ate genera and then to the totality of nature will mean executing judgments that connect particular classes to nature as a whole. Otherwise the various species would make up a random, discontinuous aggregate of classes instead of parts belonging to a coherent, law-governed system. Although judgments of species do not necessarily yield a feeling of pleasure – reflecting on the form of an organism and judging that it belongs to the species *Canis familiaris* is not, or at least not necessarily, the spark for an emotional response – pleasure is not ruled out by a Kantian-Boasian aesthetics. Boas felt that contemplating a lawfully ordered world satisfies an aesthetic desire. Kant, writing a century earlier, stated in no uncertain terms that perceiving the rational unity of natural laws "is the ground of a very noticeable pleasure, often even of admiration."[13]

Grasping how this aesthetics of nature permits the construction and contestation of taxonomical species is the task for the first three chapters of this book, which proceed from Enlightenment anthropology to its twentieth-century critics. Even as these chapters cover a considerable historical distance, they grapple with a common stance, stated succinctly in the third *Critique*, regarding the nature of anthropological categories: assigning an individual to a species or subspecies requires a concept of "*what kind of thing it ought to be* [was es für ein Ding sein solle]."[14] For example, a concept of what kind of thing a human ought to be specifies the essential characteristics for a class, which particular specimens may possess in varying degrees or not at all. Ought a human be rational or passionate? Ought humanness instead be based on physiological criteria? In either case, a determination of what kind of thing a human ought to be – in short, an ideal – defines the essence of the class and permits the designation of real individuals as members: this specimen belongs to the human species because it possesses attributes epitomized by the ideal. Then, with those attributes determined, hierarchical distinctions follow as a matter of course. One specimen is more human than another because it evinces essential characteristics in a greater degree. Aesthetics, as opposed to ethics, which typically treats questions of how humans ought to act, will serve as the primary source for these concepts of what kind of thing the modern *anthropos* ought to be. For historically it has been the case that aesthetics is the discourse where debates about form, especially the form of the human body, have intersected with ideals of taxonomical species in order to justify hierarchies of ontological value – hierarchies that impute a greater worth to a particular being or group of beings than to others.

Once normativity is introduced into a theory of nature – once "ought" is combined with "is" – the ambit of that theory can no longer be confined to nature as such, since ideals are human creations that reflect the values of their creators. Thus the question of what constitutes a taxonomical unit – be it a subspecies, species or, as we will see, a gender – is perforce a social question that weaves together fact and value, is and ought, in ways that make those components difficult to separate. Further, when that entanglement occurs in societies shaped by histories of oppression, the consequences are especially fraught inasmuch as ideological pressures distort ideals, together with the facts and values that subtend them, for the sake of factional interests. Showing how those histories have inflected ideas of the human in Black Studies and its allied fields, Alexander G. Weheliye has recently made the case that "sociopolitical processes of differentiation and hierarchization" have divided "humanity into full humans, not-quite-humans, and nonhumans."[15] On this account, humanity is a hierarchically ordered whole duly organized by distinctions of kind and degree. As a result, Weheliye concludes, "we might do well to conceive humanity as a relational ontological totality, however fractured this totality might be."[16] Throughout his analysis, Weheliye is careful to maintain a critical stance toward natural or cultural taxonomies that designate humans as members of essentially different subspecies. At the same time, his model for arranging elements into a systematic social totality relies on principles of the Kantian-Boasian paradigm that made those taxonomies possible. Judgments will have to assign individuals to general categories – fully human, partially human or not human at all – just as evaluating more or less representative humans will mean applying a standard to measure the relative completeness or perfection of particular instances of humankind. In effect, Weheliye's intervention reframes the problem so that the category "humanity" is conceived as a social construct instead of a natural truth. Significant as this shift from natural to social species may be, the mechanisms of aesthetic judgment responsible for organizing individuals and groups into a hierarchical whole are still operative. Another recent example of considerable influence illustrates this point. Frank B. Wilderson III has garnered much attention for claiming that society arrays individuals into *two species: Blacks and Humans.*"[17] In Wilderson's bracing rhetoric, society is organized such that "Blacks are the sentient beings *against which Humanity is defined.*"[18] For both of these scholars, forms and species, hierarchies and wholes remain the conceptual tools for comprehending the place of humanity in the social cosmos.

Even as these recent accounts of well-defined, hierarchical social systems recall the aesthetic science outlined in "The Study of Geography," they also hearken back to a canonical critique of regimes of racial exclusion that continues to provide lessons for our current cultural dilemmas: Franz Fanon's *Les damnés de la terre*, which illustrates with trenchancy how the dogmatic capacity of aesthetic anthropology to construct arrangements of social species interacts with its critical potential to upend them. The second sentence of Fanon's opening essay, "De la violence," lays out the practical task for opponents of colonialism in surprisingly familiar terms: "decolonization is very simply the replacement of one 'species' of humans ['*espèce' d'hommes*] by another 'species' of humans."[19] So decolonization contests the given order of things by rearranging a conventional hierarchy, substituting a particular class of humans, the colonized, for the traditional holders of power, the colonizers. Yet the monitory quotations surrounding *espèce* indicate that even if distinctions generated by the colonial situation appear to rise to the level of a taxonomical category, they are nothing of the kind. Social species are fabricated rather than natural, contingent rather than necessary, which is why one species may replace another in the theater of political conflict. But for all their subversive potential, social species are not only instrumental in challenging the colonial system. They touch the heart of the system itself: "When one sees the colonial context in its immediacy," Fanon goes on to comment, "it is clear that that which divides the world is above all the fact of belonging to a certain species, a certain race [*à telle espèce, à telle race*]."[20] No less than the aesthetic science posited by Boas, an individual in the colonial system is not an end in itself but a "specimen of the class" to which it belongs. Decolonization then overthrows that system, that parceling out of the world into parts, by inverting the order of its elements. A chief aim of the present book is to show how this dual process of construction and contestation, described by Fanon for the Francophone context, extends over a long *durée* and in a wide range of geographical settings. In opposition to influential efforts to decouple aesthetics and especially aesthetic form from history, the arguments that follow insist that the formal and aesthetic dimensions of key cultural dynamics in the twentieth century, decolonization among them, cannot be understood without coming to terms with the ideological legacies, and by implication the concrete historical and material conditions that were their cause, that descend from the eighteenth and nineteenth centuries to the decades that witnessed the emergence, flourishing and incipient decline of high modernism.[21]

But whatever the theoretical grounds for an aesthetic anthropology that organizes species and subspecies into a coherent whole, transforming ideals into a real political system is not achieved by fiat or force of persuasion alone. As the title of Fanon's essay makes clear, acts of violence both direct and more subtle impose those distinctions of kind and degree. Later in "De la violence," Fanon explains:

> in societies of the capitalist type, the education system, whether religious or lay, the formation of the moral reflexes transmittable from father to son, the exemplary honesty of workers decorated after fifty years of good and loyal service, the love encouraged by harmony and wisdom, these aesthetic forms of respect for the established order [*ces formes esthétiques du respect de l'ordre établi*], create around the exploited person an atmosphere of submission and inhibition that lightens considerably the task of the forces of order.[22]

In capitalist societies, or at least those that conform to type, certain "aesthetic forms" are the very pith and substance of the ideological apparatuses that enforce the established order. Real patterns of thought and action, these forms encompass moral responses and intellectual norms, intersubjective behavior along with affective habits. As such, aesthetic forms materially ease the burden borne by the "forces of order" since they inculcate values and attitudes that aid the regime in its functioning. Thus in Fanon's view, aesthetic form is plainly complicit in establishing an order of political violence. Yet the manner of its complicity is quite unlike the political theory of Jacques Rancière, probably the most vocal advocate in recent years for restoring an aesthetic dimension to politics. According to Rancière, distinct configurations of visibility or "divisions of the sensible" authorize modes of political subjectivity and possibilities for sensory experience. Disruptions to those divisions then enact an egalitarian redistribution of sensory parts, producing alternative relationships of political community that correspond to a different spectrum of sensations, an aesthetics of politics rooted in the classical signification of *aisthesis*: the general content of sensory experience (αἴσθησις).[23]

At various points in this study, we will have occasion to scrutinize this association between modern politics and classical αἴσθησις, since Rancière was certainly not the first to make the connection. For instance, in a prelude to a debate held in 2009 at the Institut für Sozialforschung in Frankfurt, Axel Honneth pointed out that Rancière seems to be trying to recuperate for progressive ends Walter Benjamin's famous claim that fascism aestheticizes politics – a claim that Benjamin also anchored in the classical sense of αἴσθησις.[24] In later chapters, analyzing the relationship between aesthetics and the anthropological imaginary of twentieth-century fascism will provide ample opportunity for examining these issues in detail. For now, we might remain with Fanon in order to recognize that the aesthetic forms cited in *Les damnés* – love, honesty, wisdom, respect – cannot be reduced to αἴσθησις, as they entail normative and conceptual determinations in addition to sensory content. Furthermore, in the anthropological tradition descending from Kant to Boas (an Enlightenment rather than classical tradition that nevertheless reaches into the period that coincided with high modernism), aesthetics is not a proxy for visibility or sensory experience but a discourse that arranges individuals into general categories and determines their attributes according to ideals of ontological value. Keeping these conceptions of aesthetics in mind, it is entirely fitting that Fanon concludes "De la violence" by calling for a "reintroduction of the human in the world, the total human" that might make a legitimate claim to universality.[25] Indeed, he chooses to end *Les damnés* as a whole with the peroration: "For Europe, for ourselves and for humanity, comrades, it is necessary to show a new face, to develop a new idea, to try to set on his feet a new human [*il faut faire peau neuve, développer une pensée neuve, tenter de mettre sur pied un homme neuf*]."[26] It is necessary, in other words, to make a new concept of what kind of thing a human ought to be.

Therefore if decolonization consists in substituting one class of humans for another, then Fanon himself embraces a broader set of measures for contesting the order of species established by colonialism and the aesthetic forms that are marshaled to enforce it. To that end, he augments his call for a new human by criticizing the concept of race at a later stage of *Les damnés*, taking issue with its tendency, among others, to aggregate diverse groups with divergent political interests under a single abstract heading.[27] In place of the race concept, Fanon proposes other anthropological concepts that, notwithstanding their own limitations, might stand a better chance of advancing salutary political aims: *people, nation, culture*. Tracing the links between aesthetic theory and this conceptual cluster makes up the core of Chapters 4–6 of this book, which proceed from the Herderian critique of Kant to postcolonial Ireland and antifascist theorists affiliated with the Popular Front. And in thus moving away from arrangements of species and subspecies to the concept of a people – or rather, a *Volk* – we gain distance from an aesthetic science that ranks individuals in a law-governed system. This is because in the canonical formulation offered by Herder that was later modified and modernized by Boas, a people or culture is defined primarily through internal structures and attributes – thoughts, feelings, language – that are not immediately identifiable with the external, physiological signs that were traditionally used to sort individuals into natural taxonomies. Therefore departing from forms and species arranged into hierarchies brings us closer to the affective impulse outlined in "The Study of Geography." It is appropriate, then, to bring these introductory remarks to a close by returning to Boas's essay and the affective science that, as it happens, approximates with much greater fidelity the tenets of cultural anthropology than the aesthetic science that has occupied us thus far.

Where the aesthetic orientation organizes specimens into a taxonomical system, affective inquiry eschews forms, species and hierarchies in favor of treating the individual as a whole in itself. Grounded in a subjective relationship between observer and phenomena, "the personal feeling of man towards the world," affective inquiry leaves off from ordering objects in a coherent structure. Instead, "the mere occurrence of an event claims the full attention of our mind," Boas states, "because we are affected by it, and it is studied without any regard to its place in a system."[28] In line with these axioms, a phenomenon will not be analyzed into its elements because a singular entity already qualifies as the basic unit of investigation. Nor are phenomena subsumed to general laws since the particular history of an event or entity furnishes the material for explaining its nature. In short, pivoting from the aesthetic to the affective impulse involves a thorough-going reorientation of scientific inquiry from general to specific. No longer specimens of the class to which they belong, individuals are unique beings, each possessing a distinct character.

At bottom, aesthetic science is an exercise in system building; when applied consistently, it abstracts from, and thus deliberately neglects, the particularity of parts for the sake of subordinating them to the whole. Affective inquiry, by contrast, courts the risk of devolving into granular empiricism – at least that was a criticism frequently leveled against Boasian cultural anthropology. Yet it would be an error to consign affective inquiry to the mere cataloguing of particular phenomena; for affective science, as Boas originally envisioned it, "is closely related to the arts, as the way in which the mind is affected by phenomena forms an important branch of the study."[29] That is to say, affective inquiry fosters a sensitive receptivity to the world. The psychology of the observer will therefore influence the character of the observations. Hence the affective scientist, "in treating these subjects, approaches the domain of art, as the results of his study principally affect the feeling, and therefore must be described in an artistic way."[30] Like a poet dwelling with a mood or a painter before a landscape, the affective scientist is affected by individual phenomena and moved to a response. In truth, however, the most apposite analogue for the affective scientist is not the artist, who must necessarily arrange elements into a whole in the act of creation, but rather the critic, who beholds a singular phenomenon, an artwork, and proceeds to describe, interpret and explain it for the sake of understanding.

Thus what Boas viewed as two antithetical approaches, the aesthetic and the affective, are in fact two distinct ways of applying an aesthetic method to the world. Of course, affective inquiry has little in common with the abstract organization of objects into a system of laws (aesthetic science in the narrow sense outlined earlier). But affective inquiry is aesthetic nonetheless: Comprehending phenomena and doing justice to their character means regarding natural or cultural phenomena as though they were works of art. The scientist thereby engages with the world like a discerning critic who must relate observations in a manner that is suitable for the subject, namely, in an artful manner. The discourse of aesthetics therefore points in two directions: to principles of ordering, organization and distinctions of kind and degree; or to an embodied, felt engagement with the singularity of the world. It falls to the individual chapters to follow out the anthropological ramifications of this aesthetic ambivalence.

* * *

The first chapter reassesses Kantian anthropology in an effort to correct a tendency, common in Kant scholarship and in broader cultural debates, to view Enlightenment race theory solely through the lens of moral or political philosophy. Keeping the practical stakes firmly in the frame, the chapter shifts our understanding of Kant's anthropology away from a moral register and toward an aesthetic one, arguing that *The Critique of Judgment* predicates the perfection of racialized bodies on their conformity to an ideal form or "shape [*Gestalt*]." These shapes act as templates for sorting individuals into taxonomical classes; and Kant's reasoning for employing those aesthetic shapes to define anthropological categories is treated in terms of the larger critical undertaking begun in *The Critique of Pure Reason* and completed in the third *Critique*. Even as the chapter performs a fairly focused reading of Kant, it addresses more general questions of the period: Have humans descended from a common stock or independent sources? Is the empirical variability of human appearance the product of heredity or environment? What are the defining marks of human sameness and difference? Kant's answers to these questions, at once representative of his day and strikingly original in their proffered solutions, constitute highly condensed philosophical treatments of core problems faced by theorists of human nature at the time.

Chapter 2 records the spread of an idealist aesthetic anthropology from Kant through European natural philosophy of the nineteenth century, especially Goethe, to popular anthropological works published in Victorian Britain and the American Civil War. Grounded in examination of archival materials, the chapter adduces a textual link between two influential, though largely forgotten, pieces of propaganda: *Beauty; Illustrated Chiefly by an Analysis and Classification of Beauty in Woman* (1836) by the Scottish anatomist Alexander Walker and *Miscegenation* (1864), an invidious pamphlet that pretended to promote interracial marriage in order to incite an antiabolitionist response. Translating high Kantian theory into a more quotidian, though no less potent, ideological register, *Miscegenation* and *Beauty* adapt anthropological classifications in order to circumscribe categories of race and gender. Black, white, male, female and mixed-race types epitomize species of physiological perfection. Therefore instead of conjuring a single ideal of beauty, these texts present a plurality of aesthetic ideals; and rather than reinforce the privileged theoretical status of a single perfect human, usually a white European male, they demonstrate the ideological flexibility of aesthetic anthropology and its grim efficacy when placed in the service of political ends.

The third chapter carries on into the twentieth century, arguing that Du Bois marshaled post-Kantian idealism against the taxonomical categories he inherited from Enlightenment anthropologists. The chapter departs from the standard interpretation of Du Bois as a champion of integration and a critic of the separatist nationalism advocated by Marcus Garvey. This interpretation, which relies heavily on *The Souls of Black Folk* at the expense of Du Bois's later Marxism, downplays his controversial advocacy for the self-segregation of African-American communities, an initiative that sought to capitalize on racial solidarity in order to rectify the class conflict dividing American society. Taking stock of Du Bois's legacy, Kenneth W. Warren has argued that the program for self-segregation was an impetus for a strain of particularist thought in African-American letters, which Warren tends to see as getting in the way of recognizing how economic forces drive historical change and social constitution in the wake of Jim Crow.[31] In the case of Du Bois, though, self-segregated collectives were neither a flight from economic reality nor a fetishized state of nature prior to capitalism but an indispensable weapon against precisely the material conditions that perpetuate racial injustice. Intended as spheres of free action carved out from both capitalist modes of production and predominately white social structures, these collectives, the chapter shows, evince the aesthetic autonomy theorized by the most important aesthetician working in an immediately post-Kantian vein, Friedrich Schiller, whom Du Bois admired and quoted in *Souls*. Moreover, attending to aesthetic autonomy brings to light new connections between Du Bois and cultural anthropology, another discourse commonly associated with integration. Looking past the more familiar links between Du Bois and Boas, the chapter takes up Ruth Benedict's theory of cultural patterning, which Du Bois knew, a theory that construes the ethnic specificity of Native American tribes by making a similar appeal to Schillerian autonomy. For Du Bois and Benedict, then, aesthetic arguments advance the claims of anthropological communities that need not integrate with a dominant and often hostile social milieu.

The first three chapters move from a canonical articulation of aesthetic anthropology in Kant to later instances of racialized aesthetics directly influenced by a Kantian paradigm. Each in their own way, these chapters demonstrate how a common aesthetic idiom furnished concepts for crafting categories of humankind – a neoclassical idiom grounded in notions of perfection, ideals of physiological beauty and more abstract principles such as "unity amid diversity." Associating Kantian aesthetic anthropologies with neoclassicism cuts across the usual reception of Kant, who is known for refuting the rationalist theories of judgment that undergirded neoclassical canons of taste. Likewise, a later figure such as Du Bois typically falls outside the neoclassical fold, being more frequently linked to the discourse of the sublime and folk nationalisms that align with Romanticism rather than neoclassicism. Part I reveals that the rise of so-called Romantic science in the early nineteenth century – another Kantian legacy – did not sweep aside neoclassical principles but generated unorthodox neoclassicisms that then provided the means for contriving categories of humankind. Whether by idealizing particular kinds of humans or uniting perfection with freedom, these hybrids of neoclassical aesthetics and Romantic natural philosophy provided the theoretical foundation for dividing individuals into anthropological classes as well as for contesting hierarchies of species and genera.

Chapter 4 inaugurates a second line of inquiry devoted to the concept of the *Volk*. A powerful critic of Kantian race theory, Johann Gottfried Herder argued that the "spirit of a people [*Volksgeist*]" is based on a common structure of sensibility or *Sinnlichkeit*, whose theoretical roots reach back to the notion of the *sensus communis* theorized in the early eighteenth century by the third Earl of Shaftesbury. (The *sensus communis* is one early modern instance of collective sensation being grounded in the classical notion of αἴσθησις.) After tracing the influence of British aesthetics on Herder, the chapter moves forward to consider E. B. Tylor, a towering figure of Victorian anthropology known for the evolutionary theories that displaced Herder's diversitarian model. In his magnum opus *Primitive Culture* Tylor in fact retains important Herderian premises regarding collective sensation. In turn, modernist writers such as W. B. Yeats and Arthur Symons developed a primitivist style, partly through recourse to Tylor, that valorized the Irish peasantry, as in the case of Yeats, or other anthropological groupings that were thought to be agents for reclaiming more authentic modes of sensory experience. Hence the communalist aesthetics running from Shaftesbury through Herder and Tylor leads ultimately to modernists who came of age during the *fin-de-siècle*. Influenced by Walter Pater's aestheticism and Impressionism in the visual arts, these writers used the *sensus communis* to envision novel modes of collective life just as the Victorian politics of Pater and Tylor were being eclipsed by new, more distinctly modernist forms: the rise of postcolonial nationalisms and the birth of fascism in Europe.

The fifth chapter pivots from Impressionism to its polemical successor, Expressionism, moving back to the German sphere in order to contend with the discourse of the *neuer Mensch* (new human) as it developed in German Expressionism, a movement that explicitly rejected *fin-de-siècle* refinement and Impressionist aesthetics. For Expressionists like Else Lasker-Schüler and Gottfried Benn, important contributors to the initial wave of modernist poetics in German literature, dispensing with the bourgeois pieties they attributed to nineteenth-century liberalism required imagining new anthropological entities, new humans, much in the mold of the Nietzschean *Übermensch* or, later, Fanon's *homme neuf.* In the case of Lasker-Schüler, though, the "new human" became a means for modeling a *Volk* rather than a *Mensch*, and in particular, the Jewish *Volk* at a moment when Zionism was at apogee. In her poetry and prose, the chapter argues, Lasker-Schüler defines the *Volk* by making recourse to a spatial form, the circle, whereby all parts on the circumference are equidistant from the center. Consequently, members of a *Volk* in Lasker-Schüler's writing are frequently arrayed around a single governing point, often a charismatic leader. Thus the chapter returns to the question of aesthetic form or shape, revealing how a *Volk*, not a race, is conceived along egalitarian lines rather than in terms of ontological hierarchies.

The final chapter examines how Expressionist aesthetics metamorphosed from a radical critique of bourgeois liberalism into full-blown fascism.

During his period of involvement with National Socialism, Gottfried Benn treated the *Volk* as an aesthetic object – as a work of art that could be shaped and refined through direct eugenic interventions, which Benn dubbed "art as progressive anthropology." Yet Benn's staunchest critics on the left did not dismiss his aesthetic definition of the *Volk* outright. Instead, they appropriated the *Volk* for a leftist politics. Over the course of the celebrated Expressionism Debate, which preoccupied leading critics from the German diaspora through the latter months of 1937 and into 1938, the period of Stalin's show trials and preparations for war in Europe, Marxists and liberals alike refrained from employing a vocabulary of class struggle in favor of promoting a populist aesthetics that associated the *Volk* with a distinctly anti-modernist literary mode: the realist novel. Hence the chapter takes stock of the rise of populist cultural politics on both the radical left and right at the moment when the liberal tradition descending from Kant was reaching its nadir.

Where Part I examines a neoclassical aesthetics of anthropological races, Part II pivots to the *Volk* and to a different aesthetic discourse anchored in the authentically classical signification of αἴσθησις, sense perception. In looking to the ancients, Shaftesbury recuperated a mode of aesthetic experience that he wedded to a distinct configuration of collective life. In other words, he invoked a shared *sensus* to unite individuals into a *communis*. This communalization of *aisthesis* then influenced later empiricist anthropologies that defined large-scale collectives such as nations or peoples according to a shared palette of sensory experience. Part II records the absorption of these aesthetic anthropologies into modernist culture, beginning with the initial phase of modernist experimentation in *fin-de-siècle* aestheticism and Impressionism before proceeding to the Expressionist challenge to Impressionism and then ending with the critical legacy of Expressionism, which took shape under the looming shadow of fascism. Therefore even as Part II moves between the Anglophone and German spheres, its analysis of an aesthetics of the *Volk* is trained on a central arc in the development of modernist culture.

An argument that runs from the eighteenth to the twentieth century will inevitably face problems of coverage; and there are points in this study where particular theorists and themes are given less attention than they might rightfully claim. So, for instance, an account of the modernist legacy of the Enlightenment means that the conjunction of aesthetics and anthropology in the nineteenth century, a topic that warrants an entire monograph, is limited to the second chapter and sections of Chapters 3 and 4 devoted to the reception of Enlightenment anthropology. One

figure not examined at length deserves special mention. Perhaps more than
any philosopher, Friedrich Nietzsche had a great deal to say about culti-
vating an aesthetic attitude toward life; and he frequently thinks in
anthropological terms, usually in reference to nations and peoples. Yet
partly by design, Nietzsche's reflections do not add up to a coherent
doctrine linking aesthetics and anthropology in the same way that the
arguments of Kant, Herder, Lukács and the other theoretical figures in this
study do. Furthermore, Nietzsche believed that aesthetic principles were
best realized in works of art, so it seemed appropriate to allow him to speak
through the literary writers he influenced. Accordingly, Nietzsche makes
appearances in each of the chapters in Part II, thereby providing a fair
portrait of his importance for the discourse of the *Volk* as it developed in
German and Anglophone modernism. More generally, however, the
emphasis on value and the "ontological ought" outlined earlier and analyzed at length in Part I should be read with Nietzsche in mind. It is not
sufficient, these chapters argue in a Nietzschean vein, to understand
anthropological species solely in terms of empirical data or ontological
categories; for the categorial distinctions that make up an aesthetic
hierarchy reflect value judgments about what kind of thing a human
ought to be.

A coda sums up the theoretical stakes of the investigation by reaching
back beyond the Enlightenment to reflect on the Aristotelian notion of
eusynoptos (εὐσύνοπτος): "easily taken in at a glance." In Book 7 of the
Politics, Aristotle maintains that the size of a city (πόλις, *polis*) is delimited
by the number of citizens that can be visually comprehended at a glance.
Larger collectives like a "tribe" or a "people" (ἔθνος, *ethnos*), then, do not
qualify as political entities, *sensu stricto*, since they supersede the visual
bounds of the πόλις. But what if a machine were to augment the sensory
capacities of humans? Could a political entity then be expanded beyond its
natural limits? Confronting these questions in his film theory, Walter
Benjamin claims that the movie camera can record large masses of individuals, perfectly suited for the mass politics of modernity, in a manner
impossible for the naked eye. Thus Benjamin modernizes εὐσύνοπτος,
supplementing the natural faculties of humans with machine capacities
that again call attention to the etymology of aesthetics as a form of
αἴσθησις. With this background in place, the concepts of race, *Volk*,
ethnos, mass and class are examined through an analysis of Benjamin's
idiosyncratic Marxism (dubbed "anthropological materialism" by Theodor
Adorno for its efforts to account for the effects of modern capitalism on the
human sensorium). Framing those concepts in appropriately materialist

terms and illustrating them through reports about the American reception of Nazi propaganda films, the coda develops a theory of collective spectatorship that promotes a rational politics, thereby pressing back on an irrationalist tradition in aesthetics leading from Schelling and Schopenhauer through Nietzsche to fascism.

Concluding this investigation with an affirmation of reason should not be construed as a regression to the rationalist positions that Kant at once discredited and substantially revised in the third *Critique* – ideals of beauty, perfection and order. Demonstrating the drawbacks of that aesthetic orientation, especially when applied to anthropological categories, is one of the book's principal objectives. But it would be equally mistaken to grasp at an irrationalist response, inasmuch as a union of unreason and aesthetic spectacle, which Benjamin associated with the affective excesses of fascism, is by no means a historical relic of the twentieth century and continues to make itself felt in our own. This study pursues its critical history of aesthetic anthropology by marking out those two poles and striving to navigate between them.

Part I

CHAPTER I

Anthropology from an Aesthetic Point of View

When Immanuel Kant retired from teaching in 1796, he set to work revising the notes for the anthropology course that had been one of his most popular offerings at the Albertina in Königsberg for nearly a quarter century. The book eventually produced from his labors begins by dividing the discipline of anthropology into two parts: "physiological knowledge of the human being concerns the investigation of what *nature* makes of the human being." Pragmatic knowledge, however, concerns "the investigation of what *he* as a free-acting being makes of himself, or can and should make of himself."[1] In dividing the moieties of natural and practical knowledge, Kant aligns his anthropology with the domains of nature and freedom, whose distinctness he had undertaken to justify in his critiques of pure and practical reason. As its title indicates, *Anthropology from a Pragmatic Point of View* (1798) takes the practical path, offering a sprawling compendium of the behavioral, psychological and customary practices that humans had acquired over the course of their history and that defined their character as rational beings.

Even though Kant devotes himself to observations of the pragmatic side of human life in the *Anthropology*, his reflections on the nature of *der Mensch* and, more specifically, on the physiology of human races occupied a significant place in his philosophical activities just as the critical philosophy was taking shape. An announcement for a course on geography in 1775 posits that the human species is a unified whole divided into distinct subspecies. These distinctions, known as "races," emerged through the activation of innate germs that were latent in the physiology of all humans, Kant argued, but inherited only by members of a subspecies once they were activated by environmental factors like humidity and temperature.

After expanding his announcement for print in 1777, Kant refined his theory of race in parallel with his moral philosophy. "Determination of the Concept of a Human Race" appeared in the same year as *The Groundwork of the Metaphysics of Morals* (1785). "On the Use of Teleological Principles in Philosophy," widely acknowledged as a milestone on the way to *The Critique of Judgment*, was published in 1788 along with *The Critique of Practical Reason*. These essays on race have earned Kant a curious reputation in the history of anthropology. Even though speculation about the character and customs of humans was well underway by the time Kant entered the scene, John Zammito has located the "birth of anthropology" in Kant's dispute with his erstwhile student Johann Gottfried Herder – a dispute about the correct definition of human races as well as the proper ambitions of an Enlightenment "philosophy of man."[2] And though Kant's chief innovation was to translate Buffon's monogenetic natural history, which had already used the word "race" to refer to intraspecies differences, into the sturdier conceptual framework of his teleological philosophy of nature, Robert Bernasconi has gone so far as to assign Kant the dubious status of the "inventor" of the modern concept of race.[3]

The present chapter approaches Kant less through his positive contributions to the history of anthropology, though their importance cannot be denied, than for the way his race theory raises a broader problem in the history of ideas: how to square the universalist aspirations of the Enlightenment project, where equal moral and political standing was imputed to each individual, with anthropologies that divided the species into distinct races and placed them in hierarchies of value. As both a champion of universal human dignity and one of the period's most formidable theorists of race, Kant embodies this dilemma to a degree unmatched by any other philosopher.[4]

Significant as the tension between a universalist ethics and a diversitarian race theory may be, the difficulties posed by the Kantian program cannot be restricted to the practical domain. Scholars have also used Kant's aesthetics to reckon with general problems of the period. Simon Gikandi, for example, places Kant at the head of a tradition that represses or marginalizes slavery and the black body within aesthetic discourse.[5] According to Gikandi, what defines the eighteenth-century "culture of taste," with Kant as a chief exemplar, is the systematic degradation or outright denial of blackness as a topic of philosophical consideration. There is certainly evidence for Gikandi's claim in Kant's early writing on race. "Observations on the Feeling of the Beautiful and Sublime" (1764), a precritical essay written under the influence of Rousseau, recapitulates some of the era's cruder characterizations of the "capacities of mind" belonging to non-European races and women.[6] Informed by a humoral schema where human temperaments correspond to characteristic sensibilities – sanguinity befits the charm and lightness of beauty; the choleric inclines toward the magnificence of sublimity – Kant imputes to particular human groups specific structures of feeling: men, women, peoples and races are assigned to their proper affective spheres. So we learn that French and Italians have a unique proclivity for beauty while the English, Spaniards and Germans are disposed to sublimity.

Kant would later dispense with, or at the very least modify, his impressionistic associations of emotional character with different human groups, but he remained invested in the conjunction of aesthetics and anthropology through the 1770s and 1780s, often using his anthropology lectures as a forum for discussing aesthetic topics. This entanglement of aesthetics and anthropology has been attributed to the proximity of literary and ethnographic pursuits in the period, when individual or collective character seemed especially suited to treatments that blurred the boundaries between imaginative and descriptive writing – in travel literature, say, but also in the emerging genre of the novel or the evaluative work of criticism.[7] For his part, Kant grew increasingly skeptical of literary ethnography. He admitted in *The Critique of Pure Reason* that a science of taste could not satisfy the more rigorous intellectual requirements of true philosophy. Thus he left it to others, notably his star student Herder, to take up and expand this mode of writing, which blossomed into the folk Romanticisms of the nineteenth century that defined *der Mensch* in terms of language, culture and history rather than physiology.

Kant's decampment to the more demanding terrain of critical philosophy did not mean he withdrew the prejudices contained in "Observations" – at least not at first. His belief in a racial hierarchy and the diminished mental capacities of non-European races persisted in the more sophisticated essays of the 1770s and 1780s. Yet Kant's stance on race appears to have shifted at some point in the early 1790s, the years that also found him overcoming his reservations about a systematic doctrine of aesthetics in the first two editions of *The Critique of Judgment* (1790; 1793).[8] Pauline Kleingeld has persuasively argued that the political writings culminating in *Towards Perpetual Peace* (1795) coincided with a shedding of the attitudes Kant had long held regarding the mental capacities of non-white races.[9] By the end of the 1790s, Kleingeld claims, Kant had settled on a "purely physiological concept" of race, a concept shorn of moral determinants and hierarchical implications, which he then confirmed in explicit public condemnations of both slavery and colonial exploitation.[10]

If Kant jettisoned his views on the inferiority of non-white races in light of universalist moral considerations, this chapter argues, it is because he discovered a more powerful apparatus for articulating racial differences in

"On the Ideal of Beauty," §17 of *The Critique of Judgment*. In this section Kant takes up and revises the theory of Johann Joachim Winckelmann, who had argued that each race or nation possessed a distinct ideal of beauty but that all racialized ideals were subordinated to the Greek because Greece had the finest climate and the best cultural and political institutions. Kant retains the parameters introduced by Winckelmann, yet he discards the hierarchy that ranks a European physiognomy over the appearance of other races. He also grounds both inter- and intra-species difference on the *a priori* purposiveness of racial characteristics, not on environmental factors in the manner of epigeneticists like Winckelmann or Montesquieu.[11]

Thus the theoretical breakthrough of §17 has nothing to do with vague literary affinities between aesthetics and anthropology. Rather, the aesthetic arguments of §17, made with the full force of the critical turn, serve as a more potent vehicle for Kant's views on anthropological difference than the earlier definitions he gave for human races. Aesthetic form – in particular, the shape (*Gestalt*) of the body – provides the conceptual framework for a typology of human kinds. These perfect shapes, which represent the ideal appearances of natural categories (*Naturgattungen*), are a crucial component of the Third Moment of "The Analytic of the Beautiful," which considers beauty in its relation, or lack thereof, to concepts of ends or purposes. Thus the account of physiological perfection elucidated in §17 and the surrounding sections acts as a crucial link connecting the two seemingly disparate halves of *The Critique of Judgment* – the first pertaining to judgments of taste, "The Critique of Aesthetic Judgment," and the second to judgments of organic nature, "The Critique of Teleological Judgment." Therefore far from excluding or marginalizing the topic of race and blackness in aesthetic discourse, the philosophical core of the central text of modern aesthetics, "The Analytic of the Beautiful" in *The Critique of Judgment*, contains a novel theory of the racialized ideal of beauty that doubles as a thesis about racial difference.

1.1   The Aesthetic Ought

In the third *Critique*, Kant tries to steer between what he thought were two untenable positions in the philosophy of beauty: the Scylla of aesthetic relativism where taste is the expression of personal preference and the Charybdis of rationalist arguments that derive aesthetic value from a concept of perfection. If the former descends into claims that have "no right to the necessary assent of others," the latter makes beauty into the product of logical operations at odds with the unmediated pleasure of aesthetic experience.[12] To resolve this antinomy, Kant argues that the predicate "beautiful" is assigned to an object because of a feeling of pleasure arising from the free play of the cognitive faculties. Reflecting on the form of an object, not a concept of its content, sparks the mind to take up an unrestricted activity, a "pleasure in the harmony of the faculties of cognition" that have been "enlivened through mutual agreement."[13] With judgments of taste based on a "feeling of life" caused by reflection on aesthetic form, Kant thought he had deduced a subjective yet universally valid determination of beauty.

Kant strives to overcome object-oriented aesthetics by defining beauty in terms of the operations of the cognitive faculties shared by all humans. Although objects still have their place in the critical system – something must be given to consciousness for the faculties to operate – they are treated transcendentally as representations produced by the faculty of the imagination. Nevertheless Kant admits that the concept of an object's perfection is a major obstacle to his theory: "it is of the greatest importance in a critique of taste to decide whether beauty is really reducible to the concept of perfection."[14] What tilts the scales against such a concept is the irreducibly subjective character of aesthetic judgment. Because logical inference does not entail feelings of pleasure, a concept of perfection cannot lie at the basis of pure judgments of taste.

Even as he repudiates rationalist aesthetics for the subjective universalism of the transcendental system, Kant translates the concept of perfection into language more amenable to his philosophy in the Third Moment of *The Critique of Judgment*. Sections 15–17 apply a far-ranging theory of purposiveness, which denotes a relationship between an object and a concept of its end or purpose (*Zweck*), to traditional aesthetic problems including the aesthetics of perfection that Alexander Baumgarten derived from Christian Wolff and that Winckelmann then absorbed from Baumgarten. In doing so, Kant was not merely polishing the rough edges of the philosophy of art. He was making a major intervention in a central debate of the period. Lewis Beck claims that "the only part of the 'Leibniz-Wolffian philosophy'" that became "a permanently significant contribution to modern thought was the theory of fine art" – a theory that considered beauty to be the perception of perfection.[15] Thus in rendering aesthetic perfection into the transcendental terms of the critical program, Kant was in fact grappling with the signal contribution of his two most important predecessors in the German tradition; and the theory of perfection he propounds is significant not only for its relationship to the philosophical past but also, as we will see in Chapter 2, for the philosophies descending from the third *Critique* that came to be known as German idealism.

What Kant calls "adherent beauty" – that is, beauty based on a concept of perfection – is distinct from "free beauty," which requires no such conceptual determination. Collected under the heading of adherent beauty are both organic species and inanimate objects: a horse, a church, a palace, humans, and subdistinctions within that species between men, women and children. These classes or kinds of objects require a concept to ascertain their aesthetic value. Hence adherent beauty is a property of the object and its conceptual determination instead of being the sheer feeling produced by the operations of the cognitive faculties. Accordingly, the sensation that attends the perception of adherent beauty is a satisfaction (*Wohlgefallen*) instead of the truly universal pleasure (*Lust*) arising from the play of imagination and understanding. By contrast, the beauty of a flower is free because it generates a sense of pleasure in the absence of a concept of the flower's biological purpose, namely, reproduction.

Why a horse is ineligible for free beauty is a matter Kant leaves unaddressed in §16. Indeed, what purpose a horse could conceivably serve so as to license its adherent beauty goes unstated (Schiller and Goethe, as we will see, would refine this account of the beauty of the horse only a few years later).[16] Despite the haziness of Kant's reasoning at this juncture, the upshot of his argument is that certain cases of beauty qualify as conceptual while others are free because they have no recourse to concepts of purposiveness. From this it follows that different ends or purposes entail different standards of perfection. A beautiful child would not be judged according to the same standard as a woman; nor would the concept of a horse be the measure for assessing the beauty of a man. In other words, specific purposes correspond to distinct kinds of phenomena. These unique kinds then have their own respective standards of adherent beauty: "the concept of *what sort of thing it is supposed to be* [*sein solle*] must come first," Kant writes, in order to allow for "the agreement of the manifold in the thing with this concept." That is to say: a conceptual determination of the whole permits the judgment of parts as being in conformity with that concept.

A claim about the concept of what something ought to be, a specifically aesthetic claim with ontological stakes, is therefore antecedent to the representations of perfection in a real entity. A concept of what a thing *ought to be* (*sein solle*) is required for judging parts as members of an ordered, rule-governed phenomenon. Whether the perfect object is a species or a subspecies, an organism or a distinct kind of object, what a thing ought to be determines what it is. In sum, Kant states, "the agreement of the manifold in the thing with this concept (which supplies the rule for the combination of the manifold in it) is the *qualitative perfection* of a thing."[17] On this account qualitative perfection refers to distinctions of kind. Quantitative perfection or completeness, by contrast, refers to differences of degree once the aesthetic ought has been specified: "the completeness of any thing in its own kind [*Art*] ... is a mere concept of magnitude (of totality), in which *what the thing is supposed to be* is thought of as already determined."[18] A hierarchy of value is predicated on an essential purpose. Real individuals, understood as members of a classificatory kind, may be complete in varying degrees. But these differences of degree – of quantity or magnitude, that is – assume an ideal that fully articulates what the thing ought to be. The bird perched on my windowsill may be judged more beautiful – more perfect – than the one on the branch across the street because both are measured according to a standard that embodies the totality of attributes belonging to "bird." To judge the relative perfection of the two cats resting beneath the tree requires appealing to a qualitatively different standard defined by a different end or purpose. The same can be said of other entities if they are determined according to ends. According to Kant, this includes, among other things, a horse, child, palace, man, woman, "negro" and "white."

1.2 The Kantian Ideal of Beauty

It is surprising how little attention "On the Ideal of Beauty" has received among scholars of Kant's race concept, not only because *The Critique of Judgment* crowns the critical system but also because Kant's final essay on race, "On the Use of Teleological Principles in Philosophy" (1788), is widely recognized as a precursor to the philosophy of nature and beauty contained in the third *Critique*. This lacuna is noteworthy but in no way inconsistent with scholarship on the third *Critique* as a whole. Henry Allison gives §17 only a passing glance in his study of Kant's aesthetics while Zammito remarks on the "very strange language" that crops up in the section, commenting at one point that "the more Kant develops the ideas, the more questions arise, and the less clarity remains." No less confused, Paul Guyer refers to §17 as an "argument the point of which is obscure" and an "aberration."[19] Though none of these authors discusses the racial categories in the section, there can be little doubt that Kant's racialism is the source for at least some of their perplexity.

"On the Ideal of Beauty" begins by asserting that an ideal of beauty exists as a mental construct, not a concrete artwork. To be sure, certain artworks may be "regarded as *exemplary*"; they are patterns, or models that artists may imitate.[20] Yet Kant explains that models obtain their exemplary status by being measured against a standard that exists in the mind of an observer. Kant means something along these lines: it is possible to judge the Belvedere Apollo as an exemplary model because it approaches an ideal of human beauty already present in the mind. The relationship between artwork and mental construct is stated as follows: "the highest model, the archetype [*Urbild*] of taste, is a mere idea, which everyone must produce in himself, and in accordance with which he must judge everything that is an object of taste, or that is an example of judging through taste."[21] The "highest model" is a "mere idea" produced in the observer; a work of art, what Kant here calls an "object of taste," is then judged according to that mental standard; and this judgment even includes exemplary artworks – "an example of judging through taste." For Kant, concrete instantiations of the ideal are downstream from the "ideal of the imagination" that resides in the mind and that endows certain works with their exemplary status by establishing a standard according to which their objective properties may be judged.

Kant's distinction between examples of taste and a mental archetype reaches back to some of his earliest reflections on an ideal of beauty. Along with distinguishing real works from an ideal, Kant takes steps toward elucidating how the mind constructs such an archetype in the *Blomberg Logic*, the student notes to lectures Kant likely delivered in the early 1770s: "Anyone who has seen many men forms for himself an archetype, a model of the size, of the beauty of a man, which contains the mean on all points and for all kinds of the human form."[22] Kant believes that the mind forms an average shape, or mean, which then acts as the standard of physical beauty. Such claims about ideal types can be traced at least to Plato. More proximately, Joshua Reynolds had made the case that an average form constitutes an ideal of beauty in his essay for *The Idler* in 1759, calling it the "central form" and ascribing preferences for certain forms to "habit and custom."[23] For his part, Kant gives his most sustained exposition of an average shape in the third *Critique*. At the earlier stage of his thinking recorded in the lecture notes, however, it is most important to note Kant's stance on the universal character of that average shape: the archetype of human beauty holds "for all kinds of the human form [*in allen Stücken, und Arten der Menschlichen Gestalt*]." In the *Blomberg Logic*, the archetype of human beauty is a general norm. It comprehends all *kinds*, as well as all *parts* of the human figure. As Kant hones the imaginative construction of the ideal of beauty over the next two decades, a period that coincides with his development of a theory of race, its shape will become progressively less universal, reflecting Kant's introduction of national, and in the third *Critique*, racial constraints on the appearance of the ideal of beauty.

When Kant returned to the ideal of beauty more than a decade later in his anthropology lectures from 1784 to 1785, collected as the *Anthropology Mrongovius*, he did so while working on his landmark work of moral philosophy, the *Groundwork of a Metaphysics of Morals*. In other words, at the same time that Kant was crafting arguments for the standing of all humans as members of a kingdom of ends, he was instructing his students about the nature of an aesthetic ideal – one that, at this stage in Kant's thinking, no longer reflects a universal standard of human beauty. *Anthropology Mrongovius* finds Kant engaging explicitly with Winckelmann, whose influence is felt when Kant expounds on aesthetic relationships between parts of the body: "we also get such an average of the proportion of the head to the body, the nose to the head."[24] Instead of being a mean for the entire human figure and its parts, the standard shape now includes average relationships, or proportions, between particular parts; and this narrowed focus leads Kant to make geographical distinctions: "As a consequence of this, every country has its own average size." Kant then takes another page out of Winckelmann by yoking a moral quality to a physical form: "In the Greek profiles, one finds the noses running on the same line as the forehead; that is noble." *Anthropology Mrongovius* shows that as the attributes of the imaginative shape become more specific, comprehending individual facial features along with the overall human figure, the more physical beauty corresponds to local rather than universal conditions. At this point, though, Kant thinks that the national specificity of physical appearance pertains to the proportions *between* the parts – "the head to the body, the nose to the head." In *The Critique of Judgment*, Kant takes the final step and racializes the individual physical features themselves.

The initial paragraphs of §17 in the third *Critique* suggest that Kant wishes to return the physical dimension of his ideal to a universal standard, as in the *Blomberg Logic*. He states his intent to elucidate a standard that should garner unanimity, "as far as possible, of all times and peoples."[25] With this goal in mind, Kant explains that humans alone qualify for an ideal of beauty because a human being – *der Mensch* – is the single entity that can determine its ends through reason; and he defines the shape, *Gestalt*, of the ideal human as a shape that conforms to an image for the entire species. Therefore it seems only a matter of course that all members of the human species will be measured according to the same standard shape. Kant moves in the opposite direction, though, and divides human beauty along racial and national lines, all the while insisting that he is referring to the species as a whole. To resolve this apparent inconsistency, §17 needs to be interpreted as a departure from the "monogenetic" definition of "species" that Kant argues for strenuously in his anthropological writings. Instead of races constituting subdivisions *within* a single human species (*mono-genus*), as in his anthropology, Kant's aesthetic philosophy treats racial appearance as sufficient to distinguish individuals as members of distinct species. By formulating a systematic aesthetic theory that treats racial differences on the order of species, Kant construes racial characteristics as though they denote different kinds of humans, precisely the position he argued against with his monogenetic theory of race.

As Kant conceives it, an ideal of beauty must satisfy two necessary conditions, which he calls the "normal idea" and the "idea of reason" corresponding to the physiological and moral dimensions of the ideal of beauty. In line with his earlier exposition from *Anthropology Mrongovius,* an ideal of human beauty evinces both definite relationships between parts of the body and moral qualities, a "noble" profile for instance. In the terms of the third *Critique,* the normal idea furnishes the minimal "correctness" that the form of an ideal must fulfill, whereas the moral component will "please universally and moreover positively."[26] Therefore, when Kant summarizes his theory of an ideal of beauty in the final sentence of the section, he includes both conditions together: "The correctness of such an ideal of beauty is proved by the fact that no sensory charm is allowed ... while it nevertheless allows a great [moral] interest to be taken in it." Kant devotes the bulk of his theory of an aesthetic ideal to the normal idea, the shape that defines an organism as a member of a species. The normal idea is "an individual intuition (of the imagination) that represents the standard for judging it as a thing belonging to a particular species of animal [*Tierspezies*]."[27] The normal idea, Kant specifies, refers to the entire category, "only the species as a whole [*Gattung im Ganzen*] but not any separate individual," and he links the normal idea to the shape of a biological species: "the normal idea must take its elements for the figure [*Gestalt*] of an animal of a particular species [*Gattung*] from experience." As a result, the normal idea becomes "a universal standard for the aesthetic judging of every individual of this species [*Spezies*]." The specifically aesthetic nature of Kant's claim deserves to be stressed: "*zum allgemeinen*

Richtmaß der ästhetischen Beurtheilung." Despite the fact that Kant wavers between terms – *Gattung, Spezies, Tierspezies* – his point is clear: the normal idea serves as a sensible standard that allows one to judge, and judge aesthetically, an individual as belonging to a species. This aesthetic standard for a species furnishes the basic outline, or shape, that constitutes the correctness of an ideal of beauty.

Fault lines between an aesthetic and an anthropological determination of a species are already beginning to emerge. In his anthropological, specifically natural-historical essays, Kant follows Buffon by basing membership in a species on a genetic principle: whether two organisms are able to bear fertile progeny. A doberman and a dachshund belong to a common species because they can, notwithstanding any differences in their appearance, produce offspring that can in turn propagate the species. The same goes for an African and a European. As Kant puts it in "Of the Different Races of Human Beings" (1775): "animals which produce fertile young with one another (whatever difference in shape [*Gestalt*] there may be) still belong to one and the same physical species."[28] Kant reiterates his monogenism in no uncertain terms: "all human beings on the wide earth belong to one and the same natural species [*Naturgattung*] . . . no matter what great differences may otherwise be encountered in their shape [*Gestalt*]." Appearance – the shape of an animal – is precisely what Kant eliminates from his definition of a natural species; the only criterion for belonging to a species is mutual fertility. Kant's definition of an aesthetic species in §17 takes the opposite approach, however, making shape the chief criterion: "the normal idea must take its elements for the figure [*Gestalt*] of an animal of a particular species from experience." Considered from an aesthetic perspective, shape is what allows an individual to be judged as a member of a species. These two statements of the warrant for membership in a species break in opposite directions regarding the role of shape. For a natural historian, shape is irrelevant and the laws of fertility are all that matter. For someone making an aesthetic judgment of species, shape is paramount.

To account for how such a standard shape is created, Kant again resorts to the mind's ability to construct an average form, just as he did in his logic and anthropology lectures. The imagination, according to Kant, synthesizes the normal idea by combining individual images into a single composite:

> when the mind is set on making comparisons, it even knows how, by all accounts actually if not consciously, as it were to superimpose one image on another and by means of the congruence of several of the same kind [*Art*] to

arrive at a mean that can serve them all as a common measure. Someone has seen a thousand grown men. Now if he would judge what should be estimated as their comparatively normal size, then (in my opinion) the imagination allows a great number of images (perhaps all thousand) to be superimposed on one another.[29]

The imagination assembles a variety of individual images from experience and unites them into a single representative average – the normal idea – which can thereupon serve as a standard for judging the physical dimensions of individuals. As a result, "this is the stature for a beautiful man." With this "psychological explanation," as he calls it, Kant believes he can account for the physiological component of the ideal of beauty through the idea of an aesthetic mean, an average figure representing a normative type for the species.

When Kant goes on to refine the imaginative process so that it includes individual body parts, the racialized normal idea becomes explicit:

> if in a similar way there is sought for this average man the average head, the average nose, etc., then this shape [*Gestalt*] is the basis for the normal idea of the beautiful man in the country where this comparison is made; hence under these empirical conditions a negro [*ein Neger*] must necessarily [*notwendig*] have a different normal idea of the beauty of a figure [*Gestalt*] than a white [*ein Weißer*], a Chinese person [*der Chinese*] a different idea from a European [*der Europäer*]. (Quoted from the second edition).

Differences in appearance reflect both racial and national variation. Kant first pits a sharp binary between "negro" and "white" where the phenomenological contrast takes precedent. Yet his next distinction juxtaposes the normal idea of a nationality or ethnicity, "the Chinese," against that of an entire continent, "the European," with the latter designation erasing any particular differences that may exist within Europe. In a gesture no less regrettable than it is predictable, Kant's normal idea finds all Europeans looking alike, yet essentially different from those with darker skin.

If the normal idea refers to a standard image for the "species as a whole," as Kant consistently maintains in §17, then how can the "negro" have a different normal idea from that of the "white" when both are members of the same species? Conversely, if the "negro" and "white" possess different normal ideas, and hence different aesthetic standards by which they are assigned to a species, then how can they both be judged as members of the same species? The exact steps Kant takes at this moment are pivotal for understanding the reasons that motivate him to make racial distinctions with the normal idea. First, Kant describes the average size and stature of a beautiful man [*Mann*]. He even proposes two possible means for obtaining that average. The first gives an average size by resorting to a visual analogy: "in the space where the greatest number of them [images] coincide and within the outline of the place that is illuminated by the most concentrated colors, there the *average size* becomes recognizable."[30] In addition, Kant offers a second possibility based on mathematical calculation: "if one measured all thousand men, added up their heights, widths, (and girths) and then divided the sum by a thousand." Both methods give the same result. They furnish an average standard for the overall size and stature of the "beautiful man" in general. No further qualification. At this point, Kant makes a leap: "Now *if* in a similar way there is sought for this average man the average head, the average nose, etc., *then* this shape is the basis for the normal idea in the country where the comparison is made" (my emphasis). Kant's syntax – *Wenn . . . so* – makes a clear causal link: racial and national constraints are consequent upon Kant's decision to restrict the imaginative production of a composite image so that it includes the head and face. But why does Kant add this qualification in the first place? What prevents the imagination from combining facial features, either optically or mathematically, into an average standard for the whole human species? In other words, why can't Kant imagine the face of an interracial ideal of beauty?

This passage appears to have troubled Kant. The only major revisions to his theory of an aesthetic ideal between the first and second editions of *The Critique of Judgment* – published in 1790 and 1793, respectively, precisely the years Kleingeld deems crucial for Kant's reevaluation of his views on race, were to these sentences. In the first edition the passage reads simply:

> if in a similar way there is sought for this average man the average head, the average nose, etc., then this shape is the basis for the normal idea of the beautiful man in the country where this comparison is made; hence a negro must necessarily have a different idea of the beauty of a figure than a white, a Chinese person a different idea from a European.

When in the second edition Kant adds the phrase, "under these empirical conditions" – in this translation, immediately before "a negro" – he might be conceding that someone may at some point have seen a person of a different race; under *other* empirical conditions, say if an African were taken to Europe, her imaginative synthesis would, it seems, need to reflect those circumstances. While Kant does admit empirical variation to the normal idea, the role played by empirical factors should not be overstated; indeed, the first edition makes no mention of "empirical conditions." At this moment, Kant is less interested in "the country where this comparison is made" than with the problem of where to draw the line between distinct aesthetic species, as can be seen when he immediately redoubles his commitment to aesthetic standards corresponding to individual races: "It will be exactly the same with the model of a beautiful horse or dog (of a certain breed [*Rasse*])." Kant reverts to "race" as a term derived from animal breeding, but his claim holds equally for members of human races. Kant's meaning is that phenotypical differences between races, whether human or animal, are sufficient to distinguish between normal ideas – between the standard that determines an ideal physical form and that permits an aesthetic judgment of membership in a unique category, a "species." And lest we think that over the course of his elucidation of the imaginative construction of physical beauty Kant has somehow forgotten that the normal idea refers to the species, he adds two sentences later: "It is the image for the whole species [*für die ganze Gattung*]."[31] Kant argues throughout §17 that the normal idea refers to the entire species but this claim is difficult to reconcile with the specific aesthetic standards he assigns to individual races.

Commentators typically pass over these lines as a qualification that ties the normal idea to the cultural specificity of a particular observer. Rachel Zuckert writes, "Kant argues that though all people produce such a standard idea, the specific 'look' of this idea will vary across cultures or races."[32] Guyer makes a similar assessment: "any such norm would be inextricably linked to the empirical circumstances of the individual observer, and persons in different circumstances would arrive at different norms."[33] These readings leave several major features of the passage unexplained. First, an empirical determination of the ideal of beauty would run counter to Kant's general effort to supersede Winckelmann's environmental determinism. The main task of §17 is to move past a determination of an aesthetic ideal based on local circumstance or geographical accidents. And on this point in particular, as we shall see later, Kant clarifies, "this *normal idea* is not derived from the proportions taken from experience," a statement that vitiates any claims to a strictly empirical, or culturally relative determination of the normal idea. Indeed, if the normal idea were determined solely according to empirical circumstances, it would reflect the particular experience of each individual. But that is not what Kant claims. Kant claims that the normal idea *necessarily* divides into distinct categories of race, nation and breed, an assertion he will later substantiate with arguments *a priori*, that is, with teleological reasoning meant to organize empirical differences into natural, not cultural, classes or kinds. Most problematic, therefore, is the lack of any account of the discord Kant creates between his aesthetic and anthropological use of the term "species." This is understandable for Zuckert and Guyer since their interests lie elsewhere, but David Bindman also omits any discussion of Kant's conflation of race and species even though it strikes to the heart of Kant's views on the aesthetics of racial difference.[34] The problem that requires an explanation can be stated as follows: Kant purports at the outset to show how the imagination can form a single aesthetic standard for the entire human species, and he does so regarding the overall average size and stature of the (male) human figure; but then we find him delineating species-level aesthetic standards for the facial characteristics of human races, all without missing a beat.

1.3 Race as Species

We can gain some insight into the categories of difference Kant creates in §17 by referring to "Determination of the Concept of a Human Race" (1785), an essay written during the full bloom of the critical period that provides Kant's most systematic account of the criteria for grouping individuals under conceptual headings, including those he uses in "On the Ideal of Beauty" – species, race, class, kind. For Kant, scientific inquiry into the natural world begins by observing and comparing individuals in order then to separate them into categories: "Initially, when looking only for characters of comparison (in terms of similarity or dissimilarity), one obtains *classes* of creatures under a species."[35] Consider this comparative method alongside §17 when Kant designates the mindset underlying the psychological construction of the normal idea: "when the mind is set on making comparisons, it even knows how, by all accounts actually if not consciously, as it were to superimpose one image on another." Both texts indicate an initial moment of morphological comparison. In "Determination," Kant specifies an act of observation that discerns similarities and differences and in turn produces distinctions among organisms – "one obtains *classes*." Likewise, in §17, comparison leads to a mental procedure that combines images "of the same kind" into an average standard; this standard then allows for the aesthetic judgment of individuals as belonging to a class or "species" of organism.

However, if investigation of nature is to be based on rational principles like Buffon's law, Kant argues, comparative analysis of the shapes of organisms is only the first in a two-step process. A natural historian must then find out whether there exists a common genetic source for the initial morphological similarity: "If one looks further to their phyletic origin, then it must become apparent whether those classes are so many different *kinds* or only *races*" (emphasis original).[36] If observable differences cannot be traced to a common ancestor, then the organisms qualify as different kinds, or what is the same, as belonging to different species. On the other hand, if the two organisms do share a common genealogical origin, thereby confirming mutual fertility and Buffon's law, differences in appearance may denote racial variation within a single species. A doberman and a dachshund, or an African and a European, can look different; yet despite those differences they still descend from a common phyletic origin or "stem" and therefore qualify as diverse breeds, or "races," within a single species. In order to establish the unity of the human species, the natural historian must trace apparent differences in appearance – shape – to a common source.

However, such an historical inference is precisely what Kant's aesthetic determination of species in §17 refrains from, much like the synchronic taxonomies, or "descriptions of nature," that Kant associates with Linnaeus and wishes to displace with the natural-historical approach he inherited from Buffon. For someone who refers to the normal idea, the imagination remains at the level of shape when making an aesthetic judgment of species: "the normal idea must take its elements for the figure [*Gestalt*] of an animal of a particular species from experience."[37] What Kant's terminology in §17 implies, and what the procedure outlined in "Determination" reveals, is that these aesthetic distinctions based on similar and dissimilar shapes also constitute for Kant unique aesthetic classes. In fact, the procedure from "Determination" helps explain Kant's terminological inexactness in §17. Kant wavers between *Gattung, Spezies* and *Tierspezies* because with the normal idea he is delineating aesthetic classes according to the minimally relevant mark for a classificatory distinction, which he then designates "species" with one of the available terms. Kant ends the passage in "Determination" by stating, "What is here called *kind* [in the description of nature], is often only called *race* there [in natural history]." Exactly the same holds true in §17. What is called "species" or "kind" in his aesthetic philosophy would simply be called "race" in natural history. This resolves the problem of terminology. When Kant uses the term "species" in §17, he really means "race"; but this does not mitigate the fact that the difference implied by racial appearance has risen from the status of a subdivision within a single common biological species to the status of a species proper, an elevation of classificatory status that only deepens the conceptual division between races.

This explanation would have been unnecessary had Kant simply followed the logic of his own argument. If he had been able to synthesize an average standard for the human species as a whole, including all of its facial features, it would have obviated the problem of why races have distinct normal ideas despite belonging to the same biological species. Accordingly, the method of synchronic morphological comparison shared by an aesthetic judgment of species and "description of nature" only gets us part of the way toward understanding the aesthetic categories Kant delimits in "The Analytic of the Beautiful." An explanation for why Kant elevates a category to a higher level of abstraction, from a natural-historical subspecies to an aesthetic species, does not establish the warrant for the creation of categories of difference as such; nor does it account for Kant's inability to imagine an aesthetic standard for the face of humankind. In short, the problem remains why Kant insists on racial categories in his aesthetic philosophy *at all*, especially when the mental operation that constructs a synthetic standard should erase the lines dividing one race from another by averaging out any differences in appearance regardless of the part of the body being idealized. What is it about the characteristic morphologies of races that leads Kant to assign them to distinct aesthetic classes?

1.4   Kant's Teleological Shapes

To begin, we might refer to a pair of questions Kant poses near the beginning of §17: "Now how do we attain such an ideal of beauty? *A priori* or empirically?" By all indications the answer should be straight-forward: we attain an ideal of beauty empirically. Kant himself even refers to the ideal of beauty as "the empirical criterion for the derivation of a taste, confirmed by examples, deeply buried in all human beings."[38] The normal idea in particular seems to be derived from a combination of images gained through experience: "Someone has seen a thousand grown men," Kant writes, and then the imagination synthesizes this manifold into a coherent whole consisting of an average standard; in Kant's words, "the normal idea must take its elements for the figure [*Gestalt*] of an animal of a particular species from experience [*aus der Erfahrung nehmen*]." Kant's source for the normal idea as an average shape bears out this designation; Rudolf Makkreel cites the empirical psychology of Johannes Tetens as the methodological precedent for Kant's "psychological explanation" of a synthetic average.[39]

A strictly empirical grounding for the normal idea would raise serious problems for the racial lines Kant draws between his ideal models. As two of Kant's most trenchant contemporary critics brought to his attention, the empirical evidence weighs against racial categories.[40] Herder makes this argument in the *Ideen zur Philosophie der Geschichte der Menschheit* when he writes, "there are neither four or five races, nor exclusive varieties, on this Earth. Complexions run into each other: forms follow the genetic character: and upon the whole, all are at last but shades of the same great picture."[41] Georg Forster made a similar argument with empirical data. After accompanying Cook on his journey to the South Seas, Forster wrote an extended critique of Kant's race theory in *Teutscher Merkur* (1786). Among many criticisms leveled, Forster made the obvious but nonetheless important rejoinder to Kant "that whites are more darkly colored in Spain, Mauritania, Egypt, Arabia, and Abyssinia than in Germany, Poland, Prussia, Denmark, and Sweden," as well as the fact that "the dark shading increases in approximately the gradation" of geography.[42] When skin color is the primary mark of racial difference, as it was for Kant, the data testify to the variety of human appearances and against dividing groups into separate classes. And these facts should be borne out by the imaginative construction of a synthetic average: if someone observes the faces of a thousand men and synthesizes them into an average, there will be no categorial distinctions. Complexions and shapes would "run into each other."

Kant thought he had a response to these empiricist challenges. Observation alone cannot provide insight into the real operations of nature, Kant believed; it must be guided by teleological "maxims of reason" like Buffon's law that holds in the face of the variety of observable data. Since mutual fertility indicates a real feature of the natural order – some animals really are capable of producing fertile offspring together, others are not – the categorial distinctions predicated on it were thought to reflect true natural distinctions; thus Kant referred to them as *Natur-* or *Realgattungen*. Kant believed he had a principle for assigning individuals to a race that was analogous to Buffon's law for determining a biological species: the law of necessary heritability. If certain traits like skin color are invariably inherited, then according to Kant they qualify as racial characteristics. On the other hand, if certain features like hair color or eye color are heritable, but not necessarily and only irregularly, they constitute mere "varieties."[43] Although Kant was enamored with skin color as a mark of a necessarily heritable trait because it was both easily identifiable and amenable to what he thought was a purposive adaptation to "dephlogistize" the blood, his natural-historical criterion for membership in a race is broad enough to encompass an entire phenotype. As with Buffon's law, the phenomenological character of race – a particular physical trait or a distinctive shape – is altogether absent from his definition. Kant hangs his natural history of human races on a biological principle of necessary heritability.

Even though Kant thought he had valid criteria for classifying organisms based on rational, teleological principles, he did not presume to have pulled back the curtain on the noumenal realm of nature in itself. He merely asserts that an observer must think of nature as organized according to teleological principles for it to be comprehended as a coherent system of species and genera. Teleological principles were for Kant regulative principles. What are regulative principles? Unlike the constitutive principles Kant argued for in *The Critique of Pure Reason* that underlie the possibility of experience as such – the forms of intuition (space, time) and the categories of the understanding – regulative principles manage the contents of consciousness and provide necessary coherence to the myriad data furnished by empirical observation. In other words, regulative principles lend order to sensations. They organize the particulars of given experiential content. But because such regulation requires that sensations first be given, regulative principles assume the constitution of experience according to more basic principles like causality, for instance, or the forms of intuition, space and time.

Thus teleological judgments are "empirically conditioned" since they rely on the givenness of experience. In §17, this sort of conditioning shows up when Kant refers to the racial specificity of the normal idea: "under these empirical conditions a negro must necessarily have a different normal idea of the beauty of a figure than a white." However, if a judgment is to lay claim to necessity, or if it pertains to the natural purposiveness of an organism, including the purposiveness of racial appearances, then the warrant for such necessity cannot be induced *a posteriori*.[44] On the contrary. As Kant argues in §80 of "The Critique of Teleological Judgment," empirical explanations of the natural world must be "subordinated" to teleology – to rational principles like Buffon's law and the law of necessary heritability – in order to provide true *"insight into nature."*[45] Teleology lends empirically conditioned observations their necessity, thereby differentiating teleological judgments from strictly empirical or culturally relative ones. Without rational principles to guide the mind regarding natural ends, an observer would be unmoored amid an experiential jumble and unable to detect the structure of a purposive, harmonious whole organized along real classificatory differences among organisms.

If the normal idea in §17 seems cast out of a decidedly empirical mold, the controlling influence of teleology lies behind its operations. Following the extended exposition of the normal idea, Kant appends a startling comment: "This *normal idea* is not derived from the proportions taken from experience." Instead, Kant posits the opposite: "it is the image [*Bild*] for the whole species, hovering among all the particular and variously diverging intuitions of the individuals, which nature used as the archetype [*Urbild*] underlying her productions in the same species."[46] With this sentence, Kant explains that the normal idea is not empirical, at least not strictly so; it is not an image gleaned exclusively from the subjective synthesis of culturally situated sense-data. Rather, the archetype of human beauty is a natural image, one that "nature used" in the pursuit of its ends. Kant even asserts that the empirical relevance of the normal idea is derived from its natural status: "it is in accordance with it [*nach ihr*, i.e. the normal idea] that rules for judging first become possible." According to Kant, the natural image is antecedent to any particular act of judgment; it provides the aesthetic criteria that authorize the assignment of individuals to the classes "negro," "white," "Chinese," and "European." In light of this clarification, the normal idea turns out to be a condition for the possibility of judging individuals as members of a species (read: race) based on their shape, not an inductive inference. This teleological qualification compels a very different interpretation of Kant's "psychological explanation" of the normal idea. The synthesis of images by the imagination, whether optically or mathematically, serves as a heuristic device: it points to what Kant believes is in fact a natural, *a priori* racialized shape "underlying her productions in the same species."

It is now possible to clarify Kant's reasons for introducing racial categories into his aesthetic philosophy. Teleology underlies the normal idea and the delineations Kant makes between the shapes of race, nation and breed. The logic of the normal idea functions according to *Naturgattungen*. And each natural species – "negro," "white," horse, dog, doberman, or dachshund – has its own aesthetic standard. This thesis can even be detected in Kant's inaugural statement of how the imagination constructs the normal idea: "the mind knows how ... to superimpose one image on another and by means of the congruence of several of the same kind [*Art*] to arrive at a mean that can serve them all as a common measure." A common measure is predicated on an image being of the "same kind." Different kinds of images have different common measures, an argument consistent with qualitative perfection as it is outlined in §15. Hence different races have different normal ideas because Kant thinks that from an aesthetic point of view, each anthropological race constitutes a unique aesthetic kind.

This structural logic also helps explain a notable exclusion from Kant's theory of an ideal of beauty: women. In the *Anthropology Mrongovius*, Kant follows Winckelmann by deriving an aesthetic ideal from the male body, averring that judgments of female beauty are inevitably tinged with "charm," which he wishes to eliminate both from pure judgments of taste and from the correctness that attends the normal idea.[47] Yet more is at stake in Kant's elision of a female ideal. Taking leave from the arguments of §15, where qualitative perfection refers to *any* purposive distinction between objects and organisms and, accordingly, women and children receive their own aesthetic standards alongside men, his account of the normal idea through masculine beauty in §17 is sufficient because Kant thought that women were complementary units within a single natural category, whose reproductive purposiveness licenses its status as a *Naturgattung*. Construed as members of a natural kind, women do not possess a purpose uniquely distinct from that of men, and their omission therefore poses no problem for Kant in his exposition of a teleological ideal of beauty.

Should the designations for national or ethnic difference – "Chinese" and "European" – appear to add a wrinkle to this logic since political designations of nationality do not conform to *Naturgattungen* as intuitively as biological races or species, it must be remembered that in his 1775 essay Kant considers national differences to be natural, claiming that nature "marks ethnic groups [*Völkerschaften*] forever"; he even asserts that national characteristics "would be called a race if what is characteristic did not appear too insignificant and were not too difficult to describe."[48] The core logic of §17 is now clear: *Naturgattungen* entail a unique *Urbild* for the facial features of each race or nation. Like any teleological judgment, the shapes require experiential content to be given and are not deduced from a concept as such. The crucial epistemological point, however, is that the differences between aesthetic species are necessary; they are differences of kind; and they reflect a natural standard that permits each individual to be judged as a member of a group.

Yet just as the earlier discussion of "description of nature" established the specifically aesthetic dimension of Kant's argument as an act tied to synchronic morphological comparison, here too shape displaces biology as the cardinal factor in determining race. Kant avails himself of teleological reasoning at one other moment in §17, with explicit reference to the purposive shape of the human figure:

> but the greatest purposiveness in the construction of the figure [*Gestalt*], which would be suitable as a universal standard for the aesthetic judging of every individual of this species, the image [*Bild*] which has as it were

> intentionally grounded the technique of nature, to which only the species as a whole but not any separate individual is adequate, lies merely in the idea of the one who does the judging.[49]

This single labyrinthine sentence threads together all Kant's claims regarding the epistemological status of the normal idea. Kant signals its teleological derivation by noting "the greatest purposiveness in the construction of the figure [*Gestalt*]." He also states that a particular image [*Bild*] of the species grounds the "technique of nature," which in the Kantian argot refers to a particular intention or design that nature used in the pursuit of ends. This assertion deserves special emphasis: the image grounds the technique of nature. Nature, not culture, is the operative term for the normal idea, necessary, not contingent or empirical differences. And more important, within an aesthetic framework, Kant lets *Gestalt* and *Bild* ground phenotypic purposiveness directly. In his natural history, by contrast, racial appearance is only relevant inasmuch as it acts as an empirical mark that indicates an underlying biological principle, the principle of necessary heritability, which is defined in explicitly anti-phenomenological terms. Kant makes a point, though, to remain at the level of regulative principles in the passage: the image "lies merely in the idea of the one who does the judging." According to Kant, he who judges aesthetically must think such shapes are natural.

1.5   Racism and the Aesthetics of Anthropological Difference

It is finally possible to combine the foregoing analysis, which has focused on Kant's race theory, with a more quotidian explanation for the aporia of an interracial aesthetic ideal in §17: Kant's racism. Of the variety of racist views Kant propounded over the course of his career, and there were many and they were deeply held, the most persistent was his fear of racial mixing. Jon Mikkelsen even includes it as one of the "core elements" of Kant's theory of race.[50] Kant's aversion to interracialism was born of his belief that it worked against the order of nature and leveled out natural diversity.[51] Since races constituted purposive adaptations, an activation of predetermined germs to suit particular environmental conditions, to cross races was for Kant counterpurposive; it countervailed natural ends and violated the borders between *Naturgattungen*.

Kant's antipathy to race mixing is one of the ironies of his theory of race. On the one hand, he denounced interracialism as counterpurposive; on the other, it was an inescapable consequence of his theory dubbed "the law of necessary half-breed generation": since members of a common species can procreate, and since certain traits are necessarily heritable, hybridized traits must result from interracial procreation.[52] Race entails race mixing for Kant. But as a practical matter Kant eschews race mixing as counter-purposive. And in this regard, his stance on biological interracialism as a theoretical necessity yet a practical transgression is not so different from his theory of the ideal of beauty. At the outset, the premises of §17 demand a normal idea of physical beauty for the human species as a whole, where the imagination combines images into an average shape irrespective of racial categories; in practice, though, Kant maintains what he believed were purposive divisions between the facial phenotypes of individual races.

An ideal of beauty for the human species as a whole – an interracial ideal of beauty – would constitute a violation of *Naturgattungen*, which for Kant is bad enough. But it also threatens to let the imagination overstep boundaries set for it by reason, which Kant simply cannot bear. Even though he uses biological criteria for determining the concept of a race – again, the law of necessary heritability – and is careful not to let a particular trait become a defining condition, Kant does occasionally refer to the shapes of organisms in his natural history. One such moment in "Determination" resonates with his theory of an ideal of beauty, when Kant executes an argument *reductio ad absurdum* by entertaining what he believes to be a dangerous hypothesis: What if the imagination could affect the images that underlie natural productions?

> if the magic power of the imagination or the human artifice with respect to animal bodies were granted a faculty to alter the generative power itself, to reshape the originary model of nature ... one would no longer know at all from which original nature had started, or how far its alteration could go, and into which distorted shape [*Fratzengestalt*] the species and kinds might finally degenerate [*verwildern*] given that the human imagination knows no boundaries.[53]

Zammito cites this passage as a crucial Kantian sally against *Sturm und Drang*, and the barb against a "human imagination [that] knows no boundaries" does seem aimed at Herder and his cohort.[54] But Kant himself wishes to conserve the integrity of natural images against the threat of an overzealous imagination in §17, where the mind seems poised to average out the phenotypical differences between races. In other words, Kant wants to limit the "magic power of the imagination," which might alter or "reshape" the images, or archetypes, that nature used to ground its operations; this passage from "Determination" even traffics in the language of an aesthetic ideal – an "originary model of nature." For Kant, the imagination must recognize boundaries set for it by teleological principles, which delimit real classificatory distinctions and thereby real aesthetic models, shapes or *Urbilder*; and such restraint reflects a central feature of Kant's philosophical disposition toward the natural world: "I take as my principle not to admit any botching influence of the power of the imagination on nature's business of generation, and not to admit any human faculty to effect alterations in the ancient original of the species or kinds." The imagination must acknowledge its limits; it cannot alter "the ancient original of the species or kinds," another reference to an *Urbild*. Were the imagination to synthesize a normal idea for the human species as a whole, including its facial features, it would constitute for Kant precisely such an alteration; or to use Kant's words, such a general standard would "disfigure" the "ancient original" and jeopardize the ordered system of nature with the "distorted shape" into which "species and kinds might finally degenerate." Zammito states that this passage reflects an issue of absolute foundational importance for Kant: "Kant feared for the dissolution of the two essential boundaries upon which his philosophy rested: that between matter and life, and that between organisms and man."[55] But there is a third essential boundary in Kant's natural philosophy – between races. Although Kant admitted the "law of half-breed generation" and relied on it as a confirmation of monogenism, his aversion to race mixing and his enforcement of the boundaries between organisms and man are grounded on the same philosophical commitment: compromise threatens to overstep the real distinctions, the *Naturgattungen*, that must exist for a rational, orderly conception of nature.

If Kant undertook a reevaluation of his views on race sometime in the early 1790s, as has been argued by Kleingeld, then his theorization of racial difference in "On the Ideal of Beauty" needs to be taken into account, if only for the sheer contemporaneity of the arguments in §17 with Kant's supposed reassessment. The date of Kant's "second thoughts" on race come from the Dohna Lectures on Physical Geography (1792), which are said contain Kant's final racist statements.[56] By the time Kant writes *Towards Perpetual Peace* (1795), Kleingeld shows, he had dispensed with his belief in the agential or intellectual inferiority of non-white races as well as his commitment to a racial hierarchy. All races are included under the aegis of cosmopolitan right. But Kleingeld also claims that Kant settled on a "purely physiological concept" of race, and she takes her evidence for Kant's position from his final published statement on racial difference, "On the character of the races" from *APPV* (1798):

> Instead of *assimilation*, which nature intended in the melting together of different races, she has here made a law of exactly the opposite: namely, in a people of the same race (for example, the white race), instead of allowing

the formation of their characters constantly and progressively to approach one another in likeness – where ultimately only one and the same portrait would result, as in prints taken from the same copperplate – rather to diversify to infinity the characters of the same tribe.[57]

This is an aesthetics of race, not a "purely physiological concept." What had to that point been the *sine qua non* of Kant's physiological determination of race – the biological fact of necessarily heritable traits, with skin color as its principle empirical datum – is replaced by a rumination on shape: "prints taken from the same copperplate." When Kant first imagines the appearance of the white race in this passage, he designates an image that is identical to the normal idea from §17: a synthetic image that would allow "the formation of their characters constantly and progressively to approach one another in likeness." As a result, with another distinctly artistic flourish, "only one and the same portrait would result." Yet Kant seems by 1798 to have modified the position, stated in §17, that the normal idea can serve as an aesthetic standard or *Urbild* for a race. He adds an additional law of nature that promotes *intra*-racial diversity: "she has here made a law of exactly the opposite . . . to diversify to infinity the characters of the same tribe." But if this new law seems like a departure from Kant's position in the third *Critique*, it in fact reflects his distaste for the normal idea as an "academically correct" standard. A footnote to §17 clarifies that the normal idea exhibits correctness because it "does not contradict any condition under which alone a thing of this species can be beautiful"; he then illustrates his critical discernment on the topic of correctness by referring to none other than a portrait painter: "One will find that a perfectly regular face, which a painter might ask to sit for him as a model, usually says nothing: because it contains nothing characteristic, and thus expresses more the idea of the species than anything specific to a person."[58] In §17 the normal idea of the species/race lacks anything characteristic, which is what permits it to serve as a standard for the species as a whole. As such, the correctness of the normal idea suffices as a racial *Urbild* when Kant is concerned with comparing the morphologies of multiple races. When he compares intra-racial morphology in *APPV*, Kant augments the normal idea with an additional principle so as to lend the appearance of a single race a tasteful measure of diversity.

The thesis that Kant revised his stance on race in the early 1790s gains a measure of support when Kant's final position is understood in the aesthetic terms of his last two published statements on racial difference. There is no racial hierarchy with the normal idea: essential differences exist between aesthetic standards, but Kant does not claim that the appearance of one race is superior to another, as did Winckelmann with his preference for the Greek form. And Kant does not associate the normal idea of a species with any "inner predispositions." The lack of a "drive to activity" that "makes negroes disinclined to labor," as Kant put it in 1788, would find no place in an account of racial difference based exclusively on shape.[59] There is simply no room for claims about intelligence, agency or internal attributes when racial difference is governed exclusively by external form. So if Kant's cosmopolitanism led him to discard his racism, this occurred as an adjunctive process to an aesthetic theorization of race that by the mid 1790s was well underway, probably already by 1788, when Kant introduces the motif of a portrait painter in conjunction with a discussion of Shaftesbury and the purposive dimensions of the human face.[60] After this initial gesture in 1788, Kant gave his aesthetics of racial difference its fullest articulation in §17. The political essays Kleingeld cites are indeed important; they help explain why after 1792 Kant abandoned his final retrograde attitudes, articulated in the Dohna Lectures of that year. But by then Kant had made the most important advances toward an aesthetic theory of race, which he ultimately completed at the end of his career in *APPV.*

Shape is the foundational component of the Kantian conception of race after the critical turn, a fact that has been overshadowed by the attention paid to Kant's obsession with skin color.[61] In his account of racial difference from 1775, Kant explicitly eliminates shape from his articulations of Buffon's law and monogenism. By 1785, he entertains shape as a potential mark of racial appearance – "the Mongolian particularity actually concerns the shape [*Gestalt*] and not the color"; and also, "one cannot make out with certainty whether the Kaffir shape [*Gestalt*] of the Papuans ... indicates a special race."[62] But at that point Kant still preferred skin color as the empirical condition that signified an underlying biological law. By 1788 shape played an ever more important role in light of challenges from Forster, a devotee of the anatomist Samuel Thomas Soemmering; Kant clings to skin color as the primary sign of race in "On the Use of Teleological Principles in Philosophy," his final essay devoted principally to the topic of race; but at multiple points he admits that racialized shape is a "hereditary peculiarity."[63] Then, probably in response to Blumenbach, Kant likely realized the preferability of facial shape to skin color as a discernible racial trait. So, in §17, we see Kant importing a natural-historical thesis about the essential differences between racial physiology into the aesthetic framework of his theory of the ideal of beauty, delineating racial *Urbilder* according to the shape of facial characteristics and thereby displacing the biological criteria that had there-tofore governed racial difference. Kant then extends his views to include the shape – or to use another entirely appropriate term, the aesthetic form – of intra-racial appearance in *APPV*, again with no mention of skin color. Shape conforms to a distinctly positive vector over the course of Kant's career, going from what was explicitly excluded in 1775 to the defining condition of race in the 1790s.

On this reading, rather than race constituting a "purely physiological concept," it is precisely the untenability of Kant's race theory as a physio-logical or biological fact that forces him to render racial difference in aesthetic terms. In light of the challenges from Forster, Soemmering and Blumenbach, Kant must have felt compelled to maintain divisions between racial appearances but unable to do so with the concepts, such as skin color, or the discursive apparatus he had preferred in the 1780s. So Kant transposes racial shapes into the only framework he could find to articulate essential differences, an aesthetic one, where the thesis that facial shape reflects racial categories dovetails with an argument meant to sup-plant Winckelmann's views about the classical profile.[64] And while the normal idea does indeed designate the physiology of racial character, it is not therefore a "purely physiological concept" because Kant's aesthetic framework brings all sorts of problematic cargo in tow: taste and beauty, correctness, purposiveness and, most important, a prioritiza-tion of an average shape – a stereotype – as the defining feature of a race. If anything, when translated into an aesthetic register, an average standard or *Urbild* only intensifies racial divisions inasmuch as they permit races to be judged on the order of a species.

What sort of ethics, then, is entailed by a Kantian aesthetic anthropol-ogy? First, Kant's aesthetics of race does not eliminate his racism. It expresses perforce the racist position he held most dear – his aversion to interracialism. But the ethical stakes become more vexed when Kant introduces moral value into his theory of an ideal of beauty through the "idea of reason." He relates how the ideal of beauty must accommodate "the visible expression of moral ideas," an inscription of normative value onto physical form that results "in bodily manifestation (as the effect of what is inward) their [the moral ideas] combination with everything that our understanding connects with the morally good." Kant is some distance here from giving a brief for universal cosmopolitan rights, to say nothing of willing a maxim that can be made into a universal law. He is concerned, rather, with an aesthetic representation of moral value that somehow purports to "please universally." And the moral ideas he chooses are more numerous than the "noble" profile adopted from Winckelmann and mentioned in the *Anthropology Mrongovius*. Kant cites an array of attributes that have had long, often dubious afterlives in the history of art: "goodness of soul, or purity, or strength, or repose." Thus even if the racialized ideals of *The Critique of Judgment* cannot accommodate the "inner predispositions" of Kant's earlier race theory, the outer dimensions of human shapes can nevertheless be endowed with moral value through visual representations "of what is inward."

Yet surely the most suspect feature of Kant's final stance on race has less to do with the moral ramifications of his aesthetics than with the notion of "diversity" as such, for it is based on an essentialist theory of racial character. When Kant claims in *APPV* that nature prefers to "diversify to infinity" the characters of a single race, it is but an offshoot of the same desire to promote diversity by maintaining divisions *between* races. Nature intends diversity, Kant thinks. As a result, he longs to keep races apart.

A more suspicious reading would likely invert that causal priority and interpret Kant's desire to keep races apart as the driving force behind his arguments for natural diversity. Wherever the onus for Kant's diversitarianism is placed, the rhetorical and logical purchase of his aesthetic anthropology is based on distinctions of kind and degree, qualitative and quantitative perfection. Unique ideals of beauty go hand in hand with essentially different anthropological kinds. Even though these distinctions do not necessitate the preference of one natural shape over another – "European" over "negro," for instance, as was the case for Winckelmann – Kant's method for distinguishing anthropological classes is, to say the least, a highly qualified form of egalitarianism. Not only did Kant arrive at his position after clinging to inegalitarian views on racial character for most of his career. His arguments for racial equality, such as they are, retain an aversion to interracialism and an investment in diversity that reflect an unshakeable theoretical conviction: the natural separation of races.

Compromised as Kant's position is when weighed against contemporary standards, he was considerably more advanced than many of his contemporaries and predecessors – or, as we will see in the next chapter, his successors. In addition to ranking the various normal ideas as essentially separate but fundamentally equal, Kant bestows upon every member of the species *der Mensch* the ability to determine its own ends through reason. On this point, Kant never wavers in the third *Critique*. All races enjoy the dignity of belonging to the human species. Indeed, the natural-philosophical premises of *The Critique of Judgment* require that subspecies – in this case, races – assume a place within a superordinate species and still higher-order genera. This is the core vision of a hierarchical natural order that drives Kantian teleology; and it is the same vision that Boas, to recall the argument from the introduction, construed as aesthetic. Accordingly, individuals are arranged into races that are duly assigned to a more general category – the human species. From this it follows that all individual humans, regardless of race, are in principle rational beings, though in practice their exercise of reason may be thwarted by contingent factors. So each racialized individual is human from an aesthetic-anthropological point of view, even if Kant could not bring himself to entertain how such an ideal human might look.

CHAPTER 2

Ideals of Beauty

In the end, it all depends on the *purpose* for which the lie is told.
—Nietzsche, *The Antichrist*, §56

Had Kant extended his universalist premises to their logical conclusion, he would have been forced to produce an ideal for *der Mensch* as a whole, a standard of beauty according to which all humans are measured. The dissonance in Kant's account of racialized ideals arises from the fact that his anthropological theory entails race-mixing. All humans, by virtue of belonging to the same species, are capable of procreating irrespective of their membership in a subspecies; hence the offspring of two individuals from different races will manifest attributes according to what Kant called the "law of half-breed generation." Yet Kant himself was only able to imagine perfect types that corresponded to particular races: "pure breeds," as it were, instead of a truly universal type for the species as a whole.

For all his uncertainty regarding the purposive features that signify racial difference – skin color, skull shape – Kant argued tirelessly for the transcendental status of *Naturgattungen*. Teleological judgments refer to mental operations and not to nature in itself. They are regulative, not constitutive principles. Natural philosophers working in Kant's wake, however, did not rest content with the qualified transcendentalism advanced in the three *Critiques*. In an effort to bridge the dualist chasm opened up by the critical philosophy, post-Kantian idealists rejected, or at the very least modified, the Kantian division between the world of phenomena and things-in-themselves.[1] So for Friedrich Schelling, the principles that regulated mental life were identified with the laws governing the natural world, albeit at a more fundamental philosophical level. Mind and Nature were mutually constituting polarities of an underlying Absolute. Accordingly, *teloi* could be construed as inhering in organisms themselves since mind and nature had been reconciled. For Goethe, archetypes were the ideals underlying the behavior of actual organisms in the course of their lawful development. Strictly speaking, these *Urbilder* were only intuitable in the mind and not actually encountered in experience. But they were not, therefore, any less real. On the contrary, archetypes constituted the lawful substrate of Nature itself. In a sense, then, they were more real than observations of entities because in the moment of cognizing an archetype, a fundamental unity of nature was grasped through a combination of empirical inquiry and philosophico-poetic insight.[2]

Therefore even though *Naturphilosophen* remained within a broadly teleological framework, they departed from Kant in ways that radically altered the critical enterprise laid out in the third *Critique*. These departures then opened up new theoretical horizons. To take one example, Kant followed Buffon in tending to limit his natural-philosophical reflections to the level of species and subspecies. And for good reason. It was at these taxonomical levels that laws like mutual fertility seemed to operate.[3] Once equipped with a more robust idealism, though, naturalists scaled up *Urbilder* in an effort to understand the nature of higher-order classes. So Goethe speculated about the ideal form of all plants and animals while transcendental scientists such as Lorenz Oken and Richard Owen posited archetypes for the vertebrate phylum.[4] In short, *Naturphilosophen* transgressed the limits set on the critical philosophy by Kant, but they did so in order to complete the project of constructing an aesthetics of nature: an ordering of species and genera into a coherent hierarchy of categories.

But what of the categories Kant elided or marginalized in his original analysis in §17, above all women and the mixed-race figure that would represent a true aesthetic ideal for *der Mensch* as a whole? In other words, what is the place of a specifically aesthetic *anthropology* in the expanded aesthetic science undertaken by post-Kantian natural philosophers? This chapter answers these questions by tracing Kantian natural philosophy through its initial reception, particularly in the writings of Goethe, to works of popular anthropology and cultural polemics of the nineteenth century – works that, despite their low-cultural pedigree, represent the most direct attempts to resolve the anthropological dilemmas posed by Kantian aesthetics. Indeed, the promise to theorize a genuinely human aesthetic ideal conceived in accordance with a rigorous monogenism was fulfilled less than a century after Kant published the third *Critique*, albeit in a context far removed from the lecture halls of the Albertina. In their pamphlet *Miscegenation: The Theory of the Blending of the Races, Applied to the American White Man and Negro* (1864), two American journalists named David Croly and George Wakeman contest the priority of European aesthetic standards by conceiving of an interracial ideal of beauty.[5] Rejecting the traditional attribution of superior beauty to the white race, they argue that a mixed-race type is the apotheosis of human perfection – exactly the position that a more consistent Kantianism would entail. But for all their egalitarian posturing, Croly and Wakeman had little interest in creating a more perfect human. They were, in fact, perpetrating a ruse. They published their pamphlet anonymously in the hopes that their arguments for mixed-race supremacy would incite a backlash against Abraham Lincoln's reelection, thereby offsetting the military losses being suffered by the Confederacy across the South.

Over the course of twenty chapters and seventy pages, Croly and Wakeman showcase a range of theoretical strategies: political, religious, anatomical and, not least, aesthetic. The seventh chapter, "The Type Man a Miscegen," introduces an ideal of masculine beauty rendered as a mixed-race type. The twelfth chapter, "The Miscegenetic Ideal of Beauty in Woman," shifts the gender parameters of the argument while retaining its aesthetic ambitions. "In what," the chapter begins, "does beauty consist?" Luckily for Croly and Wakeman, they had an answer ready to hand. Examination of the archival record reveals they lifted passages from another aesthetic treatise, *Beauty: Illustrated Chiefly by an Analysis and Classification of Beauty in Woman* (1836), written by the Scottish anatomist Alexander Walker (1779–1852). Published in a total of five editions including an American version in 1845, *Beauty* conjures a full-fledged philosophy of nature in support of its ideal of female perfection, drawing on a wide range of sources, some of them explicitly Kantian, in order to make its case for the nature of beauty. Under the charge of ascertaining "whether a branch of science, which is strictly founded on anatomy and physiology" can provide the basis for "judgment of female beauty," Walker derives an aesthetic theory out of contemporary biology. Along the way, he exposes the aesthetic assumptions underlying his essentialist theory of human character.[6]

The combined force of *Miscegenation* and *Beauty* demonstrates the discursive versatility of aesthetic perfection, illustrating how aesthetic science descending from Kant through *Naturphilosophen* exited the confines of high theory and entered everyday polemics not only on the European continent but in a wide swath of the Anglophone world as well. And it is precisely in these cultural zones where aesthetic anthropology could do – and did – the most ideological damage, as the persistence of the term "miscegenation," first coined by Croly and Wakeman, attests. Therefore, even as they operate at lower theoretical altitudes, the authors of *Miscegenation* and *Beauty* perform genuine theoretical work left unfinished by their more illustrious predecessors; and the solutions they provide for the aesthetic-anthropological dilemmas inherited from Kant and his contemporaries reveal with bracing clarity the very real ramifications of the idealist technicalities expounded in the third *Critique*.

2.1 Being for Pleasure

Besides ascending the taxonomical ladder from species to genera to the vertebrate phylum and even to the kingdoms of plants and animals, post-Kantian natural philosophers transformed the content of *Urbilder* from the ideals outlined in §17 of "The Analytic of the Beautiful." Where Kant argued that the normal idea was an arithmetic mean or average shape, a method with precedents in Joshua Reynolds and Johann Tetens, Goethe temporalized the archetype. Animated by a version of Blumenbach's *Bildungstrieb*, the Goethean archetype consists of a single ideal structure that contains all the permutations of an organism *in potentia*.[7] For mammals, the vertebra is the foundational organ that transforms itself into various shapes of the skeleton; and for the plant, the leaf assumes different forms at particular stages of botanical development.[8] Thus the *Essay on the Metamorphosis of Plants* (1790) begins with a description of the "various shapes [*Gestalten*]" of the seed-leaves or cotyledon before relating how those early forms become the stem leaves.[9] Concentrating on a single cycle of an annual flowering plant, Goethe then details how those stem leaves transform into the calyx but in a "very changed shape [*Gestalt*]."[10] In the main, the essay consists of intricate, often brilliant descriptions of the formal permutations that culminate in the flowering, reproduction and initiation of a new cycle of growth. A shape, on this account, is not a static "normal idea" for a species or subspecies. It is, rather, the ideal protagonist of an organic unfolding, hence the name Goethe gave to the natural-philosophical enterprise that included his reflections on both plants and animals: morphology. For Goethe, shapes possess a logic. *Morphoi* are agents of a coherent, dynamic process of development.

Published in the same year as the third *Critique*, Goethe's *Essay* was written as its author was still absorbing the force of Kantian natural philosophy.[11] An unpublished introduction to the essay notes the writings of a "new philosophical school" and cites a section from "The Critique of Teleological Judgment."[12] Elsewhere, Goethe credits his initial reading of the third *Critique* with ushering in a "most happy period of life."[13] On the core matter of how to construct an aesthetic science grounded in a rational order of species and genera, however, Goethe pulls back in the face of the problems that spurred Kant to write *The Critique of Judgment*. In a set of botanical notes written in 1788, well before publication of the third *Critique*, Goethe admits the "great difficulty of ascertaining the type of an entire class so that it fits with every category and in each species."[14] Yet Kant posited precisely such shapes as normal ideas for subspecies in §17. Looking back on his botanical researches more than four decades after the publication of the *Essay*, Goethe confesses that "the task of describing genera with confidence and placing species under them seemed to me insoluble."[15] But it was this very task that Kant set out to solve in his natural philosophy. Goethe, for all his skill in theorizing the natural world, lacked the philosophical prowess that powered Kant's teleology. Indeed, one reason for Goethe's excitement upon discovering the third *Critique* was his sense that Kant had provided a more rigorous foundation for analogies between art and nature. This philosophical support then informed the more detailed, and more empirically rigorous, examinations of the natural world that Goethe pursued in the gardens of Weimar and during his sojourns to Italy.

The Kantian contours of Goethe's project come out more clearly in the essays devoted to animals, no surprise since Kant, though interested in organisms generally, was especially keen to explain the purposive action evinced by animals and, in a more refined and rational manner, humans. In an attitude reminiscent of Kant's skepticism about strictly empirical approaches to nature, Goethe calls for a rational methodology to comprehend human and animal anatomy in the "Essay on the Shape of Animals," an unpublished fragment composed not long after his essay on plants. In the text, Goethe acknowledges the wealth of data furnished by dissection but laments when anatomical studies merely observe and label the myriad parts of bodies. Thus when he attempts to derive a *Typus* for the animal kingdom, Goethe believes he is contributing to a rationalization of nature in a Kantian spirit. An ideal type, Goethe claims with a classical flourish, should function as a "guiding thread through the labyrinth of shapes" so that "each individual observation can be put to general use" and understood as belonging to a whole. He then argues that such a regulative form

> seems to me to be the way if a general type or general schema is to be worked out and drawn up, which would subordinate humans as well as animals, along with the classes, the sexes, the species according to which they would be judged [*beurteilt*].[16]

This passage indicates the ambition of Goethe's natural philosophy as well as its Kantian foundation. No longer restricted to subspecies in the manner of §17, a *Typus* should comprehend humans, animals, and the constituent categories they contain – classes, species, sexes or any other natural distinction between individuals. And even though a hierarchy of species and genera is not worked out in detail, such a structure is implied by the claim that certain categories will be subordinated to others. In sum, Goethe expands the theoretical ambit of the teleological shapes presented by Kant in *The Critique of Judgment*. Natural types should encompass all anthropological and zoological categories – from subspecies to species to genera and beyond. At the same time, one feature remains constant for Goethe no less than for Kant. An ideal shape, whatever the scale of the morphology, is the basis for assigning parts to an organic whole through an act of judgment.

Aesthetic concepts pervade Goethe's natural philosophy. In the essays on animals, unity amid diversity is invoked as an axiom licensing the search for an ideal shape.[17] "Is there nothing more beautiful," Goethe wonders in an expansive treatment of anatomy from 1794, "than glimpsing the mysterious construction of formation [*Bau der Bildung*] that builds according to a single pattern."[18] No mere abstraction, unity amid diversity is a principle fundamentally connected to the beauty of the natural world. An underlying *morphos* furnishes a standard for judgment so that organisms may take their place in a harmonious, lawfully organized structure instead of being scattered individuals divorced from any given order. Or as Goethe writes in the "Lectures on a General Introduction to Comparative Anatomy" (1796), reflecting on the "very different parts" of animals and considering "their organic coherence" in turn produces "very beautiful results."[19] But besides finding beauty in the natural world, Goethe frequently relies on the concept of perfection and likens the scientist to the artist, or rather, the genius (*Genie*). The true scientist according to Goethe does not merely observe nature. Attuned to natural harmony, a scientist employs the synthetic sensibilities befitting a creator of coherent, rule-governed wholes – artworks – which are formed analogously to purposive organisms.[20]

Even as Goethe employs an aesthetic vocabulary in his natural philosophy, his archetypes make different claims on aesthetic discourse than the ideal forms that populate Kantian anthropology. In §17 of the third *Critique*, it will be recalled, a heuristic device allows readers to imagine a normal idea as an average shape: a clear, easily comprehensible, and most important, visually perceptible *Urbild* for anthropological subspecies. In short, it is possible to picture a Kantian type. Indeed, Kant himself stated that a portrait painter could draw its outline. Goethe also insists that the archetype is an image: "a certain general picture [*Bild*] lays at the base of all these individual shapes," he argues in the "First Draft of a General Introduction to Comparative Anatomy."[21] Writing in the "Lectures" a year later, he asserts that mammals, birds, fish, amphibians and also humans are "all formed according to one *Urbild*."[22] Paradoxically, though, the Goethean archetype is an image that cannot be seen by the eye or even pictured in the mind. No artist could ever render its form on canvas. Two features of the archetype explain this impossibility. First, since the *Typus* comprises all the various manifestations of particular organic parts, a single image would have to comprehend distinct parts at the same time. Calyx, flower, stem-leaves and all the other components of a plant at different developmental stages would need to be reduced to a common figure. Any image would therefore be but a fragmentary snapshot that fails to capture the dynamic growth of an integral whole. Second, the common form for animals must include all the constitutive shapes in a class, from humans and other mammals to amphibians, fish and birds. Inevitably any particular outline would come closer to one species and conform less well to the rest, thereby favoring a certain class as exemplary at the expense of others. That is to say, the conception of the *Typus* as a general schema for all species precludes any particular image, including the image of a human, from representing the diversity of forms belonging to a natural category. Taken together, the dynamism of the archetype and its comprehensiveness rule out a visual representation of the *Typus* in the manner of a Kantian normal idea or, later and more famously, Owen's sketch of the vertebrate archetype. Aware of these difficulties, Goethe admits in the "Lectures" that "this *Urbild* cannot be represented to the senses though it can be to the soul;" and in the "Essay on the Shape of Animals," he concedes that the unifying type "withdraws from our eye and only remains visible to our understanding."[23] The archetype, therefore, is an image in a strictly regulative sense. Itself imperceptible, the *Typus* acts as an intuitable schema that governs the formal development of organs, organisms and the species and genera to which they belong.

Yet subtracting the specifically visual content from an *Urbild* immediately raises the question of how, if at all, the *Typus* can still qualify as an aesthetic construct. How, in other words, can the Goethean archetype accommodate an aesthetic anthropology in the absence of sensory dimensions? These questions are at the center of a short essay on aesthetics Goethe wrote in 1794, just as he was returning to his studies of anatomy after a hiatus devoted to optics and at a moment when his bond with Friedrich Schiller was becoming increasingly close. Though far more cursory than Schiller's *Kallias or Concerning Beauty* (1793) and the *Letters on Aesthetic Education* (1794), two landmarks of post-Kantian aesthetics that were gestating at the same time, Goethe's "To What Extent the Idea 'Beauty Is Perfection with Freedom' Can Be Applied to Organic Nature" testifies to the intellectual proximity between the two men. Both Goethe and Schiller sought to elaborate Kantian insights first developed in the third *Critique*; and both believed that the path to a richer and more nuanced theory of beauty lay in developing a conjunction between freedom and perfection that Kant had held apart.

Seeking to overcome the hard distinction between free and adherent beauty made in the third moment of "The Analytic of the Beautiful," Goethe combines freedom and perfection through a reflection on organic form: "The parts of all creatures are so formed that they enjoy their being and maintain it and are capable of reproducing; in this sense, all things are to be called perfect."[24] At first glance, this definition appears to retain the ontological dimensions of Kantian perfection while dispensing with the value claims that anchor perfect beauty in a concept of what an organism ought to be. Organisms are defined by their sheer existence, *Dasein*, and in a sense of pleasure they derive from being in the world. This apparent absence of normative commitments is belied, however, by the statement that perfection and its attendant pleasure result from being "so formed." Creatures are products of design, it turns out. The pleasure they take in their being arises from purposive formation. As such, any assertion of design must have recourse to a rule or schema. Some conceptual guide must determine how parts ought to relate to the whole. For Goethe, of course, the archetype performs this theoretical role. The *Typus* is the standard according to which organisms ought to be formed.

Since the archetype underlies organic perfection and the ontological joy that creatures experience and propagate into the future, the dynamism of the *Typus* necessarily inflects perfect beauty. Taking leave from aestheticians in the rationalist tradition who identified beauty with perfection, Goethe maintains that beauty results from perfect formation that *at the same time* enables the free agency of the organism: "we call a perfectly organized being beautiful when upon seeing it we can think *that the free and multifarious use of all its parts is possible for it, as soon as it wishes.*"[25] To qualify as beautiful, a creature must be so formed that it appears capable of free action. Neither an adjunct added to perfect form nor an accidental attribute, freedom arises out of the very construction of an organism; and this copresence of freedom with perfection is what warrants a judgment of taste on the part of the observing subject.

Ugliness, then, results from restraints on freedom: "when the parts of an animal are formed in such a way that this creature can only express its being in a thoroughly restricted manner," Goethe writes, "we will find such an animal ugly." To illustrate the point, Goethe refers to the case of the lowly mole. Suited to subterranean existence, the mole possesses organic adaptations that serve a definite purpose: enlarged forelimbs, for instance, which aid in burrowing underground. But because an organism is a dynamic, integral totality, adaptations in one part will generate compensatory effects elsewhere in the body. Enlarged forelimbs, for example, produce a diminution in other organs. An adaptation "causes the predominance of one part so that the voluntary use of the other limbs is hindered." In the case of the mole, enlarged forelimbs mean reduced eyesight and smaller hindquarters. The ensuing imbalance between parts therefore reduces the overall coordination of the organism, compromising its freedom and thus its beauty. "This organism, since it does not have any harmony, cannot give me a harmonious impression." The mole, since it cannot freely synchronize the movements of its parts, forfeits its claim to beauty. A horse, by contrast, suffers no such structural imbalance, Goethe argues. Unlike the mole, the horse possesses parts that are so coordinated with the whole that the creature may enjoy its being and perpetuate its essence into the future while at the same time appearing to exercise free agency.

Goethe is not interested in the free play of the cognitive faculties sparked in a moment of disinterested reflection on form. He endows certain organisms with an objective attribute, freedom, that can then awaken an impression of harmony in the spectator. Accordingly, the principle of *beauty is perfection with freedom* should obtain for all animals formed according to the same archetype – moles, horses, amphibians and birds, as well as, of course, humans. While it is true that Goethe directly proceeds to apply his aesthetic principle to humans, making *der Mensch* into a privileged aesthetic being because it is the organism most liberated from natural purposes, his views on human beauty, like Kant's before him, evince a similar drift from putatively universal aesthetic standards to estimations of beauty that correspond to particular classes of humankind. But where Kant worried about maintaining racial categories in his theory of ideal beauty, Goethe's aesthetic anthropology makes categorial distinctions between the perfect form of the male and female sexes.

To be sure, Goethe was not the first to adduce sexual differences in human beauty. Kant had argued that the female form was unavoidably associated with sensual charm, which nullified claims to disinterested judgment. Still earlier, Winckelmann had associated the aesthetic ideal with the male figure, an argument that Walker sets out to refute at length in the treatise on female beauty, examined later. For his part, Goethe consistently uses the term *Mensch* – as opposed to *Mann* – when discussing humans in "Beauty Is Perfection with Freedom." At one point, he entertains the possibility of deriving "the concept of a beautiful human [*eines schönen Menschen*]"; and his essay is organized around distinctions between animals and humans, that is, inter- as opposed to intra-species distinctions. But in the "First Draft of a General Introduction to Comparative Anatomy," his sprawling text on anatomical problems written only a few months after sending the manuscript of "Beauty Is Perfection with Freedom" to Schiller, Goethe digresses from a discussion of the archetype in order to apply his anatomical insights to the case of female beauty. With uncharacteristic obtuseness, he states that "the center of the entire female existence is the womb," thus diverging from his earlier definition of organic nature in "Beauty Is Perfection with Freedom" by eliding any discussion of pleasure or self-preservation. Ontological joy and its maintenance in the present are elided in favor of perpetuating the species into the future, with females consigned to performing a distinct natural purpose: reproduction.

Notwithstanding these differing stances on organic nature – the one pertaining to all animals, the other to the specific class of females – a common aesthetic anthropology does unite the arguments of the "First Draft" and "Beauty Is Perfection with Freedom." Thus Goethe argues that the disproportionate importance of the womb in females causes a disharmonious compensation in other parts of the body: "the vital force seems to expend so much on this part [the womb] that, like in all perfect organisms, it is required to proceed more sparingly with other parts of the shape; from that I would explain the reduced beauty in women." A pure judgment of taste is not contaminated by sensual charm according to Goethe. Beauty suffers due to the purposive growth of an organ that thereupon compromises the appearance of other parts of the female figure. Crucially, Goethe does not claim that the excessive expenditure of vital force on the womb necessarily causes unfreedom, though such a sacrifice may be implied since the balance and coordination between parts will presumably be impaired by the performance of a natural purpose. He argues that the aesthetic value of females is compromised by the operations of organic perfection as such, whereby beauty in other parts is diminished in relative proportion to the increased functionality of a single organ. Why the reproductive mechanics of male anatomy do not entail a similar maldistribution is not a problem that seems to trouble Goethe. In any event, his point is clear enough. Just as the enlarged forelimbs of the mole, developed for the sake of performing a distinct purpose, disrupt the harmony and therefore beauty of that species, so, too, does the purposive growth of a particular organ in females cause a degree of ugliness that afflicts all members of that organic class.

The argument about female beauty in the "First Draft" is pitched at a general level. Goethe's comments pertain to all animals, not humans in particular, though Goethe does appear to have an eye to the aesthetic dimensions of human females – women – since he immediately goes on to assert that "through all these considerations" about female beauty as such, "we ascend finally to humans [*Menschen*]" and a specifically anthropological account of perfection. But as with so much of his writing on anatomy and the archetype, Goethe merely gestures to a more sustained account that he leaves unfinished. For all its limitations, though, Goethe's brief discussion of female beauty does present an aesthetic anthropology conceived in terms of post-Kantian *Naturphilosophie*: a theorization of beauty as a conjunction of freedom with perfection in the appearance of an object itself rather than the cognitive faculties of the judging subject. Hence his concluding statement in "Beauty Is Perfection with Freedom" lays the groundwork for a future aesthetic philosophy developed in this spirit. Goethe asserts in his final paragraph that for aesthetic discourse "to be truly useful for friends of nature and art, it must have an anatomical-physiological basis."[26] For a theory of beauty to furnish true insight into the harmony of nature itself, it must ground the principle of *beauty is perfection with freedom* in a rigorous understanding of the operations of organic life.

Therefore when Walker claims to furnish an aesthetic theory "strictly founded on anatomy and physiology" in the introduction to *Beauty: Illustrated Chiefly by an Analysis and Classification of Beauty in Woman*, he is operating well within the main line of aesthetic anthropology descending from Kant to *Naturphilosophen*. In effect, Walker elaborates the tentative, cursory anatomico-physiological theory of female beauty that Goethe offers in the "First Draft," modifying that theory to accommodate a more comprehensive set of natural-philosophical considerations as they emerged in both Britain and France in the early decades of the nineteenth century. But more generally, all of the works descending from Kant through Goethe to Walker and eventually to Croly and Wakeman attempt to address the same foundational problem for aesthetic anthropology: how to provide a general theory of human beauty while preserving distinctions between ostensibly natural classes, whether racial subspecies as for Kant, sexes in the case of Goethe and Walker, or a combination of race and gender in the theory of female beauty posited in the *Miscegenation* pamphlet.

2.2 Romantic Philosophy, Classical Aesthetics

Even though Goethe and other *Naturphilosophen* in Jena and Weimar were well situated to disseminate Kantian insights, the most consequential developments of teleological science took place outside of Germany, especially in France, where events assumed a more antagonistic cast on the floor of the venerable *Académie des sciences*. It was there, in 1830, that the teleology of Georges Cuvier was pitted against the morphology of Étienne Geoffroy Saint-Hilaire, with both men positioning their anatomical theories with respect to natural philosophy in Germany. For his part, Cuvier ridiculed *Naturphilosophie*, which for him smacked of the unhinged mysticism he associated with Geoffroy.[27] For all his churlish criticism of German science, though, Cuvier has often been considered something of a Kantian. In his classic study of comparative anatomy, E. S. Russell remarks that Cuvier "was indeed a teleologist after the fashion of Kant."[28] More recently, Philippe Huneman has argued that the great French naturalist absorbed the principles of the third *Critique* during his training in Stuttgart in the 1890s as the fires of *Naturphilosophie* were beginning to catch light.

Against Cuvier's conception of organisms as purposive, rule-governed wholes adapted to survive in the conditions of their environment, Geoffroy maintained that morphological forms illustrate unity of type irrespective of function. The wing of the bird and the arm of a human, for instance, evince a commonality of structure even though they operate for the sake of different ends. By tracing more obscure homologies – bones in the piscine jaw and the inner ear of mammals, say – fundamental unities were deduced between organisms within the four basic natural classes or *embranchements* delineated by Cuvier and accepted by most naturalists: vertebrates, mollusks, articulates and radials. Then, more controversially, morphologists sought homologies illustrating unity of type between the various branches – between mollusks and vertebrates, say, which was the case that finally drove Cuvier to launch his attacks against Geoffroy on the floor of the *Académie*. Affinities between Geoffroy and *Naturphilosophie* were not lost on contemporaries. The derivation of typological unities drove the research agendas of both "*philosophie anatomique*," as Geoffroy called his science, and Goethean *Morphologie*. As it happens, Goethe himself wrote a critical synopsis of the debate that draws out connections between Cuvier and German science even as it consistently favors the synthetic genius of Geoffroy over the analytic precision of Cuvier.[29]

In her history of the Cuvier-Geoffroy debate, Toby Appel assigns Owen the primary credit for spreading Cuvier's principles in Britain. A stalwart of pre-Darwinian science, Owen was certainly a major conduit for French science into Britain. Yet Walker had been discussing Cuvier in print as early as 1809, when Owen was still a boy. Walker also participated in the British reception of Kant.[30] He quotes from A. F. M. Willich's influential 1798 translation of the *Prolegomena* to bolster blustery "refutations" of Hume and Berkeley.[31] Further, his polemic against Berkeley invokes "the celebrated Kant" and cites a French text that describes the critical philosophy as "un Idealisme plus ou moins absolue." These statements indicate that Walker was caught up in the first wave of Kant scholarship.[32] Epitomized by the infamous Garve-Feder review of the *Critique of Pure Reason* – the review that spurred Kant to write the *Prolegomena* – early readers grappled with how to distinguish the critical philosophy from its forerunners in the idealist tradition, particularly Berkeley.[33]

Besides these points of contact with continental and specifically Kantian currents, Walker had professional ties to some of the leading representatives of Romantic science in Britain. He studied anatomy in Edinburgh with John Barclay, who was an early source for idealism in British natural science and an important influence for Owen and Robert Knox, two of the period's most prominent transcendental anatomists who also studied with Barclay.[34] After breaking off his studies in Edinburgh, Walker moved to London to work at St. Bartholomew's Hospital under the surgeon John Abernethy, whom Coleridge would later admire for his stand against materialist theories of life and the atheism they were thought to imply.[35] The same path that led Walker from Edinburgh to an apprenticeship with Abernethy was followed five years later by Knox and some fifteen years later by Owen.[36] Thus Walker must have been exposed to the same influences that shaped the thinking of better known practitioners of transcendental anatomy.

Upon returning to Edinburgh after being dismissed for pointing out a mistake Abernethy made during a surgical demonstration, Walker founded the *Archives of Universal Science*, a journal that set out to comprehend all human thought under a cosmology authored by Walker himself. In the "Plan of the Natural System" devised by Walker, the cosmos adheres to rational principles.[37] Data alone are insufficient for understanding the operations of nature, Walker argues. If facts are to provide insight into natural phenomena, they must be arranged. Therefore in the same way that Kant and Goethe worried about aimless empiricists working in the absence of regulative principles, Walker believes that reason must be a necessary adjunct to observation.[38] Hence he produces a system that should put the sciences on the path of true discovery: a foundationalist hierarchy based on metaphysics, then proceeding to physics, and finally culminating in psychology, anatomy, chemistry and other higher-order disciplines. Over the course of his career, Walker modified the constituent classes of his natural system. Fifteen years later, he classified anatomy and physiology – by Goethe's lights, the two key disciplines for aesthetic theory – as "Anthropological Sciences" instead of "Particular Physics." (*Beauty* was, in fact, later published as part of a trilogy of Walker's writings titled *Anthropological Works*.) But even though the particular classes that make up his systems submit to nominal modifications, Walker's cosmologies share a consistent architecture. The sciences, like the natural world they are meant to explain, must conform to a rational totality divided according to a hierarchy of species and genera – a vision wholly in keeping with the principles of aesthetic science.

If Walker's philosophy was proto-Romantic, his tastes were decidedly classical. Writing for the *Archives* in 1809, Walker makes a version of the aesthetic argument he would later substantiate in *Beauty: Illustrated Chiefly by an Analysis and Classification of Beauty in Woman*, his anatomically oriented treatise on female beauty: "*all the fine arts result from the muscular motions of the body*," he stresses, going on to support his thesis with bombastic descriptions of classical statuary in a distinctly Winckelmannian vein.[39] Looking to the ancients, Walker identifies the "ideal elegance and grace" of the human body. He finds "ideal correctness" and "ideal purity" in the Laocoön group and other antique statues.[40] But where Winckelmann mostly managed to sublimate his sexual urges into trenchant critical prose, Walker takes a less mediated approach. When addressing the Venus di Medici, he comments on "the admirable form of the mammæ, whence man first learns ideal beauty" – a critical estimation that combines the detachment of medical diagnosis with a pornographic gaze.[41]

Walker's contribution to the history of aesthetics cannot be appreciated without acknowledging his debts to Winckelmann, who is both precedent and foil for the arguments of *Beauty: Illustrated Chiefly by an Analysis and Classification of Beauty in Woman*: "In the details as to female beauty," Walker writes in his introduction, "it will be seen how incorrectly Winckelmann says 'In female figures, the forms of beauty are not so different, nor the gradations so various as in those of males.'"[42] As in a Kantian definition of perfection, differences of kind and degree define aesthetic judgment. A claim about specifically different aesthetic forms

combines with evaluations of gradations or degrees of value. So even if
Kant translated such judgments into the more rigorous conceptual vocabulary of qualitative and quantitative perfection in the third *Critique*, they
were very much operative in the earlier Winckelmannian discourse, which
Walker transforms into a theory of female perfection in a nearly four-
hundred-page treatise devoted to re-gendering the classical standard.

Besides substituting one category of humankind for another – a perfect
woman in place of an ideal man – *Beauty* shifts the grounds for judgments
of taste from those assumed by Winckelmann. Rather than external factors
like climate, culture and the environment being the relevant causes of
aesthetic value, Walker turns to internal, anatomical systems as the basis
for human perfection. In doing so, the warrant for judgments of beauty
shifts from obvious features – the shape of the face, the form of the breast –
to more indirect causes, namely, internal structures and functions of
the body. For instance, in the chapter that Croly and Wakeman would
later plunder for their pamphlet, Walker opens by taking a hard
Winckelmannian line on judgments of taste: "a temperate climate and
fertile soil," he writes in "Of the Standard of Beauty in Woman," are the
conditions that allowed the cultivation of beauty in antiquity.[43] Yet by the
end of the chapter, and over the course of *Beauty* as a whole, Walker
reduces environmental factors to contingencies that permit the acquisition
of more or less prominent traits. Climatological, cultural or other chance
circumstances may generate differences in appearance, but they are differences of degree and not of kind. The essence of beauty – qualitative
perfection – is instead tied to physiological functions and anatomical
structures, which are elucidated with the help of the most recent science.
Thus Walker writes in his introduction that "absolute and essential
beauty" refers to immanent properties in the object itself, not accidents
wrought by external, environmental causes:

> the different kinds and combinations of beauty, which are the objects of
> taste to different persons, are founded upon the same general principle of
> organic superiority. Nay, even the preferences which, in beauty, appear to
> depend most on fancy, depend in reality on that cause; and the impression
> which every degree and modification of beauty makes on mankind has, as a
> fundamental rule, only their sentiment, more or less delicate and just, of
> physical advantage.[44]

The vagaries of taste devolve upon a single principle: "organic superiority."
An object is beautiful because it is better, stronger, superior – because it is
more perfect. Hence the rule for judging beauty does not arise from
environmental circumstance; nor does the ability to act freely influence

the beauty ascribed to organisms. Aesthetic value on this account consists in the "physical advantage" that allows an organism to respond to environmental impulses, its fitness or adaptation to the external world. Perfection alone constitutes "absolute and essential beauty," which inheres in "objects of taste" themselves.

With this theoretical foundation in place, Walker formulates an aesthetics whose structure is tripartite and hierarchical. There exist three "species of beauty" that correspond to three – always three – distinct kinds of objects. Walker begins his exposition in *Beauty* with the simplest kind, "inanimate beings" like rocks or clouds, whose beauty manifests through their adherence to geometrical rules; the beauty of "living beings" is then tied to life and growth; finally, "thinking beings" are beautiful because they conform to rational design – symmetry and fitness.[45] So, for example, Walker praises inanimate bodies insofar as they approach the regularity of a circle while for living beings, he singles out "contrast" and "variety" since they reflect the processes of growth and change. On this model, a rose is more beautiful than a dandelion because its petals intertwine with greater frequency, a sign of life itself.

Walker then refines this ontologico-aesthetic order into a schema for comprehending human anatomy as comprised of three anatomical systems: the locomotive system for regulating movement, the nutritive for supporting life, and the thinking system of the mind and rational faculty. As with the metaphysical distinctions between kinds of objects, each anatomical system has its own respective species of beauty. A body with a highly developed physique, for instance, is qualitatively different from a figure with graceful, intellectual refinement. Walker then takes one final step. He analyzes each kind of human beauty into three "varieties." The locomotive system divides into subspecies for bones, ligaments and muscles. The other systems have their own subordinate taxa. The point is the same. Each anatomical system, whether subspecies, species or genus, has its own distinct kind of beautiful body.

After analyzing bodies into their constituent systems, Walker unites his cascading trinities into a single hierarchy of value. Higher-order organisms, he argues, exhibit their own characteristic attributes while retaining the qualities of lower-order species.[46] Plants, for example, are more beautiful than rocks because they manifest both life-preserving qualities and the geometrical regularity that characterizes inanimate bodies: "we find the trunks and stems of plants, which are near the ground, resembling most in character the inanimate bodies from among which they spring. They assume the simplest and most universal form in nature, the round one;

but as growth is their great function, they extend in height and become cylindrical."[47] Plants retain their simple circular shape while raising it into a more complicated form, the enlarging cylinder, which reflects an essential disposition toward life and growth. Higher-order organisms are thus compounds that increase in complexity, and therefore value, while at the same time preserving the autonomy of each component system – a braided chain of progressively more perfect beings.

In short, ontological and anatomical categories correspond to unique kinds of beauty. "There are ... different kinds both of beauty and of goodness," Walker believes.[48] From this it follows that "judgment can be attained by analysis and classification alone." The stakes of this taxonomical aesthetics are evident in the chapter that would later appear in the *Miscegenation* pamphlet, "Of the Standard of Beauty in Woman," which concludes by turning away from the problematic of female beauty to entertain the value of other anthropological categories, in particular, categories of race:

> in the case of the African, he is born whitish, like the European, but he speedily loses such beauty for that of adaptation, by his colour, to the hot climate in which he exists. The latter beauty is the higher and more important one, and forms for the African a profitable exchange; but the European is still more fortunate, because, in the region he inhabits, the simple and elementary beauty is compatible with that of adaptation to climate.[49]

According to Walker, a European possesses simple beauty at birth, white skin. But simple beauty is not its only relevant characteristic. Whiteness is combined with a more complex aesthetic species: adaptive beauty, which bespeaks fitness to an environment. Therefore a European possesses both simple and complex beauty while an African, by contrast, must forfeit his elementary beauty obtained at birth for an adaptive beauty that makes him fit for his climate.

In addition to evincing a slippage from feminine to masculine ideals, this entire argument is predicated on a sleight that strikes at the heart of Walker's aesthetics. The concept of what kind of thing an organism ought to be – its implicit value claim – is either repressed or tacitly redefined to suit ideological ends. In this case, Walker substitutes an alternative characteristic of simple beauty in order to preserve a racial hierarchy. When distinguishing metaphysical entities – inanimate, animate, thinking bodies – he posits geometrical regularity as the definitional characteristic: "the elements of beauty in inanimate bodies consist in the simplicity, regularity, uniformity, proportion, order, &c., of those geometrical forms."[50] Simple beauty therefore results from the extent to which a particular object conforms to geometrical principles, that is, to concepts of regularity and order, which define the sort of thing an inanimate object ought to be and, what is more, authorize the sense of satisfaction arising from the observation of an object approximating that ideal.

This definition shifts when Walker postulates whiteness as the signal mark of simple beauty. Were nonracial characteristics the standard for ranking individuals and groups – the proportions of a circle, to use the earlier example – then judgments of beauty would cut across the lines dividing anthropological classes. An African might well have a more regular face than a European, which would threaten a racial hierarchy that prefers white over black. Once skin color is elevated into the essential attribute for the species of simple beauty – once what a human ought to be is associated with pigmentation instead of shape – all individuals are valued insofar as they approach or diverge from that objective quality. Walker may then derive satisfaction from the appearance of an individual with the attributes he esteems.

A determination of what kind of thing an organism ought to be, white rather than circular, underlies Walker's hierarchy of value. The premises here are the same as those governing Kant's aesthetic determination of the concept of race. Multiple categories are differentiated according to an ontological ought. As a consequence, Walker no less than Kant must account for the necessary distinctions that divide natural kinds; or what is the same, he must justify the ontological oughts that license essential differences of qualitative perfection.

2.3 Teleological Shapes Reconsidered

Though he had long policed taxonomical boundaries, Walker would more often assert their existence than justify them with reasons.[51] The situation changed in 1815 with an essay titled "An Attempt to Systematize Anatomy, Physiology, and Pathology," which provides Walker's most rigorous argument for essential classes.[52] A key passage from the essay would be republished verbatim in the "Anatomical Principles" section of *Kalygnomia; or, The Laws of Female Beauty* (1821), an early work of aesthetic anthropology to which Walker almost certainly contributed;[53] in a long quotation from an "Anatomical Report" published in 1824 in *The European Review*, a journal Walker edited; and then in *Beauty* in 1836 where it authorizes the tripartite distinction between locomotive, vital and intellectual systems.[54] With its systematic intent announced in the title, the essay begins by surveying the field. Continental teleologists of renown are named – Blumenbach, Cuvier and Kant all receive mention. Walker then makes his case for delineating anatomical systems: "each of these classes of organs is distinguished from another by the *structure* of its parts, by the *purposes* which it serves, and by the greater or less *obviousness* of its motions [Walker's emphasis]." Classes are distinguished because of structure, purpose and obviousness. The vacuous appeal to "obviousness" may be set aside. Walker is clearly trying satisfy his insatiable need for threes.

The other two criteria, structure and purpose, correspond to the respective positions of Geoffroy and Cuvier. While it may appear that Walker equates structure and purpose – both are reasons for distinguishing classes of organs – he in fact subordinates form to function, morphology to teleology:

> not one of them [classes of organs] can be confounded with one another: for that which performs locomotion, neither transmits liquids nor sensations; that which transmits liquids, neither performs motion from place to place, nor is the means of sensibility; and that which is the means of sensibility, neither performs locomotion nor transmits liquids.[55]

Anatomical structures are distinct because they perform different physiological functions. The class "locomotive organs" contains parts united for the purpose of movement. Vital and intellectual systems serve their own distinct ends: reproduction and cognition. Of the three criteria nominated for distinguishing classes, purpose is paramount.

Walker is, at bottom, a teleologist. He defines natural kinds according to their purposiveness. Bones, muscles and ligaments are mutually dependent members of a system directed toward a common *telos* – motion. This definition cannot be restricted to anatomical systems, however. Purposiveness licenses Walker's metaphysical distinctions between inanimate and animate beings. The former are determined by physical laws, without reference to ends, while organisms respond to mechanical impetuses for the sake of maintaining life. Even Walker's cosmologies are teleological. Domains of science are unique because they are directed toward different ends. Chemistry pursues the laws regulating inanimate matter; botany and zoology seek the principles governing organic life. Thus the foundationalist hierarchies that rise up from metaphysics through physics, chemistry and other human sciences do so according to a coherent totality of species and genera defined according to ends. For Walker, teleology determines the character of taxonomical classes – anatomical, metaphysical or aesthetic.

Or anthropological. Once purposiveness is the warrant for creating independent categories of humankind, then the members of a certain class must possess the traits that correspond to their definitional purpose – the concept of what they ought to be. For Robyn Cooper, this means that Walker defines "woman" according to one purpose in particular: sexual reproduction. Women, according to Cooper, are consigned by Walker to performing their reproductive function just as Goethe believed that "the center of the entire female existence is the womb."[56] But while it is true that Walker fetishizes reproduction in the *Anthropological Works*, the trilogy that included *Beauty*, he shows no reservations when defining species of female beauty according to purposes other than, or even contrary to, reproductive function. For instance, in discussing the category of locomotive beauty, Walker embarks on extended, multipage reveries elucidating the nature of a perfect type: "the shoulders, without being angular, are sufficiently broad and definite for muscular attachments; – the bosom, a vital organ, is of but moderate dimensions; – the waist, enclosing smaller nutritive organs, is remarkable for fine proportion . . . The whole figure is precise, striking, and often brilliant."[57] Walker is imagining a perfect body, an ideal *morphos* designed to satisfy a certain purpose; and he performs an imaginative ekphrasis very much in the vein of Winckelmann. In this particular instance, organs that function for the sake of locomotion are enhanced while qualities suited for reproduction and intellection are correspondingly diminished. Walker's depiction of the intellectual type provides a useful contrast:

> In the woman possessing this species of beauty, accordingly, the greater development of its upper part gives to the head, in every view, a pyriform appearance; – the face is generally oval; – the high and pale forehead announces the excellence of the observing faculties; – the intensely expressive eye is full of sensibility . . . she boasts easy and graceful motion, rather than the elegant proportion of the first [species of beauty, i.e. locomotion]. – The whole figure is characterized by intellectuality and grace.[58]

Purpose determines essence, the qualitative perfection of a thing. And within this schema, individuals may be ranked insofar as their traits reflect a concept of what kind of thing they ought to be. A taller giraffe has an adaptive advantage in its pursuit of survival; a rose in full bloom signals life in greater measure than a wilted one; a woman with a given figure embodies her particular purpose, whatever it may be, to a certain degree – quantitative perfection follows from qualitative perfection; differences of degree from distinctions of kind.

These expositions of ideal *morphoi* return the argument to the teleological shapes that Kant describes in §17. The main difference, of course, is that Walker executes an aesthetic determination of the concept of woman while Kant was interested in the concepts of human races. Nevertheless the same theoretical apparatus operates in both cases: *Naturgattungen* – natural species – are constituted through purposive distinctions. Each essential category, defined by a concept of what it ought to be, possesses an ideal shape invested with attributes that befit the class.

For Kant, skin color was the chief mark of a human race for most of his career. As his anthropology developed through the 1780s and 1790s, however, he shifted his attention to another signifier of bodily difference, the shape of the head, which was often conflated with intellectual function, though, in §17 at least, Kant is interested solely in the outer form of the skull rather than the internal operations of the brain. Goethe and Geoffroy then extended this inward turn by making the skeleton the site for identifying homologies. Unity of type, which could now encompass higher-order taxa, referred to internal structures. Cuvier, too, designated essential differences according to internal anatomy. The structures of the nervous system licensed the division of the animal kingdom into four distinct *embranchements*. Vertebrates, mollusks, insects and radials have qualitatively different neurological arrangements. They therefore constitute essentially different classes that cannot be conflated.

Walker, by contrast, is forced to make a more complicated argument that retains an investment in surface appearances. A theory of beauty must, of course, be able to account for the surface phenomena that have traditionally been associated with judgments of taste: the contours of the face, the shape of the body, the figure of the human as a whole. Indeed, it would hardly serve for an aesthetics to refer to actual viscera; the appearance of the brain, muscles, bones or ligaments cannot be the locus of beauty. Rather, from an aesthetic perspective, internal systems are only relevant insofar as they generate phenomena on the surface, a feature of aesthetic theory that compounds its ideological potency. Physiological perfection, construed in aesthetic terms, refers to the outward appearances of putative human types – black, white, male, female. To create a viable aesthetic theory, teleological functions – the operations of internal organs – must therefore be linked to their corresponding external structures. Or as Walker puts it, "beauty results from the perfection, chiefly of external forms, and the correspondence of that perfection with superiority of internal functions."[59] Beauty is the form that makes superior function visible. So it seems that aesthetics, as opposed to the internalized natural sciences practiced by Geoffroy and Cuvier, is uniquely suited to constructing anthropological classes where individuals are distinguished by their physiognomy – by distinctions of kind and degree that inhere in surface forms.

2.4   Unity without Diversity

Though he has now fallen into obscurity, Walker managed to acquire influential friends during his lifetime. Britain's two leading transcendental anatomists, Knox and Owen, tried to secure Walker a crown pension in the 1840s; and though the effort ultimately failed, the letter of support written by Knox testifies to Walker's reputation among his contemporaries: "No one has thought more clearly on the great physiological questions than you have," Knox states.[60] Yet Walker's importance for the history of aesthetics, such as it is, rests not only with his revision of the aesthetic ideal descending from Winckelmann to Kant nor with his role in the reception of transcendental biology in Britain. He exerted an influence in his own right. Some twelve years after his death in 1852, Walker was conscripted into the cause of two Copperhead journalists, David Croly and George Wakeman, who propounded their own aesthetic typology in the hopes of swaying the outcome of the American Civil War. In advancing an aesthetic anthropology by fashioning a hierarchy of types, Croly and Wakeman return ideals of beauty to their Kantian roots as a racialized standard even though they dispense with the egalitarian essentialism that was such a central feature of the third *Critique*. But what is perhaps of more moment, they accomplish their task by theorizing precisely the human form that Kant could not bring himself to imagine: an interracial ideal.

Walker is named twice in *Miscegenation*, Croly and Wakeman's seventy-page brief for interracialism that coins the portmanteau from the Latin "*Miscere,* to mix, and *Genus,* race."[61] He is first cited as an authority on interbreeding and then as an expert on sexual attraction.[62] Yet Walker's influence is more pervasive than those citations make it seem. At various points, Croly and Wakeman lift passages from Walker's writings to support their claims about mixed-race supremacy, taking quotations by naturalists from *Intermarriage*, the sequel to *Beauty*, and availing themselves of statements by Reynolds and Richard Payne Knight for their arguments about aesthetics.[63] Passages by Reynolds and Knight that appear in a chapter of the pamphlet titled "The Miscegenatic Ideal of Beauty in Woman" show up in Walker's *Beauty* as well. Common themes also connect the texts. The chapter of *Beauty* from which Croly and

Wakeman drew, "Of the Standard of Beauty in Woman," confronts the
core dilemma staged in *Miscegenation*: "The ideas of the beautiful vary in
different individuals, and in different nations," Walker writes. "Hence
many men of talent have thought them altogether relative and arbitrary."[64]
Walker then poses the central question that would later preoccupy Croly
and Wakeman: "How, then, it is asked, amidst these different tastes, these
opposite opinions, are we to admit ideas of absolute beauty?" How, in
other words, is unity possible amid diversity?

From its opening pages, *Miscegenation* seeks to answer these questions
by striking a pose of authority, citing regional experts along with more
traditional fonts of anthropological wisdom. Croly and Wakeman discuss
the writings of Petrus Camper, the Dutch anatomist now known for
associating race with head shape, as well as James Cowles Prichard, the
leading Victorian monogenist whose science of ethnology the authors seem
interested in imitating.[65] But by the time *Miscegenation* was published in
1864, the monogenetic tradition stretching from Buffon (also mentioned)
through Kant and Prichard had been upended by the Darwinian revolution. The struggle for survival had displaced design as the mechanism
governing the natural order. Acquired fitness through time had done away
with the teleology of nature. Although it was published five years after *On
the Origin of Species*, the pamphlet fails to register these scientific innovations, and *Miscegenation*, despite its date of publication, is a decidedly pre-
evolutionary affair: Croly and Wakeman promote a fixed hierarchy of
human types with a mixed-race ideal at its summit. Yet even as its model
of nature is closer to the medieval chain of being than the evolutionary
hierarchies derived from Darwin, Herbert Spencer and E. B. Tylor, the
pamphlet does not completely lack an investment in historical change.
Croly and Wakeman argue in their second chapter, "The Blending of
Diverse Bloods Essential to American Progress," that races rise and fall
according to a cyclical process of growth and decay.

Miscegenation leans on these precedents in arguing that the "miscegen"
must assume its rightful place at the zenith of a hierarchy of physical
perfection. In their seventh chapter, "The Type Man a Miscegen," the
authors theorize their typology most explicitly, basing their claims firmly
in the domain of fact, or rather, pseudo-fact: "The most recent physiological discoveries have demonstrated that the pale, fair, light hair, mild
blue or grey eyes, and sandy, bleached complexions of the blonde or
extreme white, are far from being indications of a healthy, refined, perfected organization."[66] So whites are caricatured as a sickly race of over
intellectualized decadents. Such a fragile constitution cannot qualify as a

"perfected organization," Croly and Wakeman aver. Instead of occupying the pinnacle of a racial hierarchy, "it is among this class that scrofula, consumption, and the nervous diseases prevail." This brand of pop physiology is a staple of *Miscegenation*. The first chapter, titled "Physiological Equality of the White and Colored Races," contains familiar examples from biological race theory. Besides remarks about Camper and skull shape, the authors conjecture about the source of skin color and appeal to monogenism: "all the tribes which inhabit the earth were originally derived from one type."[67] These passages illustrate well the intellectual resources Croly and Wakeman bring to bear in crafting their race theory. Without at least some flexibility for historical change, they would not be able to rearrange the existing racial order; hence they rely on a degeneration thesis in claiming that particular tribes descend from a common type. Without arguments based on natural perfection, their hierarchy would devolve into mere personal preference or the vicissitudes of historical chance. Thus they frame their argument in teleological terms, where a single perfect type is the ideal standard, while allowing for some diachronic variation that permits the true order of things to emerge.

In its physiological argument, "The Type Man a Miscegen" drifts between scientific and aesthetic assertions, claims of fact and value. Immediately following their remark about scrofula and "nervous diseases," Croly and Wakeman state without hesitation, "the ideal of the white race – the angels of our painters, the imaginary Christ of our sculptors and artists – is not the perfect ideal of manhood. The true ideal man can only be reached by blending the type man and woman of all the races of the earth." What may seem like a non sequitur, a reflection about iconography on the heels of a statement about a dermatological malady, in truth bespeaks a necessary step in the logic of their argumentation. Science provides facts; but those facts only obtain meaning once they are schematized according to an aesthetic standard. Physiological evidence testifies that the white race is "far from" evincing a "perfected organization," but this assumes a standard is in place that ranks physical data according to their proximity to a perfect model. Thus the slippage from physical attributes like "pale, fair, light hair, mild blue or grey eyes" to speculative assertions about "the angels of our painters" exposes a central plank in the essentialist theories of race descending from Winckelmann through Kant to Walker and finally to Croly and Wakeman. A model of "the true ideal" functions as a norm that organizes physical traits into a meaningful order.

If traditional iconography mistakenly represents the figure of Christ and angels as white, Croly and Wakeman correct this error by fashioning an interracial ideal of beauty:

> The true ideal man can only be reached by blending the type man and woman of all the races of the earth. The highest conception of physical beauty possessed by the negro, by the Moor, by the Asiatic, is a model man and woman after their own race; the negro's Venus is black; his houris and gods are black; the divinity of the Hindoo is of the color of his own people; the Great Spirit of the Indian, if of any color, is copper-colored; and so through all the world, the highest conception of beauty and perfection is the noblest specimen of each particular community.[68]

The previous chapter showed Kant struggling with an analogous problem: how to account for divergent aesthetic standards while furnishing a general measure of human beauty. Still earlier, Winckelmann had relied on the environmentalism of Montesquieu to reconcile his single standard of Greek beauty with the plurality of human shapes. On that model, ideals of races and nations are a function of geography, with the most beautiful bodies arising from the finest climatological circumstances. Applying environmentalist terms in one case and a transcendental argument in the other, both Winckelmann and Kant grappled with the same quandary: how to provide a coherent theory of a single ideal for all humans while at the same time maintaining essential anthropological differences within the human species. Hence the tradition descending from Winckelmann to the *Miscegenation* pamphlet was never devoted to the problem, narrowly conceived, of assigning value to a particular human group. Theorists were occupied in equal measure with addressing the plurality of human appearances entailed by essentially different anthropological categories. Thus the discourse of the ideal of beauty is best understood as staging a dilemma: how to square natural diversity with the unity of a single ideal of human perfection.

This dilemma poses no obstacle for Croly and Wakeman. An interracial ideal of beauty solves the problem quite neatly. "Humanity's highest type, therefore, is not the white, which comprises only a comparatively small fraction of the people who inhabit the planet," Croly and Wakeman correctly point out. A standard of perfection for humanity as a whole is derived from the combination of individual instances of perfection:

> The ideal or type man of the future will blend in himself all that is passionate and emotional in the darker races, all that is imaginative and spiritual in the Asiatic races, and all that is intellectual and perceptive in the white races. He will also be composite as regards color. The purest

Miscegen will be brown, with reddish cheeks, curly and waving hair, dark eyes, and a fullness and suppleness of form.[69]

Whether in reference to physical features or to psychological attributes, Croly and Wakeman's ideal expresses the essential characteristics of a racial category – what kind of thing it ought to be. Setting aside the content of these types, the logic of Croly and Wakeman's argument is sound; its conclusions follow directly from its premises. If a theory assumes a single standard of human beauty, then that standard will necessarily entail an interracial ideal. A general standard, in classic Goethean fashion, must comprehend every individual type without privileging one particular kind or subspecies over others. Thus in a single stroke, Croly and Wakeman cut through the knot that had so vexed their illustrious predecessors. "The perfect type of the future," they insist, "will be that of the blended races."[70]

The interracial ideal proposed by Croly and Wakeman is a more consistent theoretical assertion than the ones offered by Winckelmann and Kant, who settled for uneasy compromises in order to uphold essential distinctions over against a unitary ideal. Croly and Wakeman, by contrast, simply insist on unity. And though they stop short of proposing an androgynous aesthetic ideal, the authors go about as far as possible toward resolving the problem posed by sexual difference that preoccupied Walker. Because they position themselves as proponents of heterosexual intercourse, Croly and Wakeman can claim that gendered ideals are complementary. They avoid the question of whether an ideal must be male or female by declaring the necessary existence of both – the "true ideal man" results from "blending the type man and woman of all the races." Taken together, these arguments in "The Type Man a Miscegen" offer a condensed articulation of the ideological mission of the *Miscegenation* pamphlet as a whole: transgression in theory for the sake of segregation in practice; an ideal of unity in order to create real diversity. The irony is that by violating the essential divisions upheld by Winckelmann and Kant, Croly and Wakeman come up with a more coherent theory of physical perfection with a plausible claim to universality.

2.5 Perfect Data

Even though the empirical claims of Croly and Wakeman mutate into statements about a normative type bodied forth in the guise of an aesthetic ideal, it would wrong to view the link between beauty and biology in *Miscegenation* as unidirectional. Just after their recitation of relative ideals

that culminate in a mixed-race standard as the "highest purest type," Croly
and Wakeman make an immediate appeal to scientific authority: "It is to
the credit of Professor Draper, of the New York University that he has had
the boldness to avow the physiological fact here announced." According to
Draper, a prominent physician of the period, "the extremes of humanity,
which are represented by a prognathous aspect, and by a complexion either
very dark or very fair, are equally unfavorable to intellect, which reaches its
greatest perfection in the intermediate phase." Draper links complexion to
intellect – external appearances that express internal qualities – but the
force of his claim is independent of the qualities themselves. A genuinely
universal ideal "reaches its greatest perfection in the intermediate phase," he
states. Like Croly and Wakeman, Draper glides between empirical attributes
and claims about the "greatest perfection" of an ideal human figure; and this
conspicuous oscillation between fact and value, scientific testimony and
aesthetic perfection, is no accident. It manifests the fundamental dynamic
of an essentialist theory of race in the transcendentalist discourse emanating
from Kant. Physiological facts require a normative standard if they are to
designate a type, a category, a race. A racialized ideal of perfection needs
factual support in order to pass as a real feature of the world. But even as
biology lends evidentiary weight to these classifications, the perfect standards
are themselves aesthetic – concepts of what things ought to be.

   With their invocations of the "prognathous aspect" and "the most
recent physiological discoveries," Croly and Wakeman draw on the biological racism whose genesis Andrew Curran has traced through
Enlightenment debates about the anatomical source of blackness and
hence the physiological basis for racial difference.[71] Justin Smith has also
shown how inquiry into the philosophical status of race, intertwined with
these natural scientific disputes but not reducible to them, concerned itself
with the problem of why empirical observations, any empirical observations, signified membership in a distinct category of humans.[72] But the
question that preoccupied Kant did not pertain to biological matters
narrowly construed – the "scarf skin," say, or the anatomy of the African
albino. Instead, he wished to adduce the criteria for creating classes of
organisms so that a model of nature could be constructed according to the
dictates of reason, not data collected by aimless empiricists.

   In both *Miscegenation* and the third *Critique*, a concept of aesthetic
perfection authorizes the separation of individuals into categories.
A perfect standard enables the aggregation of particular cases by allowing
them to be compared to a representative measure. An ideal of beauty is an
exemplary model, a paragon, or as Croly and Wakeman put it, the "noblest

specimen" that is valid "for each community." A norm reflects the definitional attributes of a category, including but not limited to physical attributes; a concept of what a thing ought to be includes both the normal idea and the idea of reason – qualitative perfection, in Kant's parlance. When individuals are thus measured against such a "type man," they may be judged as belonging to one class or another. More important still, such a standard of perfection licenses a hierarchy of value (quantitative perfection). Individuals approach an ideal in varying degrees. Absent an ideal of perfection to anchor the data – to allow facts to be sorted into classes, kinds or races according to a fixed norm or rule – empirical observations of particular human differences could not lay claim to a classificatory distinction. They would be the mere differences of individuals. Once a racialized type is assumed, however, those attributes can then be grouped into categories. Someone belongs to a race because that person possesses a certain facial anatomy, complexion, intellect or psychology – because that person most closely conforms to a given perfect type, or what is the same, to a concept of what kind of thing it ought to be.

In other words, biological racism becomes ideologically viable when an aesthetic typology supplies it with conceptual content. There may be racists who use biology, but over and above personal prejudice, there exists a structural logic to an essentialist theory of race. Biology and the physical sciences provide the grist, but the real determinant of racial difference is the ideal that organizes the data. Without a type that represents the essential qualities of a category, observations of physiological features would remain but unconnected examples of the particular empirical attributes belonging to individuals. The behavior of Croly and Wakeman's rhetoric, the physiological claims that flicker into standards of perfection, and from ideals of beauty back again to the "physiological fact" announced by Draper, shows that physiological arguments for racial difference are only as good as the models of perfection that subtend them.

So, to take a pair of influential examples, Linnaeus defines classes of humans according to their physical, psychological and social attributes in his magnum opus *The System of Nature*. To one variety of *Homo sapiens* he ascribes the following essential attributes: "Black, phlegmatic, relaxed. *Hair* black, frizzled; *skin* silky; *nose* flat; *lips* tumid; crafty, indolent, negligent ... *Governed* by caprice." By way of comparison, consider Linnaeus's portrayal of another variety: "Fair, sanguine, brawny ... *Hair* yellow, brown, flowing ... gentle, acute, inventive ... *Governed* by laws."[73] Far from describing anything real, Linnaeus prescribes an ideal; even as these designations remain resolutely nominalist, they body forth the characteristics of the "noblest specimen" of an anthropological class, a "type man," as it were. Consider, too, the oft-cited example from Diderot and d'Alembert's *Encyclopédie*. Written by M. Le Romain, the entry for "*Nègre*" is arguably the Enlightenment's paradigmatic definition of an anthropological category: "further away from the Equator toward the Antarctic, the black skin becomes lighter, but the ugliness remains: one finds there this same wicked people." This listing of physical, aesthetic and moral traits is no act of empirical description; it names the attributes of members of an anthropological category as an abstraction, an ideal of what kind of thing such a class ought to contain. Within essentialist anthropologies, from Linnaeus through Walker's tripartite classes of female perfection down to Croly and Wakeman, it is these imaginative determinations that provide the true conceptual grounds for human identity. An ideal limns the essential characteristics that are then endowed with the illusion of scientific veracity.

2.6   Noble Specimens

To make a race, Croly and Wakeman must construct a racial type. Given the relative paucity of mixed-race figures in the storehouse of racial typologies, Croly and Wakeman set out to create their own model of perfection that "all the world would acknowledge." They open their twelfth chapter, "The Miscegenetic Ideal of Beauty in Woman," by asking "In what does beauty consist?" They then answer by addressing matters of both form and content: "In richness and brightness of color, and in gracefulness of curve and outline."[74] Plenitude and wholeness, these attributes should be conveyed with easy grace and relaxed simplicity – Winckelmannian virtues *par excellence*. Croly and Wakeman then tether these abstract qualities to the specificity of a racialized body. Feigning egalitarianism, they pose the question, "what does the Anglo-Saxon, who assumes that his race monopolizes the beauty of the earth, look for in a lovely woman?" According to Croly and Wakeman,

> her cheeks must be rounded, and have a tint of the sun, her lips must be pouting, her teeth white and regular, her eyes large and bright; her hair must curl about her head, or descend in crinkling waves; she must be merry, gay, full of poetry and sentiment, fond of song, childlike and artless.[75]

Although the physical dimensions of a white ideal are given their due, with special attention paid to the head and face, Croly and Wakeman also specify the psychological particularities of an Anglo-Saxon type, her "childlike and artless" character. They then compare white to black: "But all these characteristics belong, in a somewhat exaggerated degree, to the negro girl." One race appears as the "exaggerated" version of another; it possesses *more* prominent characteristics, a claim that implies a norm by which differences of degree may be measured.

Despite their gestures toward relative and equal standards of beauty, Croly and Wakeman's real aim is to retain a racial hierarchy while reordering its constituent parts. "Each particular community" may have its own "noblest specimen,"[76] but those standards are nested within a unified structure with an interracial ideal as the highest model of human perfection. Examples both real and imaginary, personal and disinterested, are used to illustrate the aesthetic supremacy of a mixed-race figure: "In paintings, the artist has never portrayed so perfect a woman to the fancy, as when choosing his subject from some other than the Caucasian race."[77] With a white ideal duly subordinated, Croly and Wakeman resort to anecdotal evidence, employing the avatar of a single authorial voice: "the most beautiful girl in form, feature, and every attribute of feminine loveliness he ever saw, was a mulatto."[78] But then, yet again, the argument manifests its signal symptom, the vacillation between aesthetic and scientific registers: "By crossing and improvement of different varieties, the strawberry, or other garden fruit, is brought nearest to perfection, in sweetness, size, and fruitfulness."[79] Armed with a knowledge of interbreeding, Croly and Wakeman justify their personal taste as a scientifically verifiable aesthetic standard, leading them to describe human beauty in vegetal terms: "this was a ripe and complete woman," they write, "her complexion was warm and dark, and golden with the heat of tropical suns, lips full and luscious."[80] Whether in reference to "garden fruit" or human beings, the particular attributes are interchangeable and reflect the nature of the organism as the case may be. All along, however, the framework remains the same: perfection.

The concept of perfection implies a structural order where a single term occupies the highest rank in a hierarchy of value. As in Kant, quantitative perfection refers to the degree to which a particular individual approximates a "the completeness of any thing in its own kind." Yet if an ideal type is to carry ideological force, it must signify more than a quantitative placeholder within a formal structure. A type must have content; its qualitative perfection must be defined. Just as a strawberry "is brought nearest to perfection, in sweetness, size, and fruitfulness," so too must a human being exhibit its own essential qualities so that the kind is "complete."[81] For Croly and Wakeman, those qualities are not limited to physical appearances; and when physical features are cited, they are invariably tied to other aspects of human value: "The 'happy mean' between the physical characteristics of the white and black, forms the nearest approach to the perfect type of beauty in womanhood, and of strength and wisdom in manhood."[82] Beauty, strength and wisdom – aesthetic value, physical potential and mental ability – these are the empirical qualities by which humans are measured, the characteristics that signal an essence. The echo of Le Romain's entry in the *Encyclopédie* is hard to ignore: the "wicked people" whose "black skin" and "ugliness" set them apart act as a countertype to Croly and Wakeman's ideal of perfection. Croly and Wakeman might have cited Linnaeus verbatim, his "fair, sanguine, brawny" human type whose hair is "yellow, brown, flowing." Kant's descriptors of "purity, or strength, or repose" would not be out of place either, nor would the caricatures from "The Type Man a Miscegen" quoted earlier:

> The ideal or type man of the future will blend in himself all that is passionate and emotional in the darker races, all that is imaginative and spiritual in the Asiatic races, and all that is intellectual and perceptive in the white races. He will also be composite as regards color. The purest Miscegen will be brown, with reddish cheeks, curly and waving hair, dark eyes, and a fullness and suppleness of form.[83]

With their recitation of physical and intellectual characteristics, empirical qualities hypercathected with value and combined into an ideal of beauty as the embodiment of human perfection, Croly and Wakeman execute an aesthetic determination of the concept of race. They define the qualitative perfection of a certain kind, a mixed-race ideal, and embed that type within a hierarchy of quantitative perfection.

It would be misleading to treat the *Miscegenation* pamphlet purely as a speculative exercise, for if there was one fact of antebellum America that threatened the segregated social order it was the fact of interracialism. Race mixing was the ubiquitous material confirmation of the unity of the species. It called into question all the elaborate arguments – philosophical, religious, scientific, aesthetic – that upheld the fiction of essential differences between races. In holding to the path of least discursive resistance, Croly and Wakeman raise this absurdity to the surface: If a universal human is assumed, then the truth of racial difference vanishes. And so, on February 17, 1864, Samuel Sullivan Cox, Democrat of Ohio, a man who had earned the handle "Sunset" Cox after penning a notoriously ornate description of a sunset in the *Ohio Statesman* and who was regarded as one of the most virulent racists in the Copperhead coalition, took to the floor of the United States House of Representatives to denounce *Miscegenation* in front of his peers.

To pursue an alternative line of reasoning, what if organisms were defined not by a concept of their function or an idea of their perfect shape? In that case, how would an aesthetic anthropology conceive of an organism that ought to be free to determine its ends according to reason, taste or any other standard of value irrespective of claims to belonging to a qualitatively different subspecies? This way of framing the matter comes closer to the argument that Goethe advanced in "Beauty Is Perfection with Freedom," which was itself a development of claims about autonomy in *The Critique of Judgment*. For Kant, reflection on a given object sparks the free play of the cognitive faculties, leading to a feeling of pleasure that permits a subject to assign the predicate "beautiful" to that object. Goethe and more systematically Schiller returned freedom to the world. They invested aesthetic objects, whether organisms or political institutions constructed according to aesthetic principles, with autonomy while trying to resist a regression to precritical dogmatism. For those who wished to challenge aesthetic anthropologies grounded in heteronomy, perfection, and the ineluctability of ideal types, these more robust theorizations of aesthetic autonomy became an indispensible ideological weapon for contesting the aesthetic ideals whose legacy has now been traced from the eighteenth century to the American Civil War.

CHAPTER 3

Militant Neoclassicism

The perfect human theorized by Winckelmann and Kant, Croly, Wakeman and Walker surfaces again in W. E. B. Du Bois's *Dusk of Dawn: An Essay toward an Autobiography of a Race Concept* (1940). The final part of a loose trilogy that includes *The Souls of Black Folk* (1903) and *Darkwater* (1920), *Dusk of Dawn* consists of Du Bois's reflections on seventy years spent navigating the color line. He relates his growth from boyhood through studies at Fisk, Harvard and Berlin, his early optimism that science and sociology would solve the problems of post-Reconstruction America, and his turn to Marxism and pan-Africanism once his faith in sober fact curdled in the face of implacable race hate. In the sixth chapter of *Dusk*, "The White World," Du Bois stages a dialogue between a narrator, an avatar for Du Bois himself, and two figures who personify rationalizations for racial oppression in mid-century America. One of these hypothetical men, a reputable member of the Harvard Club and the local Episcopal church, suffers from a strain of false consciousness that blinds him to the contradictions between competing value systems: the universalism of a Christian and the exceptionalism of an American; the *noblesse oblige* of a Gentleman and the race pride of a White Man – all roles that Du Bois capitalizes to indicate their exemplarity.

But before he presents this uniquely American type, which is itself a composite of contradictory subtypes, the other figure Du Bois portrays is a more cultured advocate for the division of the races, a fictional cosmopolitan named Roger van Dieman. "His thesis is simple," Du Bois writes of van Dieman: "the world is composed of Race superimposed on Race; class superimposed on classes; beneath the whole thing is 'Our Family' in capitals, and under that is God."[1] Van Dieman subscribes to a logic of super- and sub-ordinate categories. He orders the world according to an ascending hierarchy that is analogous to the structures propounded by Walker, Croly and Wakeman. The two men in Du Bois's imaginary dialogue then discuss the content of that hierarchy, adducing the same attributes of human perfection trotted out by anthropologists since Linnaeus. Aesthetic value tops the list: "(1) Beauty and health of body. (2) Mental clearness and creative genius. (3) Spiritual goodness and receptivity. (4) Social adaptability and constructiveness." Then, as the dialectic between the men develops, van Dieman makes an ideal of beauty into a bearer of those traits, furnishing an aesthetic typology in a manner exactly equivalent to Walker and Winckelmann. Van Dieman pits the "Venus of Milo and the Apollo Belvedere" against the narrator's preference for "curly hair, black eyes, full and luscious features."[2] Hence a familiar duality emerges between racialized ideals, illustrating American racial ideology seventy-five years after the publication of the *Miscegenation* pamphlet. In the white world described by Du Bois, a post-Reconstruction world all too recognizable in the terms of Croly and Wakeman's America, the structural logic of perfection is again a primary ideological apparatus for justifying a racial hierarchy. And once again, an ideal of beauty is its chief vehicle.

By promoting an African phenotype of "full and luscious features" in a hierarchy of value, the narrator of "The White World" relies on the same ideological tactic as *Miscegenation*, where the apotheosis of human beauty is a mixed-race ideal that reconciles the antipathies of color that had traditionally organized American society. So these texts exhibit a common rhetorical gesture. They reorder the constituent parts of a system while leaving its structure intact, making empirical traits into fungible attributes for defining an anthropological group. Indeed, the texts even rely on similar language. The "full and luscious features" of Du Bois's ideal mirror the "full and luscious lips" of Croly and Wakeman's mixed-race type.[3] Imagining a white ideal of beauty, van Dieman praises "sunlight hair and sky-blue eyes" while the so-called Anglo-Saxon ideal envisioned by Croly and Wakeman must "have a tint of the sun" as well as "eyes large and bright." At the same time, however, the narrator of *Dusk* is attracted to a different palette, valuing "bronze, mahogany, coffee and gold" much as the authors of *Miscegenation* laud a complexion "warm and dark, and golden." Finally Du Bois describes the general character of beauty as consisting in "line and height and curve" where Croly and Wakeman nominate "gracefulness of curve and outline" as crucial attributes. Whether these congruities indicate that Du Bois consulted "The Miscegenetic Ideal of Beauty in Woman" when constructing his aesthetic ideals, though plausible, is largely beside the point. What is decisive is that the construction and contestation of a "white world" sets out from a disputation about the nature of ideal beauty.

Du Bois was well aware of the aesthetic dimensions of essentialist anthropology, as "The White World" demonstrates and other texts confirm. The first chapter of *Black Folk: Then and Now* (1939), published only a year before *Dusk*, disputes the "tendency to try to pick out among the different stocks some ideal which characterizes the stock in its purest form."[4] And Du Bois confronts the method of identifying "the average representative of the stocks as normal" – that is, the method of deriving a normal idea as Kant does in *The Critique of Judgment*. In other words, he takes aim at a theory of anthropological races whereby a stock – what Kant would have called a *Stamm* – is identified with its typological average, an ideal of pure form for the group as a whole. Therefore while it is true that Du Bois's narratorial avatar in *Dusk of Dawn* intervenes against racial hierarchies by refashioning an ideal of beauty – "bronze, mahogany, coffee and gold are far lovelier than pink, gray, and marble" – Du Bois himself sought to loosen the hold of human types on the imagination. Not only in *Black Folk: Then and Now* but over the course of his entire career, he worked to escape the fixed and rigid determinations of physiological races, even if not to a degree fully satisfactory to some of his more recent critics, while at the same time striving to retain the cultural aspects of race that had been gained in the struggle against oppression.

The task of the present chapter is twofold: first, to show how Du Bois moves away from an aesthetic anthropology based on physiological perfection, typological exemplarity and purposive anthropological categories; and second, to demonstrate that Du Bois crafts alternative standards for human groups that remain firmly within the discursive framework of philosophical aesthetics. This double move stages a kind of immanent critique, whereby aesthetic arguments are criticized in aesthetic terms. Definitions of collective human essence grounded in an ideal of physiological perfection, for instance, are challenged by proposing novel forms of aesthetic autonomy. By tracing the vicissitudes of a Du Boisian aesthetics, and in particular Du Bois's use of autonomy and heteronomy as aesthetic concepts, it therefore becomes possible to identify a consistent commitment to an aesthetics of freedom as a means of addressing the ills of post-Reconstruction America. Autonomy – or rather the theoretical union of aesthetic completeness and freedom – allows Du Bois to define collective human flourishing free from the constraints of both natural law and social domination.

Efforts to identify a Du Boisian aesthetics have tended to trace the influence of his Harvard instructors William James and George Santayana, whose respective brands of pragmatism and idealism found a generative alchemy in Du Bois's vast and varied writings.[5] His most widely cited work of criticism, "Criteria of Negro Art" (1926), evinces the pragmatist posture in the well-known assertion that "all art is propaganda and ever must be, despite the wailing of the purists."[6] This phrase, which has become something of a slogan for a Du Boisian aesthetics, has a tactical edge that has been overshadowed by the declarative sweep of the formulation. What purists fail to appreciate, Du Bois clarifies, is that the unequal distribution of cultural capital in America means that "propaganda is confined to one side while the other is stripped and silent." A practical problem based on racial inequity motivates the trenchant generalization "all art is propaganda," which should thus be read as an attempt to rebalance the sociocultural ledger by marshaling a universal critical judgment.

No less than Jamesian pragmatism, the axis of Santayana and Hegel has attracted considerable attention among scholars of Du Bois, and not just for its influence on his aesthetics. The most sustained effort to connect Du Bois with the German philosophical tradition has been by Robert Gooding-Williams, who has associated the idealist tenor of Du Bois's thought with a Hegelian philosophy of history that Du Bois is supposed to have absorbed at Harvard, either in the course he took with Santayana or through contact with another Harvard neo-Hegelian, Josiah Royce.[7] More recently, Gooding-Williams has expanded his reading to reflect a full-blown political philosophy that he sees descending from a Romantic tradition encompassing both Hegel and Herder. According to this thesis, called "expressivist," Du Bois commits himself to advancing "the shared attachments, purposes, and idea of the good life that essentially define the self-understanding and distinctive identity of a people, or *Volk*."[8] The stress in this definition falls on "essentially define" even though, crucially, the qualities that determine the characteristics of a *Volk* shift register, in line with their Herderian-Hegelian roots, to a historical and cultural instead of a biological one.

These Hegelian notes have been elaborated at greatest length in monographs by Stephanie Shaw and Shamoon Zamir, who detected the influence of Hegel in a key Du Boisian concept, double consciousness, as well as in Du Bois's stance on the relationship between oppressor and oppressed – or rather, master and slave – in his early writings.[9] The combined force of these readings shows that any engagement with the German philosophical tradition on Du Bois's part does not, as Adolph Reed Jr. worries, render him a "pristine idealist" whose speculative tendencies detach him from the material realities of inequality and injustice.[10]

On the contrary, Du Boisian idealism, whether in a strictly Hegelian or in a looser Romantic sense, is worthy of study precisely because it offers a theoretical weapon in the fight against the most sordid manifestations of white supremacy.

The intent of this chapter is not to add one more reading to the literature on Du Bois's contact with philosophical idealism, though by drawing out the congruities between Du Boisian autonomy and another idealist, Schiller, the chapter does contribute to this branch of Du Bois scholarship. Nor is the goal to tell a narrative of influence, even though moments when Du Bois alludes to or mentions Schiller and Goethe are discussed. The argument is more deliberately comparative. Inasmuch as Schiller is the most important post-Kantian writer on aesthetics to work in an avowedly Kantian vein, and Du Bois is the most important American (not just African-American) writer to use idealist arguments in the battle against racial oppression, these two authors, Schiller and Du Bois, are uniquely suited for an inquiry into how an aesthetics of autonomy displaces the essentialist anthropology descending from Kant through nineteenth-century theorists like Walker, or van Dieman, which Du Bois regarded as exemplary of American racial ideology.

* * *

Appreciating the subversive force of a Du Boisian aesthetics of freedom requires first situating his arguments in a history that aligns his critique of essential physical categories with the objectives of cultural anthropology, which emerged as a discipline at the end of the nineteenth century.[11] Spurred by Boas's criticisms of physical anthropology and evolutionary models of sociocultural progress, American anthropologists aimed to shift their discipline from biological problematics such as speciation or laws of evolutionary development to inquiry into the norms and traditions practiced by particular human groups. This reorientation, which, broadly speaking, turned from the study of nature or culture (singular) to the study of cultures (plural), meant that human characteristics, above all mental traits, were redescribed as the product of habits inculcated in specific cultural milieus – not as the unfolding of purposive predispositions as Kant believed, nor as the result of climate as Montesquieu maintained, nor even as the evolved behaviors, conceived in either Lamarckian or Darwinian terms, that equip an organism for survival in a given physical environment. In other words, in shifting the discipline to the analysis of acquired instead of inherited traits, Boas and his students decoupled external from internal attributes. The shape of the head, the color of the skin, the texture of the hair no longer corresponded to ethical, aesthetic or psychological qualities that had for centuries defined the character of *anthropos* and its racial subcategories. Those qualities were reimagined as the product of cultural habits.

Du Bois and Boas had passing but significant contact in the early decades of the twentieth century, the years when Boas's critique of physiological races was emerging in earnest. At Du Bois's invitation, Boas participated in a conference at Atlanta University on the topic of racial physiology; and during his visit to Atlanta, Boas addressed the class of 1906, an occasion Du Bois would later recall as a signal moment in his own intellectual development:

> Franz Boas came to Atlanta University where I was teaching history in 1906 and said to a graduating class: You need not be ashamed of your African past; and then he recounted the history of the black kingdoms south of the Sahara for a thousand years. I was too astonished to speak. All of this I had never heard and I came then and afterwards to realize how the silence and neglect of science can let truth utterly disappear or even be unconsciously distorted.[12]

Three years after their meeting in Atlanta, Du Bois enlisted Boas as an adviser for his proposed *Encyclopedia Africana*, a project he would abandon until the early 1930s when the Phelps-Stokes fund sponsored an *Encyclopedia of the Negro*. For that later iteration of the encyclopedia, Du Bois secured the support not only of Boas but also other prominent cultural anthropologists including Margaret Mead and Melville Herskovits as well as the British social anthropologists A. R. Radcliffe-Brown and Bronislaw Malinowski.[13] Though both *Encyclopedia* ventures failed to produce a more sustained collaboration between the two men, Boas did write an article for the newly launched *The Crisis* in 1910, "The Real Race Problem." Arguing in typical cultural-anthropological style, he minimizes the importance of physiological features in favor of social and cultural factors. He claims, in a manner reminiscent of the essentialist egalitarianism of Kant's third *Critique*, that any differences between races "are differences in kind, not in value."[14] The exchange of ideas between Boas and Du Bois continued in 1911, when both men contributed to the First Universal Races Congress that was held in London, a major gathering of scholars designed to address racial questions on a global scale. At the event Du Bois reported on the conditions of life for African-Americans and Boas, though not present in person, submitted a summary of his ongoing critique of physical anthropology, "Instability of

Human Types," which would be expanded in *The Mind of Primitive Man*, a work published in the same year as the Congress. In a chronicle of his London experience for American readers, Du Bois makes special note of Boas's arguments against the stability of racial types, indicating that even if he never fully embraced the fundamental pluralism of Boasian cultural anthropology, as Brad Evans has argued, Du Bois was nevertheless a firm ally of Boas on the grounds of his critique of essential physiological categories.[15]

According to George Stocking, Boas's attack on traditional physical anthropology was aided by two key scientific advances: modern statistics and Mendelian genetics. Under the influence of Sir Francis Galton and other pioneering statisticians, Boas called into question the primacy of the arithmetic mean as the measure for racial physiology – the Kantian normal idea, Reynold's central form – by applying more sophisticated techniques for analyzing large populations such as standard deviations and frequency curves.[16] These statistical methods could reveal, for example, asymmetrical distributions of traits *within* more conventional typological categories: empirical regularities corresponding to different branches of the same Native American tribe, say, that older, cruder techniques like the typological average would either erase or fail to register. Furthermore, analyses of measurements carried out under the direction of Boas at Ellis Island and in the schools of Worcester, Massachusetts, demonstrated that physiology varied according to environmental pressures. Exposure to the conditions of life in America altered the physical appearance of immigrants compared to individuals who remained in their home country, Boas showed, thus severely weakening the idea that physiological types, to say nothing of the mental and behavioral attributes associated with them, were stable categories that persisted in the face of environmental variation. Even though the turn to statistics did not do away with physiological traits as criteria of anthropological difference – on the contrary, Boas still assumed that humans belonged to separate races – the new statistical methods did cast serious doubt on the customary configurations of racial difference, both by undermining the putative immutability of human types and by discrediting the standard mechanism for typological construction, the arithmetic mean.[17]

To these statistical insights were added the innovations of modern genetics, which struck a more decisive blow to the theoretical core of physical anthropology. For Kant, it will be recalled, empirical differences only mattered inasmuch as they pointed to necessarily heritable traits. Skin color or head shape were thought to be signifiers of necessary, that is, essential and therefore natural differences between classes of humans. Gregor Mendel, whose work was rediscovered in 1900 and quickly incorporated by Boas into his critique of physical anthropology, revolutionized the science of heritability and therein overturned the principles of intergenerational physiology that had undergirded the racial theory of Kant and other Enlightenment theorists.[18] Just as Buffon's law had furnished the grounds for species distinctions, so Kant's "law of half-breed generation" had supported his claims about racial subcategories. Mendel's experiments with pea breeding, carried out at his Moravian monastery in the mid-nineteenth century, showed that offspring presented combinations of dominant and recessive genes, not blended traits. Hence claims about blends, mixes or "half-breeds" were exposed as illusions that obscured the true combinatorial logic of genetic dominance. Further, and still more decisively, the genetic revolution invalidated racial types as fundamental categories. Family lines, which cut across racial distinctions, became the basic units of genetic analysis.

Thus the doctrine of immutable *Urbilder*, which Boas at times construed in distinctly aesthetic terms, was shattered by the dual disruption of modern statistics and genetics. "Bodily form has aesthetic value," Boas writes in the second paragraph of his introduction to the 1938 edition of *The Mind of Primitive Man*. Yet he goes on to claim that "those ideals of human beauty" that had organized the antipathies of racial dogma could not withstand the scrutiny entailed by modern scientific methods.[19] This argument exemplifies a common strategy in Boasian argumentation (we will see the same move in the writings of Ruth Benedict). Boas admits the existence of racial types, which he here equates with "ideals of human beauty"; he even provides a list of attributes for the "Negro" and "East Asiatic" types that could have come from the mouth of van Dieman. But the problem, at least from a Boasian perspective, arises when these types are regarded as immutable or eternal forms. Moreover, Boas resisted attempts to derive the value of those ideals from nature – from, say, natural purposes, fitness or organic perfection. Instead the cultural anthropologist makes aesthetic value a product of habit: "the feeling of a fundamental distinctiveness of form" between racial types "is the same feeling that creates an 'instinctive' aversion to abnormal or ugly types in our own midst, or to habits that do not conform to our sense of propriety." Types, as well as individuals, may be aberrant and therefore ugly just as the table manners of a foreign guest might offend the sensibilities of a host. In either case, an unfamiliar face or an uncouth practice disturbs an observer's inculcated expectations.

More radically, Boas maintains that the feeling of difference as such, not only the difference between beautiful and ugly, arises from cultural habituation. A person is determined to belong to a different type – to possess "a fundamental distinctiveness of form" – because that person is abnormal when measured against the more common appearances within a given milieu. In each of these examples, a particular norm is established by virtue of familiarity. That norm is then the standard by which individuals may be deemed either normal or aberrant, and consequently pleasing or displeasing as the case may be. This argument does have its weaknesses. For one, Boas appears to regress to a thesis about averages, whereby a norm is ingrained sheerly through exposure to sensory data. Another problem is Boas's failure to consider whether novelty could be the cause of pleasure, as Joseph Addison insisted it must in his famous essay on the pleasures of the imagination. In short, cannot difference be attractive? Why is sameness not a source of aversion?

Whatever the weaknesses of Boasian aesthetics, it is worth reiterating that he, like Du Bois, never entirely discarded race as a scientifically viable concept. Setting aside his comments on aesthetic ideals, he asserts in *Anthropology and Modern Life* (1928) that "from a purely biological point of view the concept of race unity breaks down." At the same time, however, "the course of development of a group of children depends upon their racial descent."[20] Thus race continues to play a role, albeit an uncertain one where marks of racial physiology, understood as genetic regularities, take their place alongside cultural and environmental factors, which exert a more decisive influence on human character, especially when considering mental and behavioral characteristics that had traditionally formed the more invidious distinctions between anthropological groups. In effect the Boasian intervention redistributed the matrix of forces that define human nature. Physiology became subordinated to cultural environment. So it was for Du Bois as well: "we must all acknowledge that physical differences play a great part" in distinguishing human groups, Du Bois wrote in 1897, conceding on the one hand that biology remains relevant but insisting on the other that "no mere physical distinctions would really define or explain the deeper differences."[21] Thus both Du Bois and Boas faced a similar methodological quandary: how to account for those "deeper differences" with scientific rigor without resorting to the techniques or the conclusions of the race sciences.

Boas practiced a hard-edged empiricism derived in part from his early training in physics and geography, which he used to formulate a granular style of ethnography evidenced by his studies of the Kwakiutl tribe of the

Pacific Northwest. Du Bois also had marked empiricist tendencies, especially during the first decade of his career, which saw the publication of an array of sociological studies meant to shine the light of science onto the murk of prejudice that sustained racial divisions. One commentator has even likened *The Philadelphia Negro* (1899), Du Bois's study of black urban life, to Boasian ethnography, a valid comparison insofar as Du Boisian sociology and Boasian ethnography share a thoroughgoing commitment to empirical detail when inquiring into the character of collective life.[22] Indeed, Du Bois often bemoaned the lack of reliable data on African-Americans, going so far as to make a special plea for "anthropological measurement" of racial physiology as a necessary adjunct to the gathering of sociological statistics.[23]

But the comparison between Boasian ethnography and Du Boisian sociology obscures a closer connection between the methodologies of the two men. Like much of the research Du Bois performed in the first decade of his career, *The Philadelphia Negro* is, to use a methodological term that would gain prominence later in the century, a quintessentially "etic" study of cultural life – the author insists on a sharp distinction between observer and observed phenomena in an effort to give an objective picture of cultural life "from the outside." Though the critique of physical anthropology relied on statistical analyses of large data sets and the impartial weighing of empirical claims, ethnography under sign of Boas and his students developed an alternative method for studying human cultures, what would come to be called an "emic" approach that sought to comprehend cultural phenomena from the perspective of cultural agents themselves – including African-Americans. In his preface to Zora Neale Hurston's *Of Mules and Men*, for example, Boas lauds Hurston, whose graduate work he supervised at Columbia, for her ability to gain access to the "true inner life of the Negro," which would otherwise be denied to outsiders, particularly white ethnographers. In an analogous fashion, Du Bois depicts the texture of African-American life from "within the Veil" of race, a world whose inner contours and character he describes in works like *The Souls of Black Folk*.[24]

3.1   Critical Teleology

Given the significance of the undergraduate course Du Bois took with Santayana for scholars who detect a Hegelian influence on Du Bois's thought, it is worth dwelling on the point that in his autobiography, Du Bois names Kant, not Hegel, when reminiscing about his time at

Harvard: "I sat in an upper room and read Kant's Critique with Santayana."[25] Gooding-Williams believes it was the *Critique of Pure Reason* that was assigned in the course, though Du Bois refrains from specifying which of the three critiques he read. In any event, the fact *that* Du Bois attended a philosophy course taught by Santayana, titled "Earlier French Philosophy, from Descartes to Leibniz, and German Philosophy from Kant to Hegel," provides little insight into *what* he actually took from the experience, much less how the ideas introduced in undergraduate lectures shaped his later thinking. A letter from 1956 to Herbert Aptheker does relate how he studied with "James while he was developing Pragmatism; under Santayana and his attractive mysticism and under Royce and his Hegelian idealism." He goes on though to pivot, writing that "I then found and adopted a philosophy which has served me since," suggesting that his Harvard instructors were but waypoints on the development of his own *sui generis* philosophical program.[26]

With these considerations in mind, the present section does not trace the influence of either Kant or Hegel, or for that matter Descartes, or Leibniz, or Schiller. The task is instead to show how Du Bois, consciously or not, works against the aesthetic ideology of physiological perfection, typological exemplarity and purposive anthropological categories theorized in the third of Kant's *Critiques* and promulgated by the fictional ideologue Roger van Dieman in *Dusk of Dawn*. Put another way, the task is to elucidate what we might call a Du Boisian *critical teleology*, a theoretical enterprise distinct in both letter and spirit from Kantian critical philosophy. In contrast to the method of the third *Critique*, where teleological arguments are the epistemological grounds for necessary judgments about art and nature, Du Bois uses teleology as a more disruptive critical instrument. He makes arguments about ends and aims in order to unsettle a social order based on putatively natural human categories. He then uses such a critical teleology as the theoretical foundation for alternative forms of aesthetic collectivity.

One of the clearest examples of a Du Boisian critical teleology comes in *Dusk of Dawn* when Du Bois reflects on the first phase of his career, the period of *The Souls of Black Folk*. Looking back on his younger self, he admits his erstwhile sympathy with the ends and aims of white society: "what the white world was doing, its goals and ideals, I had not doubted were quite right." He then explains that the fault in American society lay with the fact that "people like me and thousands of others who had my ability and aspiration, were refused permission to be part of this world."[27] On this account, justice is a matter of access. Certain agents, in this case whites, enjoy their status as full members of society while others are denied that privilege. What the access model leaves unaddressed, Du Bois goes on to make clear, are the "goals and ideals" that determine the social order. "It was as though moving on a rushing express," he writes, "my main thought was as to the relations I had to other passengers on the express, and not to its rate of speed and its destination."[28] Employing the racially vexed metaphor of train travel – *Plessy* v. *Ferguson* was still the main legal basis for segregation – Du Bois declares the inadequacy of a theory that contends with the elements (the passengers on the train) but ignores the ideals that define society as a structural totality: its destination and ends.

In redirecting his scrutiny to the social whole, teleologically defined, Du Bois sees past the (re)distribution of parts within society and glimpses a more general critique of the ends that govern the social order. Yet the retrospective glance Du Bois casts on a younger self in thrall to liberal progress hardly does justice to his early political program. His writings from the 1890s through *The Souls of Black Folk* in fact execute a sustained interrogation of the social *teloi* that organize society. "If we consider what race prejudice really is," Du Bois argued in 1897, "it is the difference in aim, in feeling, in ideals of two different races."[29] This openly teleological argument, which appears in the influential essay "The Conservation of Races," combines ends, affects and ideals into a comprehensive theory of racial strife. And it is passages like these that led Eric Sundquist to identify the "*volksgeistian* definitions" of race that crop up in "Conservation," definitions that Kwame Anthony Appiah used as evidence of Du Bois's complicity in a retrograde essentialism.[30]

Even though he fails to purge outmoded racial ideas from his thinking, at least when judged by more recent critical standards, Du Bois downplays the role of physiology in "Conservation" and deploys the discourse of exemplarity in a way that actually marks his departure from the typologies characteristic of physical anthropology: "we see the Pharaohs, Caesars, Toussaints and Napoleons of history and forget the vast races of which they were but epitomized expressions."[31] In this example Du Bois names four type men; yet Napoleon is no physical specimen for the French. The physiological lines separating Toussaint from the Pharaohs and Caesar are so vague as to be inconsequential. These figures represent their respective groups because of their cultural achievement.[32] They are strictly cultural types.

Underpinning this cultural construction of a race concept is an eclectic philosophy of history where Hegelian strains contribute to more general "*volksgeistian* definitions," in Sundquist's phrase, that reach back at least to the diversitarianism of Herder, who, incidentally, also exerted a significant influence on Boas.[33] A rhetoric of racial genius together with a quintessentially Herderian appreciation of the cultural and linguistic aspects of collective life underlies one of the most stunning rhetorical gestures of "Conservation," when Du Bois declares that "for the development of Negro genius, of Negro literature and art, of Negro spirit, only Negroes bound and welded together, Negroes inspired by one vast ideal, can work out in its fullness the great message we have for humanity."[34] Here the links forged in the crucible of slavery are transmuted into bonds uniting members into a solidary whole. A group whose identity was "bound and welded" by a common history looks forward to a fuller, a more complete future. Such is the conservative force of "The Conservation of Races." Even as Du Bois eschews biological race theory, he wishes to retain a sense of racial identity as a historical construct – as a community defined by a common past and a shared future.

In thus historicizing his race concept, Du Bois sharpens his departure from the likes of van Dieman who understood human differences as reflecting an eternal, teleologically determined hierarchy of species and genera. Instead of subtending the harmonious order of nature, perfection is the endpoint implied by a diachronic process wherein each group expresses "its particular message, its particular ideal" but all groups strive "to guide the world nearer and nearer that perfection of human life for which we all long."[35] Precedents for diachronic perfectionism can be located in a variety of sources, not least in eighteenth-century discourses of progress epitomized by the Marquis de Condorcet. Stocking has argued that the evolutionary anthropology of Victorian Britain, at least as it manifested in the work of E. B. Tylor, had distinct affinities with the culture concept of Matthew Arnold.[36] However not all Victorian perfection can be reduced to Arnoldian sweetness and light. Herbert Spencer, to take only the most influential example, argued that biosocial entities – races – evolved from simplicity to complexity and environmental fitness through the pressure exerted in the struggle for survival. Even though Spencer's views are now routinely referred to as "social Darwinism," an anachronism since Spencerian evolution predated *On the Origin of Species* and relied on a Lamarckian framework, Darwin's own use of perfection can accommodate cultural evolution with little strain. "Natural selection works solely by and for the good of each being," Darwin writes at the end of *Origin*, and as a result "all corporeal and mental endowments will tend to progress toward perfection."[37] At the same moment that he destroys the old teleological natural history that treated organisms as parts of a perfect order arranged according to purposive design, Darwin reinscribes corporeal and cognitive perfection as an emergent product of the struggle for survival.

On the evidence of *The Souls of Black Folk*, which develops the notion of racial striving set forth in "Conservation," Du Bois had this decidedly pre-Boasian discourse of evolutionary anthropology in mind when invoking diachronic perfection. He writes in the ninth chapter of *Souls* that "in the future competition of races the survival of the fittest shall mean the triumph of the good, the beautiful, and the true."[38] Far from being an ideological justification for white supremacy that construes races rising through stages of savagery and barbarism toward civilization defined in predictably European terms, an evolutionary model furnishes Du Bois with the means of imagining a world where *laissez-faire* racial competition liberates groups to strive for and achieve the Platonic trinity of truth, beauty and justice. Whether articulated in Hegelian, Herderian or evolutionary terms, the upshot of Du Bois's conception of human difference is that races are historical entities whose goals remain unfulfilled because they have been denied a place in a kingdom of cultural ends.

"The Conservation of Races" was first presented as an address at the inaugural meeting of Alexander Crummel's American Negro Academy, an apt venue since the Academy influenced Du Bois's expansive conception of the black university as an institution for racial advancement. Even though other collective bodies came to exemplify Du Boisian communalism over the course of his career, from the black church and its "congregations which are the real units of race life" to the later "ancient African communism" that leavened his Marxism, it is the university that stands out as a communal ideal for African-America – in *Souls*, for example, he refers to it as "the University."[39] Such an idealization contributes, of course, to a tradition that can be traced to Cardinal Newman's "Idea of a University." Du Bois's views on higher education are also inextricable from his debate with Booker T. Washington, which pitted the vocational program of the Tuskegee Institute against the black university conceived as a bastion of spiritual fulfillment and self-mastery for a population historically excluded from "the Kingdom of Culture."

Exhaustively studied, the Du Bois-Washington debate falls easily into a kind of ready schematism: between the university and the industrial program of Tuskegee; between insistence on political and civil rights (Du Bois) and a resolute focus on economic development (Washington); between confrontation and accommodation. The biographies of the two men admit a similar opposition: Du Bois's postbellum childhood in the north and Washington's boyhood in bondage on a Virginia plantation.

Though not inaccurate, these antitheses do tend to occlude the common ground shared by Du Bois and Washington. Wilson J. Moses notes, for instance, that they both eschewed the assimiliationist message of the previous generation's most prominent race leader, Frederick Douglass, by insisting that black institutions led by African-Americans should occupy the vanguard of racial progress.[40] Even the venerable distinction between culture and economy is far from absolute. Washington admitted that academic accomplishment could encourage social progress, though he scoffed at what he thought were intellectual fashions like the training of blacks in Greek and Latin, the very subjects Du Bois taught as a young professor at Wilberforce. Indeed, Washington himself wrote movingly about receiving an honorary degree from Harvard in 1896, a testament to his awareness of cultural prestige as an index of collective achievement.[41]

For his part, Du Bois acknowledged the value of vocational skills for redressing economic disadvantages. He merely thought that higher education must supplement technical training for the general welfare of the race. Further evidence of accord between these two historical antagonists is the fact that Du Bois's views on the university, and higher education more generally, arose from his engagement with economic issues. As he argues in the report from the fifth Atlanta conference, *The College-Bred Negro* (1900), the annual meetings held at Atlanta University starting in 1896 "had a logical connection." Where the first conference studied the high death rate among African-Americans, the second was devoted to the "conditions of life" in black communities; the third and fourth meetings addressed "the hard economic struggle through which the emancipated slave is to-day passing" followed by the fifth, which turned to "the relation of educated Negroes to these problems and especially to the economic crisis."[42] Thus Du Bois's valorization of the intellect was not born out of sheer fondness for the clean air of philosophical speculation. Carving a place for African-Americans in the cultural life of the nation was, according to Du Bois, a logical response to the plight of freed slaves to secure their material livelihood.

Still, convergences between Du Bois and Washington must not overshadow the fundamental differences laid out in the third chapter of *Souls*, "Of Mr. Booker T. Washington and Others," which mixes acid commentary – at one point Du Bois refers to the author of *Up from Slavery* as "the most distinguished Southerner since Jefferson Davis" – with a sustained critique of Washington's capitulation on civil and political rights and his disparagement of the training of teachers and a cultural elite, what Du Bois would elsewhere refer to as the Talented Tenth. Moreover, the fifth chapter, "Of the Wings of Atalanta," expands the argument with Washington regarding higher education into an attack on the economic foundations of American society. In keeping with the logic of the Atlanta conferences, "the culture of the University" informs a critique of the economics of segregation and the barbarism of gilded-age industry. Significantly for our purposes, Du Bois's critique of political economy is couched in idealist terms:

> for every social ill the panacea of Wealth has been urged, – wealth to overthrow the remains of the slave feudalism; wealth to raise the 'cracker' Third Estate; wealth to employ the black serfs, and the prospect of wealth to keep them working; wealth as the end and aim of politics, and as the legal tender for law and order; and, finally, instead of Truth, Beauty, and Goodness, wealth as the ideal of the Public School.[43]

Commercial society homogenizes human striving. Diverse ideals of value are subordinated to a single, monotelic purpose: the "end and aim" of Wealth. In much the same manner, the structural logic of perfection anchors a hierarchy of value in a single standard. For Croly and Wakeman, a mixed-race ideal occupies that place. Accordingly, all individuals are ranked by their proximity to that single highest standard. For van Dieman and Walker the scope of the system broadens but the structure remains the same: "the world is composed of Race superimposed on Race; class superimposed on classes; beneath the whole thing is 'Our Family' in capitals, and under that is God."[44] Substitute Wealth for God and the value system Du Bois decries falls out as another a permutation; replace several ideals – Truth, Beauty and Goodness – with a different standard, and the essence of an institution like the university – that is, its purpose – is fundamentally altered. In order to criticize modern capitalism, Du Bois exposes how diverse ideals are leveled out in favor of a single, unitary purpose, namely, wealth: "we almost fear to question if the end of racing is not gold, if the aim of man is not rightly to be rich."[45] Like his metaphor of society as a train running toward an unknown, or rather, an unquestioned destination, Du Bois's critique of gilded-age capitalism attacks a value system that grounds a hierarchy of value in a single, immutable end.

Du Bois opposes a monotelic structure by offering alternative ends for human striving – Truth and Beauty instead of Wealth, for example – but also by insisting that a plurality of goals counterbalance any overarching purpose of human action. The task of a critical teleology is therefore twofold. It questions the ends and aims of human activity, which is to say, the content of the various ideals (Wealth, Knowledge, God). It also critically examines the relationship between the various ideals, how they interact to form a coherent value system. "Whither, then, is the new-world quest of Goodness and Beauty and Truth gone," Du Bois asks, "must that too degenerate into a dusty quest of gold?" To keep the Platonic trinity, a plurality of ends, from devolving into the single aim of wealth, Du Bois once again resorts to arguments about exemplarity:

> In the Black World, the Preacher and Teacher embodied once the ideals of this people – the strife for another and a juster world, the vague dream of righteousness, the mystery of knowing; but to-day the danger is that these ideals, with their simple beauty and weird inspiration, will suddenly sink to a question of cash and lust for gold.[46]

Justice, righteousness and knowledge are the ideals personified by the Preacher and the Teacher, figures with powerful associations in African-American history (see, for example, *The Negro Church*, which appeared in 1903, the *annus mirabilis* that also witnessed publication of *Souls* and "The Talented Tenth"). But it should be noted that the types of Preacher and Teacher mark a decisive contrast with Toussaint, Caesar and Napoleon – to say nothing of the Apollo Belvedere – that Du Bois designates in "The Conservation of Races" as exemplars of their respective groups. Where those ideals represent martial achievement, the Preacher and Teacher epitomize specifically African-American values of self-cultivation and solidarity.

In "Of the Wings of Atalanta," Du Bois mounts an idealist critique of capitalism. To execute this task, he conjures original standards, ideals both weird and beautiful that guide the actions of a people among peoples. But within the gamut of Du Boisian ideals, the black university – the University – conveys most fully Du Bois's vision for African-American spiritual flourishing. Although Du Bois's portrait of the University in "Of the Wings of Atalanta" takes Atlanta University as its model, the University represents a communal ideal exemplifying certain values of the group without necessarily conforming to any particular instantiation, just as the Preacher and the Teacher are ideals that need not be tethered to any individual. Keith Byerman has pointed out how Du Bois distinguishes the University from its surroundings.[47] Du Bois writes that "the hundred hills of Atlanta are not all crowned with factories. On one, toward the west, the setting sun throws three buildings in bold relief against the sky."[48] Set in silhouette, this trio forms a painterly counterpoint to the hills and factories that populate the Atlanta landscape. A similar spatial demarcation occurs when Du Bois portrays students streaming into the classroom. They rise up to obtain a higher plane: "the clang of the day-bell brings the hurry and laughter of three hundred young hearts from hall and street, and from the busy city below."[49]

Not only is the University set off geographically from the rest of Atlanta, it participates in a different temporal order as well. Gathered together, the students learn "nothing new, no time-saving devices." Instead of the gospel of efficient innovation, the University inculcates "old time-glorified methods for delving into Truth, and searching out the hidden beauties of life, and learning the good of living." In terms of both space and time, then, the University exists apart. It is a zone of autonomy carved out from the world that surrounds it: "here, amid a wide desert of caste and proscription, amid the heart-hurting slights and jars and vagaries of a deep race-dislike, lies this green oasis, where hot anger cools, and the bitterness of disappointment is sweetened by the springs and breezes of Parnassus."[50] Free from its environs, the University is a sanctuary of psychic convalescence that Du Bois differentiates from the real conditions that govern life elsewhere: the heteronomy of modern capitalism, the laws of the Jim Crow South. Indeed, the primary threat that Du Bois seeks to ward off is the possibility that the real might infiltrate and compromise the ideal. He warns of "the sudden transformation of a fair far-off ideal of Freedom into the hard reality of bread-winning."[51]

This Parnassian idyll of spiritual flourishing is rendered in unmistakably aesthetic terms. For instance, the initial image of "three buildings in bold relief against the sky" adheres to neoclassical tenets of aesthetic value: "The beauty of the group lies in its simple unity," Du Bois attests, finding unity amid the diversity of the architectural elements. The remainder of the description follows in the same vein:

> a broad lawn of green rising from the red street with mingled roses and peaches; north and south, two plain and stately halls; and in the midst, half hidden in ivy, a larger building, boldly graceful, sparklingly decorated, and with one low spire. It is a restful group, – one never looks for more; it is all here, all intelligible. There I live, and there I hear from day to day the low hum of restful life.[52]

This is a neoclassical tableau. Unlike, say, baroque architecture, where ornamentation would be an end in itself, the University balances diversity with unity. The two halls to the north and south are joined by a larger building in the center. A vast, single sweep of lawn comprehends contrasting colors: the red of the street and the roses; the complementary green of the grass. Indeed, it is hard to ignore the specifically Winckelmannian attributes of the scene: "noble simplicity and calm grandeur." Besides the "simple unity" of the buildings in the initial description, the halls of the

University are said to be "plain and stately" – that is, noble and simple. These forms then combine to make a "restful group," which foster a "restful life" of calm, reflective contemplation. Even the most ornamental image, the "sparklingly decorated" facade, is complemented by a "boldly graceful" shape – evoking the key classical notion of *Grazie* theorized by both Winckelmann and Schiller. In sum, Du Boisian University, its parts arrayed in formal harmony, exhibits the attributes of a work of art, or better still, a neoclassical aesthetic ideal.

However, just as Du Bois shifts the axis of the discourse of exemplarity by insisting that historical and cultural factors, not biological characteristics, determine membership in an anthropological group, so too he intervenes in the discourse of aesthetic perfection. No ideal of physiological beauty that ranks individuals according to their approximation of a perfect, natural type, the University holds open a spatiotemporal zone that harbors collective striving. Freedom supplants heteronomy. An integrated cultural whole made of diverse parts constitutes a "fair far-off ideal of Freedom" that subverts the dictates of natural law and social code.

Unity amid diversity for the sake of freedom – this aesthetic paradigm orders the ideal of the University. So, too, does it inform Du Bois's understanding of *The Souls of Black Folk* as an aesthetic object. In other words, *Souls* is itself constructed according to neoclassical standards duly revised to permit the possibility of freedom. In a short article written for *The Independent* in 1904, only a year after *Souls* was published, Du Bois takes stock of his achievement by using the very same neoclassical critical vocabulary. Addressing the oft-discussed generic heterogeneity of the book, Du Bois notes that the fourteen chapters were composed over the course of seven years and confesses that, as a result, the work has "considerable, perhaps too great, diversity."[53] The polemic against Washington in the third chapter and the celebration of Crummel in the twelfth; the idealization of the University in "Of the Wings of Atalanta" and the thick descriptions of the South in "Of the Black Belt"; the sorrow songs alongside quotations from, among others, Schiller, Lord Byron, Elizabeth Barrett Browning, Alfred Lord Tennyson and an anonymous Negro spiritual – "all this leads to rather abrupt transitions of style, tone and viewpoint and, too, without doubt, a distinct sense of incompleteness." The diversity of *Souls*, according to its author, threatens the work's aesthetic integrity, its completeness. "On the other hand," he continues, "there is a unity in the book, not simply the general unity of the larger topic, but a unity of purpose in the distinctively subjective note that runs in each essay." Subjective purposiveness unifies the book's diverse parts.

The subject's perspective, not an archetype of beauty that defines what a thing ought to be, makes the work into a whole: "in each essay, I sought to speak from within – to depict a world as we see it who dwell therein." Thus the play of the mind, a "subjective note" that is circumscribed but free within limits, lends *The Souls of Black Folk* its wholeness, its completeness.

In his early writings, Du Bois attacks the aesthetic ideology of human types by formulating a critical teleology that interrogates both the content and the structure of a hierarchy of values. Alternative ideals – Freedom, Truth, Beauty, Good – militate against a value system anchored in a single purposive ideal, be it a supreme human type or the end and aim of wealth. And this is no mere substitutive project. Du Bois does not just shuffle the parts of a hierarchy in the manner of Croly and Wakeman or Walker. He undertakes a wholesale reconsideration of the collective values that subtend the group, creating new models – countertypes, as it were – such as the Preacher, the Teacher and the University while at the same time scrutinizing the ways those ideals interact within a system of values. Skeptical of hierarchies that subordinate diverse ideals to a single highest standard – Wealth, God – Du Bois conjures a range of ideals, an assortment of ends and aims that counterbalance any single overarching purpose. In other words, Du Bois does not do away with the teleological discourses of perfection and exemplarity; rather, he motivates them for different ends. He does not rule out a neoclassical idiom; he uses it to craft a new ideal of collective autonomy. All along, Du Bois remains within the aesthetic discourse he criticizes, mounting an immanent critique of the aesthetics of human essence.

3.2 Militant Ideals

With a steady output of minor and major publications including *The Negro* and a biography of John Brown, Du Bois secured his status as a premier figure in African-American letters during the seventeen years that separate *The Souls of Black Folk* (1903) and *Darkwater* (1920), a period that also saw him gain a regular readership through his appointment as the editor of *The Crisis* in 1910. Playing up the difference between *Souls* and *Darkwater* in his autobiography, Du Bois describes the former as "a cry at midnight thick within the veil" while characterizing *Darkwater* as "an exposition and militant challenge" to a nation suffocating from the effects of racism – lynching and mob violence, the entrenchment of Jim Crow and white supremacy, the entanglement of race and class into a color-based caste system.[54] The militancy of *Darkwater*, such as it is, arises in no small measure from the trajectory of Du Bois's politics, which traced a leftward arc from a brief membership in the American Socialist Party between 1911 and 1912, through *Darkwater* and the sweeping materialist historiography of *Black Reconstruction in America* (1935), and finally to his adoption of a more inflexible Marxism that valorized Stalin and culminated in an affiliation with the American Communist Party at the end of his life.[55] *Darkwater* signals these ideological developments in chapters like "Of Work and Wealth" and "Of the Ruling of Men," which employ overtly Marxist categories and critical strategies when describing the structure of social distinctions.

The hardening of Du Bois's materialist outlook that unfolded over the latter half of his career did not come at the expense of his aesthetic commitments, however. "Criteria of Negro Art" appeared in *The Crisis* in 1926 while *Darkwater* contains his most elaborate written statement on the nature of beauty. To a degree, contextual factors explain this continued preoccupation with aesthetic problems. The flowering of the Harlem Renaissance, whose members counted Du Bois as one of their own but also consigned him to an older generation, meant that he was compelled to take a stand on debates about African-American artistic production. Alain Locke's *New Negro Anthology*, for example, precipitated "Criteria of Negro Art." But besides the climate of cultural ferment that enveloped Du Bois and his Harlem contemporaries, reasons internal to his thought suggest another interpretation for his persistent investment in cultural affairs. Because he had defined himself as a critic of the Tuskegee program, Du Bois needed to avoid the trap of a vulgar materialism that subordinated all human endeavor to the permutations of an economic base. By involving himself in cultural debates, then, he must have been motivated in part by a desire to avoid the reproach that his materialism smacked of the philistine economism he had associated with Washington.

Du Bois's most comprehensive statement on aesthetics, "Of Beauty and Death" from *Darkwater*, elevates the terms from his critical teleology into a theory of beauty in twenty brief, collage-like sections published in the shadow of the Red Summer of 1919, the paroxysm of violence that followed the demobilization of black soldiers after World War I. Counterposing elaborate depictions of the American landscape with scenes of racial violence, "Of Beauty and Death" modulates from a descriptive to a theoretical register toward the end of the chapter. "There is something in the nature of Beauty that demands an end," Du Bois writes. "Ugliness may be indefinite," he insists, "but Beauty must be complete."[56]

Enumerating the qualities that inhere in beauty, Du Bois claims that aesthetic value is predicated on the presence or absence of completeness. Beauty, on this account, requires a *telos*. "Beauty must be complete – whether it be a field of poppies or a great life, – it must end, and the End is part and triumph of Beauty."[57]

The preceding two chapters have outlined how completeness was a touchstone of neoclassical aesthetics from Kant's theory of quantitative perfection as "the completeness of any thing in its own kind," itself a retooling of the rationalism of Alexander Baumgarten and Moses Mendelssohn, to Croly and Wakeman's crasser ideal of a "ripe and complete woman." Toward the end of the eighteenth century, however, theorists turned against external standards of beauty – a determinate ratio between parts and whole, a criterion of usefulness, a model of nature whose harmony the artwork must imitate – by devising immanent criteria for judging aesthetic value. In the case of Schiller, overcoming heteronomous aesthetic standards required radicalizing Kant's doctrine of subjective autonomy, which held that the ethical behavior of the subject is determined by the free exercise of the will in accordance with reason. Mere allegiance to external laws, Kant argued, usurps the dignity of rational self-determination. Of course freedom features as well in "The Critique of Aesthetic Judgment," where the pleasure arising from the free play of the cognitive faculties is the subjective basis for ascribing beauty to an object. Like Goethe in his theory of organic perfection examined in Chapter 2, Schiller takes the concept of autonomy, which Kant had defined in subjective and transcendental terms, and restores freedom to the objective domain. The beautiful object, according to Schiller, *appears* to be free. "Beauty is thus nothing less than freedom in appearance [*Freiheit in Erscheinung*]."[58] Rather than predicating aesthetic value on the pleasure occasioned by the free play of the imagination and understanding, Schiller locates freedom in the subject's perceptual experience of the object, in its "autonomy as appearance."[59] That is not to say that the object's appearance is an anarchic jumble of warring elements. "The beautiful object may, and even must, be rule-governed," Schiller maintains. The beautiful work is complete and defined; it is shaped by the technique of the artist and the ordering influence of form. Yet any rule, end or formal delimitation cannot compromise the appearance of the object's autonomy. The artwork "must *appear* as *free of rules*" even as it is governed by them.

Making freedom into a phenomenal quality of objects means defining beauty in objective terms without regressing to the heteronomous standards that characterized pre-Kantian neoclassicism. At the same time, Schiller retains the basic connection between the nature of beauty and the essence of *anthropos* that characterizes Kant's ideal of physiological beauty in §17 of *The Critique of Judgment*. The appearance of free play in the artwork, Schiller maintains, is congruent with the ludic nature of human-kind: "humans play only when they are humans in the full sense of the word, and *they are only completely human* [ganz Mensch] *when they play*."[60] To be sure, completeness remains the conceptual basis for species being. As with Kant, humankind still conforms to a concept of what it ought to be. Yet in a brilliant argumentative move, Schiller makes anti-purposive behavior into the highest human purpose. Play, a practice undertaken *without* a specific goal or aim, is the ultimate end for *der Mensch*.

Though Schiller does not appear to have been as central to Du Bois's Harvard coursework as Kant and Hegel were, direct links with both Schiller and Goethe testify to the importance of German neoclassicism for his thinking. Fond of Faust's words to Mephistopheles "you shall forbear, forbear you shall," Du Bois quotes this line from *Faust* to conclude his description of the University in "Of the Wings of Atalanta," itself an allusion to antiquity. The chapter immediately preceding "Of the Wings of Atalanta" confirms the neoclassical influence by using a passage from Schiller's iliadic retelling of the story of Joan of Arc, *The Maiden of Orleans*, for its epigraph:

> Willst Du Deine Macht verkünden,
> Wähle sie, die frei von Sünden,
> Steh'n in Deinem ew'gen Haus!
> Deine Geister sende aus!
> Die Unsterblichen, die Reinen,
> Die nicht fühlen, die nicht weinen!
> Nicht die zarte Jungfrau wähle,
> Nicht der Hirtin weiche Seele!
>
> [Should you wish to announce your power,
> Choose those, who free of sin,
> Stand in your eternal house!
> Send out your spirits!
> The deathless, the pure,
> The ones that neither feel, nor weep!
> Choose not the tender virgin,
> Nor the soft-souled shepherdess!]

This epigraph heads the chapter titled "Of the Meaning of Progress," which recalls a summer spent teaching in rural Tennessee. In the chapter, Du Bois relates the charms of the countryside along with the value of education as a means for advancing the race – fitting, since the epigraph from *The Maiden of Orleans* comes from a soliloquy when Joan compares the rustic pleasures of youth, given over to her pursuits as a shepherdess, against her later vocation as a military leader, indeed, as the savior of France. When considered together, these allusions to Goethe and Schiller illustrate the extent to which forbearance is an active enterprise. To forbear is to marshal resources in preparation for future battle and ultimate victory.

Besides these citations of Schiller and Goethe, which appear in *Souls* in the original German, one of Du Bois's earliest defenses of university education, "Does Education Pay?," names both authors as part of a curriculum for liberal study designed to advance the interests of African-Americans.[61] After lauding higher education against "the mere technical training of the common schools," an early jab at Tuskegee, Du Bois prescribes a wide-ranging list of luminaries for a program of liberal study. The list includes only one author who qualifies as a German philosopher: Schiller. Even though "Does Education Pay?" was a speech given to the National Color League of Boston in March 1891, hardly a year after Du Bois studied philosophy with Santayana, it is Schiller – not Kant, not Hegel – that Du Bois believes must be included in a program for liberal education.

Like Goethe, whose extraliterary output tended toward the natural sciences instead of philosophy, Schiller was known mainly as a neoclassical dramatist in the nineteenth century – this despite works like Kuno Fischer's *Schiller als Philosoph* (1858), which had established Schiller's place in the pantheon of German philosophy. Therefore it may be questioned whether Du Bois had in mind the doctrine of aesthetic education when naming Schiller in "Does Education Pay?" Influential university curricula of the period did, however, instruct students on the subject of Schiller's prose. The German Department at Johns Hopkins, which set the standard for university education in German studies at the time, taught both the dramas and the prose as early as 1880; and courses on German literature were accompanied by textbooks written by Hermann Kluge and then, in 1895, Wilhelm Scherer that provide a representative synopsis of Schiller's literary identity.[62] Both books discuss Schiller's aesthetic theory.[63] Scherer's *Geschichte der Deutschen Literatur* (1883), for example, contains a sustained account of Schiller's turn to antiquity as a vehicle for a post-Kantian aesthetics of freedom.[64] Thus even if Schiller's reputation was based primarily on the tragedies in the nineteenth century, evident enough in the citation from *The Maiden of Orleans,* his role in formulating an aesthetics of autonomy was very much in the mainstream of the American curricular reception of German neoclassicism just as Du Bois was developing his own curriculum for liberal study as well as his own aesthetic theory.

"Of Beauty and Death" takes up the specifically aesthetic valences of that neoclassical tradition in no uncertain terms: "Beauty is fulfilment," Du Bois writes. "It satisfies. It is always new and strange. It is the reasonable thing."[65] What distinguishes this argument with its insistence on the rationality of beauty from the neoclassical rationalism of Winckelmann or Mendelssohn is the inextricability of beauty from freedom. "Ugliness and hate and ill are here with all their contradiction and logic," Du Bois writes, again stressing the (ir)rational character of aesthetic categories. "They will always be here," he continues, "here and eternal, while beauty triumphs in its great completion – Death."[66] Death is an elementary instance of completeness. It is the ultimate end. Yet death is also a liberation from the chains of hatred and strife. It releases a subject from the bonds of this world – the ensnarement in instrumentality and exploitation. Death, in other words, is a form of freedom. Just as Schillerian play is the purpose that frees the subject from purposiveness, death is the *telos* that dissolves teleological bonds. In sum: "Its end is Death – the sweet silence of perfection, the calm and balance of utter music. Therein lies the triumph of Beauty."[67] Calm, balance, perfection – these are quintessential neoclassical attributes. They are conceived, however, in terms of a final end that frees the subject from the plight of this world.

Schiller advances beyond pre-Kantian neoclassicism by insisting that the appearance of autonomy defines beautiful objects even though they are, in truth, rule-governed, formally defined phenomena. Du Bois accomplishes an analogous innovation. He revises a neoclassical aesthetics of perfection so that it may accommodate the possibility of freedom, little wonder given Du Bois's skepticism of the ideology of nature underlying the ideals of Winckelmann or van Dieman. This is the paradigm – completeness and autonomy – that underlies the aesthetics of *Darkwater* both in theory and in practice. Consider two of the more spectacular set pieces of the book. The first occurs when Du Bois relates a journey that took him from "the silver beauty of Seattle" to the "somber whirl of Kansas City," from Chicago to Los Angeles and the "Empire of Texas."[68] While the urban centers garner passing mention, the Grand Canyon, an emphatic example of natural beauty, elicits the following lines:

> it is a sudden void in the bosom of the earth, down to its entrails – a wound where the dull titanic knife has turned and twisted in the hole, leaving its edges livid, scarred, jagged, and pulsing over the white, and red, and purple of its mighty flesh.[69]

Figured as a wounded body, the canyon landscape registers physical violence on a geological scale. John Claborn has likened this scene to the Kantian sublime, and indeed, the magnitude of the image combined with the potency of language evokes precisely the qualities that have historically been associated with feelings of sublimity.[70] Yet the sublime, at least as Kant theorized it, is the aesthetic experience of boundlessness *par excellence*. In this case the aesthetic object is emphatically bounded. A physical wound has been cut in the Earth's crust. The "livid, scarred, jagged" borders of the canyon rim delimit the contours of a natural body. In fact, it is the idiom of natural, physical beauty that furnishes Du Bois with his descriptors in this passage, not the sublime. Referring to the Canyon, he intones that "it cannot be a mere, inert, unfeeling, brute fact – its grandeur is too serene – its beauty too divine!"[71] The noble simplicity and calm grandeur that Winckelmann found in Greek statuary is projected onto the American landscape. Like Winckelmann in *The History of the Art of Antiquity*, Du Bois describes a body in stone, a sculptural figure hewn out of the rock by the dull knife of time.

Intimations of sublimity occur elsewhere in "Of Beauty and Death." Yet even as Du Bois seems to reach for an aesthetics of boundless transcendence, he remains resolutely within the theoretical parameters of natural beauty and freedom. Describing the marine world of the Maine coastline instead of the desert landscape of Arizona, he writes that "Bar Harbor lies beneath a mighty mountain, a great, bare, black mountain that sleeps above the town; but as you leave, it rises suddenly, threateningly, until far away on Frenchman's Bay it looms above the town in withering vastness."[72] A mountain that swells in size as the viewer recedes in the distance calls to mind one of the most renowned passages in all of English poetry, the episode from the *Prelude* when the young William Wordsworth, who is also cited in Du Bois's early curriculum for liberal study, steals a boat and slips out alone on a moonlit lake:

> I dipped my oars into the silent Lake,
> And, as I rose upon the stroke, my Boat
> Went heaving through the water, like a Swan;
> When from behind that craggy Steep, till then
> The bound of the horizon, a huge Cliff,
> As if with voluntary power instinct,
> Upreared its head. I struck, and struck again,
> And, growing still in stature, the huge Cliff
> Rose up between me and the stars[73]

Like Wordsworth's cliff, the "great, bare, black mountain" of Bar Harbor ascends "suddenly, threateningly" while the viewer moves to the "far away" perspective of Frenchman's Bay. In both scenes, the visual drama consists of a mountain rearing up in the mind's eye of the observer. Further correspondences emerge if we examine the arrangement of parts in the scenes. In the *Prelude*, the cliff stands between the individual subject and the cosmos: "the huge Cliff/Rose up between me and the stars." The description of Bar Harbor establishes a congruent orientation between natural body and astral vault: "mountains hurl themselves against the stars." Likewise, sublimity appears to be the primary aesthetic valence for both Wordsworth and Du Bois. The "huge Cliff" glimpsed by the youth rises up and violates the "bound of the horizon," blotting out the points of light and breaching the boundary that had constrained the scene in the mind of the boy. In the case of Bar Harbor, Du Bois comments that "before the unveiled face of nature, as it lies naked on the Maine coast, rises a certain human awe."[74] The landscape conjures in the author a sense of the sheer force of nature unveiled.

For all the signs that the Maine landscape inspires feelings of the sublime, Du Bois retreats from an aesthetics of boundlessness. Instead, completeness prevails as the governing concept for the beauty of Bar Harbor. In contrast to the sublimity of the *Prelude*, which results from the transgression of a horizon, the section on Bar Harbor concludes by inscribing the horizon in high relief:

> We are sailing due westward and the sun, yet two hours high, is blazoning a fiery glory on the sea that spreads and gleams like some broad, jeweled trail, to where the blue and distant shadow-land lifts its carven front aloft.[75]

Du Bois draws the line where the sea meets the sky. As the boat sails west, the sun lays a track of light on the water. This "jeweled trail" then reaches its terminus where the firmament heaves up its "carven front aloft," creating rather than breaking the horizon. The horizontal plane of the sea touches the vertical expanse of the heavens. More generally, the Maine coastline is itself a borderland, a liminal domain that marks the physical ends of America. "It is a mighty coast," Du Bois writes, "ground out and pounded, scarred, crushed, and carven in massive, frightful lineaments." Like the Grand Canyon, whose bodily form was cut out of the desert rock, the physical contours of the coast have been scarred by the violent action of water and time. For both the canyon and the coastline, the lineaments of nature have been carved into the very face of the earth itself.

In a distinctly Schillerian fashion, the completeness of these aesthetic objects coexists with a condition of freedom. In other words, their beauty results from the appearance of autonomy. The lateral demarcations of the Maine landscape – horizon, coastline – do not constrain movement in the other dimension. On the contrary, verticality is emphatic. The sun blazes overhead; "mountains hurl themselves against the stars"; "the clear, impalpable air springs"; "the water flamed." Atmospheric phenomena redouble this upward trajectory: "above float clouds"; "aloft to the eastward piled the gorgeous-curtained mists of evening."[76] Vertical freedom complements horizontal boundaries – the springing air, the flaming water. And it should be noted that this dimensional complementarity also underlies the description of the Grand Canyon, which juxtaposes the lateral limit of the canyon rim with the walls that plunge down to the river: horizontal boundaries, vertical freedom. And so it is with the University, where the "the hundred hills of Atlanta" are separated off from the "three buildings in bold relief against the sky," which welcome students who rise up from the "busy city below" to reach the "broad lawn of green rising from the red street." A state of physical uplift is common to all of these scenes. Completeness coexists with autonomy. A determinate end is joined with the appearance of freedom to constitute ideals of beauty.

Thus it is imperative to understand Du Bois's intervention into debates swirling around the New Negro movement in terms of the paradigm that had consistently informed his aesthetics for decades. The theoretical claims contained in "Criteria of Negro Art," which was first presented as a speech to the National Association for the Advancement of Colored People (NAACP) in Chicago, are altogether consistent with *Darkwater*'s aesthetics of autonomy and the freedom of the University, however militant the claims to art's status as propaganda may be. Du Bois opens his argument in "Criteria" by appealing to a familiar teleological idealism: "seeing our country thus, are we satisfied with its present goals and ideals?"[77] Questioning the ends and aims that order society, he immediately asks his audience to imagine a condition of full political subjectivity. In other words, he wishes his listeners to imagine the world as it *ought to be*: "if you tonight suddenly should become full-fledged Americans," Du Bois states, "what is it that you would want?" This rhetorical question is no mere thought experiment. Du Bois compels his audience to entertain the possibility of complete social and cultural privilege. That is to say, he compels them to imagine a perfect world. And lest the aesthetic ground bass of this argument be lost amid its political overtones, he asks "what the world could be if it were really a beautiful world."[78] In imagining a beautiful world, Du Bois conjures a condition of perfection – of agents endowed with full rights in the political arena.

Within this schema, perfection is not a static rule governing the order of nature but a condition that, predictably, allows for freedom. Notwithstanding the notorious assertion about the propaganda value of art, the social or moral content of the artwork is not the only decisive factor for the artist: "free he is," Du Bois explicitly states just before his remark about propaganda, "but his freedom is ever bounded by Truth and Justice."[79] Boundedness, in this context, entails neither determination nor subordination. A concept or a moral law does not define the form or content of the artwork outright, for then the artist would be *unfree*, a prospect Du Bois expressly rejects. Boundedness means that truth, justice and freedom are complementary rather than exclusive values. They participate in a mutually reinforcing, not a monotelic, value system. So, too, when Du Bois takes up the nature of beauty. He entertains the possibility that beauty might be the single end that dominates all others: "that somehow, somewhere eternal and perfect Beauty sits above Truth and Right I can conceive." But he immediately qualifies this assertion by stating that "here and now and in the world in which I work they are for me unseparated and inseparable."[80] Du Bois does not repudiate perfect beauty. He makes beauty inseparable from truth and right at a particular historical moment. He refuses the dogmatic normativity of a totalizing monotelism and instead combines truth, beauty, justice and freedom to constitute the ideal that defines his aesthetic imagination – the "fair far off ideal of Freedom" he limned so gracefully in *The Souls of Black Folk*.

3.3   Autonomy and Self-segregation

If *Darkwater* mounted a militant challenge to a nation riven by racial strife, then the fifteen years following its publication witnessed the entrenchment of the divisions it attacked as the Great Depression exacerbated economic and racial tensions between Americans. Responding to these historical circumstances, Du Bois grew increasingly skeptical of the unilaterally integrationist posture of the NAACP, which, he argued, failed to grasp the material determinants of racism and the intransigent reality of a separated society. He therefore adopted the position that would cause his break with the organization that had been his pulpit and institutional home for a quarter century: the creation of self-segregated economic cooperatives. Along with his emigration to Ghana and his acquittal in a McCarthyite show trial in 1951, the turn to advocacy for self-segregation stands out as a major – perhaps *the* major – event of the latter phase of Du Bois's career. The final section of this chapter argues two points: first, that the aesthetic paradigm of perfect freedom informs Du Bois's stance on self-segregation; and second, that his understanding of economic cooperatives was reinforced by continued contact with cultural anthropology, which in the 1930s advanced beyond the foundational work of Boas by theorizing cultures as unified, integrated totalities grounded on their own decidedly aesthetic premises. What these two points have in common is an impetus to conceive of self-determining communal wholes, though in Du Bois's hands, these communities are continually construed in terms of his increasingly materialist worldview.

That Du Bois considered economic cooperatives to be instruments of social progress is apparent as early as 1898 and a section in the report for the third Atlanta conference documenting cooperative businesses. The twelfth conference, which took place the year after Boas visited Atlanta, was devoted exclusively to the topic of economic cooperation and produced a report on collective enterprises following a pair of epigraphs by the geographer Friedrich Ratzel, a key influence on Boas's move from geography to ethnography.[81] At this stage, however, any commitment to self-segregation was still a long way off. An article written in the same year as the twelfth conference, 1907, voices serious doubts about the viability of segregation since the demands for labor made by the world economy, Du Bois believed at the time, would draw races closer together rather than drive them apart.[82] His dispute with Marcus Garvey in the early 1920s confirms this basic alignment with the aims of integration in opposition to the nationalism that Garvey espoused and the enmities he stoked between whites, West Indians and African-Americans.[83]

However, a separatist strain had long been present in Du Bois's thought. His association with Crummel, for instance, helped him see past the assimilationist message of Douglass; and Crummel's American Negro Academy was a model for the black university, which offers an early – and especially trenchant – expression of that separatist posture. Two developments nursed these tendencies in Du Bois's thinking during the early decades of the century: his Marxist investment in class struggle, which displaced any faith in the integrative potential of capitalism; and a reading of Sigmund Freud that exposed the unconscious sources of racial antipathy.[84] When combined, these historical and intellectual developments caused Du Bois to sharpen the split in American society between distinct sociocultural "worlds." Hence the title of the chapter in *Dusk of Dawn* that contains the program for self-segregation, "The Colored World

Within," which relates the insularity of racial worlds while also envisioning economic cooperatives that take advantage of in-group solidarity in order to "eliminate unemployment, risk and profit" and dispense with "the exploitation of labor."[85] This argument makes the circumscription of racial worlds part of a project of meliorating the social effects of capitalism. The underlying forces that drive capitalist accumulation – the division of labor, the pursuit of profit – become tractable once a common commitment to racial welfare is allowed to counteract class interests.

Advocacy for self-segregation on Du Bois's part must not be understood as a celebration of segregation as such. In the articles written for *The Crisis* defending his position, Du Bois makes the indignity of life in a separated society abundantly clear. He insists just as tenaciously, though, that as long as segregation is a reality enforced by one party over another, then the subordinated group should try to bend that situation to its advantage as a means of minimizing or even overcoming the perniciousness of the social ill. In other words, one way of eliminating the color line is by creating cultural worlds populated only by a single race. This tactic, while radical in the means it prescribes, immediately courts the charge of resignation or accommodation, and large swaths of educated African America, not just rivals within the NAACP, rejected Du Bois's new tack.[86] Thus he went to great lengths to refute the claim that he was encouraging "counsels of despair" or legitimating segregation as a social institution.[87] Ultimately, Du Bois argued, the goal of voluntary segregation was reentry into the fold of an American society liberated from both racial and material strife: "this plan of action would have for its ultimate object, full Negro rights and Negro equality in America," he writes in *Dusk*.[88] The plan could even lead to a "world democracy" organized according to merit.[89] In its initial stages, though, the cooperative movement would create self-contained economic communities within, but not reducible to, a broader social milieu. The University, of course, embodied that very same mission.[90] Carved out from its immediate spatiotemporal environs and operating independently from the forces of gilded-age capitalism, the University in *The Souls of Black Folk* is a complete and self-regulating social entity – a "colored world within" that is irreducible to the laws of its surroundings.

Evidence that Du Boisian economic cooperatives possess more than a passing likeness to the University emerges in "The Negro College," which Du Bois published in August 1933, when his thoughts on voluntary segregation were coalescing into a coherent plan of action. Although he claims that his basic outlook on university training had remained unchanged in the decades since *Souls*, Du Bois concedes his disillusionment with a university grounded on universalist premises and, more generally, with the power of culture to integrate differences. Opposing his views to those of Abraham Flexner, president of Howard, who extolled the "ideal of a great institution of learning which becomes a center of universal culture," a thesis that closely resembles the one contained in "Of the Wings of Atalanta," Du Bois now commits himself to a sharpened communalism.[91] He foregoes the universalism of *Souls* that likens Howard, Atlanta and Fisk to Oxford, Yale and Leipzig and instead argues in frankly nationalist terms that "a university in Spain is not simply a university" on account of the fact that it "uses the Spanish language" and "makes conditions in Spain the starting point of its teaching." Likewise a French college is based on French culture, and according to the same logic "there can be no college for Negroes which is not a Negro college."[92] So the Herderian elements in Du Bois's worldview crop up once again, with races being equivalent to nations defined as linguistic-cultural entities. The ideological stakes are bracingly clear: "Is not this a program of segregation, emphasis of race and particularism as against national unity and universal humanity? It is."[93]

The Negro college is therefore a vehicle for self-segregation in 1933 just as the University was a site for autonomous spiritual striving in 1903. The crucial difference is that the black university in *The Souls of Black Folk* existed as a separate sphere for the sake of integrating its members into a universal kingdom of culture while the Negro college advances race consciousness and group interests above the goal of integration, now distant almost to the point of vanishing. Yet significant as this difference may be, autonomy remains the defining principle of Du Boisian communalism. The economic cooperative, like the University, gives its members the freedom they would otherwise be denied:

> instead of letting this segregation remain largely a matter of chance and unplanned development, and allowing its object and results to rest in the hands of the white majority or in the accidents of the situation, it would make the segregation a matter of careful thought and intelligent planning on the part of Negroes.[94]

Du Bois calls for the exercise of rational agency in the face of external forces – chance, accidental circumstances or worse, the active malevolence of other parties. That is to say, he prescribes autonomy: African-Americans would assert their own law (*auto-nomos*), albeit within the constraints of a preexisting social structure. Instead of remaining passive in the face of segregation, Du Bois claims for his group the right to exercise rational self-determination amid a heteronomous order. The cooperative would be an institution determined by the guiding hand of rational agents who shape the course of their development according to their own collective purposes. "We are now segregated largely without reason," Du Bois protests. "Let us put reason and power beneath this segregation."[95]

Freedom is not the only value Du Bois valorizes in imagining his racial worlds. Completeness and a resurgent teleology continue to define group life. Echoing his queries from "Criteria of Negro Art" in a commencement address held at Fisk in 1938, Du Bois asks his audience to imagine a condition of full political subjectivity: "What then is Life – What is it for – What is its great End?" He provides his own answer:

> according to the testimony of all men who have lived, Life is the fullest, most complete enjoyment of the possibilities of human existence. It is the development and broadening of the feelings and emotions, through sound and color, line and form.[96]

Complete subjectivity is the expression and appreciation of pure form – line, shape, color, sound. Continuing in an unmistakably Schillerian vein, Du Bois pronounces that "freedom is the path of art, and living in the fuller and broader sense of the term is the expression of art."[97] Hence even if the turn to self-segregation requires "inner subordination and obedience," as he puts it in "The Right to Work," those restrictions are the limits that allow for effective organization and the exercise of reason so that "we become in truth, free" – a freedom that permits the "full development of the capacities and aspirations of the Negro race" within the bounds of a well-defined, autonomous institution.[98] And over and above these Schillerian motifs, it should be noted that the acceptance of a provisional subordination or privation for the sake of attaining a fuller, freer and more beautiful future is precisely the lesson of forbearance that Du Bois had learned from the Goethe.

When advocating for the cooperative movement, Du Bois conceives of racialized "worlds" in terms of what anthropologists of the period called "cultures": particularized, coherently organized and self-sustaining social entities. The programmatic statements contained in *Dusk of Dusk*, for instance, emphasize the habituating influence of cultural milieu in a way altogether consistent with the environmentalism Boas leveled against the race sciences. "Manners are a matter of social environment," Du Bois writes, and attitudes are "the result of inherited customs." Accordingly, African-Americans are "surrounded and conditioned" by the ideas and behaviors contained in that milieu. The centripetal social forces arising from segregation, whether exerted from without or generated from within through inclinations of like to associate with like, shape the environment and therefore the psychology and behavioral traits of the members of the group. While interaction between worlds is possible – Du Bois describes "cultural contact," trait diffusion and "acculturation" *between* cultures (white and black) as well as *within* them (the contact of upper and lower classes) – segregation more often leads to the "definite crystallization of the culture elements among colored people into their own groups." The racial world is therefore "a small integrated clique because of similar likes and ideas, because of corresponding culture."

Here we have a fairly standard cultural determinism, which had filtered out from professional anthropology into mainstream ideology by the time *Dusk* was published in 1940. Yet for all the contact between Du Bois and cultural anthropology, Evans has argued that Du Bois could never bring himself to accept the "more static and descriptive notion of 'cultures' as particularized wholes" that typified American anthropology in the 1930s, when Boas's students – among others, Ruth Benedict, Edward Sapir and Margaret Mead – posited that cultures were social wholes defined by their internal coherence.[99] Because he remained committed to a basically Arnoldian concept of universal culture, Evans maintains, Du Bois "never integrated with the second generation Boasians" who advanced the pluralistic and holistic tenets of cultural anthropology.[100] Susan Hegeman draws a similar lesson from the interaction of Boas and Du Bois. She sees both men committing themselves to an assimilationist message bolstered by the cultural critique of the race sciences.[101]

While these assessments may fairly characterize the early moments of Du Bois's interaction with cultural anthropology, they neglect the later phase of his career when the pendulum swings from the universalism of *The Souls of Black Folk* and advocacy for integration *between* races to the opposite ideological position: the integration *of* racial cultures into "crystallizations" of cultural traits and the organization of those collectives into active, self-determining socioeconomic institutions. That is to say, Du Boisian segregated worlds are precisely the "particularized wholes" that anthropologists theorized under the heading of "cultures" just as Du Bois was promoting his own plan for self-segregation.

What is more: Du Bois did integrate with second-generation Boasians. He cited them as authorities and exchanged ideas with several of Boas's most prominent students. Besides recruiting Mead and others for his *Encyclopedia*, Du Bois made last-minute revisions to *Black Folk: Then and Now* after receiving comments from Melville Herskovits, changes that did not prevent an admiring but sharp review from the anthropologist's pen.[102] Showing no signs of bitterness over Herskovits's criticisms – the "Negro chauvinism" of *Black Folk* was singled out for censure along with its outdated selection of sources – Du Bois heaped praise on Herskovits's *Myth of the Negro Past* in his own review of 1942, calling the book "epoch-making in the sense that no one hereafter writing on the cultural accomplishment of the American Negro can afford to be ignorant of its content and conclusions." And far from eschewing the pluralism of cultural anthropology, Du Bois takes up and discusses the pluralist implications of Herskovits's argument. Summarizing a section on "the results of enslavement on the African cultural pattern," Du Bois notes that "the patterns of African culture, even in language, were not so diverse as to prevent understanding between individuals."[103] These sentences strike to the heart of anthropological theory among second-generation Boasians. Cultural pattern – whether the psychological types Mead and Benedict used to describe entire cultures or the linguistic regularities Sapir considered an index of cultural constitution – was a signal theoretical innovation made by Boas's students, who tried to move past the lessons of their teacher by addressing the solidary forces that bind diverse diffusionary traits, what Robert Lowie called the "shreds and patches" of civilization, into coherent, integrated wholes. Distinct configurations of cultural elements were thought to form unified patterns, "crystallizations" in Du Bois's elegant phrasing, that marked a departure from both the granularity of Boas's empiricism and the monotelic architectonics of evolutionary anthropology.

Mead claims the first written statement attempting to translate the concept of pattern into a theory of "culture and personality," though she credits Benedict with the idea and attributes its development to their collaborations.[104] Introducing a collection of Benedict's essays she edited and published in 1959, Mead also acknowledges Benedict as the figure who became associated with the study of cultures as patterned personalities. The "theory which has become identified with her name," Mead writes, maintains that "cultures could be seen as 'personality writ large.'"[105] Therefore it is unsurprising but nonetheless noteworthy that Du Bois was acquainted with Benedict's work. Corresponding with a citizen interested in scholarship on race, Du Bois calmly dismisses the reactionary Robert W. Shufeldt, author of *The Negro: A Menace to Civilization*, and instead recommends Benedict's critique of physical anthropology, *Race: Science and Politics* (1942). "You should read Ruth Benedict on *Race*," Du Bois told his correspondent.[106]

Neither as famous as *Patterns of Culture* (1934) nor as influential as her study of Japan, *The Sword and the Chrysanthemum* (1946), Benedict's second book is nevertheless her most topical work. *Race* marshals the full range of culturalist arguments, including the concept of cultural pattern, against the racial ideology of National Socialism. Proceeding in typical Boasian fashion, Benedict makes a sharp distinction between what she considered a biological phenomenon, race, and a political doctrine, racism, whose hierarchical distinctions have no basis in fact. On this account, constellations of physiological traits reflect a conventional tripartite division that is itself a function of geography: Europeans, Asians and Africans are indigenous to the Mediterranean, the Pacific and the Indian Oceans. What distinguishes this argument from the environmentalism of a Montesquieu, to say nothing of the Nazis, is its strict circumscription of specializations to physical characteristics – psychological, ethical or aesthetic distinctions are ruled out of court. Instead, cultural pattern does the work of explaining the "mental and emotional characteristics" that change over time.[107] Decoupled from biology, these "patterns of political, economic, and artistic behavior" are responsible for creating hierarchies of value – norms for action and standards for preference and aversion – which vary in the normal pluralist fashion according to historical contingencies and the particularities of a given milieu.[108] In an example that could not have been lost on Du Bois, Benedict maintains that the most "drastic change" to cultural pattern occurred among enslaved Americans whose traditions became a casualty of the middle passage.[109] Enslavement stripped its victims of the cultural achievements acquired in Africa – Benedict focuses on the Nigerian kingdoms – and replaced them with a cultural pattern more consistent with the "poor whites," as she calls them, of the American South. By no means an uncontroversial stance on the matter of African retentions, Benedict's argument nevertheless makes the force of her claim apparent. The historical mutability of cultures gives the lie to the biologically inferiority of races.

Of equal moment in Du Bois's continued engagement with cultural anthropology is his comfort with cultural pattern as a means of describing economic differences. Contributing to his regular column for the Chicago *Defender* in 1947, Du Bois admired the work of the anthropologist Oscar Lewis, whom Benedict trained at Columbia.[110] Lewis's most important contribution was the application of Boasian methods to the study of "lower class cultural patterns," as he put it in the title of a grant proposal from 1955.[111] Eventually labeled the "culture of poverty" thesis, this intervention would come under serious scrutiny from critics who charged

Lewis with mystifying economic factors by turning them into cultural traits and then imputing them to the poor.[112] The *Defender* article discusses Lewis's "Wealth Differences in a Mexican Village," an essay that has little to say about culture and personality but that was, in fact, the result of a personality study Lewis carried out with his wife in the village of Tepoztlán. In the essay, Lewis hews to basic cultural anthropological premises. For instance, he announces his strictly emic approach to understanding poverty: "Our first step in the study of wealth differences," he writes, "was to determine how wealth was defined by the villagers."[113] Operating under these premises, Lewis would elsewhere pursue the more hazardous task of recording how material differences coalesced into the behavioral regularities that constituted a characteristic pattern of poverty. Du Bois, who appreciated the empirical rigor of Lewis's study, was enthusiastic about this methodological mix of hard-boiled Boasian ethnography with a Marxist attunement to patterns of class and poverty.

Such evidence of continued Boasian influence helps explain why cultural pattern was an indispensable part of Du Bois's theoretical equipment in the 1940s. Consider the essay "My Evolving Program for Negro Freedom" (1944). Written soon before he was retired from Atlanta University by trustees hostile to their most outspoken faculty member, the essay renews the call for a comprehensive series of studies modeled on the original Atlanta conferences – a project that became a major point of contention with the Atlanta hierarchy.[114] Included in this revival would be a systematic study of "Cultural Patterns: Morals and Manners" that must, as a matter of course, take into account "scientific advance in fields like anthropology and psychology."[115] But cultural pattern is no mere topic for future research. Patterning, as the essay makes clear, is at the core of Du Bois's conception of a free and equal society. He concludes with a programmatic statement on the nature of freedom, beginning by stating his position in general terms: "by 'freedom' for Negroes, I meant and still mean, *full economic, political and social equality with American citizens* [emphasis original]."[116] Freedom, in other words, means completeness. African-Americans must be recognized as full members of society – citizens in the strong sense of the term. Yet this statement requires clarification, Du Bois concedes. He admits the vagueness of his conception of society that lies at the basis of his claim. Thus he continues, "'social' is used to refer not only to the intimate contacts of the family group" but instead "to the whole vast complex of human relationships through which we carry out our cultural patterns."[117] Society is not a conglomeration of kinship bonds; it is a vehicle for the expression of cultural pattern – or more accurately, cultural *patterns*. Du Bois claims the pluralist heritage of cultural anthropology for his own theoretical ends. He construes modern social life as a unified totality containing diverse constituent parts – complete, self-sustaining and self-determining cultural patterns woven into a complex social whole. These patterned units are the sociological content for a progressive program for human liberation whose evolution has now been traced from *The Souls of Black Folk* through *Darkwater* to his late break with the NAACP – a program where completeness exists for the sake of freedom.

* * *

Cultural pattern is therefore a concept with both practical and theoretical stakes for the late Du Bois. The revived Atlanta conferences would investigate the patterns that underlie an evolved program for freedom and the condition of full citizenship. One final move is needed to bring this chapter to a close: establishing the specifically aesthetic dimensions of cultural pattern. For this we must turn to the canonical formulation of the concept in Benedict, who, according to Mead, had laid the main foundations for her theory in essays of the 1920s later published in *An Anthropologist at Work* (1959). What is striking about these early precedents for cultural pattern is, in fact, their manifestly aesthetic nature. When Benedict first employs the term "pattern," for example, she does so in order to describe the beauty of tribal dances at Zuñi, the New Mexican pueblo where she conducted much of her fieldwork. Each dance has "its own distinctive pattern of beauty and costume and music," Benedict writes in "They Dance for Rain at Zuñi," stating, too, that each "has individuality and a history."[118] In other words, the dances at Zuñi have a personality. They are distinct, historically determined patterns that possess their own characteristic sign of beauty.

Pattern, in this context, signifies artistic form – the regular, ordered arrangement of elements in a dance. As she developed her thesis through the 1920s and early 1930s, Benedict generalized the concept of pattern without sacrificing the original formalist connotations. "Psychological Types in the Cultures of the Southwest" (1928, 1930) discusses the "highly ritualized, highly formalized" practices on the pueblo.[119] These formalized rituals, whether dances or religious ceremonies, then combine to create what Benedict calls "an intricate cultural pattern" – or what Du Bois calls "crystallizations of the cultural elements."[120] Rather than a single dance being the bearer of patterned beauty, the entire culture functions as a patterned phenomenon, with each culture having a "fundamentally different character" just as each dance is marked by its own aesthetic signature.

Through the 1930s, Benedict continued to hone her cultural formalism. Writing in 1935, she contemplates how a "folkloristic pattern" relates to broader units of social organization.[121] After puzzling over why the predominantly monogamous Zuñi possess such a preponderance of stories about polygamy, Benedict considers the ways that particular thematic patterns, mythemes, relate to categories of gender difference. The tales told by Zuñi men are filled with themes of hunting, races and gambling while the stories of the women tend to foreground domestic tasks.[122] At first glance, gendered patterns may appear to be the basic configurations that are then sublimated into mythemes. Yet the distinction between figure and ground in this model can be difficult to discern, for gender is but one more behavioral pattern. Gendered habits of mind and body are intertwined with the thematic regularities of myth yet neither is more basic. Social roles are simply one more formalized ritual inherited through the transmission of stories, customs, practices and traditions.

Generalization is therefore the main tactic in Benedict's development of cultural pattern. She moves from local instances of patterned practices, ritual dances, to a patterned whole called a "culture" that is itself made up of crystallized forms. Such an aesthetic determination of the culture concept goes well beyond the better-known, and oft-criticized, distinction Benedict makes between Apollonian and Dionysian cultures. These appellations taken from *The Birth of Tragedy* are used to describe the paradigmatic personalities of the Zuñi and the Kwakiutls – the former being quintessentially Apollonian in their measured restraint and the latter qualifying as Dionysian due to their megalomaniac exuberance. Even though Benedict was quick to point out that various cultures possess different levels of coherence and that not all evince a fully formed psychological type, Marvin Harris notes, correctly, that Benedict is working within a tradition of typological thinking that reaches back at least to Linnaeus and Kant.[123] The crucial difference, of course, is that Benedict's typologies are restricted to psychological and behavioral traits. There is no admixture of internal and external attributes. Hers are strictly cultural types.

The Nietzschean typologies Benedict employs are therefore concepts of the second order. They are names that refer to particular cultural constellations, which are themselves defined in terms of form and content, pattern and theme. Marc Manganaro, citing the feminist anthropologist Marilyn Strathern, has identified this kind of cultural formalism as one component of a "modernist anthropology" that aligns the literary experiments of modernist writers with the self-reflexivity and formal awareness characteristic of certain cultural anthropologists – a post-structuralist reading that is strengthened by the poetic aspirations of both Benedict and Sapir.[124] Taking a less linguo-centric tack, Tony Bennett has argued that the formalist implications of culture-as-pattern replaces Arnoldian sweetness and light with another basically aesthetic conception of culture.[125] These readings helpfully draw attention to a shared formalism in aesthetics and anthropology. They also gesture toward a more basic theoretical quandary that Benedict seeks to resolve in *Patterns of Culture*: If it be granted that cultures are coherent, patterned phenomena and not mere aggregations of diffused traits, then why do diverse elements take the shape that they do? It is one thing to point out the existence of formal order. It is another to give a reason for why that order emerges, and without an explanation or justification of the ordering force that transforms disparate parts into a unified whole, observations of a shared formalism must remain mere analogies between culture and art, social pattern and the unity of form.

Benedict takes a decidedly neoclassical approach to this problem. The core theoretical chapters in *Patterns of Culture* are titled "The Diversity of Cultures," which addresses trait diffusion and the heterogeneity of cultural elements, and the "The Integration of Culture," which accounts for cultural coherence. Unity amid diversity is rendered into an explicitly anthropological problematic. And given the legacy Benedict inherited from Kant – Harris makes much of her citation of the neo-Kantian Wilhelm Dilthey – it should come as no surprise that purposiveness becomes the key to cultural integration:

> The significance of cultural behavior is not exhausted when we have clearly understood that it is local and manmade and hugely variable. It tends also to be integrated. A culture, like an individual, is a more or less consistent pattern of thought and action. Within each culture there come into being characteristic purposes not necessarily shared by other types of society. In obedience to these purposes, each people further and further consolidates its experience, and in proportion to the urgency of these drives the heterogeneous items of behavior take more and more congruous shape.[126]

This passage returns us to the concepts of purposiveness and shape, types and essential characteristics that license qualitative distinctions in a Kantian framework. But where Kant understood races to be a product of the cognitive faculties, which transform the plenitude of empirical data into ordered whole of species and genera, Benedict construes cultures as deliberative agents. They are "like an individual." Accordingly, cultures are themselves able to generate characteristic patterns, both behavioral and cognitive, without their ordering impulse being justified in terms of natural law or the necessity of super- and sub-ordinate categories. Cultures possess a kind of "primitive freedom," as Benedict titled an essay published in 1942. Those cultures are then molded through contingent factors and historical causes that are immanent to a given cultural situation.[127] That is all to say, cultures provide their own laws. They regulate – or rather, self-regulate – the diversity of empirical elements to give them a progressively more coherent shape. These purposes must be obeyed, to be sure. They are laws arising from a congeries of sources: reason, tradition or unconscious drives. And they may reflect divergent values: "freedom or social cohesion or submission to authority."[128] The crucial point, though, is that these laws are not imposed from without. They are not heteronomous. Instead, the laws arise from within the culture itself and refer to the ordering of life within that milieu.

A broadly Schillerian ethos of autonomy is therefore present in both Du Bois and Benedict. The concept of cultural pattern, at least as it was formulated in *Patterns of Culture* and Benedict's essays of the 1920s, expounds on cultural types shaped by subjective purposes instead of natural types defined by the external forms of physical appearance. Patterned cultures, like collective dances, are ordered yet autonomous phenomena structured as a historical fact and not an immutable product of teleological nature. The Boasian paradigm permits a multiplicity of cultural shapes to emerge without automatically schematizing those types in a world picture of law-governed nature. Perfection, we might say, is internalized and pluralized. Form-giving intentions, the purposes of cultural members, emerge immanently from a culture and lend unity to the diversity of thoughts, practices and traditions of multifarious cultures.

The retention of autonomy is especially noteworthy in light of the increasingly inflexible determinism of Du Bois's late Marxism, which made individual behavior and social structure the products of economic forces while seeming to leave less and less room for agency or resistance to those forces. Simply put, Du Bois's "fair far-off ideal of Freedom" appears to recede into the distance as his career progresses. This chapter has aimed to show that freedom and perfection survive the Marxist turn. In fact Du Bois's militancy caused him to transform his ideal of Freedom into a program for fashioning concrete social entities, economic cooperatives, where autonomy and full political subjectivity rectify the impoverishments of American society. The late Du Bois, his pragmatism steeled by unremitting struggle, does not forgo the promise of perfection. He strives with redoubled energy to make his ideals of freedom real, thereby surpassing more familiar formulations of aesthetic autonomy, including the one posed by Schiller himself, whose notion of an Aesthetic State is circumscribed to "a few selected circles" and thus limited to a micropolitical configuration. Du Bois also takes aesthetic autonomy in a different direction than Theodor Adorno, for whom the self-referential regularities of artistic form are a means of negating the instrumental reason of capitalist modernity. Du Bois certainly negates the heteronomy of modern capital – Atalanta's lust for gold. Moreover, he refuses the constraints of a racist social order by carving out cultural wholes separate from the surrounding world. But he does not stop there. Du Boisian worlds, rationally organized, are the first step in fashioning a more total social order, unrestricted to a circle of talented elites, that replaces structural inequalities and unconscious antipathies with a collective life governed by rational self-determination. At its most infelicitous, this program makes the Stalinist state a model for a well-ordered society. More optimistically, Du Bois's vision of a complete society – be it American, pan-African or "world democracy" governed by merit – generalizes from the micropolitical perfection of economic cooperatives to a more comprehensive, perhaps even universal, human whole.

Part I of this book began with a Kantian distinction: the methodological, and theoretical, distinction between natural and practical anthropology, that is, between race and culture. In tracing Kant's aesthetic determination of a human race through its nineteenth-century inheritors, Walker and Croly and Wakeman, and then to twentieth-century critics of physical anthropology like Du Bois and Boas, we have effectively moved from one Kantian pole to the other: from nature to *praxis*, from race to culture, from heteronomy to autonomy. What has remained in place over the course of this analysis is an aesthetic paradigm where *anthropos* is a member of an ordered typological whole. The characteristics used to assign membership may vary. They may be physiological, as in the shape of the face, or behavioral, psychological and linguistic – the regularities that make up distinct cultures on a Boasian-Benedictine model. But in either case, humans are parts of rule-governed patterns. They are diverse elements belonging to unified types, whether physical or cultural.

But what if the discourse of types is discarded altogether? What if, instead of conceiving of collective human essence in terms of conformity to a pattern, the felt experience of belonging to a community is the grounds for group membership? In a way, such a *sensus communis* would radicalize the Boasian program since Boas himself turned to the subjective experience of cultural agents as a chief source of knowledge even as he marshaled those experiences as the data of empirical ethnography. His students then rationalized those data still further by arranging them into distinct cultural patterns – one more remove from the actual color of subject experience, from the qualitative texture of sensations and impressions. But the *sensus communis* need not be rationalized or typologized. For a writer like W. B. Yeats, a *sensus communis* allowed an escape from ideation through art, which he believed held the power to disclose a realm beyond the grasp of *ratio* and empirical reality. Turning away from patterned types therefore introduces a different paradigm for understanding the aesthetic essence of *anthropos*: from a *neo*classical aesthetics grounded in ideals of human beauty, to a model closer to the original etymological sense of αἴσθησις: "perception," "sensation" or, indeed, "impression," which is then collectivized to refer to distinct configurations of individuals.

Part II

CHAPTER 4

Philosophers of the Cabal

One can only reach out to the universe with a gloved hand – that glove is one's nation, the only thing one knows even a little of.
—Yeats, *Letters to the New Island*

If the discourse of perfection provides Du Bois with the means to define the nature of the Preacher, the Teacher, the Christian or the White Man, then what of the ideal Critic? In "The Perfect Critic" of 1920, T. S. Eliot addresses two interpretative traditions that had come down to the moderns over the centuries: intellectual or abstract criticism, which comprises Coleridge's philosophical hermeneutics and Horatian *ars poetica*; and impressionistic criticism, which Eliot identifies with Walter Pater and his critical heir, Arthur Symons. One charm of Eliot's essay is that he omits any explicit statement on the nature of the perfect critic, preferring instead to point out the imperfections of other critical schools while offering remarks about the "development of sensibility" or the "pure contempla-tion" that proper criticism should foster – remarks that Eliot concedes are mere "commonplaces."[1] Hence the perfect critic is adumbrated *in negatio,* a shadow cast by the light of scrutiny aimed at others.

In Eliot's telling a key problem for aesthetic critics like Pater and Symons is how to communicate their impressions to other minds. For in purporting "to exhibit to us, like the plate, the faithful record" of their impressions, these critics do not confine themselves to the realm of the senses: "the moment you try to put impressions into words," Eliot writes, "you either begin to analyze and construct ... or you begin to create something else."[2] So an alloy is introduced into the sensory ore mined from the work of art. Analysis, synthesis and language inflect the senses in the act of exhibition. But what if, to dwell on Eliot's metaphor, the aesthetic critic is not an inert plate for reproducing sensations but an active agent who responds to an artwork like a dancer moving to music? Might impressions be transmitted along other communicative channels – through the rhythm and tone of language, for example, or through the performativity of a speech act instead of its discursive content? What if creating something else is precisely the point?

For writers working in the tradition of Pater, the communication of sensory experience was a chief part of the art of criticism. "Suppose I wish to give you an impression of the Luxembourg Gardens, as I see them when I look out of my window," Symons writes in an essay on impressionist literature from 1923:

> Will it help to call up in your mind the impression of those glimmering alleys and the naked darkness of the trees, if I begin by telling you that I can count seven cabs, half another at one end, and a horse's head at the other, in the space between the corner of the Odéon and the houses on the opposite side of the street; that there are four trees and three lamp-posts on the pavement; and that I can read the words "Chocolat Menier," in white letters, on a blue ground, upon the circular black kiosk by the side of the second lamp-post?[3]

No it will not. Impressionism is not realism, a style for which Symons had little patience. And the mechanism that would "flash upon you in a new, sudden way so exact an image of what you have just seen" is not the apparatus of photography, a medium in which Symons had little interest.[4] Therefore the faithfulness of an impression is not a function of its indexical verisimilitude, its ability to provide a "faithful record" as Eliot put it. The impressionist must summon – or to use Symons's word, evoke – sensations in the reader instead of merely replicating the impulses that strike the retina or the tympanic membrane.

Impressionism at the *fin-de-siècle* jockeyed with other artistic and critical movements – Decadence, Symbolism, Aestheticism – causing uncertainty about the content of these various schools. Symons himself admits the difficulty at the beginning of "The Decadent Movement in Literature" (1893), his acclaimed essay on the French literary scene, which opens with a confession of critical vagueness: "The latest movement in European literature has been called by many names, none of them quite exact or comprehensive – Decadence, Symbolism, Impressionism."[5] For his part, Symons claims that Decadence is the central trunk that cleaves into "two main branches" of Symbolism and Impressionism, both of which "have more in common than either supposes" since both are concerned with the presentation of "*la vérité vraie*, the essence of truth" – a notion Symons takes from Pater's "School of Giorgione."[6] Yet these movements, despite their common investment in knowledge, differ with respect to the kinds of truth they offer a reader: Impressionism treats the truths of the eye while

Symbolism deals with the truths of the soul – sensation and intuition respectively. In an influential treatment of the legacy of literary decadence, Vincent Sherry has argued that historians of modernism have been complicit in subordinating one of these strains of *fin-de-siècle* art to another, namely, Decadence to Symbolism. This prioritization of Symbolism, claims Sherry, is the product of a modernist ideology that promotes renewal and a radical break with the past at the expense of decadent elements – belatedness, artifice, decay – that suffused the writings of modernists from Ezra Pound to Rebecca West to Samuel Beckett.[7] The *locus classicus* of this suppression is the early career of Symons, who retitled "The Decadent Movement in Literature" when he expanded his study into *The Symbolist Movement in Literature* in 1899 – a change that reflected the influence of W. B. Yeats, to whom Symons dedicated his volume, as well as the cultural anxieties awakened by the Wilde trial in 1895.

What gets lost in Sherry's analysis of the generational struggle between late Victorian Decadence and the modernist Symbol is the third term in Symons's triumvirate of style – Impressionism, in Eliot's view the main critical tradition descending from Pater to the *fin-de-siècle*.[8] And just as a decadent reading of modernism debunks a progress narrative at the heart of the period's self-understanding, an impressionist take on the literary practices that emerged after aestheticism helps reshape a main plank of modernism's politics: the development, epitomized by Yeats, of new nationalist sensibilities intended to counter the alienation and anomie of modern culture. By now, the story of how a young nationalist became an old reactionary besotted with eugenics has been well-told, many times, in the annals of Yeats scholarship.[9] A particular challenge for scholars has been to account for the vicissitudes in Yeats's worldview over his half century in public life: his early sympathy with Fenian nationalism and William Morris's socialism; his actions as a senator in the Irish Free State; his later admiration of Mussolini. Faced with the many moods of Yeats's politics, scholars have recurred to certain paradigmatic strategies. Beginning with Edward Said's "Yeats and Decolonization" through studies by Marjorie Howes, Declan Kiberd, and more recently Carrie Preston and Michael Valdez Moses, critics have used Benedict Anderson's well-worn notion of "imagined communities" to ground their analyses of Yeatsian cultural nationalism.[10] On this model, the nation is a figment of the mind. Therefore poets are the true nation-builders since it is they who create the tissue of shared myths and symbols that constitutes national consciousness.

Given the imaginative exuberance of the author of *A Vision*, it is little wonder that imagined communities have been a useful paradigm for understanding Yeatsian nationalism. Yet incongruities between Anderson's theory and Yeats's politics begin to emerge as soon as the conjunction is subjected to closer examination. One problem is that even as Yeats concedes that the nation is a product of the mind, he dismisses it for precisely that reason. In the final section of "A General Introduction for My Work" (1937), titled simply "Whither?," Yeats states, "I am no Nationalist, except in Ireland for passing reasons; State and Nation are the work of the intellect, and when you consider what comes before and after them they are, as Victor Hugo said of something or other, not worth the blade of grass God gives for the nest of the linnet."[11] What comes before and after the State and Nation? What is the real driving force for Yeats's politics? Though unstated in his estimation of the Nation's worthlessness, the decisive energies antecedent and subsequent to intellection can be inferred from the immediately preceding passage:

> When I stand upon O'Connell Bridge in the half-light and notice that discordant architecture, all those electric signs, where modern heterogeneity has taken physical form, a vague hatred comes up out of my own dark and I am certain that wherever in Europe there are minds strong enough to lead others the same vague hatred rises; in four or five or in less generations this hatred will have issued in violence and imposed some kind of rule of kindred.

What comes before the Nation, it seems, is a rage against the disharmony of modernity. Welling up in the obscure depths of Yeats's self, this hatred for the electric physiognomy of modern life leads to a longing for rule, concord, symmetry – a "rule of kindred" that will bring order to the heterogeneity of modernity. Though Yeats did not live to see it, it took far less than four generations for that violence to issue across Europe; and when it did, it was anything but vague.

This chapter argues that Yeatsian communities are felt, not imagined. They are "flowing, concrete, phenomenal," as Yeats writes in an earlier passage of the "General Introduction" when describing a future European religion. They are, in short, communities of impressions. In refiguring Yeatsian communities to bring out their sensory content, the aim is not to eliminate imaginative or symbolic elements from his work or from the writings of Pater and Symons, two other writers who will be discussed along the way. The goal is to show that Symbolism and Impressionism, intuition and sensation, continue to "have more in common than either supposes," as Symons put it, even after the *fin-de-siècle* was eclipsed by modernism. And what, precisely, they had in common was something quite close to what the liberal tradition has come to call a *sensus communis*, an idea theorized most trenchantly in the eighteenth century by the third Earl of Shaftesbury, the scion of Britain's most prominent Whig family of the day. While scholars of Victorian culture have done much to recuperate Shaftesburian themes for the cultural politics of the nineteenth century, modernists have tended to locate communitarian tendencies in sources more proximate to their period: in Morris and Carlyle, for instance, both of whom were major influences on Symons and Yeats.[12] Tracing the legacy of Shaftesbury's heterodox liberalism through to the twentieth century reveals how a certain empiricist aesthetics, a *sensus*, combines with a distinctively collectivist anthropology, a *communis*, to furnish twentieth-century writers with the means of envisioning new forms of collective life just as the Victorian politics that had informed Paterian aestheticism were mutating into more recognizably modernist forms: the rise of postcolonial nationalisms, a crisis of empire leading to world war, the birth of fascism in Europe.

4.1   Aesthetic Communis

Mais, sous le symbole, il faut savoir atteindre la réalité qu'il figure et qui lui donne sa signification véritable.

[But, underneath the symbol, it is necessary to learn to reach the reality that it represents and that gives it its true meaning.]
—Durkheim, *Les formes élémentaires de la vie religieuse*

In 1709, the arch Whig and renegade pupil of John Locke, Anthony Ashley Cooper, third Earl of Shaftesbury, published an essay praising raillery and wit as checks against religious enthusiasm. *Sensus Communis: A Letter Concerning Wit and Humour* prescribes linguistic play as a "remedy against vice, and a kind of specific against superstition" in the course of a critique of Thomas Hobbes and others whom Shaftesbury accuses of reducing behavior to the individual pursuit of power.[13] Though he concedes that egotism influences human action, Shaftesbury maintains that a countervailing impulse, an "associating inclination" or "combining principle," balances selfish interests through a drive for communal fellowship – a sense of the common.[14] Derived from the classical virtue of κοινονοημοσύνη (*koino* = common; noēmosune = thinking) and Roman stoics like Marcus Aurelius and Seneca, the *sensus communis* regulates behavior and authorizes standards of taste through a general ethic of "civility, hospitality, humanity toward strangers or people in distress."[15]

The classical roots of the Shaftesburian *sensus* run from the Cambridge Platonists of the seventeenth century through Roman republicanism back to the antique meaning of αἴσθησις: the general content of sensory percep-tion.[16] In a long footnote to his letter, Shaftesbury renders the Latin *sensus* with the Greek αἴσθησις, quoting a passage from Horace on manners and adding his gloss after the dash: "*Haud illud quærentes, num sine SENSU, tempore num faciant alieno. – ἀναισθητῶς.*"[17] Those without a sense of manners are anesthetic. They lack decorum and thereby suffer from a sort of social blindness – an inability to perceive the condition of others. A few lines later, the footnote returns to αἴσθησις in an effort to ward off a philological criticism: "It may be objected," Shaftesbury admits, "that the κοινός νοῦς [common mind], to which the κοινονοημοσύνη seems to have a relation, is of a different meaning." Though he does not specify the other meaning he has in mind, Shaftesbury appears to be worried about the cognitive implications of νοῦς, which might conflict with the sensory or affective shadings proper to αἴσθησις and *sensus*. Yet such an objection, Shaftesbury reminds us, overlooks "how small the distinction was in that [ancient] philosophy, between ὑπόληψις [taking in a certain sense, taking up the matter], and the vulgar αἴσθησις; how generally passion was by those philosophers brought under the head of opinion."[18] So, for the ancients, passions blended into opinion. Feeling assumed an aspect of thought. So, too, the term αἴσθησις, vulgar, apparently, due to its general applicability, is a receptive faculty for taking in the sensory world just as ὑπόληψις takes up a notion or idea in the act of interpreting, estimating or judging.

This aesthetic sense is then married to a collectivist anthropology, where the *sensus communis* refers to an innate quality of the human animal: "If eating and drinking be natural, herding is so too. If any appetite or sense be natural, the sense of fellowship is the same."[19] On this account, self-preservation and fellowship are two different but equally essential needs. Once postulated, this desire for "common affection" allows the concept of society to be recast. Instead of construing the social whole as an aggregate of actors who calculate the benefits of exchanging their liberty for the protec-tions afforded by the State, the *sensus communis* makes the social body grow organically out of this natural inclination for cooperative fellowship:

> a clan or tribe is gradually formed, a public is recognized, and, besides the pleasure found in social entertainment, language and discourse, there is so apparent a necessity for continuing this good correspondency and union that to have no sense or feeling of this kind, no love of country, community or any thing in common, would be the same as to be insensible even of the plainest means of self-preservation.[20]

An instinct that originally caused the formation of clans or tribes, and later a public commonwealth, this *sensus* retains its impetus in developed society while being directed toward new modes of collective organization – a country or community, a faction, cabal or club, even an audience gathered for entertainment. The configurations of the common are varied, yet all its many forms are downstream iterations of an elemental desire for human communion. Therefore the *sensus communis* cannot be reduced to a product of the imagination, for it is the antecedent instinct, "the force of confederating charm," that later manifests in discrete sociopolitical forms.[21]

Shaftesbury draws attention to the passionate substrate underlying viable groups. While he does not dispense with ideas altogether, he does subordinate social institutions based on ideal interests to communities grounded on shared moral, social and aesthetic sensibilities. At one point, he admits to his interlocutor, "I am writing to you in defence only of the liberty of the Club and of that sort of freedom which is taken among gentlemen and friends who know one another perfectly well."[22] Such a coterie mentality has its limitations, and Shaftesbury is quick to concede the risks of cabalism and partisanship (the gendered aporias of gentlemanliness do not detain him). But even as the flaws of in-group chauvinism are acknowledged, intimacy remains essential for encouraging individuals to unite into a common: "in less parties, men may be intimately conversant," Shaftesbury maintains. "They can there better taste society and enjoy the common good and interest of a more contracted public. They view the whole compass and extent of their community." Once again, the "sense" of the *sensus communis* conforms to the classical denotation of αἴσθησις. Members of a common may "taste society." They may take in the whole community at a glance.

As soon as the *communis* expands to include larger numbers and more abstract interests, the sensory proximity that maintains a common becomes attenuated: "the greater community falls not easily under the eye," we learn, "nor is a national interest or that of a whole people or body politic so readily apprehended." In fact, national interests may well run counter to common interests since "no visible band is formed, no strict alliance, but the conjunction is made with different persons, orders and ranks of men, not sensibly, but in idea." Real sensory contact promotes a sense of the common. When the senses are stretched beyond their natural bounds, social unions based on ideas result. And these larger social configurations develop a parasitic relationship to the *sensus communis*, distorting emotions associated with communal life by associating them with abstract ideas that diverge from the genuine interests of a common: "Thus the social aim is disturbed for want of certain scope." In the absence

of direct aesthetic contact, "the close sympathy and conspiring virtue is apt
to lose itself, for want of direction."[23] The distinction between a *sensus
communis* and communities grounded in the imagination should now be
clear. The former is a community based on intimate sensory contact while
the latter is an ideational construct of the mind. While it is true that the
sensus communis may be kindled by larger social configurations – in feelings
of patriotism, for instance – its proper domain is the small group, where
imaginary bonds are subsidiary to the scents and tastes of a circumscribed
social unit.[24]

Shaftesbury exerted an especially strong influence in Germany, where he
was seen as a major representative of British empirical psychology.[25] The
moment when Kant invokes Shaftesburian themes while discussing the
normal idea in *The Critique of Judgment* has already been noted. Later in
the third *Critique*, Kant devotes an entire section to translating the *sensus
communis* into the transcendental terms of his critical philosophy.[26]
No less an admirer of the empiricist tradition, Johann Gottfried Herder
went so far as to learn English so he could read British authors in the
original. A remarkable passage from a treatise on aesthetics Herder wrote in
1869, the *Viertes Kritisches Wäldchen*, testifies to these links between
Shaftesbury and the German Enlightenment. After alluding to Kant's
precritical essay "Observations on the Feelings of the Beautiful and
Sublime," Herder writes that the author is "truly a philosopher of the
sublime and the beautiful in humanity! and in this human philosophy,
Germany's Shaftesbury."[27] What inspired Herder to make this claim was
not Kant's prowess as a critical philosopher since *The Critique of Pure
Reason* was still more than a decade away. Rather, it was Kant's perspicacity
as an observer of human nature and his sensibility for the beautiful and the
sublime. It was, in other words, his quintessentially Shaftesburian synthesis
of aesthetics and anthropology. "Kant, the consummate social observer,
the consummate cultured philosopher, takes up the beautiful and the
sublime in his work, especially the formable nature of the human, the
social side of our nature in its finest colors and shadings." Not content to
limit his praise to Kant's social acumen, Herder lauds the "Observations"
for exhibiting "the grand and beautiful in humans and in human character,
temperaments, the sexual drives and virtues and national characters."[28]
Rarely thought of as a keen observer of sexuality and the ways of the world,
Kant is deemed Germany's Shaftesbury due to his ability to discern the
aesthetic essence of *anthropos* in its generality and its particularity – the
characteristics of humanity as a whole and the temperaments of individual
nations.

National characteristics take on a polemical edge in the *Viertes Wäldchen* when Herder addresses the *sensus communis* as it was deployed by the philosopher and aesthetician Friedrich Riedel, an affiliate of Herder's adversary Christian Klotz of Halle.[29] Though Herder's chief interlocutor in the *Viertes Wäldchen* is Riedel, who construed the *sensus communis* as an epistemological faculty for regulating shared convictions about truth rather than an instinct for sociability, the analysis of the *sensus communis* in the text is nevertheless revealing for a discussion of a Shaftesburian aesthetic anthropology. True to form, Herder relativizes the *sensus communis*. "Is it not the case," he asks, "that a nation [*Nation*] has its *sens commun* ... according to its measure of education, and with respect to its own world?" Herder then sharpens the point: "is the *sensus communis* of the Greenlander and the Hottentot in things and deeds the same as ours? And is the *sensus communis* of the bailiff [*Landverwalter*] the same as that of a scholar?"[30] No, he implies, it is not. Each group has its own *sensus*, be it a nation or an occupation that correlates with class and culture. Significantly, though, Herder does not take up communities circumscribed by αἴσθησις in this passage. In fact, he is concerned with precisely those collectives that Shaftesbury identified as threats to the healthy functioning of the *sensus communis*: "nor is a national interest or that of a whole people or body politic so readily apprehended," Shaftesbury warns his reader. Herder, without reflecting on the specificity of the sensations and impressions held in common, imputes a shared *sensus* to nations and peoples while making that sense reflect the character of the group – "Hottentot," "Greenlander," scholars or men of the land.

Two factors go into shaping the *sensus communis* in this passage from the *Viertes Wäldchen*: education (*Ausbildung*) and environment (*Welt*), the cultivation of internal faculties and the influence of external circumstances. Both of these factors were given a more sustained exposition in Herder's magnum opus and most comprehensive work of anthropological theory, the *Ideen zur Philosophie der Geschichte der Menschheit* [Ideas on a Philosophy of the History of Humanity] (1784). Along with offering a cosmological narrative that makes *anthropos* a resident of one planet among many and one creature in God's great menagerie, Herder takes issue with anthropologies that delineate racial categories within humankind. In other words, he takes issue with Kant, who, for his part, replied by penning a caustic review of the *Ideen* in 1785 and expanding his own race theory in response. The crux of the matter is stated by Herder as follows:

> So a few, for example, have ventured to call four or five divisions within the human species *races*, which were originally made according to region or

entirely according to color; I see no cause for this designation. Race leads back to a difference in descent, which in this case either fails to occur, or otherwise comprehends in each of these regions and with each of these colors the most various races. For each people is a people: it has its national formation as it has its language.[31]

On this account, the *Volk* replaces the race as the fundamental anthropological distinction within the category of the human. Instead of being a natural (sub)species descended from a common stem and defined by necessarily heritable traits, as are races in a Kantian framework, Herderian peoples are defined by their language and their *National-Bildung* – that is, their national formation.

The remainder of Books 7 and 8 elaborate on nation formation, with Herder arguing that national characteristics emerge through the conjunction of two determinants: a "genetic force" and climate. A close relative of the Blumenbachian *Bildungstrieb*, which Chapter 2 traced through the Romantic science of Kant and *Naturphilosophen* such as Goethe, the genetic force is identified by Herder as the source or "mother of all formations."[32] But where Goethe argued that a vital force caused an organism to realize its archetype through the process of *Bildung*, Herder maintains that peoples rather than plants possess an analogous drive that constitutes an "organic power," or rather, "the basis of my natural powers, the inner genius of my being."[33] Inborn and essential, this power impels *Völker* to express their national "genius" and the "type of their appearance" – that is to say, their characteristics, both internal and external, that constitute them as a people.[34] This reversion to the notion of type (*Typus*), especially since it refers to appearance, indicates that physiology has not fallen away entirely from Herder's conception of the *Volk*.[35] Yet outward appearances, while they remain a factor, are relatively insignificant when compared to the sensory and psychological dimensions of folk genius, which Herder gathers under the protean term *Geist*. Indeed, Herder follows a strategy quite similar to that of his fellow Romantics, who shifted attention away from surface phenomena like skin color to address internal structures such as the skeleton (Goethe, Geoffroy) or the nervous system in the case of Cuvier. For his part, Herder stresses the subjective dimensions of the *Volksgeist*, the mental and emotional contributions to the construction of national character. Therefore even if genius comprehends external appearances as one of many national characteristics, the Herderian *Volk* cannot be reduced to the typologies that Kant referred to as "normal ideas" or to the unities of type that Goethe and Geoffroy associated with the physical forms of species, genera or entire kingdoms of the natural world.

The counterpart to the genetic force is climate (*Klima*), which Herder defines capaciously to include meteorological phenomena, food, soil and cultural milieu – in short, the environmental circumstances that influence the degree to which innate capacities can manifest.[36] For instance, a rose will express its genetic capacity to bloom when exposed to sun and rain but wither when choked with weeds. In the same manner, the genius of a *Volk* will flourish or struggle according to the quality of its climate. Hence it is through the interaction or "strife [*Zwist*]" between these twinned forces, genius and environment, that a nation is formed and its character determined. Thus Herderian *Völker*, unlike Kantian races where innate germs are activated and then produce necessarily heritable traits in perpetuity, are quasi-organic entities whose essence unfolds dynamically, continuously through the historical process of *Bildung*. But besides departing from Kant and the doctrine of fixed racial categories, Herder also eschews the hard environmentalism of Montesquieu. The genetic force, teleological through and through, complements and counterbalances climate and the external impulses that exert their influence through efficient causation.[37]

With these general mechanisms in place, Herder then explains how the various psychological faculties that contribute to national character arise out of this combination of genius and climate. Book 8 of the *Ideen* consists of chapters, in this order, on sensation (*Sinnlichkeit*), imagination (*Einbildungskraft*), practical understanding (*praktischer Verstand*), feelings and appetites (*Empfindungen und Triebe*), and happiness (*Glückseligkeit*). Ultimately, each of these attributes of *anthropos* results from the joint operations of genetic endowment and environment. It is no accident, though, that *Sinnlichkeit* comes first in this list. According to Hans Adler, sensation was fundamental for Herder since the perception of experiential data gives rise to both the awareness of the self and the distinction between one human mind – that is, one sensing subject – and another.[38] Sonia Sikka, working in a different corner of the Herderian corpus, notes the importance of sensibility for Herder's conception of language: "Words, for Herder, are ultimately derived from sensations, which in turn belong to an embodied life moving and feeling within a specific *Klima*."[39] From this it follows that Herder's theory of language is "an *empiricist* theory because concepts are shaped by, and therefore ultimately refer to, sensations."[40] Of course, this empiricist commitment to sensation – or rather, αἴσθησις (Adler himself stresses the classical etymology) – reflects the influence of British philosophers, not least the Earl of Shaftesbury.

Much like his epistemology or his theory of language, Herder's anthropology makes sensations the elements out of which the mental life of *anthropos* is constructed. Percepts afforded by a definite environment are refined, as it were, into a temperamental disposition that comprehends both feelings and ideas. Book 8 begins by adducing the characteristic structures of sensibility shared by a people, elucidating how genetic force and climate combine to create a distinct sensory palette. For instance, continual exposure to a desert climate together with genetic endowment will result in a tolerance for hot temperatures.[41] Or, to take another example, inclinations or aversions to herbs and other edibles, which Herder calls "the most sensory, animalistic powers of humankind," will vary "with each land and climate" and wax or wane as they are "constituted and practiced."[42] That is to say, the sensory faculties reflect both the genetic force and climate: how the senses are constituted or "built" along with the manner in which they are shaped by the environment and cultivated in practice.

These structures of sensibility, fashioned through the combined influence of climate and genius, in turn subtend the higher-order psychological faculties just as sensations underlie words in Herder's theory of language: "We have no concept of a thing that resides outside the circle of our sensation," Herder writes in the first sentence of his chapter on the imagination.[43] In keeping with this frankly empiricist premise, the stories and myths that are assembled out of sensations will reflect those structures of feeling and the sensory world that determines their character: a desert people will possess few, if any, myths about snow, for example. Therefore the sensory character of a people is not lost when compounded into more complex psychological processes. The data of sensory experience are transformed, so to speak, without losing their connection to a *Sinnlichkeit* defined by genius and climate. In sum, the Herderian *Volk*, despite being a large-scale collective unconstrained by direct sensory contact, is a community of impressions no less than the Shaftesburian *communis*. At bottom, a nation is founded on the basis of shared sensations. The imagined dimensions of these national communities, their symbolic systems and governing myths, will then grow out of the soil of this common *Sinnlichkeit*.

Returning, now, to the analysis of the *sensus communis* in the *Viertes Wäldchen*, it is remarkable how Herder's early text on aesthetics anticipates the anthropology later developed in the *Ideen*. Just before his statement on the *sensus communis* of the "Greenlander" and the "Hottentot," Herder posits a thesis about the nature of the sensing subject:

> Is the feeling for beauty innate? If you like! but only as an aesthetic nature that has the capacity and tools to perceive sensuous perfection, that has the

pleasure to develop these abilities and use these tools, and to enrich itself with ideas of this kind. All lies within him, but only as a seed for development.[44]

Like a plant whose powers reside in seed, humans possess an "aesthetic nature" whose innate capacities must be nourished if they are to thrive. One of these powers is the ability to "perceive sensuous perfection," a Baumgartian formulation for the faculty more commonly known as "taste." An analogous power, it stands to reason, is the ability to feel desire for and pleasure in communal contact with others – in other words, the ability to perceive a certain *sensus* with respect to the *communis*. Thus it is no surprise that "a nation has its *sens commun* . . . according to its measure of education, and with respect to its own world," as Herder goes on to argue in the next paragraph, because the *sensus communis* is a structure of *Sinnlichkeit* that varies according to the cultivation of genius and the climate that contains it.

For Shaftesbury, a drive for communal fellowship was as fundamental as the need for food and drink. To lack a *sensus communis* was more than a mere aberration. It violated the very essence of the political animal that is *anthropos*. Herder, notwithstanding his diversitarian tendencies, does not dispute the generality of the *sensus communis*. Each people may indeed possess a shared *sensus* just as all humans have eyes, ears and a sense of taste. The significant difference between the two theories rests with the specificity and the scale of the *sensus*: Shaftesbury adduces a universal need for communion that manifests most clearly in small groups; Herder pluralizes the *sensus* so that it reflects the national *communis*. But even as he attributes characteristic constellations of sensibility to entire nations and peoples, Herder does not forego all claims to universality: "It is possible to break the habit of that innate and acquired stubbornness," Herder contends, "to detach oneself from the irregularities of a too specific situation and, finally, to appreciate the beautiful without national, temporal, and personal tastes."[45] It is possible, in other words, to escape the tyranny of habit and enjoy pleasures unconstrained by particular interests. He who remains constrained by parochial tastes, however. "He who is attached to local and national beauties, or to the virtues of his club." He, Herder writes, is a "philosopher of the cabal."

4.2 Strange Empiricism

> It is always necessary to affirm that nationality is in the things that escape analysis. We discover it, as we do the quality of saltness or sweetness, by the taste, and literature is a cultivation of taste.
> —Yeats, "Samhain 1904 – First Principles"

Over the course of the nineteenth century, Herderian anthropology advanced along two main lines: the comparative linguistics pioneered by Wilhelm von Humboldt and the science of *Völkerpsychologie*, which fleshed out the nature of the folk mind that Herder had sketched in the *Ideen*.[46] Even as these disciplines studied different albeit related aspects of the *Volk*, namely, the systems of thought embedded in language and the mental characteristics of peoples, they both operated within a Herderian paradigm where "each people is a people: it has its national formation as it has its language." Influential as Herder's anthropology was for contemporaries, its historicist and anti-racialist legacy reached well into the twentieth century through the efforts of Boas, who substituted immersive field work and the rigorous study of "cultures" (read: peoples) for the travel reports that had acted as Herder's primary source for ethnographic data. Surveying Boas's debts to the German anthropological tradition, Matti Bunzl identifies two key figures linking the Romantics – Herder and the Humboldt brothers, Wilhelm and Alexander – with the young Boas, who, it must be remembered, was very much a man of the nineteenth century despite his decisive importance for the twentieth.[47] The two figures were Theodor Waitz and Adolf Bastian, scientists whose chief contributions were made around the middle of the century, before evolutionary models had swept the field. Elaborating, respectively, the linguistic and the psychological strains of post-Herderian thought, Waitz and Bastian added empirical precision to the concept of the *Volk* through their accounts of what Waitz called "Naturvölker [natural peoples]" or what Bastian referred to as "Völkergedanken [folk thoughts]." Of the two, Bastian was probably the more significant since his outspoken criticisms of Darwinism, which Boas absorbed during his training with Bastian at the *Königliches Museum für Völkerkunde*, shaped the anti-evolutionary aims of cultural anthropology.

Yet the intellectual genealogy leading from Germany to Boas and American anthropology bypasses precisely those anthropologies that informed the literary primitivism of Yeats and his contemporaries in the Irish Revival: the evolutionary theories of E. B. Tylor and his successors Andrew Lang and James Frazer among others. Though Tylor was not the only Victorian to translate Darwin's theses into an anthropological idiom, *Primitive Culture* (1871) marked a watershed for its coordination of arguments now associated with the evolutionary paradigm: the staged development of peoples "from savage through barbaric to civilized life"; the notion of cultural "survivals," which held that beliefs and practices of so-called primitive peoples are "carried on by force of habit into a new state of society different from that in which they had their original home";

or the overarching thesis that human culture develops according to laws
that are as valid as those of the natural sciences: "laws as definite as those
which govern the motion of waves, the combination of acids and bases,
and the growth of plants and animals."[48] But even though Tylor shifted
the theoretical parameters of anthropology from a diversitarian to an
evolutionary model, the German tradition did not cease to offer lessons
for anthropologists working in the wake of Darwin. In his preface to
Primitive Culture, Tylor singles out two works – and only two – for special
mention: Bastian's "Mensch in der Geschichte [Human in History]" and
Waitz's "Anthropologie der Naturvölker [Anthropology of Natural
Peoples]" – the same works, with titles indicating their Herderian pedigree,
that connect Boas with German Romanticism.

One of the most significant interventions in *Primitive Culture*, and one
that has obvious resonances with a Herderian model, pertains to the
relationship between sensation and mythology.[49] Arguing against the
nominalism of Max Müller, the philologist whose "Aryan thesis" established a common linguistic heritage for Eurasian peoples through the study
of ancient Sanskrit texts, Tylor stakes out a position quite close to the
theory of the imagination in the *Ideen* – duly modified, of course, to suit
evolutionary principles. Synthesizing his commitments to German anthropology with an unmistakably British empiricism, Tylor maintains that "as
we recede more nearly toward primitive conditions, the threads which
connect new thought with old do not always vanish from our sight."[50]
Following from this genealogical premise, such historical threads constitute
"clues leading back to that actual experience of nature and life, which is the
ultimate source of human fancy." In the final estimation, Tylorian fancy
arises from experience in the same way that *Einbildungskraft* emerges out
of *Sinnlichkeit*. Sensations and impressions, furnished through direct contact with the world, are the materials out of which the mind creates its
imaginative products. "Impressions thus received," Tylor writes, "the mind
will modify and work upon, transmitting the products to other minds in
shapes that often seem new, strange, and arbitrary." Myths, concepts,
symbols, images and shapes both strange and new are assembled from
the raw data of sensory experience. Finding the key to all the world's
mythologies requires, therefore, identifying the experiential causes that
generate imaginative effects. So while it is true that Tylor ventured a
different intellectual framework for comprehending the nature of *anthropos* – evolutionary instead of teleological, unified rather than diverse – he
espoused a distinctly Herderian brand of empiricism where sensations are
the basis of the mental life of peoples.

And this conception of sensation worked its way into the anthropological imaginary of Yeats despite its seeming incongruity with his skepticism regarding the empirical sciences. Scholars have already established several points of contact between the Irish Revival that flourished at the end of the nineteenth century and the anthropological discourses that were circulating at the time.[51] Focusing on the case of Herder, Barry Sheils has argued that a counter-Enlightenment tradition, with Herder at its head, later informed Yeats's mystical fetishization of the Irish folk.[52] On this reading, poetic language is irreducible to reason, analytic inquiry and the detached observation of the intellect. Thus by tapping into the sensory resources contained in poetry, especially the poetry of the folk peasantry, anthropologist and poet alike may escape modernity's ineluctable drive toward rationalization – a considerable desideratum for Yeats, it must be said. But along with obscuring the heterodox empiricism that Herder picked up from Shaftesbury, whose *sensus communis* was at once a child of Locke and Hobbes and a rejection of their materialist and individualist excesses, a strong counter-Enlightenment reading runs against the epistemological grain of evolutionary anthropology, which exercised a powerful influence on the Irish Revival and furnished a thick theoretical basis for the revivalism that lent the movement its name.

Surely one of the crowning achievements of Enlightenment rationality, evolutionary anthropology offered a comprehensive theoretical framework for conceiving of more originary forms of social practice – Tylorian survivals – that had managed to endure the onslaught of modernity. These vestiges of the past are not irreconcilable with a rationalized world. They are integral components of modern life that retain the mark of their earlier, more primitive nature. For instance, Tylor interprets modern games of chance as survivals of ancient divination rites such as the casting of lots.[53] Salutations occasioned by a sneeze – in English, *God bless you* – are relics of magical utterances intended to ward off the spirits thought to enter and exit the bodies of the sick.[54] These practices are not just fossilized fragments of the anthropological past, however. Even though survivals are products of a deep cultural history, they can and often do modulate from "passive survival into active revival."[55] A revival – a technical term for Tylor – does not denote mere cultural retention. It is the positive cultivation of primitive ideas. Early modern belief in witchcraft revives the practices of sorcery common among primitive peoples.[56] Spiritualism, which Tylor considered a contemporary analogue to early-modern witchery, represents a "direct revival from the regions of savage philosophy and peasant folklore."[57] Hence, in a revival, past and present combine to form a palimpsest of cultural practices. Primitive and modern, secular and divine, savage and civilized intermingle much in the way that Yeats, a revivalist of the first order, believed that "natural and supernatural are knit together," as he stated in "A General Introduction for My Work."[58] This synthesis, not a rejection of one for the other, reanimates a world bled of its mystery; it may also inspire an artistic renaissance: "our imaginative movement," Yeats wrote in 1928, "has its energy from just that combination of new and old, of old stories, old poetry, old belief in God and the soul, and a modern technique."[59]

Sinéad Garrigan Mattar has shown, though, that evolution was a Janus-faced theory for Yeats. Not only did the gradualism of evolutionary change have little in common with his sense of discrete historical ruptures, the sterility of the scientific method failed to satisfy his need for an inspired, enchanted world.[60] For these reasons, Mattar suggests that the anthropologist who most appealed to Yeats was Andrew Lang, a folklorist working in a Tylorian vein who supplemented his anthropological studies with literary aspirations and a robust investment in the occult.[61] Yeats owned copies of Lang's *The Making of Religion* (2nd ed., 1900) as well as volume 2 of *Primitive Culture*; and judging by his marginalia, which consist of strokes marking passages on several pages, Yeats read sections from Lang that submit the theory of sensation advanced in *Primitive Culture* to sustained critique – less in order to overturn the empiricist premises underlying the Tylorian project than to expand them so they include mystical and other "supernormal experiences" like trance, hallucination and hypnotic reverie.[62] What results is not a theory of "sense as the seventeenth century understood it," a position Yeats attributed to Locke in an article of 1932.[63] Lang ventures a more capacious empiricism that aligns with Yeats's own brief for a philosophy of the future, which he appended to a late essay on another of empiricism's more unorthodox minds, George Berkeley. After surveying some recent developments in the field, Yeats states that "future philosophy will have to consider visions and experiences such as those recorded in *An Experiment with Time, An Adventure* and in Osty's *Supernormal Faculties*" – occult works, one of which alludes to the doctrine of the supernormal in its title, that had captured Yeats's interest.[64] Accordingly, the task for the mystically inclined anthropologist, poet or philosopher is to discover a broader, stranger range of sensory data – "visions and experiences" – in a world where nature and the supernatural have been spun into a single thread.

This supra-empiricism, as it might be called, rests on a theory of sensation that Lang took from the German psychologist and aesthetician

Max Dessoir. In a summary of Dessoir's results, which Yeats also marked in his copy of *The Making of Religion*, Lang begins by recapitulating empiricist tenets: "in every conception and idea an image or group of images must be present. These mental images are the recrudescence or recurrence of perceptions."[65] This model of mind makes ideas the product of antecedent impressions. Thus when the mind is presented with an idea, "the original perception of them returns, though of course more faintly."[66] At this point, Lang retains the standard empiricist order of priority where sensations precede ideas and the operations of the mind – *Sinnlichkeit* comes before *Einbildungskraft*, experience before fancy. Furthermore he adheres to the distinction between impressions and ideas posited by David Hume himself: the former are "strong and vivid," Hume writes in the *Enquiry*, while the latter are "naturally faint and obscure."[67]

But where a conventional empiricist would apply the scientific method when following Hume's dictum, "we need but enquire, *from what impression is that supposed idea derived*" in order to resolve philosophical disputes, Lang identifies an alternative means for tracing ideas to their sensory sources: a sort of psychological revival. Referring again to the ideas that are in truth recrudescent impressions, Lang maintains that "these revived mental images would reach the height of actual hallucinations (so that the man, dog, or tree would seem visibly present) if other memories and new sensations did not compete with them and check their development."[68] According to the Lang-Dessoir thesis, a din of mental activity distracts the mind and retards the formation of particular ideas. Crowded out by other stimuli, any single image-complex is prevented from obtaining its full articulation – unless, that is, the sensing subject passes into a supernormal state. Upon entering a trance, for example, the mind is quieted so that "the competition of new sensations and other memories is removed or diminished." Liberated from the pressures of waking life, "the idea ... does become an actual hallucination." No longer a faint impression, the image-complex moves back across the psychological threshold separating it from a sensory experience: "the hypnotized patient sees the absent object which he is told to see, the sleeper sees things not really present." Trance imbues ordinary ideas with supernormal intensity. The dreamer or hypnotic sees ideas as though in a vision.

Lang immediately attaches an anthropological corollary to these psychological arguments: "our primitive state, before the enormous competition of other memories and new sensations set in, would thus be a state of hallucination." Thus what constitutes "our normal present condition, in which hallucination is checked by competing memories and new sensations, is a suppression of our original, primitive, natural tendencies." He then concludes, "hallucination is man's original and most primitive condition."[69] Lang, who amply acknowledges his debts to Tylor, remains within an evolutionary framework where primitive and civilized peoples are distinguished according to a developmental schema. At the same time, he transposes the Tylorian notion of revival, which typically refers to cultural practices and beliefs, into a specifically sensory register. Supernormal experiences revive impressions acquired at earlier historical junctures. Impressions, once buried, reemerge. Therefore trance and hallucination are not divergences from psychological normality. In fact, what usually counts as a normal mental state – sober, rational, conscious – suppresses a still more basic condition that folds hallucinations and impressions, ideas and sensations into a single perceptual field. In a supernormal (or primitive) state, the world radiates in a vision. Therefore if Lang retains empiricist tenets he inherited from Tylor and Herder, claiming that sensory experience precedes ideas that are in truth weak impressions, he also reverses the usual empiricist circuit between impressions and ideas. In moments of psychological revival, ideas are transmuted back into their original sensory bases. Fancy becomes experience. Imagined entities – symbols, myths, concepts, perhaps even national communities – become sensible once more.

4.3   Seeing Together

If, as Yeats claimed in 1932, John Locke provided a theory of sense for the seventeenth century, then Lang and Dessoir furnished a theory that Yeats would apply to *anthropos* some two hundred years later. Supra-empiricist arguments show up in his writing just as he was approaching the "mid-career turn" that is said to have led him away from the enthusiasms of his youth to a harder edged, more concrete sensuality.[70] Certainly, the critical prose of the first decade of the century offers bracing statements of a sensualist aesthetics: "All art is sensuous," Yeats proclaimed in 1907, "but when a man puts only his contemplative nature and his more vague desires into his art, the sensuous images through which it speaks become broken, fleeting, uncertain."[71] Art, according to Yeats, speaks the language of the senses. Intellectual activity then causes those sensate images to crack and fade. A different essay from the same collection makes an even stronger case: "art bids us touch and taste and hear and see the world, and shrinks from what Blake calls mathematic form, from every abstract thing."[72] Here again αἴσθησις provides the conceptual ballast for the

argument. Not only is all art sensuous, particular artworks prompt a reader
or viewer to engage with the world as a sensory construct – as a tactile,
visual, audible or, rather, as an aesthetic phenomenon.

Determining precisely when Yeats underwent his turn, if he did so at all,
is a hazardous enterprise given the fluidity of his thought.[73] Nevertheless,
one precedent for the earthier sensualism of the middle phase is the
Impressionism of Symons, though it should be said that Yeats was never
entirely convinced by what he called "the poetry of cigarettes and black
coffee, of absinthe, and the skirt dance."[74] Although he preferred his more
muscular blend of mystical heroism and archaic myth, Yeats testified in his
autobiography that the Rhymers Club, which met at the Cheshire Cheese
in the early 1890s, espoused a poetics that shunned abstraction in favor of
sensations gained in London's music halls or in the streets of Paris.
"Symons fresh from Paris would sometimes say, 'We are concerned with
nothing but impressions,' but that itself was a generalization and met but
stony silence."[75] The problem with Impressionism, at least for the
Rhymers, was that it was not impressionistic enough. Later in the decade,
Yeats regularly associated himself and his cohort with the "poets of sensation" that Arthur Hallam had aligned against Wordsworth and "poets of
reflection," who were accused of tainting their verse with political or moral
commentary.[76] Despite rechristening poets of sensation like Keats and the
early Tennyson as members of an "aesthetic school," a phrase not in
Hallam's original that implies the inclusion of Pater, Yeats retains the
key distinction between sensation and reflection and places it in the service
of his critical polemics of the period: on the one hand, a commitment to
the senses for the sake of beauty above all; on the other, the didacticism of
Victorian rhetoric and the literary propaganda of the Young Ireland
movement.[77]

One commentator has recently argued that another impetus for the
mid-career turn was "that strong enchanter" Friedrich Nietzsche, whose
work Yeats likely knew as early as 1896, when Symons published Havelock
Ellis's landmark introductions to Nietzsche in the *Savoy*.[78] Only in 1902,
though, did Yeats admit to reading the philosopher, a date that coincides
with his engagement with Lang and Dessoir:

> A certain learned man [Dessoir], quoted by Mr. Lang in his *Making of
> Religion*, contends that the memories of primitive man and his thoughts of
> distant places must have had the intensity of hallucination, because there was
> nothing in his mind to draw his attention away from them – an explanation
> that does not seem to me complete – and Mr. Lang goes on to quote certain
> travellers to prove that savages live always on the edges of vision.[79]

All the elements of the Lang-Dessoir thesis appear in this passage from "Magic" (1901): hallucination as a supernormal intensification of ideas; a revivalist impulse that reanimates distant thoughts; the emphasis on the sensory dimensions of primitive life. Yeats, like Lang, moves freely between the sensory and the visionary realms. Weaving sensation and imagination into a single psychological cloth, he imputes to the primitive mind a capacity for reclaiming aesthetic experience from the frigid ratiocination of the modern intellect.

Yeats withholds his full support for the Lang-Dessoir thesis for reasons left unspecified, an omission that does not prevent an inference of at least some of his reservations from the surrounding sentences. In effect Yeats levels a Herderian critique of Lang and Dessoir. Their theory of sensation is incomplete because it fails to consider education and environment, the same factors that shape the *sensus communis* in the *Viertes Wäldchen*:

> We cannot doubt that barbaric people receive such [occult] influences more visibly and obviously, and in all likelihood more easily and fully than we do, for our life in cities, which deafens or kills the passive meditative life, and our education that enlarges the separated, self-moving mind, have made our souls less sensitive.[80]

Yeats begins by restating the supra-empiricist argument for the heightened sensitivity of a primitive, or in this case, a barbaric *Volk*. He then departs from Lang, who when referring to "our primitive state" and "our normal present condition" means humanity at large, by juxtaposing a "we" of the cities with other *Völker* – presumably those peoples that live in the countryside or, in line with a primitivist logic, in darker parts of the globe. For Yeats, the city-dweller and the peasant possess distinct structures of sensibility (Herder made an analogous distinction between the *sensus* of the scholar and the bailiff, the "Hottentot" and the "Greenlander"). Furthermore, the cause responsible for altering this *sensus* is not a general tendency of the mind to stifle ideas through its immanent activity as Lang maintained; nor does Yeats invoke evolutionary pressures exerted over time in a Tylorian fashion. The immediate environment shapes sensibility. The urban milieu dulls the senses through the force of habit. *Klima*, in other words, determines *Sinnlichkeit*. And whatever modern education may have accomplished in expanding the rational faculties, humans have paid a heavy price with their unfeeling, anesthetic souls.

Something like a "genetic force" exerted its own influence on the Yeatsian *Volk*, and not only in the notorious late pamphlet *On the*

Boiler, which combines eugenic speculations with ruminations about the "old folk-feeling" of the Irish.[81] An essay written in 1892 during the first flush of Yeats's cultural nationalism ends by deploying the organic metaphors so prized by Herder and his Romantic contemporaries:

> We must know and feel our national faults and limitations no less than our national virtues, and care for things Gaelic and Irish, not because we hold them better than things Saxon and English, but because they belong to us, because our lives are to be spent among them, whether they be good or evil. Whether the power that lies latent in this nation is but the seed of some meagre shrub or the seed from which shall rise the vast and spreading tree is not for us to consider. It is our duty to care for that seed and tend it until it has grown to perfection after its kind.[82]

This peroration relies on both the relativism and the organic essentialism of Herderian anthropology. No individual character is superior or inferior to any other. Each nation has its own proper essence, its unique claim to perfection. Accordingly, the nationalist must cultivate those latent powers so they may flourish according to their kind. Less than a year later, in an essay published as "Nationality and Literature," Yeats elaborated on those botanical metaphors to great effect: "We are gardeners, trying to grow various kinds of trees and flowers that are peculiar to our soil and climate; but we have to go for the art of gardening to men who grow very different flowers and trees in very different soils and climates."[83] Character, whether of a nation or an organic species, assumes its shape amid a given environment, or more specifically, amid the definitively Herderian determinants of soil and climate. Thus it follows that "not only is this literature of England different in character from the literature of Ireland, as different as the beach tree from the oak, but that the two literatures are in quite different stages of their development." A nation develops according to the laws of *Bildung*, proceeding along very different developmental paths but developing nonetheless. National character, while remaining within the bounds of genetic kind, is formed by the quality of the environment and the skill of the gardener.

Throughout his career, Yeats made recourse to this Herderian paradigm, albeit with modifications to accommodate his distinctive habits of mind. Chastising that bastion of Anglo-Ireland, Trinity College, he wrote in 1895 that the institution "has been the mother of many verse writers and of few poets; and this can only be because she has set herself against the national genius, and taught her children to imitate alien styles," by which he obviously means English style.[84] A decade later, in an article defending the Abbey Theatre, Yeats argued that nationalist playwrights were able to move past the subject of the peasantry. They could take up more traditional dramatic scenarios such as the drawing room in order to "see if there is something characteristic there, something which our nationality may enable us to express better than others."[85] At first glance, this statement appears to deviate from a relativist stance. If one nation can express a theme better than another, does that not imply superiority? In truth, though, such a claim is consistent with the theory of national character developed by Herder in the *Ideen*. Desert peoples, to return to an earlier example, would be better equipped to find water in an arid climate than peoples accustomed to a rainforest, who would possess their own set of skills appropriate to their milieu. In neither case is a particular skill inherently preferable; nor is one people innately superior. Each *Volk* has a range of abilities that reflect the specificity of their genetic endowment and climate. Irish dramatists, therefore, should try their hand at another form to see if it suits their national character. Later, during his tenure in the Irish Senate, Yeats struck a more forceful Herderian tone by alluding to "those among us who think that all things should begin with the nation and with the genius of the nation."[86] And in 1919 he answered the materialism of the *Communist Manifesto* by posing the eminently Herderian question: "but what of those problems of the relative importance of heredity and environment?" – of genetic force and climate, to use an older but no less apposite idiom.[87]

These two pillars of Herderian anthropology – heredity and environment, genetic force and climate – mixed in uncertain and varying proportions over the course of Yeats's life, though it should be said that the hereditarian strains did gain strength as he aged.[88] Still, even after joining the London Eugenics Society in 1936, Yeats was tilting against those electric signs above O'Connell Bridge, which for him represented the baleful influence of the modern metropolis on the human spirit. This longstanding antipathy toward urban modernity served several purposes for Yeats: It satisfied his nostalgia for the summers he spent in Sligo as a youth; it also confirmed his anti-progressive tendencies, which identified the city as a source of change. No less decisive was his conviction that human sensibility had suffered from its exposure to the urban environment. We have already seen how the city deadens the senses and anesthetizes the soul in "Magic." Later in the same essay, Yeats renews his plaint by comparing "persons of our own time who have lived in cities" unfavorably to "the more sensitive people of ancient times."[89] He then goes on to press the Lang-Dessoir thesis in an original, more provocative direction. To their primitivist anthropology, he adds an aesthetics where the act of artistic creation is a mode of supernormal experience. Yeats begins by depicting a primal scene of αἴσθησις:

> Instead of learning their craft with paper and pen they [artists] may have sat for hours imagining themselves to be stocks and stones and beasts of the wood, till the images were so vivid that the passers-by became but part of the imagination of the dreamer, and wept or laughed or ran away as he would have them.[90]

Rather than revive impressions from the past, this exceptional psychological state imbues present images with supernormal intensity. Stones, animals and plants obtain the vivacity of an actual hallucination, reaching such a pitch that passersby are drawn into the field of the artist's powers. On this account, supernormal states are not passive experiences for the dreamer or hypnotic. Impressions are not merely summoned up before the mind's eye. The artist-magician actively commands those images. He controls his immediate environment.

In this scene of aesthetic sorcery, Yeats presents a moment of mental communion between primitive artist and audience. Passersby who happen to cross the path of the artist-magician are absorbed into his imagination. Duly bewitched, these individuals behave like images in a waking dream, or rather, like characters in a play acting under the instruction of a willful director. But the mental traffic in "Magic" runs along other, stranger channels too: "just as the musician or the poet enchants and charms and binds with a spell his own mind when he would enchant the mind of others, so did the enchanter create or reveal for himself as well as for others the supernatural artist or genius, the seeming transitory mind made out of many minds." First enchantment joins the mind of the magician with the objects of his spell. Then, in an analogous manner though on a larger scale, the spell elicits a greater mental entity, a collective mind made out of plural minds. Earlier in "Magic" this entity is described as a "great mind and great memory" as well as "a single mind, a single energy."[91] Elsewhere Yeats gives this collective mind a more famous designation: the *Anima Mundi*, or world-soul, a term he took from the Cambridge Platonist Henry More.[92] Of course, we have already seen versions of this collective mind at earlier historical junctures. Working from the very same Cambridge sources, the Earl of Shaftesbury derived the *sensus communis* from the notion of a κοινός νοῦς, which he marshaled against the atomized epistemologies of Locke and Hobbes. Somewhat later, Herder nationalized that common mind and called it the *Volksgeist*.

The common mind invoked by Yeats takes myriad forms in "Magic," ranging from the world-soul to more familiar manifestations.

The artist-magician, we immediately learn, "kept the doors too, as it seems of those less transitory minds, the genius of the family, the genius of the tribe, or it may be, when he was mighty-souled enough, the genius of the world."[93] Yeats scales up the *communis* in this passage, moving from intimate groups circumscribed by direct sensory contact, the family or the tribe, to the world as a whole. In doing so, however, he overleaps the one configuration of collectivity we might most expect him to mention, to wit, the genius of the nation. This aporia, whether due to a reluctance to freight occult theses with political categories or a belief that the attributes of family and tribe sufficiently covered national characteristics, should not be taken to mean that the Yeatsian κοινός νοῦς cannot accommodate the nation. Far from it. Reflecting on his occultism in "Hodos Chameliontos," later collected as part of *Autobiographies*, Yeats recasts this common mind in explicitly national terms. Soon after referring to the *Anima Mundi*, and shortly before criticizing Locke, he sets out his views in the form of rhetorical questions: "is there nation-wide multiform reverie, every mind passing through a stream of suggestion, and all streams acting and reacting upon one another, no matter how distant the minds?"[94] Evidently, an entire nation may pass into a supernormal state. This condition of collective reverie induces particular minds to form a single psychological current, which obeys an uncanny physics of action, reaction and attraction at a distance. Yeats then asks, or rather asserts in the interrogative mood, "was not a nation, as distinguished from a crowd of chance comers, bound together by this interchange among streams or shadows; that Unity of Image, which I sought in national literature?"[95] So the nation, as opposed to a crowd aggregated by chance, is a mental entity that coheres due to supernormal forces operating on a national scale. Literature is the spell that conjures this national consciousness. And for Yeats, the artist is its high priest.

At various points in his exposition of mental communion, Yeats claims that the imagination acts to bind individuals into a national whole. Indeed, in the passage just cited he goes so far as to identify the nation as such with Unity of Image. These appeals, though they associate the nation with imaginative processes, point up an alternative relation between imagination and nationhood than the one posited by Benedict Anderson, who argues that the imagination gains its political significance because sensation is unable to comprehend a national polity. The nation "is *imagined*," Anderson emphasizes, "because members of even the smallest nation will never know most of their fellow-members, meet them, or even hear of them."[96] In other words, they cannot in their totality form an aesthetic *communis* in the Shaftesburian sense of the term. Faced with the impossibility of direct sensory contact but nevertheless "connected to people they have never seen," members of a nation must fall back on a different cognitive operation, which Anderson calls the imagination, in order to make their union psychologically salient. Shaftesbury, as we have seen, made much the same point when distinguishing a *communis* from a nation that is formed "not sensibly, but in idea." In either case, the mind fills the ideological vacuum opened up when the senses can no longer comprehend the group. Whether through imagination or ideation, mental operations furnish the nation with its psychological reality.

Rather than substitute the imagination for senses unable to grasp the totality of a nation, Yeats combines imagination and sensation in a manner much closer to the supernormal synthesis of impression and vision advanced by Lang or, for that matter, the interlocking faculties of *Einbildungskraft* and *Sinnlichkeit* in the *Ideen*. Consider the remarkable account of mental communion included in *The Celtic Twilight*, the collection of fairytales and popular lore Yeats published in 1893. Early in the text, Yeats relates a trance he experienced in the company of a man and a young girl who was especially attuned to the occult. After the girl begins to feel otherworldly influences, Yeats reports that "I too had by this time fallen into a kind of trance, in which what we call the unreal had begun to take upon itself a masterful reality, and I had an impression, not anything I could call an actual vision, of gold ornaments and dark hair." At this point, the trance had not yet attained supernormal intensity. Yeats saw dark hair and the color gold but those impressions were not quite visionary. Still, the event clearly left a mark since Yeats returned to the passage thirty years later in order to add a footnote elaborating on the sensuousness of the trance: "the girl was, however, fully entranced, and the man so affected by her that he heard the children's voices as if with his physical ears. On two occasions, later on, her trance so affected me that I also heard or saw some part of what she did as if with physical eyes and ears."[97] This is a *sensus communis* considerably more radical than anything ventured by Shaftesbury. Trance allows impressions to cross over into other minds. Sensation and imagination merge in a moment of vision. Distinct individuals – Yeats, the young girl, the man – see through common eyes.

If trance can induce a *communis* between two or three sensing subjects, might something similar occur for an entire nation? Can the nationwide reverie Yeats described in "Hodos Chameliontos" take on sensory dimensions? At the very least, that is the effect the national artist should strive to achieve, Yeats believed. Only a month before publishing "Magic," in a lecture titled "Ireland and the Arts" first presented to the National Literary Society and then printed in *The United Irishman*, the nationalist paper edited by Arthur Griffith who went on to found Sinn Féin two years later, Yeats assigned to the national artist the following task:

> I would have our writers and craftsmen of many kinds master this history and these legends, and fix upon their memory the appearance of mountains and rivers and make it all visible again in their arts, so that Irishmen, even though they had gone thousands of miles away, would still be in their own country.[98]

The difficulty that Anderson considered insuperable and that forced him to substitute imagination for sensation – the distances that separate members of a nation and bar direct sensory contact – is overcome in a moment of national αἴσθησις. A world becomes visible, though not as an artifact of the imagination. A national art binds artist and nation just as Yeats was magically united in a common *sensus* with the young girl in *The Celtic Twilight*. First the artist records characteristic sensations: the Irish landscape, or more generally, the genius of the place. Once translated into works of art, those impressions may evoke – or rather revive – the same sensations in the nationalized (and gendered) folk: Irishmen may see their homeland no matter how far they are from each other and their native soil – "no matter how distant the minds," as Yeats put it in "Hodos Chameliontos."

In practice, such a nationalist art might look like this, taken from Yeats's regular column for American readers published in the Boston *Pilot*:

> I do not head this letter "The Celt in London" as my wont is, for I am back in Ireland for the time being, and writing out on the lawn of an old Irish thatched farmhouse. An apple tree covered with red apples shakes softly before me in the sunlight, and the paper on which I write rests on the stone top of a sundial. Behind me in the hedge a grasshopper has just lifted his shrill song. To talk of books at all on this green clover spotted grass seems sadly out of keeping, unless, indeed, it be some dreamy romance like *Marius the Epicurean,* whose golden sentences, laden as with sleepy sunlight, I have been reading slowly and fitfully since morning, taking the book up for a moment and then laying it down again, and letting my mind stray off to the red apples and the shadowing leaves before me.[99]

Returned from his urban exile, this self-appointed Celt allows his reader to see Ireland through his eyes. Assuming the role of the young girl in "The Celtic Element in Literature," Yeats entrances his readers. He affects them in such a way so that they may see and hear Ireland as though with physical eyes and ears; and the citation of *Marius* only confirms that Yeatsian αἴσθησις runs in the main line of the aestheticist tradition, even if Yeats himself undertook to harden the delicate and often insubstantial impressions of the *fin-de-siècle* in the hotter flame of his poetic soul.

The nationalist edge to this aesthetic program was sharpened in "The Galway Plains" (1903), which elaborates on the links between imagination and sensation as they relate to national consciousness. Referring to the west of Ireland, Yeats argues that "there is still in truth upon these great level plains a people, a community bound together by imaginative possessions, by stories and poems which have grown out of its own life, and by a past of great passions."[100] Two elements bind a people *qua* community: imaginative possessions and passion. Yet the stories that contribute to collective consciousness do not float free in some rarified mental ether. They grow out of the soil of common experience, emerging from the life of a people just as myths do in the anthropologies of Tylor and Herder. Other examples of this experiential rootedness crop up in Yeats's prose of the period. Writing for *Samhain*, the official organ of the Irish National Theatre Society and then the Abbey Theatre, he argued in 1904 that for great artists of the past, "everything that their minds ran on came on them vivid with the colour of the senses, and when they wrote it was out of their own rich experience."[101] In a different issue of *Samhain*, he describes "rhythmical movements that seem to flow up into the imagination from some deeper life" – from some repository of experience that subtends imaginative action. Thus the imagination does not so much compensate for sensation as combine with it as part of a more holistic folk psychology.[102] In sum, the nation is constituted out of a broader range of psycho-sensory mechanisms that cannot be reduced to the master category of imagination: *Sinnlichkeit* underlies *Einbildungskraft*, which is in turn complemented by other components of the Herderian *Volksgeist* – feelings and appetites (*Empfindungen und Triebe*), for example, or what Yeats called the "great passions" that bind a community, which he would later associate with the "old folk-feeling" of traditional Irishry. But not every human group enjoys this spiritual vitality. In "The Galway Plains," Yeats goes on to comment that "England, or any other country which takes its tunes from the great cities and gets its taste from schools and not from old custom, may have a mob, but it cannot have a people."[103] Afflicted by that double scourge of modernity, education and environment once again, England, a mere country instead of a nation, has been shorn of a past nourished by custom. It has therefore forfeited its claim to peoplehood and is populated by a different anthropological entity: a mob rather than a people, a crowd not a community.

For Herder no less than for Yeats, a second dimension of natural character augments the impressions, ideas and passions that constitute collective consciousness: language, often considered the defining attribute of national identity. According to Herder, the variety of languages testified to the basic diversity of humankind while Yeats had to navigate the fraught linguistic currents of anti- and post-colonial Ireland as a son of the Anglo-Irish Ascendancy and an inveterate English speaker. Although he generally supported efforts to revive Irish, Yeats produced his best-known statement on linguistic politics in response to Douglas Hyde's "The Necessity for De-Anglicising Ireland" (1892), a speech laying out the principles of the Gaelic League that Hyde would launch in the following year.[104] Though linguistic revival was its most important component, Hyde's program entailed a comprehensive resuscitation of customs that ranged from traditional dress and sport to the reclamation of place names and the rejuvenation of cultural practices, not least literature and music.

Much like Yeats, Hyde tried to position himself athwart the transformative forces of modernity that he believed were destroying Irish culture and eroding the values that could act as a bulwark against English imperialism. Thus Hyde deplores the "decay of our language" while observing bitterly that the artworks "of one of the quickest, most sensitive, and most artistic races on earth are now only distinguished for their hideousness."[105] According to Hyde, this decline of language and culture had contributed to Ireland's absorption into England since the demise of customs and a common heritage hollowed out any independent national identity that might check assimilation. Arresting such decadence therefore required reviving traditional folkways and reclaiming a more glorious past in order to steel Ireland in its struggle against England.

At bottom, Hyde's revivalism is a restorative enterprise. He begins "The Necessity for De-Anglicising Ireland" by enjoining his audience to "take a bird's-eye view of our island today, and compare it with what it used to be"; and he concludes by pronouncing that "upon Irish lines alone can the Irish race once more become what it was of yore."[106] Yet in the moments of his speech when he gestures to "the restoration of a German-speaking Greece" as a model for Irish revival or calls for the "restoration of our place-names" that have been swept away by English imports, Hyde is not interested in parlor-game antiquarianism.[107] He intends these restorative measures as sallies in cultural combat against a nemesis that had spent centuries erasing Irish national consciousness. Thus Hyde strikes a more aggressive posture with his revivalism by recalling the days when Celts rivaled Rome and held sway over half of Europe, an argument whose implicit imperialism, directed against England, would show up more forcefully a decade later in D. P. Moran's *The Philosophy of Irish Ireland* (1905).[108] Yeats, too, looked to a bygone flowering of Irish culture, though not for the sake of building a new Rome on the banks of the Liffey. In a manner more reminiscent of Tylor and Lang, Yeatsian revivalism mines experience for primitive elements that have held out against modernity and retained the stamp of a more authentic mode of responding to the world.

Over and above the differing accents they laid on the past – Hyde's restorative emphasis, Yeats's primitivism – these two nationalists diverged with respect to the content of their revivalism, that is, with regard to precisely what should be recuperated from historical experience. Where sensations and the texture of *aisthesis* were paramount for Yeats, Hyde was more concerned with counteracting the deleterious effects of the English language on the mental traits that he considered characteristic of the Irish people. Thus in a single breath he mourns the loss of "language, traditions, music, genius, and ideas"; and he asserts that England "has definitely conquered us, she has even imposed upon us her language, that is to say, the form of our thoughts," a comment that feigns defeat as a rhetorical gambit for spurring listeners to support his cause.[109] Therefore when Hyde talks about restoring the Irish language, he wishes for native ideas to flourish once the English molds that had shaped Irish minds have been smashed. On this account, linguistic revivalism and its cultural correlates should allow the Irish people to discover – or more accurately, rediscover – their own authentic ways of thinking about the world. "The revival of our Irish music" and other traditional practices, Hyde argues, "go hand in hand with the revival of Irish ideas and Celtic modes of thought."[110]

In its way, Hyde's stress on the mental hygiene of a people, on the way that right thinking might be mediated through language and literature, is no less Herderian inasmuch as characteristic habits of mind distinguish nations in the *Ideen*. What a specifically Yeatsian nationalism in all its idiosyncrasy helps reveal is a more fundamental stratum in Herder's anthropology: the empirical core of sensations that combine to form language, symbols and other cognitive content that rides on top of sensory data. It is telling, then, that Yeats and Hyde break in different directions when it comes to the nature of national sensibility. In "The Necessity for De-Anglicising Ireland," Hyde maintains that Ireland is "at once the most assimilative and the most sensitive nation in Europe" – assimilative *because* it is sensitive, Hyde implies.[111] As a consequence, "we must teach ourselves to be less sensitive" in order to halt and ultimately reverse absorption into the British fold.[112] Of course, this call for a deliberate desensitization of the Irish people responds to the stock characterization of a hypersensitive and emotionally labile Celt (as opposed, predictably enough, to the principled rationality of the Saxon). In other words, Hyde at once concedes this stereotype and seeks to refute it by reengineering the *Volksgeist*, strengthening a people in its fight against assimilation by reclaiming a distinct cultural and linguistic heritage. For his part, Yeats takes a different tack. Following Lang and Dessoir, his aesthetic anthropology universalizes that characteristic sensitivity, making it an attribute that all humans possess in a primitive condition. Yeats then radicalizes that supernormal sensitivity by making its cultivation the task of artistic production.

For all their differences, Yeats and Hyde certainly agreed on one point: the harmful effects of certain modern forms of literary production. So, for instance, Hyde reflects on the cultural practices of the peasantry and remarks that "many of them read newspapers indeed, but who reads, much less recites, an epic poem, or chants an elegiac or even a hymn?"[113] Yeats, for one, was an avid chanter of verse, though he was certainly not of the peasantry. Nevertheless, he understood his poetry and the early drama associated with the Abbey as growing out of popular cultural traditions, which he then wielded as a corrective against the deadening influences of modern journalism. In a salvo against newspapers published in *Samhain* in 1904 (the article was titled "First Principles"), Yeats declaims, "one is indignant with those who would substitute for the ideas of the folk-life the rhetoric of newspapers, who would muddy what had begun to seem a fountain of life with the feet of the mob."[114] The impersonal pronoun in this sentence does not disguise the fact that Yeats's own indignation is roused against those who substitute ephemeral media and dead rhetoric for more lasting, vital traditions such as fairytales and folklore. Therefore even if the newspaper furnishes the cultural grist for a large-scale collective politics, it does so by advancing the interests of the mob, that debased cousin of a people or a community. Yeats then turns to the matter of language, asking, "is it impossible to revive Irish and yet to leave the finer intellects a sufficient mastery over the more gross, to prevent it from becoming, it may be, the language of a Nation, and yet losing all that has made it worthy of a revival, all that has made it a new energy in the mind?"[115] Tortured syntax aside, as far as Yeats is concerned, writing and printing newspapers in Irish would denude the language of the spiritual energies that made it attractive in the first place.

The vulgarization of life and language that Yeats found so threatening might be staunched by art, as long as that art retains its rootedness in sensory experience. The writer who came to represent this Yeatsian ideal was John Synge, whose knowledge of Irish made him a more qualified observer of the peasantry than Yeats himself, who was dependent on translations or friends like Lady Gregory to mediate his contacts with Irish speakers. It is therefore fitting that near the end of "J. M. Synge and the Ireland of His Time" (1910), the memorial essay composed for his fellow Abbey director, Yeats leaves off from his treatment of Synge in order to make a more sweeping declaration about method: "the imaginative writer shows us the world as a painter does his picture, reversed in a looking-glass that we may see it, not as it seems to eyes habit has made dull, but as we were Adam and this the first morning."[116] The true artist, Yeats believes, returns us to our original sensory condition. Works of the imagination revive our ability to see the world. Even though this passage generalizes about the imaginative writer as such, the implicit referent is Synge; yet we are also dealing with a moment aptly described R. F. Foster: "as so often, he was talking ostensibly about Synge but really about himself."[117] In fact Yeats was channeling the same investment in αἴσθησις that runs from Rhymers Club Impressionism through the supra-empiricism of Lang and Dessoir to the claim in *Discoveries* that "all art is sensuous." Thus it should come as no surprise that the apotheosis of this aesthetics is stated in personal terms in "Swedenborg, Mediums, and the Desolate Places" (1920):

> an impulse towards what is definite and sensuous, and an indifference towards the abstract and the general, are the lineaments, as I understand the world, of all that comes not from the learned, but out of common antiquity, out of the 'folk' as we say, and in certain languages, Irish for instance – and these languages are all poetry.[118]

Definite, concrete, sensuous – these are the attributes of the Yeatsian *Volk*, their language, their art. With an ancient past anchoring common sensations, the national artist must activate this impulse toward sensuousness – must reverse the mirror so we may see the world anew.

Yeatsian nationhood, that chameleonic ideological construct, rests on anthropological premises quite consistent with the theses of Herder, who constructed the *Volksgeist* out of sensations compounded into higher-order psychological operations – imagination, feelings and appetites, practical understanding, even happiness. Hence the most suitable designation for the Yeatsian nation is not an imagined community but rather a configuration of collectivity that Yeats himself denominates, ironically enough, in one of the very few essays he published in a language other than English. Contributing in 1898 to *L'Irlande Libre*, the journal affiliated with Maud

Gonne's *L'Association Irlandaise*, Yeats concludes a review of the Celtic poet Fiona Macleod (William Sharp) by surveying the nationalist movement:

> Une communauté de sentiments, non seulement entre ces deux peuples [les Celtes irlandais et écossais], mais encore avec les Celtes gallois, sera peut-être l'un des résultats décisifs du "Movement Celtique," et bien des événements sociaux, politiques, aussi bien que littéraires, en peuvent dériver.[119]

> [A community of sentiments, not only between those two peoples [the Irish and Scottish Celts], but further with the French Celts, will perhaps be the one decisive result of the "Celtic Movement," and moreover of the social, political, and literary events that can be derived from it.]

A community of sentiment transcends political divisions – the individual nations of Ireland, Scotland and France – and achieves unity through recourse to an anthropological entity: a people, in this case, the Celt. At the same time, Yeats's longstanding investment in collective αἴσθησις justifies a divergence from a strictly literal translation of *communauté de sentiments* in order to call attention to the characteristic *Sinnlichkeit* of the Yeatsian folk: A *community of sense* is the most decisive result of the Celtic Movement and its social, political and literary offspring.

If, recalling Yeats's agreement with Hyde, the newspaper deadens national consciousness and stifles the creative forces that promise a revitalization of Irish art, then what are the cultural forms that animate communities of sense? Two obvious candidates would be poetry and drama since these are the genres in which Yeats was expert. Indeed in his writings on tragedy Yeats makes heavy use of the supernormal experiences theorized by Lang and Dessoir: "tragic art, passionate art, the drowner of dykes, the confounder of understanding, moves us by setting us to reverie, by alluring us almost to the intensity of trance."[120] This passage from "The Tragic Theatre" (1910) cannot be understood, however, without qualification: "if the real world is not rejected altogether, it is but touched here and there, and into the places we have left empty we summon rhythm, balance, pattern, images that remind us of vast passions."[121] When passions confound the mind but leave intact a fragile link with reality, rhythmic images and primal feelings fill the spaces vacated by ideas. These patterned rhythms may ultimately be molded into language. In that case, poetry and drama would indeed become vehicles for communities of sense; but those patterns may also assume a more bodily form, namely as dance, a wordless art that occupies a prominent place in Yeats's verse and his plays.

The next section argues that collective movement in Yeats combines an anthropology of the *Volk* with Paterian aestheticism in order to form communities of sense; yet the cosmopolitan and Francophile refinement usually associated with the *fin-de-siècle* is replaced with a more unsettling amalgam of primitivism, postcolonial nationalism and the fascist tendencies that have continued to dog Yeats's reputation.

4.4 Communities of Sense

> The dream of my early manhood, that a modern nation can return to Unity of Culture, is false; though it may be we can achieve it for some small circle of men and women, and there leave it till the moon bring round its century.
>
>   —Yeats, "The Tragic Generation"

Coming to terms with the anthropological significance of communities of sense is aided by attending to the philological content of one of the sacred texts of the *fin-de-siècle*: the conclusion to Pater's *Studies in the History of the Renaissance*, which opens with an epigraph from Plato's *Cratylus*: "Λέγει που Ἡράκλειτος ὅτι πάντα χωρεῖ καὶ οὐδὲν μένει." In his edition of the *Studies*, Matthew Beaumont notes that both Benjamin Jowett, Oxford's Regius Professor of Greek who censured Pater for corresponding with an openly homosexual undergraduate, and Pater himself offered translations of this passage.[122] Pater renders the Heraclitean adage in *Plato and Platonism* as "all things give way: nothing remaineth." For his part, Jowett gives the considerably less inspired "Heracleitus is supposed to say that all things are in motion and nothing at rest."[123] Where Jowett drains the force from χωρεῖ with the flat nominalization "are in motion," Pater opts for the more dynamic, and accurate, "give way." From χῶρος – "space," "place, spot"; "(freier, leerer) Raum, Gegend, Land"; "espace libre" – the verb χωρέω denotes "make room for another, give way, withdraw" – to make space, as it were.[124]

Citing Émile Boisacq, Chantraine suggested that χῶρος descends from the root *gher-*, which it shares with χορός, a noun that can mean either "a place for dancing," thereby aligning with the spatial designation χῶρος, or simply "the dance," especially the circle dances performed in cult rituals.[125] Whether or not Pater was aware of a semantic congruity between χορός and χῶρος – Georg Curtius had traced an etymological link between χορός and χόρτος ("enclosed place") as early as 1858 – his translation of the *Cratylus* does intimate something of the dance.[126] By rendering χωρεῖ as "give way," Pater indicates that the subject of the phrase, πάντα, is met by a counterforce. All things are not merely in motion as Jowett would have it. They give way to an external impetus. They make space for another. It is as if, according to Pater's rendering, all things dance.

Heraclitean motifs pervade the "Conclusion" and inflect the metaphors Pater uses to describe human experience in aestheticist terms. At one point, he writes of the "impressions unstable, flickering, inconsistent, which burn and are extinguished with our consciousness of them."[127] This impressionistic flux, unique to each subject, constitutes Paterian experience, which is elaborated in the same Heraclitean vein:

> To such a tremulous wisp constantly reforming itself on the stream, to a single sharp impression, with a sense in it, a relic more or less fleeting, of such moments gone by, what is *real* in our life fines itself down. It is with the movement, the passage and dissolution of impressions, images, sensations, that analysis leaves off, – that continual vanishing away, that strange perpetual weaving and unweaving of ourselves.[128]

Αἴσθησις is temporalized here. A dynamic, living stream of impressions, experience in its most pristine state – which is also its most real state – remains untainted by the analysis Eliot believed must spoil pure sensation. Yet for all its ebullience, mental life on this account is a decidedly lonely affair. After all Pater admits that "every one of those impressions is the impression of the individual in his isolation, each mind keeping as a solitary prisoner its own dream of a world."[129] Faced with such dispiriting solipsism, it is useful to recall the epigraph from the *Cratylus* and wonder whether the perpetual weaving and unweaving of the Paterian self can be transformed from a solitary into a social event. In other words, is the aestheticist mind constituted as mere motion? Or, rather, might it give way and respond to another?

Pater's acknowledged heir among English critics was Arthur Symons, whose *Symbolist Movement in Literature* supplemented the doctrine of *l'art pour l'art* with a theory of the symbol that Symons had imbibed from Yeats (the two friends shared rooms in the Temple in the winter of 1895; and the following year, they traveled together to western Ireland). Nowhere are Symons's debts to Pater clearer than *Studies in Seven Arts* (1906), which opens with a quotation from "The School of Giorgione" that Symons elevates into "a kind of motto for my book": "each art brings with it a special phase or quality of beauty, untranslatable into the forms of any other, an order of impressions distinct in kind."[130] Taking such medium-specificity as his starting point, Symons sets out to survey the various arts – Rodin's sculptures, Wagner, Whistler, French cathedrals – in an effort to syncretize those modes into a "universal science of beauty."

Although *Studies* never coheres into a general theory, Symons does venture a more comprehensive thesis about aesthetics in "The World as Ballet," a pendant to the collection first published in 1898. Draped in the many-layered sensuousness of the *fin-de-siècle*, the balletic world limned by Symons reflects its original date of publication. Describing a group of dancers "as they dance, under the changing lights," Symons thinks "they seem to sum up in themselves the appeal of everything in the world that is passing, and coloured, and to be enjoyed; everything that bids us take no thought for the morrow, and dissolve the will into slumber, and give way luxuriously to the delightful present."[131] Summoning a different mood when discussing a waltz, Symons recalls the self-reflexive solipsism of Pater's "Conclusion": "in its winding motion it raises an invisible wall about us, shutting us off from the whole world, in with ourselves." But if Pater argued in "The School of Giorgione" that each art, whatever its claim to medium specificity, strives to attain the condition of music, Symons takes a different tack, privileging dance as the ultimate art: "all this really primitive feeling, all this acceptance of the instincts which it idealizes, and out of which it makes its own beauty, is precisely what gives dancing its pre-eminence among the more than imitative arts."[132] Yeats could not have said it better himself. No longer is the disembodied sensuousness of music the aestheticist ideal. Dance, which celebrates primitive instinct, becomes the art of arts.

Beginning in 1892, Symons served as the music hall critic for the *Star*, and during his period of cohabitation with Yeats in Fountain Court, he was passionately involved with a dancer whom he had met at the Empire Theatre.[133] Yeats's interest in dance, though consistent over the course of his career, was a more strictly literary affair. Surveying the juvenilia, Richard Ellman cited two instances of dance – a song from *The Island of Statues* and a speech from the dramatic poem *The Seeker* – while the play Yeats was writing on his deathbed, *The Death of Cuchulain*, features a speech by the character generally considered to be an avatar for the author.[134] "I promise a dance," the Old Man announces. "I wanted a dance because where there are no words there is less to spoil."[135] So the final literary testament of the poet contrasts the purity of dance with the perishability of language.

Frank Kermode set a powerful precedent for scholarship on Yeats and dance when he argued that one particular choreographic figure, the solo dancer, represents nothing less than "the central icon of Yeats and of the whole tradition" of aesthetic philosophy that rejects the intellect in favor of sheer embodied presence, beauty made flesh.[136] This "emblem of the perfect work of art," as Kermode calls the lone dancer, makes notable appearances in Yeats's plays as well as his verse. The landmark modernist drama *At the Hawk's Well* (1917) included dances by Michio Ito in the character of the Guardian of the Well; and the mid-career mystical poem "The Double Vision of Michael Robartes" (1919) features a "girl at play" flanked by a Sphinx and Buddha:

> O little did they care who danced between,
> And little she by whom her dance was seen
> So she had outdanced thought.
> Body to perfection brought[137]

Kermode identified the dancer of this poem with Salomé, the *femme fatale* and icon of the decadent movement immortalized by Wilde and Aubrey Beardsley. The more apposite allusion, however, might be the sacrificial victim from Nijinsky's legendary staging of *Le sacre du printemps* six years before – a girl who danced herself to death and signaled the birth of a new aesthetic era:

> And right between these two a girl at play
> That, it may be, had danced her life away,
> For now being dead it seemed
> That she of dancing dreamed.

Other developments in modernist choreography explain the critical pre-occupation with the solo dancer in Yeats. Isadora Duncan, the paragon of early modern dance, performed alone as a means of escaping the traditions of ballet. Since antiquity stage dance had been associated with pantomime, the wordless physical imitation of characters or events, which was codified by Lucian in his second century treatise, *de Saltatione*.[138] Seeking to leverage the prestige of the ancients, eighteenth-century choreographers like John Weaver and Jean-George Noverre preserved the mimetic character of ancient dance while shifting their productions toward dramatic narrative. In his *Letters on Dancing and Ballet* (1760), Noverre argued that ballet could imitate nature just as well as poetry and painting, part of his effort to raise the prestige of professional dance. Noverre's own *ballets d'action*, as well as those choreographed and danced by his contemporary, the celebrated Marie Sallé, were organized around the narration of events, a signal departure from the bawdy entertainment of the Commedia dell'arte, the popular showpieces of the Paris Opera, or the *ballet de cour* and other courtly dances that arose during the reign of Louis XIV. Deeply influenced by David Garrick, Noverre transformed dance into a properly dramatic art, and his writings were a theoretical touchstone for the classical ballet of the nineteenth century. Duncan responded to the theatrical trappings of ballet by shunning mimesis, narrative and classical technique in favor of the rhythms of embodied movement.[139] Thus the anti-mimetic and self-reflexive character of early modernist dance seems to suit the general spirit of poetic innovations of the period, which also assumed a critical stance toward formal artifice and inherited traditions while frequently condensing multiple perspectives into a single impersonal subject.

Though Yeats was at least tangentially aware of Duncan's work, receiving descriptions of her dances from his father who had seen her perform in America in 1908, he makes no mention of Duncan in his poetry.[140] On two other occasions, though, Yeats does name modern dancers; in "His Phoenix," he notes the acclaim enjoyed by stage performers – Gaby Deslys, Ruth St. Denis and Anna Pavlova – and he devotes an entire section of "Nineteen Hundred and Nineteen" to Loïe Fuller, the only solo dancer whose fame could rival Duncan's. Fuller developed her serpentine dances out of popular music-hall traditions, yet the aesthetic innovations of her choreography were similar to those of Duncan. The solitary body in motion displaced the spectacle of the group. Yeats's adaptation of Fuller's dances in "Nineteen Hundred and Nineteen" breaks in a different choreographic direction, however:

> When Loie Fuller's Chinese dancers enwound
> A shining web, a floating ribbon of cloth,
> It seemed that a dragon of air
> Had fallen among dancers, had whirled them round
> Or hurried them off on its own furious path.

These dancers move as a group, with the stress on their plurality, "whirled them round/Or hurried them off." The stanza then ends with a still more general figure, "All men are dancers and their tread/Goes to the barbarous clangour of a gong." Unlike Stéphane Mallarmé's rapturous responses to Fuller's solo performances, Yeats depicts her ensemble choreography. He incorporates modernist dance into his verse yet in doing so prefers the rhythms of collective movement to solo dance.

A similar confusion has attended readings of "Byzantium," one of Yeats's most important reflections on the act of artistic creation. Critics have elevated the poem into an apotheosis of solo dance because it presents the autogenic play of a moving figure, though the dancer itself is replaced by the element of fire.

> At midnight on the Emperor's pavement flit
> Flames that no faggot feeds, nor steel has lit,
> Nor storm disturbs, flames begotten of flame,
> Where blood-begotten spirits come
> And all complexities of fury leave,
> Dying into a dance,
> An agony of trance,
> An agony of flame that cannot singe a sleeve.[141]

Assuming that the fire moving across the imperial χορός can be identified with dancers, the choreography of this scene once again favors the collective over the singular. Flames flit across the floor even if they are born from a single source. Furthermore the syntactic evidence of the intricate sentence confirms the stress on collective agency since "spirits" and "complexities" – rather than "flames" or "flame" – are the most proximate subjects that die into a dance, extinguishing themselves in anguished impotence. Within this place marked out for dancing, the supernormal and merely human come and go, intimating that the movement of one gives way to another. The next and final stanza of "Byzantium" maintains this emphasis on collectivity while calling still greater attention to the aesthetics of the χορός:

> Astraddle on the dolphin's mire and blood,
> Spirit after spirit! The smithies break the flood,
> The golden smithies of the Emperor!
> Marbles of the dancing floor
> Break bitter furies of complexity,
> Those images that yet
> Fresh images beget,
> That dolphin-torn, that gong-tormented sea.

Images carved in the Emperor's dancing floor breed more images much like the generative fire in the previous stanza (or like the magical visions that rush into the mind of a suitable medium). Although Yeats himself was probably ignorant of the semantic proximity between "dance" and "place for dancing" contained in the Greek noun χορός, his concluding reflection on aesthetic creation places that duality at its heart. The dancing floor, constituted in images, becomes animate and generates still newer sensations.

If, as Kermode maintains, the solitary dancer represents a Romantic tradition running from Blake through Pater to the poets of the 'nineties and Yeats, then the "Conclusion" to the *Studies in the History of the Renaissance* also records the bleak side of that ideology: the solitary mind locked in its particolored prison; the solipsism of mere, endless motion; the isolated impressions that make up the dreamworld of an alienated subject. Yeats, it turns out, had a more social conception of dance than the critical literature has allowed, as the previous examples demonstrate. In fact, cases of group dancing outnumber instances of solo dance in his poetry. Therefore by recalibrating Yeatsian choreography toward the group, the anti-discursive elements that Kermode attributes to the lone dancer – the rejection of ideas, the intellect and abstraction in favor of sheer rhythmic motion – are brought into alignment with the aesthetic anthropology underlying communities of sense, where direct sensory contact in a group provides a collective, instead of individual, release from the hypertrophied intellection that Yeats associates with modernity.

In *The Wanderings of Oisin* (1889), Yeats's most expansive poetic treatment of Irish mythology, the eponymous poet-hero travels to the Island of Dancing accompanied by Niamh, daughter of the Celtic god of love, chronicling events that "are supposed to have taken place rather in the indefinite period," Yeats explains in a note, "made up of many periods, described by the folktales."[142] Recalling his time with the daughter of Aengus, Oisin begins by recollecting "bowls of barley, honey, and wine,/ Those merry couples dancing in tune,/And the white body that lay by mine" (ll. I.8–10), a reference to Niamh. Meanwhile, Niamh tries to entice Oisin with tales of women "who when they dance to a fitful measure/Have a speed like the speed of the salmon herds" (ll. I.97–98), thereby antici-pating the "salmon-falls, the mackerel-crowded seas" that would later drive an old Irishman, youthful reveries long behind him, to sail to Byzantium.

Following their brief courtship, the two lovers spend a hundred years on the Island of Dancing, a world saturated with sensory stimuli – a place where "The damask roses, bloom on bloom,/Like crimson meteors hang in gloom" (ll. I.305–306), where "the sun in a saffron blaze/Was slumbering half in the sea-ways" (ll. I.394–395), and where "Joy drowns the twilight in the dew,/And fills with stars night's purple cup." This sensate density stands in marked contrast to the Island of Forgetfulness, a later destination for the couple. There, Oisin and Niamh are met with a more muted palette: "And we rode on the plains of the sea's edge; the sea's edge barren and grey,/Grey sand on the green of the grasses and over the dripping trees" (ll. III.13–14).

On the Island of Dancing, events culminate with a "wild and sudden dance" (ll. I.290) that breaks out after Oisin and Niamh, visiting a "house of wattles," meet a druid armed with "a sceptre flashing out/Wild flames of red and gold and blue" (ll. I.249, 251–252). Tracing its course over the

landscape, "the dance wound through the windless woods" (ll. I.320) until
the ensemble reaches a hilltop:

> gathered in a panting band,
> We flung on high each waving hand,
> And sang unto the starry broods.
>
> . . .
>
> 'You stars,
> Across your wandering ruby cars
> Shake the loose reins: you slaves of God,
> He rules you with an iron rod,
> He holds you with an iron bond,
> Each one woven to the other,
> Each one woven to his brother
> Like bubbles in a frozen pond.
>
> (ll. I.324–326, 329–337)

In these lines, Christian cosmology fades into Enlightenment science.
Slaves of both God and Newton, the stars are bound by iron laws enforced
by a sternly phallic iron rod – a natural order reflected by social forms since
the brothers that form the "the starry broods" are frozen into a fixed,
unchanging fraternity. The panting band is united by different bonds:

> Unchainable as the dim tide,
> With hearts that know nor law nor rule,
> And hands that hold no wearisome tool,
> Folded in love that fears no morrow.
>
> (ll. I.338–341)

This dancing band is not beholden to mere motion – the eternal, unchanging course of the stars across the heavens. The dancers enfold themselves
in love. They hold their partners with hands that know no toil. They give
way in response to each other. On the Island of Dancing, then, a critique
of law manifests not as a lone body that has "outdanced thought" but as a
dancing band that implores the stars to be slaves no more.

Three years after *The Wanderings of Oisin*, "Who Goes with Fergus"
presented dance as an explicit refusal of the solipsism implied by a solo
dancer. Replacing the sexual link between Oisin and Niamh with a
generalized man and woman, the poem opens with the image of a
χορός, a place for dancing:

> Who will go drive with Fergus now,
> And pierce the deep wood's woven shade,
> And dance upon the level shore?

> Young man, lift up your russet brow,
> And lift your tender eyelids, maid,
> And brood on hopes and fear no more.

When the poem begins, the young man and maid look downward, each consumed with their own thoughts. Look up, the speaker instructs, suggesting gestures to follow in tandem, raised heads and joining eyes. The bodies must mirror one another, their movements encouraged by chiastic bonds: "Young man, lift ... lift your tender eyelids, maid,/And brood on hopes and fear no more./And no more turn aside and brood." Only by facing each other may the man and maid banish their fear, just as on the Island of Dancing the dancers are "folded in love that fears no morrow." Consisting of three sentences, the poem begins by posing the question "Who will go drive with Fergus ... and dance upon the level shore?" This query is not met with an answer, however, but a command, "Lift up your russet brow." The interrogative mood is not completed by the indicative to make a closed unit of meaning. It is parried by the imperative, deflecting the impulse together with the poem's most insistent formal feature, the anaphora at the onset of the lines. Four of six begin with "And," a concatenation that runs from the first through the second and final stanza, spanning the break and the full stop that concludes the initial exposition:

> And lift your tender eyelids, maid,
> And brood on hopes and fear no more.
>
> And no more turn aside and brood
> Upon love's bitter mystery;
> For Fergus rules the brazen cars,
> And rules the shadows of the wood,
> And the white breast of the dim sea
> And all the dishevelled wandering stars.

Here the stars do not move according to iron laws. They wander, disheveled like two lovers. This brief, highly condensed lyric records something like the formation of a proto-*communis*: The principal figures overcome their solipsistic posture, evidenced by downcast glances, and meet the eyes of another. They sense the presence of their counterpart. This transition from solitude to communion is consummated by an implied semantic shift in the poem's core term, *brood.* The meaning opens out from the mind that broods "upon love's bitter mystery" and moves through the whole arc of animal fertility: the mother that broods on her unborn young, the brood of children born. Do not turn aside and brood, the poem commands. Go dance with Fergus on the level shore.

The dance aesthetics presented in "Fergus" cuts to a deeper layer of Yeats's poetic and political sensibility in the longest poem contained in *The Rose*, "Cuchulain's Fight with the Sea," which introduces the figure that would become a major Yeatsian symbol for the revival of national culture and Ireland's perpetual struggle against England. At various points in his career, Yeats explicitly associated Cuchulain with dance. For instance Susan Jones has noted a letter to Olivia Shakespear from 1929 that envisions a dramatic adaptation of the myth:

> The play begins with a dance which represents Cuchullan fighting the waves, then after some singing by the chorus comes the play which for its central incident the dance of the goddess and of Cuchullan, and then after more singing is the dance of the goddess mourning among the waves. The waves are of course dancers.[143]

In this choreography, collective movement complements solo dances. Choral singing acts as a counterpoint to the goddess and hero; and the rhythmic actions of the group mimic the motions of nature. In the earlier version collected in *The Rose*, the basic outlines of the myth Yeats used as a template are as follows: Having been betrayed by her husband, Cuchulain's wife Emer seeks revenge by sending their son Conlaech to challenge his father in battle. Cuchulain accepts without recognizing his challenger and kills his son, who announces himself just before he dies. Beset by grief, Cuchulain returns to the camp of the Red Branch band whose king, Conchubar, realizes the danger posed by the aggrieved father and directs his druids to enchant Cuchulain in order to prevent him from claiming more lives. Thus Cuchulain wanders out to sea where he expends his sorrow in fighting against the waves.

"Cuchulain's Fight with the Sea" narrates events in couplets of iambic pentameter, with the main conflict commencing when Conlaech relays his challenge through a messenger: "he gives his name/At the sword-point, and waits till we have found/Some feasting man that the same oath has bound." Submitting to a specific form of bondage, Conlaech suppresses his name and thereby forfeits any mark of social belonging: his status as Cuchulain's son or, indeed, as the member of a lineage of Irish kings. But even though Conlaech himself is unaware of the fact, the oath connects him to his father, who responds by crying "I am the only man/ Of all this host so bound from childhood on." This iron bond, fixed from youth to maturity, in turn removes Cuchulain from the idyll of collectivity represented by the Red Branch band: "Among those feasting men Cuchulain dwelt,/And his young sweetheart close beside him knelt … And all around the harp-string told his praise,/And Conhubar, the Red Branch king of kings,/With his own fingers touched the brazen strings." In obeying a filial-paternal blood bond, Cuchulain forsakes the erotic and aesthetic fulfillment of a *communis* gathered on the level shore for a contest that will end only on the point of his sword.

As father and son engage each other in combat, "fighting in the leafy shade" that recalls the χορός of "Fergus," it requires little imagination to see in this scene of paired movement a version of a *pas de deux* (historically, dance and the martial arts have had a long association).[144] With the two men facing each another, Cuchulain addresses his son during a brief pause in the fight, juxtaposing the erotics of "Fergus" with their own struggle: "He spake to the young man, 'Is there no maid/Who loves you, no white arms to wrap you round,/Or do you long for the dim sleepy ground, That you have come and dared me to my face?'" Instead of folding himself in love that fears no morrow, Conlaech does the bidding of his vengeful mother; and rather than match the glances of his maid, this young man meets the face of his enraged father. In effect, "Cuchulain's Fight with the Sea" inverts the dance aesthetics of "Fergus," employing an analogous poetic choreography for opposite ends. Through the choreographed movement of the characters, Yeats records the decline of communal belonging, following a regressive trajectory from the bliss of the Red Branch band to paired combat between father and son and then finally to the solitary, compulsive motion of Cuchulain.

It is fitting, then, that the revelation of Conlaech's identity causes the two figures to become one: "Cuchulain I, mighty Cuchulain's son," Conlaech utters at the end, thus continuing to suppress his own name in order to merge with his father in a moment of syntactic parallelism. Conchubar then warns that "Cuchulain will dwell there and brood/For three days more in dreadful quietude,/And then arise, and raving slay us all." As Cuchulain broods, he inclines to deeper solitude. So Conchubar sends his druids to cast their spell, which completes Cuchulain's descent into madness. The hero wanders out to sea where he moves with the periodic rhythms of nature: "Cuchulain stirred,/Stared on the horses of the sea, and heard/The cars of battle and his own name cried;/And fought with the invulnerable tide." Of course madness, too, is a form of supernormal experience, though one of its loneliest varieties. In this scene of repetitive, rhythmic motion, Cuchulain performs a kind of solo dance that conveys the tragedy of his fate through the content of sensory experience. He sees horses and hears the sounds of warfare. But unlike the *sensus communis* that Yeats records in *The Celtic Twilight*, where different individuals perceived through the same eyes and ears, Cuchulain senses in solitude. He alone can hear his name.

Other early poems choreograph their figures much in the manner of *The Wanderings of Oisin* through "Fergus" and "Cuchulain's Battle with the Sea." "The Stolen Child" from *Crossways* is spoken by a group of fairies who "foot it all the night,/Weaving olden dances,/Mingling hands and mingling glances" while the concluding poem of *The Rose* (1893), "To Ireland in the Coming Times," includes an image of "faeries, dancing under the moon." *The Wind Among the Reeds* (1899) pluralizes Fergus's man and maid in "The Host of the Air," when a piper accompanies "young men and young girls/Who danced on a level place," another instance of a χορός. Then in "The Fiddler of Dooney," the *Volk* itself becomes the agent of collective movement: "When I play on my fiddle in Dooney,/Folk dance like a wave of the sea." By the time of *In the Seven Woods* (1904), dance had become a straightforward signifier of the Irish people: "the Danaan kind/Wind and unwind dancing when the light grows cool/On the island lawns." These lines from "The Withering of the Boughs" remove any pretense that the Island of Dancing, a χορός rendered on a geographical scale, is anything other than a metonym for Eire itself.

A choreographic distinction between solipsism and collective movement remained in place even in later years. "The Collar-Bone of a Hare," a poem originally published in *The Little Review* in 1917 and later collected in *The Wild Swans at Coole* (1919), may have given Yeats a chance to work through personal associations given that "hare" was his sobriquet for Iseult Gonne. In any event autobiographical allusions do not compromise the overall effect of the poem, which opens with the speaker announcing a wish:

> Would I could cast a sail on the water
> Where many a king has gone
> And many a king's daughter,
> And alight at the comely trees and the lawn,
> The playing upon pipes and the dancing,
> And learn that the best thing is
> To change my loves while dancing
> And pay but a kiss for a kiss.

This scene hearkens back to the Island of Dancing published nearly three decades before, when the hero-poet did in fact travel across the seas with

Niamh, the daughter of a god, Angus, rather than a king. In this case the speaker longs to sail to a χορός where members of a chain dance trade their partners with ease. The second stanza then shatters this carefree spectacle:

> I would find by the edge of that water
> The collar-bone of a hare
> Worn thin by the lapping of water,
> And pierce it through with a gimlet and stare
> At the old bitter world where they marry in churches,
> And laugh over the untroubled water
> At all who marry in churches,
> Through the white thin bone of a hare.

Crude, compulsive repetition coupled with *vers libre*, a rarity in Yeats, diverges from the high artifice of "Fergus," injecting a note of menace. In this poem, rhythm is implied by the imagery rather than operating explicitly through meter. Lapping water has eroded the collarbone, introducing a rhythm, the period of the waves, that contrasts with the movement of the dancers, who take their cue from the pipes and thereby create an artistic, not natural, cadence all their own. Both in its mood and the events it narrates, "The Collar-Bone of a Hare" pivots on a cryptic gesture. The speaker punctures the bone and turns it into an optical device. Holding the filter up to his eyes, the brooding voyeur looks back on the "old bitter world" where the mystery of love, solved in "Fergus," remains an enigma. Hence the difference between a wished-for world of erotic fulfillment and the cold reality of marriage and institutional orthodoxy is mediated through an optical device, the collarbone of a hare, as though two specific kinds of communal organization, with the lone speaker caught in between, correspond with two different forms of sensory perception.

Yeats refashioned his poetic choreography into prose in order to contest the stereotypes of the Irish promulgated by Matthew Arnold and Ernst Renan. The argument in "The Celtic Element in Literature" is straightforward. Attributes usually imputed to the Irish – love of nature, imagination, melancholy – are in truth possessed by all humans in their primitive condition. So, for example, "Arnold quotes the lamentation of Llywarch Hen as a type of the Celtic melancholy," Yeats writes, "but I prefer to quote it as a type of the primitive melancholy."[145] Therefore in the same way that "barbaric peoples" had a finer sense for occult influences, so too primitive humans share a characteristic structure of feeling, in this case melancholy; and just as "Magic" conjures a primal scene of artistic creation, "The Celtic Element in Literature" summons up an aestheticized state of nature:

> Men who lived in a world where anything might flow and change, and become any other thing, and among great gods whose passions were in the flaming sunset, and in the thunder and the thunder shower, had not our thoughts of weight and measure.[146]

These noble savages are of a decidedly 'nineties vintage (the essay was first published in 1897). Unburdened by the principle of mensurability or anything resembling analysis and intellection, the denizens of this Heraclitean cosmos bask in the glow of their blazing passions. But where Pater staged *Marius* in the sun-drenched radiance of Augustan Rome, a classical setting that suits the novel's conflict between paganism and early Christianity, Yeats prefers an ancient milieu that calls to mind the Celtic χοροί of his early poetry. Those men that live in a state of flux "worshipped nature and the abundance of nature, and had always, as it seems, for a supreme ritual that tumultuous dance among the hills or in the depths of the woods, where unearthly ecstasy fell upon the dancers." These dancers rise to the summits of hilltops; they "pierce the deep wood's woven shade"; and their ecstasy, not their melancholy, befalls them as a group. In her reading of this passage, Mattar traces anthropological influences to Lang and Müller, arguing that "The Celtic Element in Literature" marks a "definitive step away from 'Celticism' and toward a broader primitivism."[147] Yet this primitivist idyll that acts as a set piece for the entire argument retains the choreography of the most expressive examples of the early Celticism, *The Wanderings of Oisin*, "Who Goes with Fergus" and the harmony of the Red Branch band in "Cuchulain's Fight with the Sea." Then in "The Withering of the Boughs," a poem published just as Yeats's primitivism was about to reach apogee in "Magic," Yeats translates those primitive elements back into their Celtic originals: "the Danaan kind/wind and unwind dancing when the light grows cool/On the island lawns." Therefore this "supreme ritual" of group dance is less a turn away from Celticism than a refiguring of folk attributes so they fit into a more general primitivist framework, an adaptation that, on the one hand, allows Yeats to resist the restrictive typologies of Arnold and Renan by claiming that folk attributes are universally primitive; on the other, Yeats can still single out the cultural production of certain peoples, such as the Irish, who carry those primitive characteristics into modernity by preserving, unlike the English, their connection with tradition, customs and rituals of the past.

If poetry was a generic vehicle for a Yeatsian dance aesthetics, then drama offered its own choreographic possibilities, especially after Pound introduced Yeats to Japanese Noh in 1915. Although the mid-career "dance plays" – *At the Hawk's Well* (1917), *The Only Jealousy of Emer* (1919), *The Dreaming of the Bones* (1919), *Calvary* (1920) – represent Yeats's most sustained engagement with staged choreography, dance had been a feature of his plays from the start: "Who Goes with Fergus" first appeared as a lyric in *The Countess Cathleen* (1892); and *The Land of Heart's Desire* (1894) sets a circle dance, once again, in a clearly demarcated χορός: "the faeries dance in a place apart,/Shaking their milk-white feet in a ring." Yet the 1916 premier of *At the Hawk's Well*, which was held in the drawing room of Lady Cunard with Pound and Eliot in attendance, broke with these early plays and with the cultural nationalism of the Abbey more generally. Spurred by the youthful Pound, Yeats was pursuing what he called an "unpopular theatre" – a theater that embraced avant-garde experimentation and required "an audience like a secret society where admission is by favour and never to many."[148]

For all the stylistic innovations of *At the Hawk's Well* – Ito's dancing, masks by Edmund Dulac, an austere musical accompaniment – the dance plays upheld certain tenets of the Abbey's cultural politics. Preston argues that the adoption of Noh did not mean forfeiting anticolonial ambitions, while Moses has claimed that the turn to "aristocratic political tragedy" can still "resonate in unexpected ways with the most advanced postcolonial critiques of the nation-state."[149] These caveats have equal purchase when it comes to the dramatic choreography in the dance plays, though group dance in "Certain Noble Plays of Japan" (1916), a critical primer for *At the Hawk's Well*, is a medium for national culture rather than a means for criticizing nationhood. Striking familiar notes, Yeats bemoans the decline of poetry before adducing the same tendency in dance: "movement also has grown less expressive, more declamatory, less intimate." Yet all hope for a revival has not been lost:

> When I called the other day upon a friend I found myself among some dozen people who were watching a group of Spanish boys and girls, professional dancers, dancing some national dance in the midst of a drawing-room. Doubtless their training had been long, laborious, and wearisome; but now one could not be deceived, their movement was full of joy.[150]

These dancers perform in a χορός far from the hills and woods of Tír na nÓg. Nevertheless this drawing room is a venue for a national dance, indeed, for something of a supreme ritual, as Yeats and his friends combine to form an "audience like a secret society." And whatever suffering the dancers may have endured during their training, it is joy or, rather, ecstasy that rewards them for their labor.

Immediately after this observation about group dancing Yeats addresses the choreography of Ito: "my play is made possible by a Japanese dancer whom I have seen dance in a studio and in a drawing-room and on a very small stage." Attending to the place of the dance as much as the dance itself, Yeats invokes, if inadvertently, the dual sense of χορός. In fact we can now venture an explanation for the remarkable appeal of the χορός for Yeats. Drawing room, level shore, imperial floor, island lawn, small stage – these χοροί create an aesthetic *communis* as a matter of course. Proximity, enforced by the setting, becomes a structural feature of the performance, which restores the intimacy that had been lost with the lapse into modernity. With this choreographic schema in place, Yeats then sums up his response to Ito's dance: "One realized anew, at every separating strangeness, that the measure of all arts' greatness can be but in their intimacy." If all art is sensuous, as Yeats claimed in *Discoveries*, then the value of that αἴσθησις derives from its intimacy. Therefore Ito may well epitomize a Yeatsian dance aesthetics, but he does so not as a token of the auto-telic quiddity of art. Instead he is a lone dancer that generates a sense of the common through the ecstasy of ritual.

Yeats's final play *The Death of Cuchulain* provides a suitable finale to this survey of communities of sense by lending those collectives a more radical cast. George Yeats was perhaps the first to note the inadequacies of *The Death of Cuchulain*; and the play cannot be considered one of Yeats's best.[151] Nevertheless, the character of the Old Man, a double for Yeats himself, activates political potentialities that were latent in earlier instances of communities of sense but that only manifested with full force in this uninhibited literary valediction. In a bilious prelude to the action, the Old Man declares "I wanted an audience of fifty or a hundred, and if there are more, I beg them not to shuffle their feet or talk when the actors are speaking." Desiring an unpopular theater, the Old Man choreographs the actions of the audience, instructing them to remain mute and directing the movement of their feet. He then lurches into more extreme territory: "if there are more than a hundred I won't be able to escape people who are educating themselves out of the Book Societies and the like, sciolists all, pickpockets and opinionated bitches."[152] If forty or fifty form an audience, more than a hundred make a mass, a collective body ruined by modern education and popular culture. We have been warned about this kind of reaction: Herder depicted the philosopher of the cabal as a blinkered pedant clinging "to local and national beauties, or to the virtues of his club"; and the *communis*, Shaftesbury noted, can always devolve into "the spirit of faction."

Yet the ravings of this old man suggest a more substantial departure from an authentic *sensus communis*, where direct sensory contact fosters an ethos opposed to religious zealotry or nihilistic individualism that construes all human endeavor as the sheer pursuit of power. That is to say, the *sensus communis* in its initial formulation is a liberal entity that cuts across the main line of liberal theory descending from Hobbes to Locke and John Stuart Mill. Likewise Herder advanced an unconventional liberalism at once critical of Kant but committed to the values of *Bildung* and cultural pluralism. The ideology of the Old Man calves off from the liberal tradition altogether, indicating that the debasement of the *communis* that worried Shaftesbury and Herder can assume a distinctly twentieth-century guise, namely, the fascist valorization of the collective. The antiliberal dictates of the Old Man were presaged by Yeats's own warm response to Mussolini and Eoin O'Duffy's Irish Blueshirts. These personal affinities for fascism bring out the darker undertones of *The Death of Cuchulain*. They also illustrate how a heterodox liberalism, in this case in a Shaftesburian or Herderian guise, can turn against itself and consume any remaining liberal elements: the politeness, decorum and tolerance of the original *sensus communis* have vanished in the Old Man's preface, replaced by a dictatorial factionalism that aligns the chosen few against the many. At this point the ideological trajectory of Yeatsian communities of sense reaches an end. Ecstasy and the gaiety of young love, previously the emotional core animating communities of sense, curdle into the caustic brooding of a sterile old man.

CHAPTER 5

Prometheus Found

An ideological cousin to the new nationalism of Yeats was born in Berlin around the year 1910: the "new human" of German Expressionism, an artistic movement usually dated to the second decade of the century, which burned hot before being eclipsed by the frank realism of the New Objectivity and the still more extreme disruptions of Dada.[1] Like their contemporaries in Britain and Ireland, Expressionists rejected what they understood to be the bankruptcy of an old, exhausted humanism that found its most trenchant critic in Friedrich Nietzsche – a philosopher whose influence on Expressionism equaled his importance for Symons and his contemporaries.[2] But in contrast to Yeats in his more nationalist moods, Expressionists favored a warmer universalism that the eminent critic of Expressionism Walter Sokel dubbed "communionism": a conception of collective life grounded in a neo-Christian ethos, which Sokel distinguished from materialist social theories – that is, from Communism – as well as from a Zarathustrian message of heroic individualism.[3] All belong to a common humanity. Art is thus a medium for conveying this shared bond; and spreading the gospel of universalism becomes the task for a "messianic Expressionism."[4]

Despite the stylistic diversity of artists associated with Expressionism, two overlapping tendencies have been identified as organizing the movement as a whole: a full-throated emotionality that generated experiments with artistic form; and a program for social renewal epitomized by the discourse of the "new human."[5] The latter tendency is usually singled out as the more baleful of the two. With its overheated moralism, its unrestrained declamations of fellow feeling, and its enthusiasm for fashioning a better world through sheer emotive force, the discourse of the "new human" has made a large target for later critics. Silvio Vietta offers a representative critique when he laments the "vague communal pathos" of the *neuer Mensch*, which he disparages as a social program that tried "to create human brotherhood on the irrational grounds of the ego."[6] Thomas

Anz takes a similar view, writing that "the 'new human' became an empty formula, which let itself be fulfilled by longings and wishful dreams of all kinds" – including dreams of a reactionary or proto-fascist cast.[7]

This chapter aims to give a more precise account of the "new human" by tethering the irrationalist and religious dimensions of the *neuer Mensch* to an aesthetic-anthropology of *space*. That is to say, a distinct spatial ideal, the circle, becomes the standard by which the "new human" is measured.[8] At first glance, space may seem to be a counterintuitive way of defining the nature of *der Mensch*. But as Chapter 1 showed, anthropologists had long used archetypes of beauty to sort individuals into categories – races – based on spatial relationships: the proportions of the head or the face, for example. For an Expressionist like Else Lasker-Schüler and her allies in the *Neue Gemeinschaft*, one of Germany's foremost utopian communities at the turn of the century, the racial distinctions inherited from physical anthropology were objects of scrutiny, not emulation, particularly when they correlated with social status and distinctions of rank. Hence Expressionists resorted to a purer, still more ideal conception of spatiality in order to determine the nature of the "new human": the properties of three-dimensional space defined according to the axioms of Euclidean geometry. The circle, a figure that makes all points on the circumference equidistant from the center, captures the essence of the *neuer Mensch*. All humans may be considered equal as long as they orient themselves with respect to a single definitional point – the center.

An aesthetic anthropology of space returns the argument to themes introduced in earlier chapters though for different purposes, namely, to show how anthropological entities may be conceived along egalitarian lines instead of in terms of ontological hierarchies. And in the same way that Kant provided the most rigorous exposition of how an anthropology of space renders human bodies into elements that can be assembled into hierarchies of species and genera, the theoretical stakes of the spatial turn among Expressionists become clearest by consulting Kantian arguments. (As will become clear, Expressionist theorists themselves owed considerable debts to Kant.) In the "Transcendental Aesthetic" from *The Critique of Pure Reason*, Kant maintains that space and time, and only space and time, are *a priori* forms of intuition that structure human consciousness. On this account, the regularities of Euclidean space are not induced through observations of empirical figures. In other words, the relationship between a circle's center and its circumference is not established by measuring various chords and then generalizing those measurements for the figure as a whole. Such an inference could never provide the apodeictic certainty characteristic of geometrical proof. Therefore, according to Kant, the properties of Euclidean space must be legislated by the mind so that experience conforms to necessary spatial laws (the aesthetic component of the famous "Copernican revolution" achieved in the first *Critique*). One consequence of this reorientation of mind and world is that appearances of particular objects are downstream from antecedent mental structures. Sensations are already organized by the mind in the moment they manifest in consciousness. In Kantian terms, then, space and time are aesthetic categories more fundamental than the archetypes of organic species theorized in the third *Critique* since they constitute, rather than merely regulate, sensory experience.

It is at this point that a phrase can be introduced that will become increasingly important for the remainder of this study: "the aestheticization of political life," a phrase Walter Benjamin used in his essay "The Work of Art in the Age of Mechanical Reproduction." The details of Benjamin's argument will be examined in due course. For now, suffice it to say that Benjamin considers "aestheticization" to be a process that replaces the real determinants of political life – that is, property relations (*Eigentumsverhältnisse*) – with sensations, impressions or feelings associated with political activity and group constitution. Strictly speaking, sensations are epiphenomena generated by material factors. When mere appearances replace real causes, Benjamin maintains, a sort of false consciousness emerges that warps reality and blocks effective political action. Even though Benjamin identifies mass rallies, the aura of charismatic authority and other political spectacles as examples of aestheticized political life, there is no need to limit the force of his critique to these particular cases. The argument is more general. Aestheticization is an intellectual strategy whereby aesthetic effects, whether discrete sensations or more general categories like space and time, are substituted for material causes.

Therefore it needs to be acknowledged at the outset that an aesthetic anthropology grounded in the primacy of space courts the risk of a Benjaminian critique, for the aestheticization thesis targets any prioritization of aesthetic categories over material ones. Granting the force of this critique would, in turn, cast serious doubt upon the value of construing anthropological categories – *Mensch*, race, *Volk* – along spatial or any other aesthetic lines. That is because for Benjamin the aestheticization of politics was inextricable from the rise of fascism, a political movement that allowed its followers to voice their grievances while maintaining the property relations that were the true source of social ills. In fabricating the appearance of redressing those ills, fascism, whether in the guise of Italian

Futurism or National Socialism, offered a satisfying illusion that wrongs were being righted even as it preserved the existing economic order.

As an artistic movement supported by a social ideology, Expressionism is especially vulnerable to the charge of harboring fascist potential through its aestheticization of political life. Indeed, this accusation helped ignite one of the most important debates on the prewar cultural left in 1937, the so-called Expressionism Debate that will be the topic of Chapter 6. For his part Benjamin himself explicitly notes how fascism cultivates expressive behaviors that in turn generate an aestheticized false consciousness: "fascism tries to give the masses *expression* [*Ausdruck*] while preserving those [material] relations. This follows necessarily to an aestheticization of political life."[9] Fascism, in other words, promotes the externalization of internal resentments without affecting the material sources responsible for creating animosity in the first place. This is the conservative or, rather more accurately, reactionary core of aestheticization. Mere appearances, collectivized and concretized in expressive acts, provide an outlet for feelings, sensations and ideas and thereby misdirect attention from true – that is, material – causes.

From this it follows that Expressionism does not somehow eliminate the sensory dimensions of collective life that Herder and Yeats believed were fundamental for *Volk* and nation. But unlike Impressionism or the aestheticism examined in Chapter 4, where sensations are rendered with phenomenological nuance and psychological depth, Expressionism begins with the resources of internal life and then projects them outward, reversing, as it were, the order of priority. In its purest state, the self becomes the source for creating an aesthetic world, reorienting subject and object to prioritize the former. This Expressionist inversion of an Impressionist aesthetics ought therefore to prompt a more critical interpretation of the spatial metaphor of the circle. Read according to the aestheticization thesis, the circle is not a perfectly rational shape that captures the nature of equality with geometrical neutrality. In truth the circle is a rationalized externalization of an internal longing for an egalitarian order. Thus the "communal pathos" and "wishful dreams" that critics have noted when describing the discourse of the *neuer Mensch* do not disappear when translated into an aesthetic-anthropology of space. They are the latent subjective content that manifests as an ideal arrangement of elements organized around a single governing center.

If Benjamin insists that fascism thrives by giving the masses the means for political expression, then this chapter and Chapter 6 will show that Expressionism relied on another, more richly anthropological form of collectivity: the *Volk*, the same concept that energized Yeatsian nationalism. In this respect, the new humanism of Else Lasker-Schüler is especially revealing since in her poetry and prose, Lasker-Schüler translates the spatial anthropology of the *neuer Mensch* into a means of defining the *Volk*, and in particular, the Jewish *Volk* as it grappled with the social forces that would culminate in National Socialism and the foundation of the State of Israel. Born to an assimilated family in Wuppertal, Lasker-Schüler came into contact with leading figures of the Jewish Renaissance that flowered in Berlin during the late Wilhelmine and Weimar periods. Martin Buber published one of her first poems in his journal *Ost und West*. And he would later be an important interlocutor for matters relating to Judaism.[10] In 1942, for instance, Lasker-Schüler confessed to Buber, "I am no Zionist, nor Jew, nor Christian; I believe, though, I am a human, a very deeply sad human."[11] Yet she also called Theodor Herzl an "angel" and spent her final years living in Mandatory Palestine. Over the course of Lasker-Schüler's career, the discourse of the "new human" in fact runs together with the cultural condition of the Jewish people, producing a spatialized new humanism that expresses the condition of a very old *Volk*, the Jews, as it worked to imagine itself anew amid a rapidly globalizing modernity.

The chapter begins by examining Lasker-Schüler's writings from the first decade of the century, before the emergence of Expressionism proper but informed by the same intellectual currents – in particular, vitalism and utopian communalism. Focusing on the concepts of *Mensch* and *Volk* in Lasker-Schüler's poetry as well as her prose, Section 5.1 discusses the early work in conjunction with the new humanism of Heinrich and Julius Hart, the two leaders of the *Neue Gemeinschaft*. The chapter then turns to the main phase of Expressionism with an extended history of its rise, an excursus warranted by the fact that Expressionism, at least in English-language literary history, has not attained the same recognizability as its contemporaries and ideological kin Italian Futurism, Wyndham Lewis's Vorticism or the high modernism of Yeats. Attending to questions of gender, which are especially important given the contemporaneous development of first-wave feminism and its concomitant discourse of the "new woman," the long Section 5.2 situates the concepts of *Volk* and *Mensch* with respect to Expressionist art more generally. Finally the chapter concludes with a reading of the short story *Der Wunderrabbiner von Barcelona* [The Miracle-Rabbi of Barcelona]. Published after Expressionism had mostly burned itself out, *Der Wunderrabbiner* (1921) connects the promise of social renewal associated with the *neuer Mensch* with the territorial aspirations of Zionism, providing a model for diasporic consciousness that relies on the spatial humanism first expounded by the *Neue Gemeinschaft* and then realized during the full bloom of the Expressionist period.

5.1 Reconciliations

From Lasker-Schüler's earliest work through her later, more famous collection *Hebrew Ballads* (1913), folk poetry served as a vehicle for lyric innovations. One of her first published poems, "Volkslied [Folk Song]," conjoins popular verse and proto-modernist techniques despite initially bearing a title that mutes the allusions to folk traditions in favor of a more diffuse psychological tenor, "Vorahnung [Premonition]." Only with her debut volume *Styx* (1902) did she change the title to "Volkslied" and make the links to popular song explicit, thereby complementing the references to classical antiquity in poems such as "Αθάνατοι" and "Sterne des Tartaros [Stars of Tartarus]." "Volkslied" begins in action, opening with a verb whose subject is only given at the end of the line. The poem then moves through a fractured image complex overlain with the emotional strains of family:

> Laughs at me teasingly the whirlwind
> – My child, it is heaven's child
> With locks, like sunshine.
>
> I sit crying under the roof,
> Am awake and feverish at night
> And sew shirts out of linen.
>
> My mother's birthday is today,
> Both father and mother are dead
> And no longer saw the little one.
>
> My mother once had a heavy dream,
> She did not look at me without sighs
> and without secretly weeping.
>
> [Verlacht mich auch neckisch der Wirbelwind
> – Mein Kind, das ist ein Himmelskind
> Mit Locken, wie Sonnenscheinen.
>
> Ich sitze weinend unter dem Dach,
> Bin in den Nächten fieberwach
> Und nähe Hemdchen aus Leinen.
>
> Meiner Mutter Wiegenfest ist heut,
> Gestorben sind Vater und Mutter beid'
> Und sahen nicht mehr den Kleinen.

Meine Mutter träumte einmal schwer,
Sie sah mich nicht an ohne Seufzer mehr
Und ohne heimliches Weinen.][12]

Just as the poems of *Hebrew Ballads* are ballads in name only, lacking, as they do, the attributes that define the ballad form in a strict sense, the extent to which "Volkslied" is a popular song is open to question. There is no narrative organizing the content of the poem. The meter is fairly regular but without the musical lilt one would expect from a song. At the same time, the "Wirbelwind" and "Himmelskind" allude to the lines the children sing upon meeting the witch in Hänsel and Gretel: "*der Wind, der Wind,/das himmlische Kind.*"[13] Further, a degree of musical regularity does come through in the rhyme scheme, couplets followed by a rhyme linking the stanzas, though the strong early caesuras – "Mein Kind, das ist ein Himmelskind/Mit Locken, wie Sonnenscheinen" – never quite resolve into an easy meter. And despite the absence of a narrative arc, the four stanzas do give fragmentary vantages on a domestic scene, indicating that even if "Volkslied" is not a strict imitation of a folk song, it is playing with the conventions of popular verse.

For all the presence of death in "Volkslied," a countervailing impulse illustrates the vitalist tendencies that Gunter Martens argues were crucial for Lasker-Schüler's early verse and for the later Expressionist movement.[14] Elements like fire (*fieberwach*), water (*Weinen*) and wind (*Seufzer*) are rendered as psychosomatic events – fever, tears and sighs – which are then invested with emotional valences that reinforce a constitutive tension between death and life: the mourning for the departed parents and, by contrast, the hope for a future generation, the *Himmelskind*, that is not without its own frisson of death, "heaven's child." Such thematic complementarity is a common feature of the family poems in *Styx*. "Chronica" refers to parents who have died but "shower their force" down from heaven. "Youth [*Jugend*]" opens with a scoff at Death, the *Sensenmann*, as he hammers together a coffin. The speaker then responds by marking time in an altogether different rhythm, the throbbing of life itself: "My heart plays with the young light of dawn/And dances in the swarming sparks of the sun's glow." Far from dragging the verses into the solemnity of elegy, the presence of death allows life to resound with greater intensity, with the family acting as a chain linking past generations with the present.

"Volkslied," while it shares these tonal and thematic contrasts, strikes more dissonant chords in each of its successive stanzas. After the initial jolt of the opening, maternal affection shifts to despair in the second stanza.

Then in the third stanza despair shades into grief before concluding with the tears and sighs of the final tercet. Amid this emotional tumult, there is a definite center to the poem. The main image, the whirlwind, is a motion whose energy is oriented around a central point – very different, then, than the generic wind that Hänsel and Gretel sing in the Grimm Brother's tale; and still less like the sheer radiation of life that Martens identifies as vitalist.[15] This wind has shape and structure. Its movement is focused, organized, centralized. In fact, its form can be generalized onto the poem as a whole. Through their lexical and sonic proximity, the whirlwind and the *Himmelskind* are the physical and emotional centers of "Volkslied." They are the points around which the poem spins.

Concentration coupled with disruption, this polar physics continues to inform Lasker-Schüler's literary imagination. In her first major work of prose, *Das Peter Hille-Buch*, the character of Tino, a proxy for the author, watches birds as they "circle through the air like a silver whirlwind."[16] Another scene contains a circle dance whose center is occupied by the novel's protagonist, Petrus, the first of many charismatic leaders that will populate Lasker-Schüler's prose: "they danced dances around him as though around a stone idol."[17] As this passage illustrates, the materials that converge on a point are not only natural entities – animals or elements like wind, water and fire. More often they are political subjects, even members of a *Volk*, who are held together by the galvanizing presence of Petrus himself.

Written in memory of Peter Hille (1854–1904), the writer, journalist and *bohémien extraordinaire*, *Das Peter Hille-Buch* arose from Lasker-Schüler's association with the *Neue Gemeinschaft*, a back-to-nature collective led by the brothers Heinrich and Julius Hart. Located first in Berlin and then on the nearby Schlachtensee, the *Neue Gemeinschaft* counted among its affiliates some of the more progressive minds in contemporary German culture. Gustav Landauer was briefly involved, though he soon soured on the Harts's freewheeling hedonism.[18] Herwarth Walden contributed to the group's cultural offerings (he appears in *Das Peter Hille-Buch* as Goldwarth); and Lasker-Schüler was a frequent guest at the community, where she gave readings from her poetry. Of all the colorful individuals affiliated with the *Neue Gemeinschaft*, it was Hille who exerted the greatest influence on Lasker-Schüler. A crucial early advocate for her work, Hille came to represent something of an ideal artist for the young poet. Through his notorious penury and the breadth of his literary endeavor, he seemed to be someone who lived the sincerity of his vocation. One contemporary, commenting on Hille's place in the avant-garde, called him "the most homeless man in Berlin [*der heimatloseste Mensch in Berlin*]."[19]

Lasker-Schüler published *Das Peter Hille-Buch* two years after her mentor's death at the age of fifty caused by a fall at the Zehlendorf train station.[20] The events of the narrative, in keeping with the ideology of the *Neue Gemeinschaft*, bask in a Zarathustrian glow. After emerging from the earth like a chthonic god, Petrus leads a merry band of disciples as they wander through the mountains and countryside. Evidence for the influence of Nietzsche, who has been suggested as a source for the book's ebullient language as well as its peripatetic plot, is indirect but nonetheless convincing.[21] Besides being exposed to the philosopher through the *Neue Gemeinschaft*, where Nietzsche was a guiding light, Lasker-Schüler participated in the "Nietzsche Evenings" organized by Walden under the auspices of the *Verein für Kunst*, a cultural forum he founded in 1904 shortly after his marriage to Lasker-Schüler. These evenings, held on three occasions while *Das Peter Hille-Buch* was being composed, consisted of readings from Nietzsche's works often accompanied by musical arrangements performed by Walden on piano (one of the evenings took place at the Nietzsche Archive in Weimar).[22] Any explicit connections between Lasker-Schüler and Nietzsche, which are not altogether absent, postdate *Das Peter Hille-Buch*.[23] In her kaleidoscopic portrayal of the Berlin cafés titled *Letters to Norway* (1911–1912), she mentions Nietzsche along with Goethe as someone who believes that "art is conversation with God," a statement that may have been inspired by *Human, All Too Human*.[24] Only much later did she write a short sketch titled "Der kleine Friedrich Nietzsche [The Little Friedrich Nietzsche]" (1929), in which she relates a tale of youthful heroism by the twelve-year old Friedrich she claimed to have had heard from a childhood friend of the philosopher. Her story of enjoying a personal audience with the invalid Nietzsche during a trip to Weimar in her youth is considered by her biographer to be apocryphal.[25]

Whatever the philosophical influences on *Das Peter Hille-Buch*, the literary history that informs the novel is decidedly eclectic. Zarathustrian strains, including a moment when Petrus tells of an Old Iranian prophet who "formed the new human [*den neuen Menschen*]" out of the "midday sun of his homeland [*Heimat*]," take their place alongside religious, especially Judeo-Christian references.[26] Sokel believes the Bible is a precedent for Lasker-Schüler's paratactic style.[27] He even classifies the book as a form of Christian hagiography. Popular allusions waft through the book's fantasyland atmosphere too. At one point Tino says she must "don the dress of Scheherazade" while strolling through a magical garden, where she spies the "hedge behind which Sleeping Beauty lay for a hundred years in her magical slumber."[28] She then meets one of Snow White's dwarves, showing the extent to which the Brothers Grimm remained a touchstone for her work – as they would continue to be in later years. In 1910, for example, she described Max Brod as a character out of the *Kinder- und Hausmärchen*: "In Grimm's fairy tales he [Brod] is painted, the way he looked as a child, in Hänsel and Gretel."[29] Such heterogeneity in the literary-historical background of *Das Peter Hille-Buch* is entirely consistent with the book's disjunctive, episodic plot, which swerves from one event to the next without any real direction or development.

Absent a coherent narrative or a consistent thematic register, Petrus acts as the book's indisputable center. Of forty-seven chapter titles, his name appears in thirty-three.[30] In one of the more overtly Nietzschean chapters, "Petrus in the Mountains V," the protagonist illustrates his magnetic power over others. Acting as narrator, Tino first admits to assuming a peculiar orientation with respect to the prophet-leader Petrus: "I lay like a ring around his foot, which was like stone." Tino forms herself into a circle around the foot of Petrus, which holds the shape's center. This odd image, evoking at once physical embrace and a ritual display of supplication, stages the relationship of center and circumference through the interposition of two bodies: the fixed, stone foot of Petrus; the flexible figure of Tino that encircles him. Once this arrangement of bodies is in place, "Petrus spoke to the noisy crowd, but I didn't hear his words over the drone of his voice, but the people down below next to the water listened spellbound while the forests all around [*ringsum*] them rustled."[31] The listeners, constituted as sheer noise (*die Lärmenden*), are immediately identified as a *Volk* that assumes a distinctly passive posture with respect to the speaker. They are spellbound, *gebannt*, as the words wash over them. Yet Petrus's voice has the opposite effect on the natural elements in the scene. When he speaks, the leaves of the trees, which form yet another ring, rustle (*rauschen*) as though blown by a wind. That is to say, the words disturb the leaves while fixing the attention of the *Volk* on the person of Petrus.

The politics of *Das Peter Hille-Buch* have not failed to cause concern among Lasker-Schüler's readers.[32] Along with noting the conventional gender politics, the paternalistic Petrus attended by the fawning Tino, Marion Adams labels the book "conservative," a generous estimation given the *Führer-Volk* dynamic between Petrus and his followers.[33] Yet for all the proto-fascist elements in *Das Peter Hille-Buch*, which are too pervasive to be ignored, the book emerged out of more progressive political soil – what

Adams calls *Gefühlsozialismus* or Seth Taylor, in his survey of the politics of Expressionism, describes as "left-wing Nietzschean": a fundamentally subjective aversion to bourgeois society, which certainly reflects the worldview of the *Neue Gemeinschaft*.[34] Given that Hille was not without leftist credentials – he had edited socialist newspapers and his own debut novel was titled *Die Sozialisten* – the political vectors of Lasker-Schüler's collective imaginary need to be understood in terms of their engagement with Marxism or materialist thought more generally.[35] The chapter "Petrus and the Workers," which intimates potential ideological sympathies in its title, provides one of the clearer reflections on the solidary bonds that unite individuals to a common cause.

The chapter begins with Petrus and Tino entering a claustrophobic urban landscape: "springtime cannot bloom and is suffocated between the narrow houses." Met by a group of workers with "hands clenched and threatening," Petrus and Tino watch as the crowd chants socialist slogans and events incline toward violence.[36] Only when addressed by their leader, a character named Sennulf probably based on the firebrand anarchist and advocate for worker's rights Senna Hoy (Johannes Holzmann), are the workers mollified:

> his words whirled [*wirbelten*] over the freedom-hungry *Volk*, which were like early spring leaves before the thunderstorm. And at the end of the evening, several individuals approached Petrus, among them a poet-worker named Damm. And many of the youths had come on account of the honored guest.

Here we have a moment of collective disintegration and reintegration. When Sennulf speaks, his words whirl over the listeners, rustling them like leaves in the wind. Yet their movement does not remain disjunctive. Once again, a double motion is apparent. The words dissolve the bonds of the workers, rendering them into individuals (*einzelne*), whereupon those newly liberated actors gather around a different center, Petrus, who assumes the authority formerly enjoyed by Sennulf.

Besides offering an example of collective disruption followed by immediate reintegration around a new center, this scene stages a qualitative shift in the character of the collectivity at hand. When Petrus and Tino first behold the workers, they chant slogans that draw attention to their material grievances: "we don't want to be put off until heaven," they cry, "we want to have it on earth, just like the rich!" The divisions that animate the crowd are therefore material. They pertain to worldly desires that correspond to a distinction between rich and poor. In fact one of the chapter's first images is of children whose impoverishment has warped their visage: "children play on the playgrounds, the poor ones [*die armen*] with elderly faces and crooked joints." When Sennulf addresses the crowd, however, the collectivity loses its connection to material deprivation. Instead the crowd becomes a "freedom-hungry *Volk*," a designation that replaces a plight associated with the poor, physical hunger, with a more abstract longing – a hunger for freedom. But this newfound need, legitimate as it may be, is not resolved by granting autonomy. In other words hunger for freedom is not satisfied by giving freedom. Rather, the need for freedom is rendered moot, supplanted by obedience inasmuch as the individuals gravitate toward a leader, the figure of Petrus.

In "Petrus and the Workers," the potential for (violent) revolutionary action is defused by stripping a collective entity of its material character, that is, by transforming the nature of its hunger and substituting an alternative means, in this case the charismatic force of Petrus, in order to create solidary bonds between parts and whole. As such the chapter provides a stark example of a Benjaminian aestheticization of politics. Material divisions are erased and replaced by a fundamentally affective connection between a leader and followers. Petrus, however, is no member of a *sensus communis* in the manner of the Yeatsian dancers in *The Wanderings of Oisin*, who allow themselves to be swept up in the sensation of group movement. Rather Petrus is the fixed point around which followers trace their orbit. He is the center that orders elements in space. "The boys and the girls," Tino relates, "danced dances around him as though around a stone idol [*Urgestalt*]." Petrus is himself an archetype. He has the power to form the content of sensible experience.

With this exposition of Lasker-Schüler's early prose in place, we can now elucidate points of contact between her writings and the discourse of the *neuer Mensch* as it was formulated in Germany at the beginning of the century. Consider the collection of essays published by Heinrich and Julius Hart in 1901, *Das Reich der Erfüllung* [The Kingdom of Fulfillment]. Volume 2 comprises lectures delivered by the Brothers Hart at the *Neue Gemeinschaft* including "Der Neue Mensch" by Julius, which lays out the new humanism guiding their utopian experiment. Before turning to the text of Julius's lecture, it is worth noting some general tendencies in the worldview of the brothers. One of the most prominent is a longing for reconciliation – or as Heinrich puts it, "the connection, fusion, and marriage" between individuals, concepts, entities or dualisms of all sorts.[37] This conciliatory ethos is readily apparent in "Die Neue Gemeinschaft," which opens with the following programmatic statement by Heinrich:

> *In the intimate fusion of religion, art, knowledge, and life, the New Community seeks the ideal human and the ideal of humanity, the realization of the completion of individual and collective.*[38]

A synthetic enterprise through and through, the *Neue Gemeinschaft* strives for its ideal human by uniting disparate domains. Contradictions, Hart maintains throughout the lecture, are but figments of the mind. They fall away in the pursuit of life and sheer action, which are not subject to the laws of logic. Through impassioned living with others, antitheses dissolve – including antitheses between social groups. Hence the *Neue Gemeinschaft* seeks an "ideal beyond all divisions of status, folk, race," but not by dispensing with those concepts altogether. He adds in the next sentence that the *Neue Gemeinschaft* is "an over-people over the peoples, a new humanity [*ein Übervolk über den Völkern, eine Neumenschheit*]."[39] In a single breath, Hart grafts the concept of the *Volk* onto the Nietzschean superman. A new humanity, or its proxy the *Übervolk*, resolves antagonisms that had traditionally divided German society – race (*Rasse*), status (*Stand*) and ethnicity (*Volk*).

In "Der Neue Mensch," Julius Hart develops this new humanism by deploying motifs that would later show up in *Das Peter Hille-Buch*. At one point, he conveys his optimism by stating that "the hedge of thorns that had surrounded Sleeping Beauty has turned into a wall of flowers."[40] We also learn that the new human, much like Petrus, is a sort of divine artificer that can "mold, form, and shape" the world, a point echoed by Heinrich who refers to an "original power to shape [*Urgestaltungskraft*]" possessed by humankind (Heinrich also uses the phrase "den neuen Menschen" in his lecture).[41] But there is more to the argument of the Harts than vague sentiments of union and mystical brotherhood that Vietta singles out for censure in his analysis of the *neuer Mensch*. Julius defines the new human by invoking a specifically spatial ideal: the circle, a shape that implies its own kind of egalitarianism, with points on the circumference arrayed at equal distances from the center. "Your essence is center and your essence is circle," Julius writes of the new human.[42] He then proclaims in his peroration, "we call for the new human, the world-shaping! . . . Center and circle, God and creator of things."[43]

A circle is not the most obvious way of defining the nature of *anthropos*. At least Kantian archetypes referred to human physiology whereas the circle, as Julius Hart understood it, is a configuration of elements arranged

according to Euclidean geometry. Appreciating the theoretical import of
the circle as an ideal for *anthropos* requires attending to Hart's rather
elaborate reading of the Copernican revolution, which he makes a guiding
thread for the lecture as a whole. "Our poor earth was torn from its central
place and installed in its distant peripheral courses," Hart writes. As a
result, "we humans have moved out into those peripheries," and the
"anthropocentric lie [*anthropozentrische Lüge*]" can no longer be maintained.[44] But even as Hart admits that humans have been displaced from
center to periphery, such a reorientation obtains merely in the realm of
what he calls "scientific truth."[45] Only the natural sciences have wrested
humans from the center of the cosmos and placed them in the outer orbits.

In the realm of spirit, however, humans retain their primacy. "We are
the core and center [*Kern und Centrum sind wir*]." Consequently "the
world circles around us on the axis of our ego."[46] So the *neuer Mensch* is
defined as having two aspects: spiritual and natural, corresponding to
central and peripheral places in the cosmos. Unmistakably Kantian notes
ring through this argument, recalling both the Copernican revolution of
the first *Critique*, which relocated the metaphysical grounds for reality to
the mind instead of the world, as well as the famous conclusion of *The
Critique of Practical Reason*: "two things fill the mind with ever new and
increasing admiration and reverence ... the starry sky above me and the
moral law within me."[47] For Heinrich and Julius Hart, however, a general
spiritual and creative dignity plays the role of Kantian Law in their cosmic
anthropology even as they hew to the idealist split between nature and
spirit, world and self that descended from Kant through Fichte and Hegel.
But where Kant held those two autonomous spheres apart, and the post-
Kantian idealists tried to reconcile them through dialectical striving, the
Brothers Hart take a different approach. They invoke a spatial figure, the
circle, in order to represent those dual aspects as parts of a single theoretical
construct. On their own, Julius Hart goes on to argue in "Der Neue
Mensch," neither the purely spiritual nor the strictly natural aspect –
neither center nor periphery – can comprehend the full measure of the
new human. "The spirit within us must die that always rises from the
middle of things and projects itself as mere nothingness." Thus is spiritual
man condemned, just like natural man in the next sentence: "we must
strike down the human of the periphery," Hart declares. However, "out of
its blood rises up the new human, the founder of new times and new
kingdoms, who acts as his own God and his own word, substance and
form, center and circle."[48] The circle coordinates the antitheses of core and
periphery. If alone neither aspect suffices, together they combine to make

an ideal shape that allows both aspects of humanity to be present at the same time. Hence the new human is both spirit and nature, center and circumference, core and periphery.

For the Brothers Hart, the circle is a theoretical instrument that can help address a range of dualities – nature and spirit, substance and form, as we have just seen, but also, as they argue in the first volume of *Das Reich der Erfüllung*, "individualism and socialism, nation and humanity, conservative and revolutionary ... optimism and pessimism, right and wrong, good and evil." So, for instance, "nation and humanity relate to each other like a smaller circle does to a larger one, by whose periphery it is circumscribed." Once again the circle translates two concepts, nation and humanity, into spatial terms. Yet instead of representing those concepts as complementary parts of a single figure, center and circumference, this example renders them as two similar figures differentiated by size. The nation is a smaller circle contained by a larger one, humanity. So construed, the discursive tension or threat of contradiction between particularism and universalism, nation and humanity is eliminated by fiat. In this version of a spatial turn, a conceptual difficulty is not transcended or resolved as much as redescribed in order to simplify the problem out of existence.

Circular motion was a frequent motif in Lasker-Schüler's writing, as we have already seen, and it often appeared in the form of whirling motion reminiscent of the winds of "Volkslied." In the story "Der Derwisch [The Dervish]," for example, a character "blows the whirling sand"; and a short piece about the theater describes "whirling applause."[49] The first major work of prose to follow *Das Peter Hille-Buch*, *Die Nächte Tino von Bagdads* [The Nights of Tino of Bagdad] (1907), then inflects this figure with Lasker-Schüler's characteristic blend of Orientalism and folktale. One early chapter finds Tino "dancing an endless dance that stretches like a dark cloud over Baghdad." The text continues: "I dance over the waves of the sea, whirl up the sand of the desert and before the palace the people listens [*lauscht das Volk*]." Here, the orientation between Petrus and his followers is revised so that Tino now occupies the center of the circle. But despite this change of character, her dance has the same effect, fixing the attention of the folk, which beholds her whirling movement.

Die Nächte relates Tino's adventures through a plot of loosely organized stories – *1001 Arabian Nights* is an obvious precedent – and includes an array of figures whose power is associated with the east: khalifs, sultans, khedives, a Jewish field marshal, a Great Mogul, even a Grand Vezier. In the chapter "Der Khedive," the name for an Egyptian prince,

Tino enters a foreign kingdom along with her companion, Mohamed Pascha:

> He [Pascha] sits on his heavy elephant and rides above the motionless bodies of the dignitaries and slaves and they shall never forget the hour. And, until the moon sets, they must always speak his command, which turns in their mouths, a holy dance. And as the great caravan entered the green city and the *Volk* on the street asked the name of the princess [Tino] with the glittering eyes, they spoke the command of their master.[50]

Elevated above the people, his authority marked by a spatial distinction, the prince transmits his power through an aesthetic device that moves in the mouths of the otherwise motionless bodies – "a holy dance." At first the slaves and dignitaries – that is to say, those who must obey – are the elements on which Pascha exerts his power. But the force of that authority is immediately transferred to the *Volk*, which repeats the command of their master, or rather, their lord (*Herrn*). At the end of the chapter, alliances between the major characters are confirmed at a royal festival, where "the princes and princesses danced, and everyone in the palace danced right down to the goatherds. And the walls of the gardens began to turn and the entire city danced all the way to the banks of the river."[51] Instead of enforcing a constitutive distinction between master and slave, as in the case of the lordly Pascha, princes and princesses, upper classes and lower move as parts of the same harmonious dance. Even the city itself, its physical architecture of walls and gardens, spins in time with the music.

Besides thematizing circular motion, Lasker-Schüler cultivated the conciliatory ethos of the *Neue Gemeinschaft* as Peter Hille himself pointed out in a famous essay of 1902. Now known mainly for Hille's characterization of Lasker-Schüler as "the black swan of Israel," a phrase that did much to establish her reputation as a spokesperson for Jewish culture in Germany, the essay is in fact more invested in identifying a cultural synthesis in Lasker-Schüler's work.[52] Hille proclaims in his emphatic style that she "romps about with the august Jahweh." But he immediately adds that she is "touched by something like German folkways [*Volksweise*]." It is as though her verses come "from a book of fairy tales." So Lasker-Schüler merges Judaism with a sensibility attuned to the German *Volk*. She marries Jewish and German traditions, here equated with the genre of fairy tales, into a distinctive folk hybrid. Gottfried Benn, writing half a century later, expounded on the same cultural synthesis in a lecture devoted to Lasker-Schüler's poetic legacy. Referring to the poem "Mein Volk," which we will have occasion to analyze later, Benn detects "a complete fusion of the Jewish and the German; it is the expression of a true community of being at the highest level."⁵³ Whether Benn knows it or not, he is relying on the letter and the spirit of the *Neue Gemeinschaft*. He finds the expression of a communal essence that fuses distinct cultural traditions to produce a higher collective ideal – an *Übervolk*, as it were.

Such a poetics of reconciliation, present if not yet fully developed in *Styx*, came to fruition in the subsequent collections *Der Siebente Tag* [The Seventh Day, 1905] and *Meine Wunder* [My Miracles, 1911], titles that signal both the leisure and creative license of a Judeo-Christian God. A poem like "Wir Beide [We Both]" represents reconciliation as a state of prelapsarian bliss:

> The evening wafts longing out of sweetened blossoms,
> And frost burns on the mountains like a silver diamond,
> And the heads of angels look over the strip of sky,
> And we are both in paradise.
>
> And to us belongs the whole colorful life,
> The great, blue picture-book with stars,
> With cloud animals that chase each other in the distance
> And hey! the circle winds that lift and spin us round!
>
> Our dear God dreams his child's dream
> Of Paradise – of his two playmates,
> And the great flowers look on from their thorny branches . . .
>
> The darkened earth still hung green on the tree.
>
> [Der Abend weht Sehnen aus Blütensüße,
> Und auf den Bergen brennt wie Silberdiamant der Reif,
> Und Engelköpfchen gucken überm Himmelstreif,
> Und wir beide sind im Paradiese.
>
> Und uns gehört das ganze bunte Leben,
> Das blaue, große Bilderbuch mit Sternen,
> Mit Wolkentieren, die sich jagen in den Fernen
> Und hei! die Kreiselwinde, die uns drehn und heben!
>
> Der liebe Gott träumt seinen Kindertraum
> Vom Paradies – von seinen zwei Gespielen,
> Und große Blumen sehn an von Dornenstielen . . .
>
> Die düstere Erde hing noch grün am Baum.]

In the first stanza, a union is achieved through a blending of the senses. Sensory differences are overcome as scent mingles with taste in the first line, "sweetened blossoms." Sight is then fused with touch in the second: ice that burns like a diamond. By the third line, though, synesthesia has given way to the optical register since angel-voyeurs gaze into paradise, where they witness a condition of prelapsarian union. The characters of the poem – the implied referents of the pronoun *we* – are in paradise, a place of circling winds and dreams of children. They reside there as though it is their home. At the same time, the poem suggests that paradise is itself a state of being together – the condition before the fall into strife and contradiction, which plagues those who have eaten from the tree of knowledge.

In a letter to Julius Hart from 1900, Lasker-Schüler confesses that "Eden was too small for me" – she is referring to the *Neue Gemeinschaft* – "and not the true paradise."⁵⁴ Even though she remained in touch with the community through at least 1902, her attention increasingly turned to the cafés of Berlin, where she would leave her mark as one of the city's foremost bohemians and a fixture on the Expressionist scene. It is therefore appropriate, by way of concluding this section, to turn to a poem that captures the conciliatory ethos of the *Neue Gemeinschaft* while looking forward to the decade that would define Lasker-Schüler as an Expressionist poet: "Versöhnungstag," which can be translated as "Day of Reconciliation," or, in a more ethnic vein, as "Day of Atonement," that is, Yom Kippur. First published in *Der Sturm* in 1910, the poem was later collected in *Hebrew Ballads* as "Versöhnung" and then in *Das Hebräerland* (1937), Lasker-Schüler's travelogue written after a stint in Palestine, where it appears under its original title:

> A great star will fall in my lap . . .
> We want to wake the night,
>
> And pray in languages
> That are carved like harps.
>
> We want to reconcile the night –
> So much God overflows.
>
> Children are our hearts,
> They wish to rest tiredsweet.
>
> And our lips wish to kiss,
> Why do you hesitate?
>
> Does my heart not verge onto yours –
> Your blood colors my cheeks red.
>
> We want to reconcile the night,
> If we embrace, we do not die.

A great star will fall in my lap.

[Es wird ein großer Stern in meinen Schoß fallen ...
Wir wollen wachen die Nacht,

In den Sprachen beten
Die wie Harfen eingeschnitten sind.

Wir wollen uns versöhnen die Nacht –
So viel Gott strömt über.

Kinder sind unsere Herzen,
Die möchten ruhen müdesüß.

Und unsere Lippen wollen sich küssen,
Was zagst du?

Grenzt nicht mein Herz an deins –
Immer färbt dein Blut meine Wangen rot.

Wir wollen uns versöhnen die Nacht,
Wenn wir uns herzen, sterben wir nicht.

Es wird ein großer Stern in meinen Schoß fallen.]

With a rough-hewn parataxis foreign to the mellifluousness of "Wir Beide," these couplets record a fall from grace. A single star lands in the lap of the speaker, intimating a loss of innocence. In this world, as opposed to paradise, a moment of hesitation delays the kiss. One heart verges, or more literally borders (*grenzt*), on the heart of another. A distance now separates the subjects. *We both* have become *you and I*. Yet, in the last couplet, a moment of reconciliation is intimated: "If we embrace, we do not die." An act of union, the fusion of two into one, grants a moment, however fleeting, of immortality. The final line then completes the circle, ending the poem where it began.

Reconciliation is thus a restoration of prelapsarian wholeness. It is the experience of Eden in this world. If Lasker-Schüler practiced a form of messianic Expressionism, to return to Sokel's designation of the strain of Expressionist ideology that includes the discourse of the new human, she did so *avant-la-lettre*, before Expressionism coalesced into an artistic movement and in concert with the new humanist ideology of the *Neue Gemeinschaft*. But her poetics of reconciliation, especially the reconciliation of cultural traditions, persisted into the following decade, the decade of Expressionism, even as the spirit of renewal and the optimism of the *Neue Gemeinschaft* was shattered by the reality of world war and genuine political revolution.

5.2   Reconciliation and Reciprocity

Since advances in the visual arts preceded the rise of literary Expressionism, debates about modernist painting set the parameters for the reception of Expressionist writing in Germany, including for Lasker-Schüler, who was both an accomplished artist and the friend of progressive painters like Oskar Kokoschka and Franz Marc. The inception of modern art in Germany can be dated to the 1890s and the creation of organizations, known as secessions, designed to act as institutional counterweights to the academies that had traditionally supported artistic production in the German states. According to Peter Paret, a crucial juncture for the establishment of the Berlin Secession arose when the *Verein Berliner Künstler*, a body with close ties to the Prussian Academy of Fine Arts, invited Edvard Munch to present his work in Berlin – without, however, being acquainted with Munch's heterodox style. After conservatives led by the emperor's favorite Anton von Werner saw the paintings and voted to close the show, a substantial minority of *Verein* members protested, causing a schism that would culminate in the formation of the Berlin Secession in 1898.[55] For the next decade and a half, the Secession would be a bulwark for modern art in the capital and, by extension, for Germany as a whole.

The reasons for the split between Academy and Secession ran deeper than disagreements about style. Although the tension between academic realists and modernists who favored an assertive use of color and the disruption of line associated with French Impressionism was considerable, not all secessionists were modernists.[56] Some were stylistically quite conservative, and Paret argues that many were simply fed up with exhibition practices based on an annual salon that prioritized commerce over culture and the welfare of the mass of painters trained according to Academy standards over individual talent.[57] Secession exhibitions, which began in 1899, observed a curatorial ethos intended to promote a more reflective viewing environment by limiting the number of works on display. Informed viewership was cultivated in equal measure by Paul Cassirer, the influential gallerist who managed the Secession's business affairs and became a prominent advocate for modern art in the early decades of the century (he would later preside over a publishing house that issued Lasker-Schüler's collected works). Shows at the Cassirer gallery would pair secessionist painters like Max Liebermann or Walter Leistikow with interlocutors from abroad such as Renoir and Degas, effectively educating the public about modern art in a cosmopolitan setting that provided an escape from the bustle of the salon. Writing in 1910, Lasker-Schüler reports on a

Kokoschka show at the Cassirer gallery that signaled the rise of a new generation of painters, a generation that would come to be called Expressionist, who would eventually eclipse the Secession and the Impressionist style of its leading members.[58]

Lasker-Schüler's emergence as a poet coincided with the period of the Secession's greatest influence – approximately, the turn of the century to the onset of World War I – and her connections with the organization were myriad. In the mid-1890s, before the Secession was formally established, she studied drawing with Simson Goldberg, a rabbi who had resettled in Berlin to pursue an artistic career that included training with both Liebermann and Werner.[59] According to Lasker-Schüler, "Prof. Liebermann considered him [Goldberg] the best technical draftsman in Berlin."[60] She also recalled trips with Goldberg to the Berlin Zoo, where the two would observe "the exotic shows of peoples [*exotischen Völkerschau*]" that were displayed alongside the exhibitions of animals.[61] Hence the illustrations that accompany Lasker-Schüler's later writings, often orientalist sketches in a loose impressionist style, have a visual pedigree that can be traced through Goldberg to the Secession and its leading protagonists. After her marriage to Walden in 1903, she would have had contact with the Secession through the *Verein für Kunst*, which hosted lectures by the curator and critic Harry Graf Kessler, an important supporter of the Secession, and Lovis Corinth, a prominent Secessionist and director of the group following Liebermann's resignation in 1910.[62]

At around this time, the old guard of Impressionists were beginning to feel the pressure of the younger Expressionist generation. After a Secession jury rejected a group of painters for its 1910 exhibition, the offended parties responded by forming a splinter group, the New Secession, that staged their own show in 1911 (Lasker-Schüler mentions the show twice in the *Letters to Norway*).[63] It was in this context that "Expressionism" entered critical discourse. At first the term was used to refer to a group of French painters, Braque and Picasso among others, who were featured in the 1911 Secession exhibition.[64] Soon though Expressionism came to stand for a general wave of artistic innovation that encompassed the New Secession, the Dresden-based Brücke group, and the Blauer Reiter in Munich.[65] Accordingly, "Expressionism" is best understood as a generational designation. It denotes a second phase of modernist panting that reacted against the initial Impressionist break with realism.

For better or for worse, stylistic attributes were quickly attributed to Expressionism. As its name implies, Expressionism signals a departure from the phenomenological representation of nature, taken to be quintessentially Impressionist and epitomized by *plein-air* painting, in favor of a greater degree of abstraction meant to reflect internal states and moods.[66] In this respect, Van Gogh, who was an important influence on the Expressionist prose of Carl Sternheim, can be considered as marking an important transition, though similar tendencies were already present in Munch.[67] Put simply, Impressionism signified a move *from* the external world *to* internal phenomena. Expressionists moved in the other direction: from the inner to the outer. Kurt Hiller, though he was referring chiefly to literary Expressionism, articulates the position with trenchancy, recalling the doubts voiced by T. S. Eliot regarding Symons and aesthetic criticism:

> Those aesthetes who only know how to react, who are only wax plates for impressions [*Eindrücke*] and finely-tuned description machines, (just like the "pure theorists" in philosophy), seem to us to be genuinely inferior. We are Expressionists [*Expressionisten*]. For us it's all about content, desire, ethos.[68]

Not satisfied with reproducing their impressions of the world, Expressionists projected the sheer pathos of inner experience onto the canvas or, later, onto the page.

The critical disputes that had animated the reception of German Impressionism reignited against modern art, Expressionism included, when over a hundred artists contributed to a polemic led by the landscape painter Carl Vinnen.[69] Even though Vinnen labors to give due credit to foreign influences in the introduction to his rabidly anti-modernist *Protest deutscher Künstler* (1911), his real aim is to attack what he saw as the perniciousness of French style, which he construed as being devoted to superficiality and mere appearance whereas "the characteristic of our *Volk*," he avers, is disposed instead to "depth, fantasy, sensitivity of the soul," a strangely inapposite assertion since Expressionism, as we have just seen, was taken to be a turn to inwardness that, by Vinnen's lights, should comport with this stereotype of Teutonic profundity.[70] In any event, Vinnen believed that the threat posed by international modernism was comprehensive: "where foreign influences wish not only to improve, but also to change from the ground up, there lies a great danger for our people [*Volkstum*]." Rather than try to derive a so-called Nordic modernism from the work of Expressionists like Emil Nolde, as Goebbels would later do, Vinnen hews to a more reactionary position. He unites nation and *Volk* in the service of a cultural conservatism opposed to aesthetes (*Ästheten*) and other elites who were thought to stifle native intuitions in the arts.

The ideological fissures in this reception history, which would culminate in National Socialism's disdain for *Entartete Kunst* and so-called Asphalt Literature, were already implicit in the early reaction to the Berlin Secession. The fact that two Jews, Cassirer and Liebermann, directed the Secession had stoked antisemitic anxieties that merged with a Prussian national pride skeptical if not downright hostile to influence from abroad, especially France, the nation's adversary in the Franco-Prussian war.[71] Thus it should come as no surprise that established defenders of modern art like Liebermann and Cassirer quickly countered Vinnen with the *Answer to the "Protest of German Artists"* (1911). The younger generation of Expressionists, no less hostile to Vinnen's retrograde views, contributed to the response as well. Marc, for instance, chides Vinnen for waving "the flag of Germanness and the art of the homeland" and celebrates the influence from abroad.[72]

Lasker-Schüler, no stranger to antisemitism herself, was not shielded from these currents in German culture.[73] Setting aside the racist abuse she would suffer at the hands of the *Völkischer Beobachter* after receiving the Kleist Prize in 1932, Lasker-Schüler was smeared in a 1911 article that accused her of "total softening of the brain [*vollständige Gehirnerweichung*]," a slight that targets the supposed decadence of modern art and hints at the syphilitic symptoms associated with the moral looseness of the city.[74] Even a friend like Marc, whose relationship with Lasker-Schüler had cooled by the time of his death in 1916, would comment in a letter to his wife that Lasker-Schüler is not "hysterical or neurotic, – for that, she's too gifted; but she's long past her prime, overgrown and wild, 'decayed' [*entartet*]" – a pointed irony given that Marc's work was included in the infamous *Entartete Kunst* exhibition held by the Nazis in 1937.[75] Thus the atmosphere surrounding the reception of modern art in Germany, charged as it was with both nationalist and racialist currents, did not subside in the decades after Expressionism. On the contrary, many of the arguments later used in the fascist reaction against modernism were honed in the debates from earlier in the century.

Even though Expressionism had its roots in the visual arts, it soon encompassed both painting and literature, with the term signifying a generational break with earlier styles of modernist writing in the same way that Expressionist painters were seen as taking leave from Impressionism. Literary Expressionism, especially for those writers born in the late 1880s and 1890s, departed from two currents in the initial wave of modern literature: naturalism on the one hand, especially the works of Henrik Ibsen and Gerhart Hauptmann, and *fin-de-siècle* tendencies such as

Jugendstil on the other. While individual Expressionists retained features of those earlier movements – Döblin developed a hard-edged descriptive style shorn of psychological inwardness that recalled naturalist modes; Lasker-Schüler never quite shed all of her connections with *Jugendstil* – the overall trajectory of Expressionism was away from the probing social commentaries and predominantly realist style of naturalism, and the filigreed refinement of what Symons would have called the decadent movement in German art. Instead Expressionists ventured a more emotionally bracing, morally strident reckoning with the psycho-social condition of modernity.

Hiller was the first to use the term "Expressionist" in a literary context (quoted earlier) when referring to a group of Berlin writers around the *Neue Club* and the *Neopathetische Cabaret*, two key arenas for the development of German Expressionism. Writing for *Der Sturm* in 1910, Lasker-Schüler describes an evening at the *Cabaret*. "Suddenly, up fluttered a raven, a shining black head that looked darkly over the edge of the pulpit. Jakob van?"[76] Though she failed to catch the name of the promising young talent, Lasker-Schüler is surely referring to Jakob van Hoddis, the writer whom Hiller nominated as a leading example of Expressionist verse in 1913.[77] Kurt Pinthus was no less aware of van Hoddis's importance, despite the brevity of a career cut short by a schizophrenic break (van Hoddis was later deported, as Patient No. 8 of the Bendorf-Sayn Asylum, and murdered by the Nazis).[78] Pinthus chose van Hoddis's "Weltende" (1911) to open *Menschheitsdämmerung*:

> The man's hat flies off his pointed head,
> The airs echo as though with cries.
> Roofers fall and break in two,
> And on the coasts – one reads – the tide is rising.
>
> The storm is here, the wild seas leap up
> On land, and smash the thick dams.
> Most people have a cold.
> The trains fall from bridges.
>
> [Dem Bürger fliegt vom spitzen Kopf der Hut,
> In allen Lüften hallt es wie Geschrei.
> Dachdecker stürzen ab und gehn entzwei,
> Und an den Küsten – liest man – steigt die Flut.
>
> Der Sturm ist da, die wilden Meere hupfen
> An Land, um dicke Dämme zu zerdrücken.
> Die meisten Menschen haben einen Schnupfen.
> Die Eisenbahnen fallen von den Brücken.][79]

With lines whose velocity mimics the urgency of the scene and a miasma of thickening anxiety hanging over the urban landscape, "Weltende" does well to capture the Expressionist mood. But despite the finality implied by the poem's title, "End of the World," there are signs, however faint, of the rebirth and renewal associated with the discourse of the *neuer Mensch*.[80] The destruction in the poem is resolutely future-oriented. The storm has arrived but not yet ended; the rising tide suggests patterns of growth and decay; a disease afflicts most humans, to be sure, but not all. Some might survive the apocalypse, just not the ridiculous *Bürger* in the first line. The end of this world does not preclude the rise of another, a better one.

Lasker-Schüler's "Weltende" strikes a more meditative tone than van Hoddis's trumpet blasts of urban modernity. Though it was originally collected in an anthology of modern German verse published in 1903, Lasker-Schüler's poem retained enough subversive force for Karl Kraus to claim it could "elicit a smirk from the rationalized visage of the German observer of art" when he reprinted "Weltende" in *Die Fackel* in 1910, only three months before van Hoddis's poem of the same name appeared in *Der Demokrat*.[81]

> There is a weeping in the world,
> as though our beloved God has died,
> and the leaden shadows that fall,
> weigh graveheavy.
>
> Come, we want to hide ourselves closer . . .
> Life lies in all hearts
> As though in coffins.
>
> You, we wish for a deep kiss . . .
> A longing pounds on the world,
> on which we must die.
>
> [Es ist ein Weinen in der Welt,
> als ob der liebe Gott gestorben wär,
> und der bleierne Schatten, der niederfällt,
> lastet grabesschwer.
>
> Komm, wir wollen uns näher verbergen . . .
> Das Leben liegt in aller Herzen
> wie in Särgen.
>
> Du, wir wollen uns tief küssen . . .
> Es pocht eine Sehnsucht an die Welt,
> an der wir sterben müssen.]

If van Hoddis's world ends in calamity, strife and transgression – the image of "roofers falling down and splitting in two"; the seas leaping up onto land and breaking the boundaries that divide water from earth, "the thick dams" – Lasker-Schüler's eschatology, by contrast, evinces the spiritual erotics familiar from her early work. The poem concludes with two lovers meeting in a kiss, or at least the wish for it, an erotic reconciliation that acts as a consolation for the finitude of this world.

In the years before World War I, the coterie of intellectuals and artists associated with the *Neopathetische Cabaret* found their home in the cafés of Berlin, where Lasker-Schüler was a key member of the circle around *Der Sturm*, the journal Walden founded in 1910 and turned into a leading venue for Expressionist art. Besides publishing occasional essays by his wife and longer prose like the *Letters to Norway*, Walden featured much of Lasker-Schüler's poetry written between 1910 and 1912, the year the couple divorced after ten years of marriage.[82] Yet, Lasker-Schüler was also something of an outsider on the Expressionist scene, having established herself as a poet in the previous decade. Both van Hoddis and Georg Trakl, a friend and correspondent until his own untimely death, were eighteen years her junior. Benn, who became the object of her affections following her split with Walden, was seventeen years younger. Walden himself was a decade younger than his wife.

More than her age, Lasker-Schüler's gender marked her out from contemporaries. As the only woman included in *Menschheitsdämmerung*, her place in the Expressionist canon is beyond dispute, though she was not the only woman to have shaped the development of German Expressionism. Emmy Hennings and Claire Goll are two other well-known examples, and even during her *Neue Gemeinschaft* days Lasker-Schüler was one of several women who read their poems at community gatherings.[83] Lasker-Schüler's relationship to first-wave feminism, however, was ambivalent at best.[84] Christanne Miller has shown that Lasker-Schüler maintained a muted distance to the women's rights movement, but it needs to be acknowledged that she did at times stake out more progressive positions on issues affecting the welfare of women.[85] During the Weimar Republic, for example, she opposed a controversial abortion law, commenting that "only female judges should decide about these paragraphs, since obviously *men have never in their lives brought a child to term*" [emphasis original].[86]

To be sure, Lasker-Schüler failed to conform to the more mainstream feminist movement that was available to her at the time. Miller argues that instead of aligning herself with first-wave feminism, Lasker-Schüler adopted various gender-bending personae that may have been a means of self-assertion in an otherwise male-dominated environment.[87] The poet's most famous alter-ego was Jussuf Prince of Thebes, a name she used in everyday discourse as well as in her published writings (*Der Prinz von Theben* is the title of a collection of stories published in 1914). Miller discusses other male names used by Lasker-Schüler over the course of her career, though, curiously, she does not mention the poet's decision to retain her maiden name upon her first marriage to Berthold Lasker. Itself a masculinized noun for *schoolchild* (as opposed to *Schülerin*), "Schüler" was the second half of the hyphenate that would be the poet's legal name for the rest of her life. In this context, it is worth quoting the application submitted by the *Staatspolizei* to the *SS* in 1938 to revoke Lasker-Schüler's citizenship:

> The Jewish emigrant Else Lasker [*sic*] possesses German nationality. She was a typical representative of the "emancipated woman" that appeared in the post-war period. Through lectures and writings she attempted to disparage the spiritual and moral value of the German woman.
>
> Following the seizure of power she fled to Zürich, where she expressed her anti-German attitude by circulating horror stories [*Greuelmärchen*]. She continued writing and publishing articles in the famously anti-German *Pariser Tageblatt*. Furthermore, she published writings in the anti-German *Oprecht Press* in Zürich, whose entire production stands on the list of disgraceful and undesirable literature.
>
> Therefore I propose revoking the citizenship of the Jew Else Lasker [*sic*].[88]

Along with robbing Lasker-Schüler of her German patronymic, this letter winds gender, race and nation into a single thread of odium. But what seems to worry the author even more than the unspecified "*Greuelmärchen*" that Lasker-Schüler supposedly spread during her time in Switzerland is the threat she posed to German womanhood – that is, the way that she embodied the liberatory promise of the "new woman." Through her decision to live as an emancipated woman, placed in scare quotes in the original, Lasker-Schüler jeopardized the moral standing of German society.

Gender was certainly a factor in the reception of Lasker-Schüler's poetry among more reliable critics. Benn, whose affair with National Socialism will be a topic for Chapter 6, held her in genuine esteem. He dedicated *Söhne* (1913) to Lasker-Schüler with a quotation from *Mein Herz*, the book version of the *Letters to Norway*. Decades later, Benn would write that she was "the greatest lyricist Germany ever had," praise tempered

somewhat by the use of the feminized noun *Lyrikerin*, roughly equivalent
to "poetess," which consigns her to a more minor category in the history of
Germany verse.[89] Hiller provides a still more infelicitous example. In his
essay "Meetings with Expressionists," Hiller boldly schematizes all poetry
according to three criteria: the sensual, the sentimental and the mental.
"By our honored Else," Hiller writes in a tone whose familiarity shades
into condescension, "the third, the mental, is lacking."[90] So Lasker-Schüler
is regarded as a mere poet of feeling while Stefan George and Goethe are
said to exemplify all three categories. One of Lasker-Schüler's most avid
supporters was Kraus, who called her "the strongest and most unavoidable
lyric event of modern Germany," an estimation untarnished by the gendered limitations of Hiller and Benn.[91] Kraus considered "Ein alter
Tibettepich [An Old Tibetan Carpet]," published in *Der Sturm* in 1910,
one of the finest poems in the history of German verse:

> Your soul, the one in love with mine
> Is wound with it in a carpet-Tibet
>
> Ray in ray, besotted hues,
> Stars, that woo each other heavenwards.
>
> Our feet rest on that luxuriousness
> Stitches thousands yet thousands long.
>
> Sweet Lama's son on that herbal scented throne
> How long then does your mouth kiss mine
> Cheek to cheek through those color-woven times.
>
> [Deine Seele, die die meine liebet
> Ist verwirkt mit ihr im Teppichtibet
>
> Strahl in Strahl, verliebte Farben,
> Sterne, die sich himmellang umwarben.
>
> Unsere Füsse ruhen auf der Kostbarkeit
> Maschentausendabertausendweit.
>
> Süsser Lamasohn auf Moschuspflanzentron
> Wie lange küsst dein Mund den meinen wohl
> Und Wang die Wange buntgeknüpfte Zeiten schon.]

One would be hard pressed to find a more consummate union of headlong
formal experimentation – flagrant neologisms, acute parataxis, outrageous
inversions – with an erotism of such a pure distillate – true modernist love.

Lasker-Schüler's efforts to fuse Jewish culture and modern German
verse culminated in 1913 with *Hebrew Ballads*, which was published by

A. R. Meyer in Berlin, also the publisher of Benn's *Söhne* and the *Futuristische Dichtungen* (1912) of Filippo Marinetti.[92] Bringing together new poems with work that had already appeared in earlier books and journals, *Hebrew Ballads* consists mainly of religious portraits – all but four of the twenty poems take up characters from the Old Testament – including biblical women who anchor the book's second half: Abigail, Esther, Ruth and Sulamith. But these are portraits only in the loosest sense. Rather the characters are templates for Lasker-Schüler's variations on a mood. Bauschinger notes, for example, that a poem like "Ruth" shares little with the biblical figure other than its name:[93]

> And you look for me before the gates.
> I hear your steps sigh
> And my eyes are heavy dark drops.
>
> Your glances bloom sweet in my soul
> And fill up,
> When my eyes change into sleep.
>
> On the well of my homeland
> Stands an angel,
> He sings the song of my love,
> He sings the song of Ruth.
>
> [Und du suchst mich vor den Hecken.
> Ich höre deine Schritte seufzen
> Und meine Augen sind schwere dunkle Tropfen.
>
> In meiner Seele blühen süß deine Blicke
> Und füllen sich,
> wenn meine Augen in den Schlaf wandeln.
>
> Am Brunnen meiner Heimat
> Steht ein Engel,
> Der singt das Lied meiner Liebe,
> Der singt das Lied Ruths.]

In the poem, love and religious ardor are mutually reinforcing emotions. The final lines, which achieve an incantatory force altogether absent in an early poem like "Volkslied," combine excess and repetition by breaking the bounds of the stacked, three-line stanzas – the form of "Volkslied" and the most common stanza in *Hebrew Ballads*. The angel first sings the song of love. Then, in substituting "Ruth" for *Liebe*, the poem identifies its female protagonist with eros itself.

In titling her collection *Hebrew Ballads*, Lasker-Schüler again signals her fondness for popular traditions, in this case the tradition of balladry associated with arch-Romantic collections of folk art like *Des Knaben Wunderhorn*, the Ossian poems or, indeed, the tales gathered by the Brothers Grimm. That said, the poems have little, if any, connection with the ballad form, strictly defined. In the same way that biblical figures are a backdrop for the characters in *Hebrew Ballads*, balladry is relevant for its ability to conjure the spirit of popular art, not its instantiation of a particular verse form. Thus it is fitting that Lasker-Schüler chose the poem "Mein Volk [My People]," which had already appeared in *Der Siebente Tag*, as the first poem in a volume devoted to the art of the people:

> The rock is rotting,
> from which I spring
> And sing my hymns . . .
> Suddenly I fall from the path
> And, wholly within myself, trickle
> down, alone over mourning stones
> To the sea.
>
> So I've flowed away
> from my blood's
> Musted-ferment.
> And always, always still the echo
> In me,
> When, horribly, toward the east
> The rotten rock-bone,
> My people,
> Cries to God.
>
> [Der Fels wird morsch,
> Dem ich entspringe
> Und meine Gotteslieder singe . . .
> Jäh stürz ich vom Weg
> Und riesele ganz in mir
> Fernab, allein über Klagegestein
> Dem Meer zu.
>
> Hab mich so abgeströmt
> Von meines Blutes
> Mostvergorenheit.
> Und immer, immer noch der Widerhall
> In mir,
> Wenn schauerlich gen Ost
> Das morsche Felsgebein,
> Mein Volk,
> Zu Gott schreit.]

The poem begins with the genesis of a lyric subject. A rotting rock, symbol of the Jewish people, gives birth to a singer who sings the songs of God. Yet any signs of independence in this opening are illusory since, in fact, the birth inaugurates a logic whereby the whole entity, the *Volk*, and one of its constituent parts, the poet, are united in bonds of mutual possession. In the language of the poem, *people* is the object of the possessive pronoun *my*. "Mein Volk" makes the people belong to the poet. However the title is also a self-declaration of membership. The poet belongs to the people. Thus in "Mein Volk" the bonds between poet and *Volk* are reciprocal – both belong to each other.

The possessive pronoun *my* marks the most emphatic statements of possession in "Mein Volk," but the negotiation between whole and part assumes other forms in the poem. In the second half of the first stanza, the singer abruptly departs from a common course, "Suddenly I fall from the path." An allusion to the first lines of Dante's *Divine Comedy* – arguably the greatest poem of the Christian tradition, indicating Lasker-Schüler's continued interest in reconciliation – this passage signals a departure from a shared path of righteousness while at the same time initiating another transformation in the constitution of the lyric subject. Originally sprung from stone, the subject assumes a different physical state by the end of the stanza. The self becomes liquid, a transubstantiation that occurs as an internal event, "wholly in myself." Thus transformed from solid to liquid, the subject is thereupon compelled by an external force, gravity, which draws the flowing self down over "mourning stones," or more properly "wailing stones [*Klagegesteine*]," in a course toward the sea – a totality that would absorb the solitary speaker into its greater body. Once again, the part flows back to the whole. The concluding lines then reiterate, or rather echo, that directionality: "Zu Gott schreit" compared with "Dem Meer zu." In the final gesture, the *Volk* projects its cries out toward its lord. It emits a sound that is more than mere noise but not quite song. A poetics of the *Volk*, at least as it manifests in "Mein Volk," consists of the divergences and convergences between part and whole, individual and collective: the self that streams away from the blood but back to the sea; the singer that departs from, but returns to, the collective body; a *Volk* that declines but seeks communion with God.

* * *

In leaning east while crying to God, "Mein Volk" employs a classic Expressionist trope, the primal scream of humanity, in order to convey the condition of the Jewish people. Neil Donahue points out that the Expressionist cry, canonically rendered by Munch and adapted for the stage by Expressionist dramatists, represented the "rage and revolt" epitomized by "the central Expressionist theme of the reborn 'New Man.'"[94] Donahue's gendered translation of *Mensch* notwithstanding, the scream is at once a cry of protest and an utterance expressing the more fundamental longings of a self straining for life. For her part, Lasker-Schüler bends this trope to the purposes of a new *Volk* rather than the *neuer Mensch*. She imagines her own people, the Jews, as it strives for spiritual renewal.

In giving the cry an easterly orientation, Lasker-Schüler introduces a host of cultural-geographical allusions: to the flight of the Israelites from Egypt; or to Adam and Eve's original banishment from paradise. The conclusion also looks forward to a paradise, of sorts, that was in the process of being regained: Palestine, the promised land, a place that would exert an increasing hold on Lasker-Schüler's literary imagination in the latter half of her life (her productive years align, roughly, with the period from the first Zionist conference, held in 1897, to the foundation of the State of Israel in 1948). Of course these allusions to the east contribute to a broader orientalist sensibility that pervaded her work from the start. An early poem like "Sulamith," for example, ends by conjuring the "evening colors of Jerusalem." *Die Nächte Tino von Bagdads* revels in its oriental settings. Lasker-Schüler even published a scenario for a silent film in 1914 titled *Plumm-Pascha: An Oriental Comedy.*

Although she practices an ebullient brand of Orientalism, Lasker-Schüler cannot be fit into the interpretive schemas descending from Edward Said through postcolonial criticism – at least not without remainder. The most salient incongruity arises from Said's omission of German Orientalism from his classic study, an aporia that Said himself concedes but justifies by subordinating Germany to its European neighbors, England and France, whose extensive colonial holdings provide a better illustration of the entanglement of academic Orientalism with power relations arising between colonizer and colonized.[95] Suzanne Marchand has recently leveraged the history of German Orientalism into a forceful response to Said, arguing that the institutional situation of Germany – the specifics of its colonial exposure; the proximity of biblical scholarship and orientalist studies at the universities – inspired a range of political positions, some conservative but others critical, that need not be construed as inescapably complicit in the institutionalization of empire.[96]

To be sure, Anglo-French Orientalism did leave its mark on German Expressionism. One of the most important genealogies for Expressionist prose runs from Gustave Flaubert, especially *Salammbô*, through Filippo Marinetti's *Mafarka – Le Futuriste: un roman Africain* (1910).[97] With its nod to Flaubert's Carthaginian novel in its subtitle, *Mafarka* then influenced writers of the *Sturm* circle like Alfred Döblin, who called *Die drei Sprünge des Wang-Lun* (1916) "ein chinesischer Roman [a Chinese novel]" in recognition of his debts to both Flaubert and Marinetti. Although she was well situated to absorb these influences, Lasker-Schüler took a different tack with her representations of "the Orient." Despite knowing Döblin from his association with *Der Sturm* (he appears on two occasions in the *Letters to Norway*), she chose the genres of fantasy and folktale as her vehicles for the east rather than the historical novel, which Döblin used for *Die drei Sprünge* and Flaubert for *Salammbô*. And while she must have been familiar with *Mafarka* – Walden apparently had an agreement with Marinetti to translate the novel, though the project never came to fruition – she draws on biblical and Judaic traditions, "the evening colors of Jerusalem," rather than the overtly colonial vocabulary of Marinetti (or Flaubert for that matter).[98] Of course these idiosyncrasies do not mean that Lasker-Schüler was insulated from more familiar forms of Orientalism. She paraded around Berlin in fanciful eastern costumes while calling herself Jussuf Prince of Thebes. Rude as those cliches may have been, they were combined with German and Jewish traditions to make an eclectic Orientalism irreducible to a strict Anglo-French lineage or to the tropes passed from Flaubert through Futurism.

Die drei Sprünge and *Mafarka*, touchstone novels of Expressionism and Futurism, respectively, are important for other reasons, not least for their canonical examples of modernist "new humans": Wang-Lun, the charismatic leader of a religious movement on the order of Petrus and Zarathustra; Gazurmah, the machine-man sired by Mafarka to epitomize the conquest of technology over nature.[99] Each of these new humans has analogues in Lasker-Schüler's writing, and we have already seen how Petrus heralds the secular religion of the *Neue Gemeinschaft*. Charismatic messianism manifests in another Petrus-like figure, the rabbi Eleasar, who is the protagonist of the short story *Der Wunderrabbiner von Barcelona* [The Miracle-Rabbi of Barcelona], which Lasker-Schüler published with Cassirer in 1921. Set in medieval Barcelona when the city was known as a haven of religious tolerance, *Der Wunderrabbiner* begins by disabusing its reader of expectations to multicultural comity. After an opening lyric titled "Gott hör [God hear]" – an evocation, perhaps, of the cries uttered at the end of "Mein Volk" – the narrative begins by relating the racial strife between Jews and Christians:

> The population of Barcelona busied itself persecuting the Jews in the weeks that Eleasar spent piously contemplating in Old-Asia. It was them again, the ones that hindered the trade of Spanish merchants with inflated prices, and at the same time made themselves known with their messianic spirit among the city's lower, poor classes. Apostle figures preached equality and brotherhood and they broke their heart in their breast and gave it to the poor like Jesus of Nazareth shared with them the bread of his heart.[100]

Respected by Barcelona's Christians and revered by his congregants, Eleasar is the crux of a fragile peace in the city. When he departs for his annual pilgrimage to "Old-Asia," a designation that combines both space and time while shifting the locus of action from west to east, his absence catalyzes the antagonisms between the Spanish merchants, elsewhere identified as Christian, and the Jews who spread their message of equality and brotherhood among the poor, or rather, the "lower classes." Thus Eleasar embodies the conciliatory spirit of the *Neue Gemeinschaft*. He is the talisman that holds the city together despite its "divisions of race, status, ethnicity," to recall the social categories of Heinrich Hart. This conciliatory ethos is then confirmed by two youths whose love transcends differences of creed: Pablo, the son of Barcelona's Christian mayor, and Amram, "a poet [*Dichterin*] among the Jewish people" and a clear avatar for the author.[101]

Compared to Lasker-Schüler's earlier prose, particularly a text like "Petrus and the Workers," *Der Wunderrabbiner* unites class, religious, ethnic and national differences into a much tighter weave. Whereas Petrus resolved material grievances by transforming a group of agitating laborers into a "freedom hungry folk," *Der Wunderrabbiner* stages a series of conflicts between the Spanish bourgeoisie, the merchants who enjoy political representation by a Christian mayor and the Jews who find their home amid the working class. This retention of material distinctions reflects a broader shift in Lasker-Schüler's social consciousness in the years since *Das Peter Hille-Buch*. By the 1920s she had in fact become quite comfortable adopting the language of the left. For instance in 1925 she implored her fellow artists, "let's organize like the workers, let's make our art state-sponsored." This pronouncement, which appears in the essay *Ich räume auf! Meine Anklage gegen meine Verleger* [I'm Settling Up! My Charge against My Publishers], was prompted by a falling out between Lasker-Schüler and Cassirer over what the author perceived to be exploitative practices in the publishing industry. Yet the essay soon leaves off from airing personal grievances to stage a reckoning with the immiseration of artists in the Weimar Republic. If artists were to organize, Lasker-Schüler asserts, "all literatures would bestride the stage of the revolution like workers, would wear a red ribbon as an emblem of blood in our buttonholes."[102]

These revolutionary notes should not be taken to mean that Lasker-Schüler was following the path from Expressionism to Marxism charted by Johannes R. Becher, Bertolt Brecht or even Herwarth Walden, who perished in a Soviet labor camp after emigrating to escape the Nazis. For the most part Lasker-Schüler hewed to a form of apolitical bohemianism that was punctuated by outbursts of *Gefühlsozialismus,* to recall Adams's label for the poet's politics, or what Georg Lukács would have called bourgeois anti-capitalism. For instance, in a letter of 1937, she went so far as to assert that "I am unpolitical."[103] In the same year, she penned an open letter to the *Neue Zürchner Zeitung* following withering criticism of her play *Arthur Aronymus und seine Väter:* "It would never have occurred to me to be politically active in a host country," she admits rather defensively, "neither in actions nor in words nor in the flower of poetry." These denials of political commitment may have been motivated by the conditions of exile – Lasker-Schüler had fled to Switzerland in 1933 – when overt statements of political sympathy often entailed existential risk.[104] But they also reflect a more general disposition, tenacious but by no means absolute, to remain aloof from political affairs.

Whatever Lasker-Schüler's reluctance to involve herself in politics, the evidence of *Der Wunderrabbiner* demonstrates the entwinement of ethnic and material categories in her social imaginary. As the disjunctive plot of *Der Wunderrabbiner* unfolds, the narrator abruptly announces that "one day a large ship stood in the marketplace." This magical irruption of a ship into the narrative, which goes unexplained, leads to a crisis since "men, horses, and oxen were not able to move the mysterious vehicle out of the city, which disrupted the market and trade."[105] Once again a disruption to commerce contributes to a deterioration of relations between religions in the city. What began, however, as the persecution of Jews due to their apparent obstruction of trade becomes, by the end of the story, a holocaust of violence that claims the lives of Barcelona's Jews, their rabbi, as well as the city's Christians, who are destroyed when Eleasar pulls down the walls of a palace in the story's finale.

Since the presence of the ship in the marketplace has halted commerce, the mayor appeals to Eleasar for assistance in removing the magical vehicle from the city. When the rabbi refuses, the "mass of followers" that had been led by the mayor morphs into a confused Christian mob – "*die verwirrten Christen*" – that vents its rage against the Jews.[106] Unlike the crowd of workers in *Das Peter Hille-Buch* that is mollified through the combined efforts of Petrus and Sennulf, this mass of Christians reaches a point of inflection, whereupon violence can no longer be avoided. As a result, "in the night, the pogrom began":

> And all the Jews, who were always roused by the name of Jehovah, lay around on the streets, where the poor had been driven like cattle, mutilated, chewed up, faces separated from bodies, hands of children and little feet, most delicate human foliage.

With hands and feet strewn through the streets, the victims are scattered like leaves in the wind. Their bodies disintegrate. Faces are torn off, separated from the whole. These lurid images are reminiscent of the battle scenes and orgiastic frenzies of Döblin's *Die drei Sprünge*, where armies, crowds and other masses of individuals are made into the bearers of narrative action. This technique, where pluralities replace the self-reflective protagonist of the realist novel, was one of the key lessons Döblin learned from Marinetti and that Marinetti took from the battles of *Salammbô*.[107] Lasker-Schüler, for her part, also included brief scenes of combat in *Der Malik* (1919), the sequel to the *Letters to Norway*; but in *Der Wunderrabbiner*, she employs collective characterization for different ends: namely, to represent the perpetrators and the victims of social violence – the confused Christian mass, the "human foliage" spread in the streets, the poor herded like livestock through the city.

As if to stress the senselessness of the pogrom, the ship that was the ostensible cause of the violence has already made its miraculous departure from the market. While Amram and Pablo play onboard the vessel, "the immense ship, moved by love ... gently disappeared through the gate of the city like a ceremonious bridal car."[108] Thus the pogrom comes to pass when its cause has vanished but also, more to the point, when the conciliatory force of Amram and Pablo's love has left the scene. Eleasar, the other potential source of reconciliation, is absent too. Fleeing the violence, he takes refuge in a palace. There, alone, he reads from a holy book, *The Atlas of Creation*, that tells of the formation of the earth and its peoples. In other words, the rabbi and the reader escape ethnic violence by fleeing into a frame narrative, in this case, a creation myth:

> in the beginning the father pressed together the world from earth and water, his "wedding manna cake," with all the golden ingredients of his heavenly blood and that of men. He took the great worldly form and, with all his

might, produced therefrom the peoples and the peoplespeoples and the peoplespeoplespeoples and invited them all to a common meal.

[in der Anfänglichkeit der Vater aus Erde und Wasser die Welt, seinen "H ochzeitsmannahkuchen," ballte, mit allen goldenen Zutaten seines himm- lischen Blutes und des Menschen der großen Weltenform entnahm und aus ihm wieder mächtig holte die Völker und Völkervölker und Völkervölkervölker und lud sie ein alle zum gemeinsamen Mahle.][109]

The social tensions tearing apart Barcelona are resolved within the frame. A paternal demiurge takes human blood and mixes it with water and earth to make a "wedding cake" from which he draws the world's peoples. In this moment of Promethean fashioning, the religious leader Eleasar cedes his place as a "new human" to a still more primal *Urgestalt*, a true paternal God who synthesizes the various peoples while giving the world its shape. Julius Hart, in his peroration to "Der Neue Mensch," conjures the following figure as the apotheosis of his new humanist credo: "we call for the new human, the world-shaping! ... Center and circle, God and creator of things" (ellipsis original). In *Der Wunderrabbiner*, Lasker- Schüler answers that call. She imagines a deity who shapes the world and its peoples, its peoplespeoples, its peoplespeoplespeoples – an *Übervolk* rendered lexical. And whatever hint of separation may lurk in the distinc- tion between *Völker* and *Übervölker*, peoples and peoplespeoples, it is quickly removed by the concluding invitation to a common meal.

What of the center and circle? As the title of the creation myth indicates, the spatiality of Lasker-Schüler's new humanism has lost none of its purchase since her time with the Brothers Hart. *The Atlas of Creation* conceives of the formation of the cosmos as a spatial-geographical event – as something that can be recorded in an atlas. Further, the main story of *Der Wunderrabbiner*, not just the frame narrative, is organized according to its own spatial logic, where a European and ostensibly cosmopolitan metropolis, Barcelona, is counterposed to a distant site of religious pil- grimage, "Old-Asia." Such an arrangement, it bears noting, conforms to a conventional orientalist schema. At the same time, the usual ideological content of center and periphery has been reversed: "Old-Asia" is the origin and font of knowledge – the core, as it were – while Barcelona is the peripheral area belatedly declining into anarchy.

In his chapter-length study of *Der Wunderrabbiner*, Jonathan Skolnik argues that the spatial order of the story conforms to what Gilles Deleuze and Felix Guattari call "deterritorialization."[110] According to this model, Lasker-Schüler resists identifying a people, the Jews, with a particular territorial homeland, Palestine, and instead prefers language as the chief means for defining the group. Allison Schachter has made an analogous argument in more general terms by applying a "nonterritorial" paradigm to diasporic culture and Jewish writing in the modernist period.[111] For Schachter, language best captures the contours of the diaspora, not political territory, with the tension between Yiddish and Hebrew generating the main fault lines, not the vexed spatial or territorial claims associated with nationhood.

Even though the arguments of Schachter and Skolnik helpfully correct for a tendency to associate territoriality and Jewish modernism with the cultural politics of nationalist Zionism, *Der Wunderrabbiner von Barcelona* configures diasporic consciousness in emphatically spatial, indeed, territorial terms. For instance, the narrator states that Barcelona's Jews are "everywhere strewn [*Überall verstreut*]," thereby invoking the strict sense of diaspora as a spreading or dispersion in space (Gr. διασπορά, "scattering," from διασπείρω "to scatter," "to spread about," "to disperse," from σπείρω, "to sow," "to engender, beget," "to scatter like seed").[112] No incidental detail, this dispersion is inseparable from the historical subordination of European Jewry: "Everywhere strewn ... an entire *Volk*, humiliated for centuries" – humiliated, to be sure, and worse, as when the bodies of Jews are strewn through the streets of Barcelona like "human foliage."[113]

Of course, these moments of ethnic dispersion take their place in a longer history of dispersive physics reaching back to the whirlwinds of "Volkslied" and Lasker-Schüler's early work. Accordingly, we should expect to find a countervailing impulse toward centralization; and in *Der Wunderrabbiner*, Palestine performs just such a centralizing function. Despite dissension among the Jews about the proper course of action in response to their persecution, the narrator states that in "all of them rose the longing after their lost land," a phrase employing that potent German word, *Sehnsucht*. Moreover, the Jews "count the days and hours that separate them from Palestine," another wedding of space and time like the "Old-Asia" of the opening lines. Finally, Eleasar remarks at one point that "whoever does not carry the promised land [*das gelobte Land*] in his heart will never obtain it," indicating that Palestine is both a territory, a land at once lost and promised, and a psychological locus that focalizes the longing, the *Sehnsucht*, of a people.[114] But, crucially, rather than a character acting as the charismatic point around which the Jews take their shape – Petrus, for example, or Eleasar, who by the end of the story is powerless to stop the pogrom – the centering principle is territorialized. A specific geographical location is the organizing center for the consciousness of a *Volk*. Dispersed to the periphery, the Jews find their psycho-social core in Palestine.

Let us now examine that homeland more closely. After relating the formation of the earth and its various peoples, *The Atlas of Creation* turns to the topic of a *Heimat* for both Jews and Gentiles. For non-Jewish peoples, the demiurge "prepared a homeland [*Heimat*] between the green foliage of the summertime-earth, on the rolling, restful waters, and under the pure winter snow."[115] In keeping with *The Atlas of Creation* as a whole, this description fixes the *Heimat* of the Gentiles in territorial terms: "on the waters," "under the snow," "between the green branches of the summertime-earth" – another conjunction of space and time.

When *Der Wunderrabbiner* turns to the Jewish homeland, though, the *Heimat* is mapped along more uncertain coordinates. In *The Atlas of Creation*, the Jews are designated the "people of the prophets" and made to "serve in every land, in every people, on all paths," suggesting a continuation of the diasporic dynamics. When the narrative departs from the frame, however, and returns to Eleasar in his palace, the narrator offers a more specific localization of the Jewish people, stating cryptically "that *Palestine* is only an *observatory* of their home [daß P a l ä s t i n a nur die S t e r n w a r t e ihrer Heimat sei]." This obscure metaphor of Palestine as an observatory – a *Sternwarte*, which combines the word for star, *Stern*, with the term *Warte*, which is an elevated piece of land or a vantage point – contains at least one allusion to scripture: Moses on Mount Nebo glimpsing the promised land. Therefore, in the same way that the leader of the Israelites could see the place of his people's salvation while knowing he would never himself attain it, so too is Palestine in *Der Wunderrabbiner* a place, a promontory for observation like Mount Nebo, that implies postponement or temporal deferral. (*Warte*, both sonically and etymologically, suggests the verb *warten*, "to wait.") Thus Palestine is both a location for viewing – an elevated vantage point – and a place for waiting.

In the final estimation, then, Palestine is a territory – a fixed location for gazing at the stars – that, paradoxically, allows for the transcendence of territoriality. Palestine is a geographical place for observing the *Heimat*, now identified with the heavens instead of the earth. In one sense this metaphor supports the methodology of Schachter and Skolnik. Lasker-Schüler clearly has no interest in equating Palestine with the site of a future Jewish nation. Furthermore she directs the gaze of a people outward, beyond the horizons of the earth and the limitations of the globe. On the other hand, language in not the chief means for ordering peoples.

Both Jews and Gentiles are oriented in the world according to their connections with territories. Physical geography, a form of territoriality even more emphatic than nationhood, identifies and gives meaning to peoples: the "summertime-earth," the *Atlas of Creation*, Mount Nebo and the *Sternwarte* itself – all arranged according to an orientalist schema where a people, dispersed through the world, leans to the east in the hopes that God will hear its cries.

Another way of interpreting the final metaphor of the *Sternwarte* is by looking back to Julius Hart's "Der Neue Mensch," where the Copernican revolution furnishes a theoretical vocabulary for comprehending the modern human condition. New humans, it will be recalled, are both spiritually central and naturally peripheral. They possess a creative spiritual core; yet they are located, in physical terms, in the distant orbits of outer space. Palestine, in an analogous manner, is a psychological and emotional center for the Jews: the core that must be held in the heart if it is to be attained in this world. At the same time, it is also a geographical center, an observatory, from which the *Volk* may behold the most distant periphery of all – the celestial sphere, a place where the stars, strewn across the sky, do not wander according to earthly laws. They reside as parts of a coherent, harmonious whole, moving in sidereal time. Palestine is thus a territorial-ized representation of the modern Jewish *Volk*: the center that grants a glimpse of the homeland circling above.

The circle is one paradigm for shaping both the "new human" and an old *Volk* that is striving to form itself anew. Another way of fashioning new anthropological entities, whether humans or peoples, is by making direct interventions into their physiological constitution – eugenics, in a word, which was a topic of considerable importance for the late Yeats as well as for Benn's Expressionist aesthetics, as we will see in Chapter 6. For present purposes, comparing the Expressionist "new human" with its close con-temporary and ideological kin the Futurist machine-man allows for closer scrutiny of this interventionist methodology. Although the mechanized new human sired at the end of *Mafarka* is an important instance of this techno-anthropological hybrid, precedents can be found at least as far back as Mary Shelley's *Frankenstein*. Lasker-Schüler contributed her own vari-ation on the theme in a minor text published only a year after *Der Wunderrabbiner*.

The occasion for the essay "The Revolving World-Factory [*Die kreisende Weltfabrik*]" was a survey in the *Vossische Zeitung* asking artists to reflect on Berlin as a site for artistic production.[116] The metaphor Lasker-Schüler uses for her title, which can be translated more literally as "The Circling

World-Factory," reappears in the body of the essay to represent modern urban life:

> This Berlin, circling world-factory. Tempo: the inhabitants walk on wheels, are worn down or understand themselves to be de-organicized, they can become mechanical.
>
> [Dieses Berlin, kreisende Weltfabrik. Tempo: auf Rollen laufen die Einwohner, entnerven oder verstehen sich zu entorganisieren, vermögen maschinell zu werden.][117]

Berlin is a "world-factory," a sort of territorial proxy for the demiurge of *The Atlas of Creation* that replaces the divine artificer, a model of the ideal artist, with the foremost institution of modern industrial production, the factory. Within this urban landscape, mechanized humans roll through the streets and thereby mimic the circular motion of the city itself. Lasker-Schüler, who does not often venture into theoretical speculation, continues her meditation on mechanical reproduction by commenting that "the aestheticians [*die Aesthetiker*] like to flee to the comfortable emptiness to compose their poem (but whether the aestheticians are only photographers among the artists – maybe)."[118] Despite the confusing syntax, this statement appears to associate aestheticians with their external environment. They flee to a placid landscape to write their poetry; they record impressions of the world with the help of the camera. True artists, by contrast, generate the world out of themselves: "We artists are creators, the material lies within us."[119]

The distinction Lasker-Schüler makes between artist and aesthetician hews to the standard Expressionist theory of artistic production advanced by Hiller, noted earlier, that pitted the genuine artist – that is, the Expressionist artist – against the "aesthetes [*Ästheten*] who only know how to react, who are only wax plates for impressions [*Eindrücke*]." Thus the Impressionist is an aesthete who reacts and the Expressionist an artist who creates. While Lasker-Schüler seems to accept this basic distinction, she offers a still more modern technique for reproducing the sensations of urban life: photography, which requires an apparatus for processing external impressions through the combination of light, lens, film and mechanical parts, very different, then, than a neutral medium like the wax plate that receives a stamp of the world through brute force. Yet the machine, as the essay makes clear, is capable of more than mere reproduction. Technology expresses the condition of humanity in modernity:

> but the human, a single human, the human that I love, the nearing light. From our great city rings out the cry of humanity, the roar of technology.

[aber der Mensch, ein einziger Mensch, der Mensch, den ich liebe, das nahende Licht. Aus unserer großen Stadt schallt der Schrei der Menschheit, das Getöse der Technik.][120]

In this passage, Expressionist and Futurist new humans merge into one. The human scream, an Expressionist scream, blends with the roar of technology, combining to make a single sound emitted from the modern city. Therefore if Palestine granted a glimpse of paradise regained, of unity and wholeness circling above in the starry sky, then Berlin is the center and source of a different form of circular motion: the industrial regularity of urban modernity, the routines of labor and cycles of production. In this godless metropolis, the cries of inhabitants go unheard. Human scream and mechanical noise ring out into the empty atmosphere.

Beginning during her time at the *Neue Gemeinschaft* and continuing through the main phase of Expressionism, Lasker-Schüler developed a new humanism that synthesized cultural traditions, both German and Jewish, in an effort to imagine novel configurations of *Menschen*, *Völker*, *Übervölker*. While there is certainly no lack of emotional exuberance in Lasker-Schüler's poetry and prose, her new humanism emerged from a more sophisticated theoretical matrix than the sheer irrationalism usually imputed to the discourse of the *neuer Mensch*: a spatial ideal, the circle, takes the measure of the "new human" in both its spiritual and natural aspects. Nevertheless this spatial aesthetic-anthropology remains open to a Benjaminian critique that levels the charge of aestheticizing politics. The primary categories for this new humanism are Kantian categories from the "Transcendental Aesthetic" – space and time instead of history and class consciousness, for example. Indeed the progressive elements of this aesthetic ideology – the resolution of status, racial or ethnic differences – gain their subversive force by organizing parts of the social whole according to a spatial orientation, center and periphery, that is readily occupied by a charismatic leader and an adoring *Volk*. Accordingly, the paradigmatic figure of Petrus is significant not so much for an ability to inspire reverence among a crowd of followers; nor is he a *Führer* with privileged access to the nature of the *Volksgeist*. His political function is, in a certain sense, more fundamental still. He is the necessary locus that gives an egalitarian spatial order its meaning. He is the center around which the points on the circumference trace their orbit.

The materialist theory underlying the aestheticization thesis would doubtless construe status, race and ethnicity, together with the social ills they produce, in different terms – as idealist epiphenomena generated by material causes, whose melioration would require more than elevating a benevolent leader to the center of the circle, fashioning a new spatial order, or seeking salvation in a promised land. Yet the aestheticization thesis itself is not immune to scrutiny, for the assertion that fascism aestheticizes politics is only valid if it can lay claim to a legitimate theory of realism that reveals the aesthetic distortions of political life. That is to say, only if Benjamin's materialist premises are granted does his critique obtain its force. Hence it is necessary to turn now to the theory of realism that licensed his famous reading of fascism, a theory that received its most decisive articulation in 1937, when Marxists led by Lukács mounted a sustained attack on the politics of Expressionism – on modernism as such – even as they worked to claim the *Volk* for the political left.

CHAPTER 6

Socialist Realism, Socialist Expressionism

Ein Volk mußte geschaffen sein, für den Geist zu streiten
[A people had to be created for the spirit to fight]

—Heinrich Mann

In a famous opening set piece to *The Theory of the Novel* (1916), a work written at the height of the Expressionist decade not usually associated with Expressionism as such, Georg Lukács tries to convey the sense of wholeness and integrity enjoyed by the Greeks in classical antiquity: "Blessed are those times when the starry sky is the map of passable paths ... The world is wide and like a home, because the fire that burns in the soul is of the same essential kind as the stars."[1] As in the concluding metaphor of *Der Wunderrabbiner von Barcelona*, the celestial sphere is made into a model for home. An individual's place in the cosmos is mapped in the heavens above. Lukács then elaborates on this metaphor by turning to the shape of the circle: "All action of the soul becomes meaningful and rounded," he writes, "and finds its own center and draws a closed circumference around itself." So the ideal Greek is struck from the same mold as the Expressionist "new human." At home in the world, *anthropos* is both center and circumference.

Lukács later repudiated *The Theory of the Novel* after his move from idealism to materialism, a process that gathered strength in the twenties, marked by the publication of *History and Class Consciousness* in 1923, and continued to harden in the 1930s during his Soviet exile. One of Lukács's most synthetic statements on cultural policy emerged during the Expressionism Debate of 1937, a signal moment in the history of modernism that began when Alfred Kurella, a Marxist who had fled the Nazis to Moscow, alleged that Expressionism had been complicit in the rise of fascism. Following this initial broadside, critics from across the German diaspora, Lukács foremost among them, took up the question of whether aspects of Expressionist art – self-reflexive formal experimentation, irrationalism and the celebration of extreme affects, a distinctly bourgeois brand of anti-capitalism – were harbingers of National Socialism, indeed, whether they were directly complicit in its rise.

The ensuing debate quickly evolved into a full-blown reckoning with the ideology of modern art and the politics of style. Commenting on the expanded scope of the arguments, the editors of *Das Wort*, the Moscow-based journal that served as the primary venue for the debate, noted that "our discussion is a typically German reflection of the great dispute between formalism and realism that, quite rightly, occupied intensely for months and continues to occupy literary theorists and historians, critics, writers, and not least a wide reading public in the Soviet Union."[2] Scholars have followed the editors by interpreting the Expressionism Debate as much more than a dispute about Expressionism narrowly construed. Astradur Eysteinsson believes the polarities that emerged exemplify a paradigmatic tension within the concept of modernism; Fredric Jameson goes so far as to call it the "Realism/Modernism controversy."[3]

Important as they were, the stylistic contours of the debate have tended to overshadow disagreements that struck at the conceptual roots of the *Volksfront*: disagreements about the *Volk* and its derivative *Volkstümlichkeit* (popularity, folksiness). Touchstones of fascist aesthetics, *Volk* and *Volkstümlichkeit* became unlikely axioms of the realist program promulgated by leftists like Lukács and Kurella. For instance, the editor of *Das Wort* in Moscow, Fritz Erpenbeck, commented that "*Volkstümlichkeit* is absolutely the central practical problem of our artistic production."[4] In part a response to the withering of the left's authority in the face of the racialized nationalism of the Nazis, members of the *Volksfront* tried to reclaim the mantle of popular art, often foregoing the language of class struggle in favor of a head-on confrontation with the right about the content of a populist aesthetics.

Such a left populist aesthetics grounded in the concepts of the *Volk* and *Volkstümlichkeit* as they were theorized in the 1930s refigures more familiar versions of the cultural politics of the period – including the Benjaminian theses introduced in Chapter 5. In the months he spent with Brecht during the tense summer of 1937, Benjamin acted as a sounding board for his friend's polemics against Lukács.[5] But for all the sympathy that existed between Benjamin and Brecht, the famous interpretation of fascism in the Work of Art essay has a decidedly Lukácsean ring: "The masses have a *right* to change property relations; fascism tries to give the masses *expression* [*Ausdruck*] while preserving those relations. This follows necessarily to an aestheticization of political life."[6] On this account, fascism transmutes politics into the sound and smoke of pure subjective experience; and these distortions to the reality of material relations elicit a clear response: "Communism replies with the politicization of art."

Lukács, whose *History and Class Consciousness* Benjamin had long admired, made the same arguments against Expressionism, first in 1934 in an article for *Internationale Literatur* and then in the Expressionism Debate.[7] Refining Kurella's Marxist anti-modernism, Lukács alleged that the chief theorist of Expressionism, Ernst Bloch, had confused a bourgeois critique of society that focused on the subjective experience of life under capitalism with an objective and properly materialist account of society as an economic totality. Subjective flights into modernist montage – or primitive cultures, or idealist categories like space and time – give the impression of disruption and critique but come to grief because they misunderstand the object of critical scrutiny, namely, society constituted through economic relations, *and* because subject-centered critiques fail to provide a credible strategy for exiting capitalism, an event Lukács reserves for genuine proletarian revolution – or, at any rate, for the Party that acts as the executor of the proletariat's revolutionary potential. In other words, the aestheticization of politics that Benjamin sees in fascism and that Lukács identifies with Expressionism vitiates real political change by confounding subjective effects – impressions arising *from* the social order – with the objective causes *of* that order: property relations. Therefore Benjamin's assertion that fascism gives expression to popular sentiments was informed, at least in part, by left critiques of modern art: Lukács's initial sally against Expressionism was published two years before Benjamin wrote the first draft of the Work of Art essay; the Expressionism Debate occurred while he was revising the version he entrusted to George Bataille before fleeing to Marseille and then, finally, Portbou.

Rather than fashion a synthesis of aesthetics and politics out of claims about sensibility – αἴσθησις in the classical sense, which informed the aesthetic anthropologies of Impressionism – this chapter argues that in the 1930s critics from across the political spectrum theorized the *Volk* as an anthropological entity whose revolutionary promise was inextricable from its aesthetic determination as a purposive totality – as a subject of history embodying a social rather than natural teleology. While the conceptions of totality expounded during the Expressionism Debate certainly look forward to postwar theories of totalitarianism where the state apparatuses of Nazi Germany and the Soviet Union pursue complete control over the lives of their subjects, the fault lines in the cultural politics of the 1930s had not yet ossified into the Cold War polarities that underlie the totalitarianism thesis of Hannah Arendt and others of her generation. In the Expressionism Debate, totality refers not to the state but to the *Volk*, the traditional font of popular sovereignty that then legitimates the exercise of state power. Thus the Marxist critical theory advanced by the *Volksfront* derives its force not from politicizing art in the manner of Benjamin and the tradition of engaged criticism he helped promote but from recognizing the subversive potential within the discourse of aesthetics itself.[8]

The chapter begins by examining the work of Gottfried Benn and the responses he generated in *Das Wort*. One of Expressionism's brightest lights, Benn eventually joined Martin Heidegger and Carl Schmitt in that ignominious fraternity of elite intellectuals who placed their talents in the service of National Socialism. Though Benn's idiosyncrasies as a poet and social critic disqualify him as either orthodox Expressionist or doctrinaire Nazi, his role as a key figure for early Expressionism, his status as a primary target in the Expressionism Debate, and his writings on art and the *Volk* in the 1930s make *der Fall Benn,* the case of Benn, an unavoidable topic for any evaluation of the Expressionist *Volk*. The chapter then turns to the Expressionism Debate and efforts to theorize an aesthetics of the *Volk* that is capable of combatting fascism.

6.1 The Genius of the People

The cultural legacy of the 1910s and 1920s had become pressing for *Volksfront* critics due to the political fortunes of Benn, the only poet of stature to throw in his lot with the National Socialists. Benn's rise had begun in 1912 with *Morgue and Other Poems,* a collection that scandalized the German literary public and announced its author as a major lyric voice.[9] Channeling a Baudelairean attunement to the sordid beauty of urban life through a bracing, analytic style shot through with medical jargon, the *Morgue* poems tapped into what Benn would later call "the creative side of objectivity."[10] Unsparing poems about autopsies, bodily decomposition and human decay lyricized the "coldness of thought, sobriety, the last sharpness of a concept" inculcated by Benn's medical training at the Pépinière, the Prussian military academy in Berlin.[11] Though his debut was condemned in the same terms that Carl Vinnen used to inveigh against modern art in *Protest deutscher Künstler* – one reviewer derided its "decadent and aestheticist soul" – Lasker-Schüler called *Morgue* a "terrible artistic miracle" and described Benn's poetry as having "the bite of a leopard, the leap of a wild animal."[12] Later, after Benn dedicated *Söhne* (1913) to Lasker-Schüler, she commented to Franz Marc that the poems were "moon-red, earth-hard, wild twilight, hammered in blood."[13]

During the war, Benn was awarded the Iron Cross for participating in the invasion of Antwerp. Then, while serving as a staff doctor at a hospital for prostitutes in occupied Brussels, he contrived his alter ego Dr. Rönne, the protagonist of the *Brains* novellas. According to Wolfgang Emmerich, this character allowed Benn to examine modern man's rejection of "reality and its bourgeois surrogates" in favor of an "un-reality principle [*Irrealitätsprinzip*]."[14] Motivated by this anti-realist outlook, Rönne's kaleidoscopic, ecstatic counter-worlds chart the psychic terrain of modern Europe. After the war, as Germany was reeling politically, economically and spiritually from the losses suffered in the trenches, Benn began to translate his anti-realist, anti-bourgeois art into a critical theory of civilization. Fueled by readings of Nietzsche, Benn's jeremiads against rationalization and philistine commercialism lack Nietzsche's trenchancy and critical self-awareness even as they emulate the philosopher's bravado. A passage from "Das Moderne Ich [The Modern Ego]" (1920), the only nonfiction collected in the *Gesammelte Schriften* of 1922, captures the pitch and tenor of Benn's heady, dissociative prose: "Pain, a fist's strike against the cheap life of the frayed maul of hedonistic democracy, pain, chaos that sweeps over and exterminates the sewage fields of bourgeois reason and, destroying, forces the cosmos to fold itself anew."[15] Later, during his fascist phase, Benn would remark that "Das Moderne Ich" gave voice to the "hatred of the scientific Utilitarian, knowledge turned mercantile, the state as pure caretaker, the human as pure pensioner, of everything mechanical in life," a critique of bourgeois decadence that for Benn would crest in the "creative force [*schöpferische Wucht*]" of National Socialism.[16]

Benn's general disdain for popular culture and its political surrogates, the people conceived as rights-bearing individuals and consumers in the cultural marketplace, went hand in hand with a theory of artistic production indebted to the concept of genius, that quintessentially alienated figure who stands apart from the masses. For Benn, the artist is an exceptional being isolated from the norms that govern everyday social intercourse. The poet "has no social requirements," Benn writes in "Zur Problematik des Dichterischen [On the Problem of the Poetic]" from 1930. "His social requirements do not concern him." Not only are social entanglements irrelevant for the poet, "there exists a chasm" between the "great man" and the middling agents of rational progress who are beholden to empirical laws, historical contingency and the constraints of ego psychology.[17] The genius, by contrast, plunges beneath ideation to a more fundamental, essentially irrational realm: "the body is the final compulsion and the depth of necessity," not the mind. "There is," Benn continues, "just one necessity: the body."[18] As Benn himself admitted, much of his theory of poetic creativity as somatic event had already been worked out by Nietzsche.[19] Reason and the ego as epiphenomena, the primacy of corporeal and instinctual impulses, the great man as antidote to modern mediocrity and democratic leveling, all these components of sensualist vitalism had been theorized by Nietzsche and become standard features of Expressionist aesthetic epistemology.

For all they share, Benn diverges from Nietzsche when it comes to the kinds of collective experience that stoke the flames of aesthetic rapture. In *The Birth of Tragedy*, a lodestar for Expressionism, a Dionysian drive dissolves the *principium individuationis* in moments of intoxicated revery. Kindled by the ecstasy of collective rituals – group dances, for example, that were codified as the chorus of classical tragedy – Dionysian experience has a social corollary for Nietzsche: "singing and dancing, man expresses himself as a member of a higher collectivity." Nietzsche elaborates on these group bonds: "Not only is the association between human and human [*der Bund zwischen Mensch und Mensch*] united again under the magic of the Dionysian: but also alienated, hostile, or subjugated nature celebrates again its festival of reconciliation with its lost son, mankind [*dem Menschen*]."[20] A natural drive, equally cosmic as it is corporeal, Dionysus unites individuals with others and with their own truer human nature. Later, in §8 of *The Birth of Tragedy*, Nietzsche extends this collectivism into an account of poetic creation: "a poet is only a poet by virtue of seeing himself surrounded by forms [*Gestalten*] who live and act before him, and into whose innermost essence he peers." Mediated by the image-giving influence of Apollo, this dream-like impression of group membership underpins both poetic creation and aesthetic reception: "Dionysiac excitement is capable of communicating this artistic ability to an entire mass of people, the ability to see themselves surrounded by such a band of spirits."[21] Though this communalist aesthetics is most apposite when referring to the assembled groups of dramatic spectacle – the players, the chorus, the audience – Dionysian experience is capacious enough to comprehend other arts including music, dance, lyric poetry, even cinema.

Where for the young Nietzsche, the antithetical forces corresponding to Dionysus and Apollo were cosmic-corporeal drives with psycho-social ramifications, Benn gives the collectivity of aesthetic rapture an anthropological and biological, indeed a neurological turn.[22] Hewing to his theory of the isolated genius, Benn views artistic creation as a solitary event. The poet employs a self-reflexive "geological principle" that excavates progressively more primitive psychic strata, tunneling down through layers of historical experience that have accumulated and solidified as neurological structures: the more recent, higher-order faculties in the cerebrum, the brainstem that houses deeper, irrational drives.[23] Yet Benn's neuropoetics has an anthropological edge: "we carry the early peoples [die frühen Völker] in our soul and when the more belated reason is loosened in dreams and intoxication, they rise up with their rites, their pre-logical modes of thought [Geistesart]."[24] Drawing on theories of contemporary scientists like the Hungarian neurologist Constantin von Economo, Benn treats the historical experiences of Völker, the sum total of their sensations and impressions, as fossils deposited within our collective cognitive endowment. Poiesis, then, taps into these psychic reserves, activating what is latent and conjuring primitive experiences through language.

"Zum Problematik der Dichterischen" presents a more detailed exposition of the anthropological body as font of poetry:

> There resides in the body a dream, an animal, from far away; from far away, it is loaded with the mysteries of those early peoples who carried within themselves the primeval times, the origin, with their wholly foreign sense of the world, their mysterious experiences out of preconscious spheres, in whose bodies the inner consciousness was still labile, the constructive strength of the organism still free; this means that consciousness and the organization's center were still accessible, still tractable, though it has long since lost its capriciousness and become a different biological type from us.[25]

Boring down through successive layers of accrued experience, the poet has access to the deepest zones of human consciousness, reaching into the "visions, ecstasies, the peoplehood of the dawn [Völkerschaft der Frühe]" that lurk below the rational superficies. For all the myriad references to Völker in Nietzsche's later writings – his loathing for Germans and preference for Mediterranean cultures is well known – the Dionysian collective in The Birth of Tragedy is a humanist Bund.[26] Benn recasts this "higher collectivity," however, replacing the revery of collective aesthetic practice with a poetics that plumbs the irrational depths of the völkisch brain.

Benn's theory of genius evinced a primitivism that Klaus Mann singled out for reproach in his reckoning with Benn's fascism in Das Wort. Citing the poem "Gesänge" (1913), Mann targets what he sees as a key psychological motif for the Expressionist movement as a whole, an "atavistic complex" conveyed by the poem's opening lines: "Oh that we might be our great-great-grandfathers./A clump of slime in a warm bog [*O daß wir unsere Ururahnen wären./Ein Klümpchen Schleim in einem warmen Moor*]."[27] Benn practices a rather diffuse, free-floating identification with the "South" as the locus of primal experience, which Joshua Dittrich has claimed was shaped by concerns about the decline of Germany's status as a colonial power after World War I.[28] Despite occasionally anchoring his primitivist geography in particular locations, Benn tends to invoke a more atmospheric sense of southern culture illustrated by the concluding lines of "Karyatide," a poem that apostrophizes a figure from classical statuary, the caryatid, which is a column carved in the shape of a woman in mid stride. Here, in the final stanza, the poem moves from apostrophe to a direct address to the reader:

> Spread yourself, blossom, oh, let bloom
> the soft garden from your great wounds:
> behold, Venus of the doves
> girds herself with roses around her hips, love's portal –
> behold the last blue breath of summer drifts
> on aster seas to the distant
> tree-brown banks; dawning
> behold these last fortunate-false hours
> of our southernness
> vaulted high.

> [Breite dich hin, zerblühe dich, oh, blute
> dein weiches Beet aus großen Wunden hin:
> sieh, Venus mit den Tauben gürtet
> sich Rosen um der Hüften Liebestor –
> sieh dieses Sommers letzten blauen Hauch
> auf Astermeeren an die fernen
> baumbraunen Ufer treiben; tagen
> sieh diese letzte Glück-Lügenstunde
> unserer Südlichkeit
> hochgewölbt.]

Benn conjures images that contribute to the poem's auratic effect, what Benjamin would later call "the unique appearance of distance, however near it may be": images that float on the "distant/tree-brown banks" and the blue breath of the cryptic "aster seas" that call to mind the wine-colored waves of Homer's οἴνοπα πόντον.

Since the genius must resuscitate the long-lost impressions of early peoples, distance, whether spatial or temporal, is a necessary condition for Benn's poetics. In other words, the geological principle developed in the essays on genius implies the presence of distance. As a consequence, any rigorous study of primitive life would be counterproductive for Benn since empirical data would fill the constitutive gap between past and present, here and there that poetic introspection is meant to bridge. Nietzsche, by contrast, employed philology in order to peer into the cultural past; and Yeats sought actual contact with putatively primitive cultures in the west of Ireland. For all the flaws and insufficiencies of their respective methods, these authors at least attempted to grasp the alterity of primitive cultures through firsthand exposure or by studying their linguistic or artistic products. For Benn, however, serious empirical inquiry would usurp the role of the genius, whose express purpose is to break the chains of induction by means of poetic introspection. For Benn, the genius makes recourse to a geological principle – not the collection of artistic, ethnographic or philological data – in order to activate the primal substrates lodged in the vital centers of the brain.

6.2   "Art as Progressive Anthropology"

Benn's essays on artistic production from 1930 reveal a commitment to *völkisch* thinking that would flourish during his affair with National Socialism – an affair that lasted until the summer of 1934, when Hitler consolidated power through a spate of extrajudicial killings, known as the Röhm Putsch, that disabused Benn of his naive faith in the creative promise of the Nazi movement.[29] At the beginning of the decade, though, Benn was not yet the pariah he would soon become despite coming under pressure from leftist critics like Johannes R. Becher, a former Expressionist turned Marxist, and Egon Erwin Kisch, who published a letter in *Die neue Bücherschau* railing against Benn as "a snob entangled in his own diseased (schizophrenic) scruples."[30] Benn's riposte, "Über die Rolle des Schriftstellers in dieser Zeit [On the Role of the Contemporary Writer]" (1930), redoubles his commitment to the radical independence of the artist, this time as a sally against critics on the left who insisted on the historicity of artistic production. Even though the spat with Becher and Kisch foretokened the critical assessment of Expressionism that would take place in *Das Wort*, Benn managed to retain professional contacts with figures who would later become instrumental in the left-liberal front against fascism. In March 1931 he gave a speech celebrating the sixtieth birthday of Heinrich Mann; and in January 1932 Benn was elected to the literary section of the Prussian Academy, where he joined both Mann brothers, Alfred Döblin and Ricarda Huch as a member. While Benn's election to the Academy signaled his entry into the highest echelon of German letters, it also sowed his downfall. Two weeks after the burning of the Reichstag on February 27, 1933, Benn helped draft a document for his Academy colleagues that demanded "loyal cooperation with the constitutionally required national-cultural tasks in light of the changed historical situation."[31] Thomas Mann and Döblin resigned in response (Heinrich Mann had already resigned for political reasons). With those titans of German letters out of the way, Benn oversaw their replacement with lesser lights sympathetic to the Nazi cause.

Benn's activities at the Prussian Academy stand as his most material contribution to cultural *Gleichschaltung*, the act of aligning an institution with Nazi policy. At the same time, due care must be taken when correlating Benn's politics with Nazi ideology. Unlike Heidegger and Schmitt, Benn never joined the Nazi party; and his advocacy for the new German state never devolved into the legal apologetics of Schmitt or the sublimated antisemitism of Heidegger.[32] Indeed, scholars who have studied Benn's involvement with National Socialism have stressed this lack of antisemitic tendencies, which is notable given the robustness of his racial imagination. Ultimately these points of heterodoxy exposed Benn to attacks from more activist fascists like Börries von Münchhausen, the balladeer and leader of a faction of cultural conservatives who published a broadside against Benn and other Expressionists for, among other things, "severing literature from the spiritual life of the people."[33] Notwithstanding their *völkisch* overtones, then, Benn's anthropological musings failed to insulate him from a right critique that targeted the elitist strains of Expressionist art and invoked an alternative, populist interpretation of the *Volk*. For a time, though, his energetic efforts to justify cultural pursuits under the Third Reich held the field as a means of yoking together art and the aims of the state.

In over a dozen essays and radio addresses, Benn fortified reactionary tendencies that had been implicit in his pre-Nazi writings. Reminiscent of the *völkisch* collectivism contained in his essays on genius, Benn's broadcast from April 24, 1933, "Der neue Staat und die Intellektuellen [The New State and the Intellectuals]," adapts verbatim Nietzsche's conception of group identity from *The Birth of Tragedy* but torques Dionysian collectivity to serve anti-Marxist ends. Benn asserts that National Socialism "wishes to dissolve the unproductive Marxist conflict between employee and employer into a higher collectivity [*eine höhere Gemeinsamkeit*]."[34] While it is true that Nietzsche remains Benn's theoretical touchstone during his fascist phase, his view of human groups hearkens back less to the Dionysian dancers of *The Birth of Tragedy* than to the anthropological types, more Apollonian than Dionysian due to their status as aesthetic ideals, theorized so powerfully by Enlightenment naturalists such as Kant and Goethe.[35] Benn calls for a "new idealistic anthropology" and celebrates the "new biological type," the "new typological variant" birthed by the fascist revolution.[36] Over and above employing a familiar essentialist typology, Benn conceives of fascism in teleological terms, writing in one of his several essays on eugenics that "the meaning of breeding can only be the *Volk* itself; the goal of all talent is once again only the *Volk*."[37] In the preface to a collection of essays published in 1934, Benn writes that "all political efforts of the new state are directed toward one inner goal: enrichment of a new human substance in the *Volk*."[38] Thus it should come as no surprise that the structural logic of perfection accompanies Benn's teleology: "the decisive factor with respect to all breeding perspectives is the moral will of a *Volk* to breed, its belief in a drive to perfection."[39] Benn even incorporates claims about perfection into the most comprehensive reflection on poetry from his fascist period, "Bekenntnis zum Expressionismus [Declaration on Expressionism]," which attempts to fend off the criticisms of Münchhausen by reconciling Expressionist aesthetics with Nazism. In a passage that Klaus Mann would cite in his critical essay in *Das Wort*, Benn marvels at the "enormous biological instinct for racial perfection" ushered in by the rise of National Socialism.

For all their commonalities, it would be a mistake to identify Benn too closely with Kantian anthropology, for his espousal of the mutability of human types flies in the face of Kant's argument that *Urbilder*, like the anthropological categories they stand for, are natural shapes (*Gestalten*) that individuals may conform to, or diverge from, but not alter in their essential character. Benn demands "the formation of a new higher type."[40] He wishes to form, in the strict sense, an altogether new kind of human. And the mechanism for enacting this formalist imperative is *Züchtung*, a term with both biological and political senses (*züchten* = "to breed"; *Zucht* = "breeding" or "discipline"; *Zucht und Ordnung* = "law and order"). For Benn, breeding means:

> to set the *Volk* in motion, because only out of it [*aus ihm*, i.e. *das Volk*], out of its own new experiences and beliefs arises the siring and generative will [*stellt sich der vorwerfende und zeugende Wille ein*]. Indeed, everything that Germany experiences today will enter into that will: its unity, the political unification and the metaphysical community, and thereupon the imagination of its still unfulfilled destiny, alone among the peoples of Europe;

further still the discipline [*das Disziplinäre*] of its current leadership [*Führung*] and the intransigent will to self-formation.[41]

Benn arrogates to the *Volk* what Kant reserved for nature, the creation of human types. No ideal shape that artists may imitate, a perfect human type on Benn's account is subject to the "self-formation" of the *Volk* through a will to form. Inseparable from a drive to perfection, this will propels the *Volk* toward the fulfillment of its physico-political destiny. Unlike Kant, who insisted on the stability of a natural order grounded in rational principles, Benn decouples teleology and perfection from the ineluctable heteronomy of nature. Yet Benn does not take the path chosen by Schiller and Du Bois, which privileges autonomy as freedom *from* natural law. On the contrary – the will to form bends the underlying order of nature itself so that it conforms to a social or political concept of what a people *ought* to be.

In a manner directly reminiscent of the Old Man who choreographs the movements of the dramatic audience in *The Death of Cuchulain*, to say nothing of Yeats's own personal interest in eugenics, Benn asserts control over the human group, the *Volk*, conceived as an aesthetic body. He demands self-formation through *Züchtung*, disciplined breeding. Lending an Apollonian cast to Nietzsche's claim that Dionysian experience renders "man an artist no more, he has become a work of art," Benn conceives of the *Volk* as an aesthetic object, a work of art that can be manipulated and modified, crafted and formed through *Züchtung*: "breeding and art" stand as the "symbols of the new Europe," Benn proclaims in an essay commemorating Stefan George.[42] In order to give still greater specificity to his collectivist aesthetics, Benn makes artistic form the engine of political action, evincing what Philippe Lacoue-Labarthe calls the "national-aestheticism" of the Nazi movement.[43] He regards "form and breeding" as the "new gods" of a fascist world. In a speech given to honor Filippo Marinetti during his visit to Berlin in 1934, Benn expounds on the politics of form, or more accurately, on politics as form:

> Form – everything that you see in the new Germany was fought for in its name; form and breeding: the two symbols of the new Reich; breeding and style for both the State and for Art: the basis of the imperative worldview that I see coming. The entire future that we have is this: the State and Art.[44]

Such a formalist political-anthropology does not construe collectivity as an aggregation of social units – a *fasces* in the conventional sense of the term. Benn conjoins the quantitative aspect of the *Volk* with its qualitative character: "The special situation of Germany with respect to the eugenic question is that it wishes not merely to increase its population, since it has no room, no colonies, and already has quite a high population density. It wishes to maintain its stock and to improve it qualitatively." Quality and quality are inextricable when breeding a *Volk*: "The program of Germany is not only to increase the number of the population but also to improve it."[45]

Thus Benn's *völkisch* aesthetics regards the *Volk* as a coherent rather than aggregate whole, a total work of art rather than an aesthetic *fasces*, which can be crafted and shaped like a sculptural ideal, not through the sculptor's hammer and file, but by an Apollonian drive to breed perfection, by "art as progressive anthropology" as Benn put it in the title of the final section of his essay *Doric World: An Examination of the Relationship between Art and Power* (1934).[46] So absolute is Benn's unification of aesthetics and politics that it exceeds even the famous diagnosis of fascism as the "aestheticization of politics" made first by Benjamin and developed in the Heideggerian reading of Lacoue-Labarthe. For Benn, politics is not the primary category that is then aestheticized. Aesthetics and politics are categories equally foundational. The *völkisch* nation, the social body, is born through the will to form: "when both these truths meet, when political and aesthetic aspects unite, then the nation can truly rise."[47]

6.3   The Organic Proletariat

Benn and his obsession with form remained at the center of the dispute that unfolded in the pages of *Das Wort*.[48] Setting the tone for later contributors, Klaus Mann reminds his readers of those "who have used the concepts 'form' and 'breeding' as the most audacious justification for an incomparable excess of atrocities."[49] Appearing well before the most heinous Nazi crimes, Mann's reading of the historical trajectory of *völkisch* formalism intimates the horrors still latent in a program of "art as progressive anthropology," which Mann construes as replacing the traditional content of liberal society – values like progress, reason or justice – with a fetishization of artistic form as such. Yet for all his rabid anti-liberalism, Benn does not so much reject bourgeois themes as appropriate them for reactionary ends. After all, his cultural program relies on that eminently bourgeois concept of genius. Mann overlooks these tensions and, in keeping with his polemical mood, depicts Benn as a fascist aggressor against a liberal cultural politics exemplified best by his uncle and *Volksfront* stalwart Heinrich.

Over ten months and eighteen essays, two factors conspired to expand the Expressionism Debate beyond its original concern with the case of

Benn: a lack of consensus among leftists regarding the parameters of a properly Marxist critical theory, which forced authors to make programmatic declarations of their positions, and contemporary historical events. The historical circumstances are especially noteworthy. Only weeks before the debate commenced in *Das Wort*, the notorious "Degenerate Art" exhibition opened in Munich in July 1937. Featuring paintings by Franz Marc, Wassily Kandinsky, Oskar Kokoschka and other artists of the Expressionist generation, the exhibition condemned Expressionism in no uncertain terms, thus marking a shift away from Goebbels's earlier assertion, written in 1920 but published in 1929, that "our century is thoroughly Expressionistic in its inner structure. Nowadays we are all Expressionists."[50] Though Kurella later claimed to have written his essay before the opening of the Munich exhibition, he published his polemic against Expressionism in the September issue of *Das Wort* and thereby caused an awkward alignment between the anti-modernism of the Soviet faction of the *Volksfront* and the official hostility toward modern art preached by the Nazis.[51] This uncomfortable proximity between left and right anti-modernism was not lost on participants in the Expressionism Debate: Bloch made it a feature of his critique of Lukács; Herwarth Walden cited Nazi antipathy to Expressionism as evidence of its political merits.[52] Lukács and Kurella therefore had to refine their theoretical stances in order to differentiate their own allegations that Expressionism was "decadent" (Lukács), or the "self-decay [*Selbstzersetzung*] of bourgeois thought" (Kurella), from the National Socialist accusation that Expressionism represented "cultural decay [*Kulturzersetzung*]," as Adolf Hitler averred in his remarks on the opening of the Munich exhibition.[53] The theoretical positions that emerged now stand as some of the most trenchant statements on behalf of socialist realism in the canon of Western aesthetics.

For its principal antagonists, Munich cast a long shadow over the Expressionism Debate. Dieter Schiller has shown how the conflicts of political orthodoxy and cultural sensibility sparked by Kurella's initial essay threatened to split the eastern and western flanks of the Popular Front.[54] Tensions were especially high between the Moscow circle around Lukács, which included Kurella, and writers whose exile lay outside the Soviet Union like Bloch and Brecht – the former an outspoken defender of Expressionism who bore the brunt of Lukács's intra-left polemics, the latter an editor-at-large for *Das Wort* and one of the most prominent artists in the *Volkstfront*. These personal and intellectual dynamics shaped the trajectory of the debate while also influencing the contributions of individual authors. Brecht, for example, withheld publishing his critique of Lukács in the interests of maintaining a unified front.

Yet as the Munich affair illustrates, the political tensions that played out in the Popular Front cannot be reduced to rivalries on the left. In a survey of the Front's literary production, Birgit Schmidt has detected a kernel of nationalist sentiment that could qualify as a general rightward lurch in the politics of the movement. Ranging from a rather traditional attitude toward gender and sexuality to declarations of national pride that verged into chauvinism, the conservatism within the common front against fascism reveals a genuine, if partial and often repressed, alignment on social issues between the political left and right.[55] Dubious as they may be, these ideological infelicities cannot be said to have compromised the basic commitments of the *Volksfront*. Stalinism, which had entered its most severe phase just as the Expressionism Debate was getting underway, exerted considerable ideological pressure on the Moscow faction. To take but one example, the director Vsevolod Meyerhold had been censured in *Pravda* in December 1937 for practicing a "stylised, mystical, formalist theater of the aesthetes."[56] Then, at the height of the Expressionism Debate, Bela Balász published an essay in *Das Wort* titled "Meyerhold and Stanislavsky," which leveled a party-line attack against Meyerhold for "empty formalism" and translated the terms of the Expressionism Debate into those of Soviet cultural policy.[57] Meyerhold was arrested by Soviet authorities in the summer of 1939 and executed by firing squad on February 2, 1940.

The Marxist credentials of Kurella, though, were beyond reproach (he had been an employee of the Soviet State Library and would later become the most authoritative voice on cultural policy in East Germany as the leader of the *Kulturkommission*). By Kurella's lights, the most objectionable aspect of Expressionist art was its stylistic syncretism. African sculpture, classical epics, "sketches of Leonardo, Indian temples, Scythian gold work" congeal into a farrago reflecting bourgeois commodity culture run amok (the distance between this claim and the culture-industry thesis of Horkheimer and Adorno, which targets the homogenization, not diversification, of cultural production is worth noting).[58] With the ferocity typical of a convert – Kurella had once sympathized with Expressionism but later turned to Marxism – he fulminates against the eclecticism of modern art, "the cloudy, burbling, bottomless stream of the self-decay of bourgeois thought" that reached its zenith in World War I, when the imperialist phase of capitalism collapsed on the fields of France and Belgium.[59]

Kurella's pronouncements on Expressionist style, categorical as they are, fade into claims about literary history freighted with significance for the Popular Front as well as for intra-left disputes of the 1930s. Spurred by a need to identify which aspects of bourgeois culture could be recuperated for a classless society, and moreover by a desire to repudiate Nazi appropriations of German culture, leftists and their liberal allies grappled with what was known as the *Erbe* problem – the problem of determining the political legitimacy of the cultural past (*Erbe* = legacy, inheritance).[60] Hence Kurella excoriates Benn and his Expressionist cohort for literary historical transgressions alongside their stylistic affronts, most notably against the tradition of German classicism. According to this line of thought, which in a manner reminiscent of Du Bois reclaims Winckelmann for a left-liberal aesthetics, the cultural arbiters of the middle classes are implicated in betraying the ordering influence of the classics in favor of ostensibly decadent experiments with artistic form. In marked contrast to T. S. Eliot, who saw in the classical architecture of *Ulysses* a means "of giving a shape and a significance to the immense panorama of futility and anarchy which is contemporary history," the classics of Schiller and Goethe are but one more victim of the anarchic forces unleashed by the modernizing bourgeoisie, who are accused of unmooring art from a coherent, realist tradition and replacing the legacy of neoclassicism with the renegade Hellenism of *The Birth of Tragedy* or Benn's own *Doric World.*[61]

Besides the twin elements of style and literary history, themselves epiphenomena of class struggle and the decline of the bourgeoisie for Kurella, a third component rounds out this cultural calculus: the *Volk*. Concluding his essay with three "catechism questions" – it is here that the Stalinist context is most evident – Kurella conveys the programmatic character of socialist realism while also testing the orthodoxy of his readers:

Antiquity: "noble simplicity and calm grandeur"– do we see it that way?

Formalism: the true enemy of a literature that strives for greatness – are we agreed on this?

Proximity to the people and popularity: the basic criteria for any truly great art – do we affirm this absolutely?[62]

So construed, Expressionism violates all three tenets of socialist realism. The putative formalism of Expressionist montage diverges from the nobility that Winckelmann ascribed to classical statuary, just as the calmness of the classics is at odds with Expressionism's hot-blooded subjectivity, what Balász calls its "emotional unrestraint."[63] Only in the final tenet does Kurella enumerate the basic criteria of artistic greatness and aesthetic value, however: *Volksnähe*, literally "nearness to the people," and *Volkstümlichkeit*, which denotes an artwork's thematic or stylistic conformity to popular sensibilities – "folksiness" in English, or "popularity" so long as the Latin root *populus* (people) remains at the front of the term's semantic palette. Yet while *Volksnähe* and its antonym *Volksfremd*, "foreign to the people," capture the orientation of art to audience through a spatial metaphor, nearness and distance, *Volkstümlichkeit* introduces a more unstable range of meanings to Kurella's socialist account of cultural reception.

In contrast to the word *Volk*, which has deep linguistic roots, *Volkstum* and its derivatives *volkstümlich* and *Volkstümlichkeit* have a much more recent lexical pedigree.[64] Attestations begin in the early nineteenth century with Friedrich Ludwig Jahn's *Das Deutsche Volksthum* (1810).[65] Jahn, a veteran of the Napoleonic wars and the founder of the gymnastics movement in Germany, channeled national pride through a work of amateur ethnography. In his introduction, Jahn recounts the genesis of his coinage. Just as the words "national, nationality, national characteristics, nation-specific [*National, Nationalität, Nationaleigenthümlichkeit, Nationgemäß*]," so too with words referring to the people: "folkdom [*Volksthum*] is likewise formed from *Volk*, and from this we arrive in the most natural way at folksy [*volksthümlich*] and folksiness [*Volksthümlichkeit*]."[66] A product of the nationalist sentiment that arose in Germany in response to Napoleonic domination, *Volkstum* finds its closest cultural analog in Romantic-era balladry, a quintessentially *volkstümlich* art, which exerted a powerful influence in Britain through the Ossian poems and in Germany with the collection *Des Knaben Wunderhorn* (1805).

Under the Third Reich, conservatives like the balladeer Börries von Münchhausen revived demotic poetry for a twentieth-century readership, conscripting *Volkstümlichkeit* for a "blood and soil" ideology that prescribed a return to the land and primitive folkways. In a study of National Socialist literary theory, Klaus Vondung traces the infiltration of these ideological themes into philology and criticism during the years of Nazi rule, citing the fate of the renowned journal for literary history *Euphorion* as a telling example of cultural *Gleichschaltung* within the professional humanities.[67] In 1934 the journal's title was changed to suit the new historical circumstances. In justifying the title *Dichtung und Volkstum*, the editors Julius Petersen and Hermann Pongs indicate the connotations surrounding *Volkstum* in the Third Reich:

> With the new year the journal *Euphorion* enters into a new relationship with the sciences of culture and the spirit of research. It gives up its name *Euphorion* and with it the overemphasized dependence of German letters on

humanist learning. The new name *Dichtung und Volkstum* wishes to express that literary scholarship, too, keeps folkdom [*Volkstum*] in view as the basic value that supports and nourishes all aesthetic, literary historical, and historical values. The eternal concept of the people [*Volksbegriff*] in its historical development, as Herder saw it and as it is lived and experienced anew in Germany today, is the living ground [*Lebensgrund*] for all strong poetry to rise.[68]

Taking leave from the humanist tradition, Petersen and Pongs posit folkdom as the collective soil of cultural production. Despite bending logic by being both a timeless, "eternal concept" and subject to "historical development," the *Volk* is the vital source of artistic energies, the "living ground" that nourishes the fruits of culture. What is more, folkdom undergirds a monotelic hierarchy of values, being the "basic value [*Grundwert*]" that supports all others.

Therefore when Kurella, too, postulates *Volksnähe* and *Volkstümlichkeit* as the grounds for aesthetic value – "the basic criteria [*Grundkriterien*] for any truly great art" – he cuts a socialist theory of reception from the same discursive cloth as his fascist adversaries. Furthermore, the vitalist motifs insinuated by Petersen and Pongs burst forth *fortissimo* in Kurella. He alleges, for instance, that modern art has become "uprooted, creatively exhausted, since it has been robbed of the last connection to the living forces of the people."[69] He returns to the organic metaphor in a coda to the Expressionism Debate published ten months after his initial essay, claiming in his penultimate paragraph that "our German art in particular has lost the living connection with the great problems of our people. Expressionism and the other anti-realist artistic movements," Kurella continues, "have dissolved the concept 'Volk,' if they ever even knew it to begin with."[70] Torn from the loam of the *Volk*, the arts and letters of a nation are severed from the wellsprings of popular culture: "our German art" is uprooted from "our people." No longer circumscribing his argument to the case of Benn, or even to Expressionism, Kurella makes anti-realist art as such an enemy of the people.

Usually regarded as an epigone of Lukács – Klaus Berghahn reduces him to a "mouthpiece" for the Hungarian theorist – Kurella distills Lukácsian aesthetics to its programmatic essence while adding a polemical bite to suit the exigencies of Stalin-era cultural politics.[71] The master, though, was no less devoted to the *Volk* than his pupil. With a trenchancy unmatched by his *Volksfront* colleagues, Lukács takes up the problem of *Volkstümlichkeit* in his tour de force contribution to the Expressionism Debate, "Es geht um den Realismus [It's About Realism]." Employing the same vitalist rhetoric as Kurella, Lukács makes a sweeping declaration about the social purpose of art: "the living relationship to the life of the people, the progressive development of the masses' own life experiences – that is indeed the great social mission of literature."[72] For now it suffices to note the equivocation between "mass" and *Volk* in this passage. More to the present point, Lukács invokes "life" three times in a single sentence, using the term in at least two senses. He first describes a "living connection" that joins literature and the life of the *Volk* just as Kurella does when lamenting the deracination of German culture from its people; he then asserts the development of the "life experiences" of the masses as the social task of art.

As they appear in Lukács's theory of *Volkstümlichkeit*, the terms "life" (*Leben*) and "living" (*lebendig*) are not immediately recognizable as belonging to a Marxist idiom; they do not refer to Marx's distinction between living and dead labor, for example. Nevertheless certain conclusions can be drawn from Lukács's vitalist rhetoric. For instance the link between art and *Volk* seems to qualify as a "living relationship" because culture partakes in the unfolding of the dialectic of history. The dynamism of the dialectic colors every aspect of Lukácsian popular culture, animating the *Erbe* problem as it relates to the people: "in every living relationship to the life of the people, *Erbe* means the moving process of progress, a real participation, a taking up [*Aufheben*], a preservation, a development of the living, creative forces in the traditions of the life of the people."[73] Here Lukács surpasses Kurella by rendering *Erbe* as a dynamic process rather than a fixed repository of Winckelmannian glories. *Erbe* sublates the living forces harbored by the people, taking up while preserving the creative energies contained in popular traditions.

Organic rhetoric shades into more potent biological metaphors as the exposition of *Erbe* turns to the tie that binds the individual author to the historical *Volk*: "the possession of a living relationship to *Erbe* means to be a *son of one's people*, carried on the current of the development of the people."[74] Once the individual author is figured as a metaphorical blood relative of the social group – Lukács cites Thomas Mann, Maxim Gorki and Romain Rolland as exemplary sons of their respective peoples – the *Volk* can exert an influence on its members that is genetic in its intimacy: the nature of the *Volk* determines the character of art. "The content and tone of their works," Lukács continues, "descend [*stammen*] from the life, from the history of their people; they are an organic product of the development of the people [*ein organisches Produkt der Entwicklung ihres Volkes*]."[75] So many shoots off a common stock, popular writers transmit, and thereby conserve, the traditions of their respective fatherlands. As parts of an organic social whole, these elements of a dynamic, dialectical totality can meaningfully be described as being conjoined in "living relationships."

The second sense of "life" only compounds the organicity of Lukácsian *Volkstümlichkeit*. "The life of the people, the progressive development of the masses' own life experiences" should furnish the subjects of realist fiction. Lukács concerns himself here with thematics, with prescribing the proper content of literary art. To take but two examples, realists like Balzac or Mann "provide access to the many sides of the life experiences of the reader who comes from the broad masses of the people [*Massen des Volkes*]."[76] Again slipping between "mass" and *Volk*, Lukács calls for an art that mediates society, for a literature that, in the words of an essay from 1936, narrates rather than merely describes the nuances, tensions and contradictions of society conceived in its totality. Therefore in the act of reading realism,

> readers clarify their own experiences and life events; they expand their human and social horizons and are thereby prepared by means of a living humanism to accept the political message of the *Volksfront* and to realize its political humanism; through the mediated understanding, provided by realistic art, of the great progressive and democratic era in the development of humankind, a fertile soil [*ein fruchtbarer Boden*] will be prepared in the soul of the broad masses for the revolutionary democracy of a new type.[77]

As outlined here, a two-step process comprehends the interaction of society and literature. Realist fiction imparts mediated knowledge of democracy, whereupon the act of reading prepares the masses for a new kind of politics. The order of priority is important: "living humanism" makes the masses "a fertile soil" for the flourishing of "political humanism." First, cultural production anchored in the concrete experiences of the masses; then realization in political praxis. Therefore while the position of Lukács diverges from that of Petersen and Pongs with respect to content – left-liberal humanism versus fascist anti-humanism – their arguments are rhetorically equivalent and structurally analogous. Popular art and political revolution blossom from the soil of the *Volk*.

How, then, to reconcile Lukács's vitalist *Volk* with his Marxist materialism? To be sure, Lukácsian *Volkstümlichkeit* evinces what Paul de Man identified as the "organic continuity which Lukács seems unable to do without" in his literary theory, a point also made by Terry Eagleton who notes that a "vein of 'organistic' thinking about the art object runs through much of his criticism."[78] But it is one thing for Lukács to ascribe organic unity to works of art, as de Man and Eagleton maintain, and it is quite another for him to theorize society and cultural concepts like *Erbe* as organic phenomena. One reading might consign the vital *Volk* to a tactical rhetoric designed to appeal to liberals by eliding the jargon of class struggle. The phrase "revolutionary democracy" would thus be an especially conciliatory locution since it softens the tenor of Lukács's well-known Blum Theses, which had formulated a program for "democratic dictatorship" in the wake of the Hungarian Revolution.[79]

On the other hand, the theoretical robustness of Lukácsian *Volkstümlichkeit* suggests that conceptual rather than merely rhetorical factors are at work. In this respect the figure looming over Lukács's invocation of the *Volk* is, of course, Hegel. By describing culture as being carried along the "current of the development of the *Volk*," Lukács appears to regress to an idealism that he himself criticizes in *History and Class Consciousness* when distinguishing two competing conceptions of the subject of history: the proletariat and the Hegelian "spirit of a people [*Volksgeist*]." Whereas the *Volksgeist* is a "'natural' determination of the World Spirit," the proletariat is a revolutionary class defined by praxis, a product of capitalism and the social relations between humans.[80] In other words the proletariat is a constructed entity, not a product of nature conditioned by the World Spirit. Therefore when Lukács makes realist fiction an "organic product" of the *Volk,* and the *Volk* itself a subject of history united in "living relationships" with the social totality, his theory of *Volkstümlichkeit* shows every sign of a recrudescent Hegelianism that naturalizes the *Volk*, a regression that would revert to a pre-Marxist (i.e. bourgeois) theoretical stage and void any claims on materialist premises.[81] A theoretical blunder of such magnitude seems unlikely, not least because Lukács had adopted a more uncompromising stance toward idealism in the fifteen years since the publication of *History and Class Consciousness*.

There is another possible explanation, however, which saves the core of Lukács's materialism while at the same time accounting for his vitalist rhetoric, namely, that the Lukácsian *Volk* is both a made entity, a product of praxis and social relations analogous to the proletariat, and an organic, but not necessarily natural, phenomenon. That is to say, on a theoretical level, the *Volk* is a work of art. Only as an aesthetic object can the *Volk* be both constructed and organic, both a made entity and a part reciprocally bound with the whole. Conceived in these terms, an aesthetic subject of history resolves the contradiction between vitalism and materialism.

Inasmuch as the *Volk* is an artifact with a claim to organic wholeness, it activates the foundational tension that Theodor Adorno ascribes to all works of art in *Minima Moralia*, his collection of aphorisms written during the height and aftermath of the fascist horror the Expressionist Debate anticipated. In one of his later reflections, Adorno posits an "insoluble contradiction" in every artwork arising from its dual status as a made object, "an artifact inseparable from instrumental reason," and as a whole whose parts are organized toward an immanent end, "a creation of second nature" analogous to an organism.[82] For Adorno artworks are both made and seemingly natural. They are coherent ends in themselves and products of intentional design. Hence they body forth a specifically second nature that mimics the autotelism of the first, an imitation brought off by the purposive activity involved in the act of human making. Such a conception entails a dialectical contradiction because the artwork appears to be both made and not-made, or rather natural, at the same time. Given his stance on the quasi-naturalness of the artwork, it is entirely appropriate that Adorno, too, slides out of a materialist register to adopt the same vitalist rhetoric that characterizes the left aesthetics of the Expressionism Debate. He immediately elaborates on this definitional tension by arguing in almost Goethean terms that "the contradiction of the made and the existing is the life element of art and circumscribes its law of development."[83] The contradiction between making and being, artifact and organism, animates something like a *Bildungstrieb* translated into an aesthetic idiom, a vitalizing element that catalyzes artworks into following a law of formal development.

Although Adorno derives his foundational contradiction from the Kantian principle of "purposiveness without purpose," his more proximate interlocutor when defining the essence of art was, in fact, Lukács and the doctrine of second nature worked out in *History and Class Consciousness.* In that earlier work, second nature refers to the reified operations of modern capitalism, which through the hardening of ideology assume the lawlike regularity of nature itself. Hence Lukácsean second nature is an epistemological corollary of capitalism, a feature of false consciousness that makes an economic order, the product of history and human choice, appear to be an eternal and ineluctable natural entity. In response, Adorno posits a redemptive mode of second nature whereby artistic creation crafts a new world that is purposeless – that is, autonomous – since all parts of an artwork are organized for an immanent end instead of external purposes such as the use- or exchange-value fetishized by capitalism and the culture industry. Therefore the law of development that Adorno sees emerging out of the contradiction between aesthetic being and making is an autonomous law opposed to the reified pseudo-lawfulness of the capitalist order.

These divergent positions on second nature extend the theoretical horizon of the *Volk* as a conceptual vehicle for social theory. At least before

Boas and the innovations of cultural anthropology, the *Volk* had usually been considered a natural modality of human collectivity, whether in the Hegelian *Volksgeist* mentioned earlier or in the notion of "Naturvölker" developed by anthropologists such as Theodor Waitz and later absorbed by writers like Yeats. Though not as biological as a "race," the *Volk* had been rooted in the conditions of its natural environment and, according to Herder, subject to genetic laws of natural development much in the manner of Goethean plants and animals that grow according to the model of an archetype. In effect, Lukács and his allies in the Expressionism Debate inherited this conceptual legacy of the *Volk*, a natural entity of the first order, and transformed it by creating a second nature that endows the *Volk* with the artifactual character of the proletariat. On this account the *Volk* is not reducible to the first nature of Hegelian and pre-Marxist anthropologies; nor is it a mere conglomeration of material parts. The aesthetic *Volk* synthesizes these two positions to produce an aesthetic anthropology that embodies a historical law of development rooted in the praxis of human making. If this synthesis does not resolve the "insoluble contradiction" that Adorno identified with artworks, it at the very least invests the *Volk* with a vital energy that drives a progressive response to the specious naturalism propounded by fascists and capitalists alike.

Yet in rendering the *Volk* as an organic proletariat does Lukács aestheticize politics? Or if not, does he have recourse to a deeper connection between aesthetics and politics in the manner of Benn, the ostensible antagonist in the Expressionist Debate whose aesthetic anthropology epitomized the cultural politics of National Socialism?

6.4   Lifeless Masses and the Living *Volk*

The allegation that Expressionism shunned popularity finds ample support in writing of the Expressionist period – much of the poetry in *Menschheitsdämmerung*, for example, or Döblin's *Die drei Sprünge des Wang-lun* – which set aside aspirations for popular assent in favor of attracting a readership that tended to come from the educated bourgeoisie. Populists from across the political spectrum responded by heaping scorn upon the pretensions of this self-appointed cultural elite. On the right, a common epithet for this kind of art was "Asphalt Culture [*Asphaltkultur*]," which the eighth edition of *Meyers Lexikon* (1936), dubbed the "Brown Meyer" for its fascist tendencies, defines as follows:

> Asphalt Culture: culture that is foreign to the people, which emerged in the years after the First World War. – Asphalt Literature refers to works of

rootless metropolitan literati; fashionable before 1933 and a symptom of decline, partly of degraded origin.[84]

The racial innuendo intimated in *Meyers* is amplified by Münchhausen, who sneers in his denunciation of Expressionism that Döblin, a writer of Jewish descent, has a "racial right to the city and to Asphalt Art."[85] But the coterie mentality fostered by Expressionists earned no less ire from Lukács, who, without stooping to racist invective, leveled an equally damning indictment of the decline of art marked by the spread of Expressionism.

Even though they could hardly deny that Expressionism thrived among an urbanized avant-garde, defenders of Expressionist art were not indifferent to charges that they had abandoned the *Volk.* Two of the movement's most prominent spokesmen, Walden and Bloch, rebutted populist aggressors by linking Expressionist primitivism to the traditions of folk art. In his contribution to the Expressionism Debate, Bloch plays up the receptiveness of Expressionists to peasant art, Slavic folk art, the art of children, convicts and the insane, summarizing his position by asserting that Expressionism "went to folk art; it loved and honored folklore."[86] Walden takes a more extreme line: "it is historically demonstrable," Walden declaims, "that everything that qualifies as dance, music and poetry goes back in its origin, thus in its originality, to the so-called *Volk,* to the masses."[87] Equating "mass" and *Volk* in the familiar fashion, Walden advances a theory of art that recalls Benn's *völkisch* appropriation of *The Birth of Tragedy*: "the so-called *Volk*" is the primal font of art. Hence Bloch and Walden derive a theory of popular culture by revising the concept of *Erbe* along primitivist lines. Unlike Kurella, who grounded popularity on the union of progressive humanism with realist neoclassicism, they argue that Expressionism circumvented the legacy of high art altogether and established a direct genealogical link with the people.

These arguments rankled Lukács, who responded by attacking his opponents for their pretensions to popularity (*Volkstümlichkeit*): "popularity is not the ideologically indiscriminate, variety-act, snobbish reception of 'primitive' products. Real popularity has nothing to do with all of that." Besides offending against Lukács's conviction that realism was the privileged form of popular art, Bloch's celebration of primitive culture tapped into a deeper disagreement about the constitution of the social order. According to Lukács, Bloch was operating on the mistaken premise that grappling with subjective effects generated by material causes constituted a legitimate means of understanding capitalism and contesting its hold over modern life. From this it follows that the experience of alienation or fragmentation, which Bloch associated with modernist montage, is merely an epiphenomenal response to capitalism, not an attempt to come to grips with a coherent, self-perpetuating economic system much less provide a critique of that system. By the same token, the fetishization of primitive cultures reflects a nostalgic longing for some earlier, presumably less burdened condition, which might serve as an alternative to a rationalized world. In either case, montage and primitivism are stylistic products reflecting subjective states, alienation or nostalgia respectively, and not the objective determinants of capitalism – property relations or class consciousness, for example, the knowledge of which Lukács believed literature should mediate.

Uncertainty about basic terms of analysis in the Expressionism Debate compounded these ideological differences, resulting in a confused theoretical vocabulary regarding topics of considerable moment. Most conspicuously, the wavering between mass and *Volk* among left theorists of popular culture bespeaks more than a rhetorical idiosyncrasy. It is a chronic feature of the debate that crops up in arguments of apologists and antagonists alike. Staking out one rhetorical extreme, Walden identifies "people" and "mass": "compared to imitations by educated or trained poets, folk art has a more direct effect since its content expresses what the people as mass wanted to say."[88] Others gave a more nuanced account of *Volk* and mass as collective subjects of cultural history. Kurt Kersten, a minor critic who won the praise of colleagues for his measured assessment of the politics of Expressionism, claims that Expressionists "remained, in spite of their efforts, without any relationship to the masses, to the *Volk* whatsoever." He then qualifies that assertion, "but it would be wrong to say that the majority of them sided with the domination of the propertied classes over the *Volk*."[89] Kersten first glosses "masses" by invoking the *Volk*. He then introduces a third form of group identity, class. The *Volk*-mass is opposed to the "propertied classes." This clarification indicates that Kersten, like Lukács, considers the *volksnah* masses to be a proxy for the proletariat. But the fact that Kersten must spell out the class position of the *Volk*-mass demonstrates the indeterminacy of those terms within an economic framework. That is to say, "mass" and "*Volk*" are not *prima facie* identifiable as an economic group, and by aligning them against capital, Kersten resolves the uncertain status of the "masses" within a socioeconomic structure by situating the conjunction of mass and *Volk* within a class hierarchy.

From a purely semantic standpoint, it is indeed difficult to see how "mass" or "the masses" could admit of internal classificatory distinctions, economic or otherwise, since the terms imply a group defined solely by its quantitative aspect. A mass is a collection of units, an aggregation of individuals that connotes a strictly physical meaning – mass as quantity of matter. Stepping out of the theoretical landscape of the Expressionism Debate for a moment, we might recall that Hannah Arendt, an anti-fascist theorist from the generation after the Popular Front, reaches a similar conclusion when she writes that "the term masses applies only where we deal with people who either because of sheer numbers, or indifference, or a combination of both, cannot be integrated into any organization based on common interest, into political parties or municipal governments."[90] Without common interests – economic, civic, national, religious – the masses are defined by "sheer force of numbers" and not by ideology or institutional affiliation.[91] Arendt defines the masses as a strictly quantitative and therefore underdetermined social unit, which lends a very different inflection to the conspicuous slippage between *Volk* and mass in left theories of popular culture. Instead of indicating synonymy, the equivocation of the terms betrays an attempt to define the masses by association. Whether by aligning the masses with a class or with the *Volk*, authors are working to give a strictly quantitative group the qualitative content, otherwise lacking, that would render the mass a political agent with its own character, ends, purposes and interests.

The effort to endow the masses with political character manifests most clearly in an essay by Rudolf Leonhard, the erstwhile leader of the *Schutzverband Deutscher Schriftsteller im Ausland* [Union of German Writers Abroad]. Leonhard concludes his contribution to *Das Wort* by responding to Kurella's three catechism questions. To the question, "proximity to the people and popularity ... do we affirm this absolutely?" Leonhard answers with an emphatic affirmative, but only insofar as *Volksnähe* and *Volkstümlichkeit* "are really and in every sense a 'natural growth' and if the *Volk* is the reality of the living masses."[92] With subject and predicate neatly stated, Leonhard lays bare a specific difference between the two terms. The *Volk* is the vitalized incarnation of the masses. Brecht, whose contributions to the Expressionism Debate have come to represent the ideological antithesis to Lukács even though their posthumous publication prevented any influence on the debate itself, makes the same distinction in "*Volkstümlichkeit und Realismus* [Popularity and Realism]". Though he uses no organic metaphors, Brecht too moves from the inertness of the receptive masses to an engaged political *Volk*. According to Brecht, *Volkstümlichkeit* means:

> intelligible for the wide masses, taking up and enriching its forms of expression, taking up its standpoint, solidifying and correcting the progressive part of the *Volk* so that it can take over leadership, and thus also be

intelligible to other parts of the *Volk*, connecting with the traditions, continuing them, and transmitting to the part of the *Volk* that is striving to lead the accomplishments of the part that is currently leading.[93]

Brecht defines *Volkstümlichkeit* by moving from the masses, understood as passive object, to the *Volk* conceived as active political subject. First Brecht designates the masses as a recipient of culture: *Volkstümlichkeit* means works of art that are generally intelligible. The first clause therefore concerns issues of reception and artistic style. After that Brecht describes the task of the *volkstümlich* writer: "solidifying and correcting the progressive part of the *Volk*." Shifting his terminology from mass to *Volk*, Brecht gives the popular writer the task of enhancing progressive tendencies within a particular sector of the *Volk* itself. Even though he resists limiting the artistic options for popular writers to a single style, realism, Brecht nonetheless shares with Lukács a conviction that popularity requires tapping into and developing the unfulfilled political promise of the *Volk*. At this point, Brecht's definition takes one more turn. He pivots from the popular artist to political *praxis*. The artist refines progressive tendencies so that the *Volk* may "take over leadership." On this account cultural traditions inform and propel political action. Past accomplishments, recorded in works of art, act as a heuristic device for "the part of the *Volk* that is striving to lead." From the masses treated as an object of artistic reception, to prescriptions for the popular writer regarding the *Volk*, and finally to the *Volk* itself animated by a practical end, Brechtian *Volkstümlichkeit* modulates from the masses to the *Volk*, therein imbuing the collective subject of cultural history with a political mission.

The distinction between mass and *Volk* is therefore a difference between object and subject, between passive and active historical agent, between the lifeless masses and a living *Volk*. This distinction brings us back to Benn's aesthetic anthropology, which theorized the *Volk* as an artwork that could be formed in both its quantitative and qualitative aspects. Left theorists of *Volkstümlichkeit* pursue a similar project. "Solidifying and correcting the progressive part of the *Volk*" and "enriching its forms of expression," Brecht and Lukács look to enhance the latent political potential of the *Volk*; they wish to refine the *Volk* and "improve it qualitatively," to use the language of Benn. But the qualitative concerns of *Volksfront* theorists run deeper still, requiring a transformation between two essentially, that is qualitatively, distinct kinds of phenomena: the mass or masses understood as sheer quantity, like the population (*Bevölkerungszahl*) discussed by Benn, and a social organism – an aesthetic subject of history endowed with a revolutionary task. It should therefore come as no surprise that for Lukács "real *Volkstümlichkeit*" requires "finding directives and slogans that awaken a new, politically efficacious life."[94] Popularity means discovering the "life awakening, popular progressiveness" that catalyzes the qualitative change from physical, inert social object – the masses as political matter – to a living subject of history, the *Volk*.

Hence it is now possible to answer the question posed at the end of Section 6.3 in the negative. When rendering the *Volk* as an organic proletariat, Lukács does not so much aestheticize politics as follow his materialist premises to their necessary conclusion, which happens to be an aesthetic conclusion. The *Volk* is at once a product of concrete forces of production and defined by its reciprocal relations with the whole, namely, the totality of capitalism. Not a political entity that is then aestheticized, the *Volk* is by its very nature both made and teleological, a subject of history that meets the sufficient conditions for a work of art. This answer then poses its own questions in turn: What kind of world ought to issue from this revolutionary subject and what are the legitimate means for achieving that end? Benn, it should be remembered, was no less committed to a revolutionary overthrow of the bourgeoisie than Lukács. Yet for all his belief that popular authors bear an organic, even genetic relationship to their *Volk*, Lukács does not prescribe eugenic interventions in the biological constitution of a people (the means) in order to bring about a perfect State (the end). For Lukács, society replaces nature as the determining instance of the *Volk*. Capitalism is the unity comprehending the diversity of forms. Consequently this aesthetic anthropology distinguishes the Lukácsean *Volk* not only from Benn's eugenics but also from the Herderian *Volksgeist*, whose characteristics emerge out of a convergence of genetic endowment and climate. In Lukács's account an economic totality, not Nature divided into a coherent hierarchy of species and genera, determines social parts through reciprocal causality with the whole.

These theoretical innovations lead to alternative means of bringing about political ends. According to Lukács's theory of *Volkstümlichkeit*, comprehending reality through the medium of literary art furnishes a living humanism that then prepares readers for a humanist politics. In other words, reading realist novels is the means by which a new political reality is disclosed, a world where humans are connected in coherent, organic relations that are nevertheless parts of a social totality conceived along materialist lines. Compelling as this aesthetic praxis may be, it would be seriously compromised if an alternative art could better capture the nature of modern reality – an art, for example, like cinema. And it is therefore with this art, which makes its own claims to popularity while harboring its own political implications, that this study must conclude.

Coda
Eusynoptos

Despite their various political orientations, the aesthetic theories of human essence examined in this study face a common problem: how to expand a group from the felt intimacy of a small community into a larger social entity. Two canonical examples illustrate the point: Friedrich Schiller concedes in the final letter of *On the Aesthetic Education of Man* that an Aesthetic State may exist in a "few selected circles"; and Shaftesbury defines the *sensus communis* as an innate faculty for fellow-feeling that flourishes in small communities held together by shared sensory contact.[1] In each case, small groups foster the sensory immediacy that binds individuals into a collective whole, which immediately raises the problem of how to formulate a large-scale aesthetic group. For their part, Schiller and Shaftesbury evaded the problem, preferring to elaborate the nature of the small group as an ideal of aesthetic community. Later theorists did not do much better. Du Bois expounded at length on the close-knit coordination of autonomous economic cooperatives but only gestured to an American social order based on perfect freedom. And Yeats, in a manner that lays bare the difficulty at hand, transformed small sensory communities epitomized by group dances into a national *sensus* only by invoking the powers of magic.

Such a preference for the micro-political has a classical pedigree. Reflecting on the quantitative dimensions of the *polis*, Aristotle posits the "best standard [ὅρος ἄριστος]" for the size of the city as "the greatest multitude for self-sufficient life that may be easily taken in at a glance [εὐσύνοπτος; *eusynoptos*.]"[2] Just as Shaftesbury delimits the *communis* by inscribing a visual boundary – members may "view the whole compass and extent of their community" – so too Aristotle circumscribes the size of the *polis* by means of a perceptual, that is, an aesthetic limit: the power of the eye to take in the whole population with ease.[3] Should a people or a "political multitude" expand beyond those synoptic bounds, then the human organization, such as it is, qualifies as a different entity:

> It is customary for the beautiful [τό καλὸν] to come into being through number and size. So, too, for the city to which the stated definition regarding size applies, this is necessarily the most beautiful ... One that is too great is self-sufficient in necessary things like a nation, but still it is not a city [ὥσπερ ἔθνος, ἀλλ᾽ οὐ πόλις], since the government [πολιτείαν] cannot easily exist. For who will be the general of such an excessive multitude, and who will be herald if not Stentor?[4]

Framing his definition in terms of the proportions that befit the πόλιν καλλίστην, the best or most beautiful city, Aristotle predicates political power on the perceptual capacities of those who are ruled: their ability to hear the voice of the herald. Expansion beyond those perceptual limits does not just compromise the beauty of a collective body. It also jeopardizes the governability of the *polis*. That is to say, the political constitution of the city, *sensu stricto*, is threatened by the supersession of aesthetic limits. By contrast, an *ethnos* – a term that may be translated as "nation" or "tribe" and, together with its semantic proximity to γένος (Lat. *genus*), can refer to heritable qualities and common descent – possesses the basic self-sufficiency of a city but without the same aesthetic measure that restricts the city's size.[5] An *ethnos*, in other words, is unbounded by the sensory limits that circumscribe the *polis*.

Therefore when Shaftesbury distinguishes the *communis* from the nation, designating the latter as a group formed "not sensibly, but in idea," he makes an Aristotelian distinction between the community as an aesthetic-political entity and the nation as a super-communal group ordered according to criteria other than sensory ones.[6] A neoclassical communitarianism therefore marks the political spirit of the *sensus communis*, as it does Schiller's Aesthetic State and the University in *The Souls of Black Folk*. These writers, in addition to making recourse to neoclassical aesthetics, rely on an Aristotelian conception of the eusynoptic collective as a standard for envisioning a viable communal body. Each in their own way, small sensory communities are the apotheosis of a well-governed collective. Even writers less inclined to cite Greek antiquity show an affinity for the micro-political nature of the *polis*. For instance Yeats, long a devotee of clubs and cliques, uses the character of the Old Man in *The Death of Cuchulain* to choreograph the movements of a theatrical audience, a consummate eusynoptic group.

Yet several of these cases of neoclassical communitarianism execute a telling double move. They allude to the harmony of the *polis* while violating the basic distinction that defines the city in the *Politics*. Whereas Aristotle holds the *ethnos* and the *polis* apart, distinguishing the former from the latter for quantitative reasons, modern authors blur the lines between ethnic and political groups. Yeats's eusynoptic audience coexists with his interest in eugenics; Du Bois extrapolates from the intimate autonomy of the Black University to the folk at large. Lukács and Benn identify an aesthetic subject of history with an organic *Volk*. In each case the distinction between ethnic and aesthetic-political determinations of collective life crumbles. National or genetic categories – *ethnoi* – are defined as aesthetic entities with political force. One reason for this conspicuous synthesis of *ethnos* and *polis* in modern accounts of collective life is that it solves the problem of scale posed earlier. Combining aesthetic conceptions of collective life with anthropology – the two main discourses examined over the course of this study – helps theorize large-scale social entities according to the aesthetic essence that unifies the *polis*. In other words, ethnologizing the eusynoptic group scales up the collective. Nation, race, *Volk* or *Volksgeimeinschaft* – all these configurations of collectivity are, quantitatively speaking, on the order of the *ethnos*. Yet aesthetic justifications of these configurations of collectivity lend them, however speciously, something of the solidary force that binds small-scale entities into a unified whole.

There is an alternative solution to the problem of scale, however, that avoids the problematic elision of *ethnos* and *polis* and achieves its theoretical aim by modernizing eusynoptos as a means of determining group constitution: Walter Benjamin's theory of the cinematic masses in "The Work of Art in the Age of Mechanical Reproduction." Following the discovery of a longer version of the Work of Art essay – known as the *Zweite Fassung*, which was thought lost until the publication of the final volume of the *Gesammelte Schriften* in 1989 – scholars have come to appreciate how a vexed editorial history shaped the essay's argument both in response to objections leveled by Theodor Adorno and Max Horkheimer and with respect to the evolution of Benjamin's own thinking in the final years of his life.[7] Four versions of the essay are extant, three in German and a French translation prepared in collaboration with Pierre Klossowski that was published in the *Zeitschrift für Sozialforschung* in 1936.

The epilogue of the best-known, third version collected in *Illuminations* (1955) moves briskly from a statement about property relations to the famous declaration that "fascism leads necessarily to an aestheticizing of political life."[8] By *aesthetic*, here, Benjamin means a general theory of perception tied explicitly to the term's classical sense. Immediately preceding the epilogue in all but the final version, Benjamin links the most modern of artistic practices, namely cinema, to a classical conception of aesthetic theory: "film proves at present to be the most important object of that theory of perception called aesthetics by the Greeks."[9] Modern aesthetics, understood in classical terms as a theory of perception, finds its privileged object of inquiry in the art of film, or rather, in the art of mass reproduction. Therefore the aestheticizing impulse, which renders the world in sensory terms and manifests most potently in fascism, translates modern political life into a neoclassical aesthetic problem: how to understand an age of technical reproduction by means of a theory of perception.

By the autumn of 1935, when Benjamin first drafted the Work of Art essay, he had absorbed Lukács's critique of Expressionism, which had first been leveled in 1934 and then developed in the Expressionism Debate.[10] For both Benjamin and Lukács, as we saw in Chapters 5 and 6, fascism reduces politics to a spectacle of subjective experience that gives expression (*Ausdruck*) to popular sentiments while preserving the material relations that organize society. At the same time, the specifically aesthetic character of fascism, its perceptual or sensory aspect, is somewhat thinly drawn in the Work of Art essay, at least in the epilogue of the third version. Even though Benjamin invokes the concept of *Ausdruck* and includes a long quotation from the Expressionist favorite Filippo Marinetti, there is no elaborate theory of form as was the case for Benn, no critique of immediacy as in Lukács. The first, handwritten draft of the essay, though, provides a more sustained exposition of fascist aesthetics that was reduced to a footnote in later versions. Reflecting on what Siegfried Kracauer called the "mass ornament," Benjamin connects the medium of film, that privileged object of modern αἴσθησις, to the dynamics of fascist collectivity. He writes:

> mass reproduction [i.e. film] accommodates the reproduction of the masses, especially when considering newsreels, whose propagandistic meaning cannot be overestimated. In the great festival parades, the monster assemblies, in mass sporting events and in war that are all supplied by the camera today, the mass looks itself in the face.[11]

Documentary newsreels distill the aesthetics of fascism. Whether martial or recreational, images of the masses are presented to an audience assembled in a theater. But the propaganda value of newsreels derives not, or at least not only, from their discursive content. The political value of cinema is more direct. The camera, *die Aufnahmeapparatur* in Benjamin's point-edly technical diction, turns the mass into an aesthetic object, an image on the screen, and *therein politicizes* a collective body. Through an act of technological portraiture, wherein the camera allows a mass to see itself, to look at its own face, a collective body *may be easily taken in at a glance*. The mass becomes eusynoptic, perceiving itself *qua* mass. Benjamin's French makes the intimation of mass eusynoptos in this passage clearer still. Rather than the mass "look itself in the face [*sieht die Masse sich selbst ins Gesicht*]," as the German puts it, the original publication in the *Zeitschrift für Sozialforschung* reads: "la masse se regarde elle-même dans ses propres yeux."[12] Gazing through the camera's mechanical eye, the cinematic mass looks into its own eyes, "ses propres yeux," as it beholds itself onscreen. So when Benjamin continues by asserting that "des rassemblements de centaines de mille hommes se laissent le mieux embrasser à vol d'oiseau," he revives and expands an Aristotelian "best standard" for the size of the most beautiful city, τήν πόλιν καλλίστην, by positing the bird's-eye view as the *best* optic for embracing and encompassing the whole extent of a mass at a glance.[13]

Even though Benjamin uses the term *Leben* (life) in his famous condem-nation of aestheticization – "fascism leads necessarily to the aestheticization of political life" – his analysis of the fascist mass remains truer to a strict Aristotelianism than the theory of popular art in the Expressionism Debate, for he refrains from the telling conflation of ethnic-genetic and aesthetic-political configurations of group constitution. There is no rhetorical slippage between *Volk* and mass in Benjamin's argument, for example, which was certainly the case for the *Volksfront* critics who held forth in *Das Wort*. And there is certainly no vestige of the Kantian organicism that places subspecies, species and genera in a hierarchy of natural categories in the manner of Walker or Croly and Wakeman. With that said, the trenchancy of Benjamin's account of the relationship between technological apparatus and modern perception arises in large part from the way the camera reengineers the nature of human perception. Central to the Work of Art essay is its "anthropological materialism," a phrase used by Adorno to describe Benjamin's conviction that "the human body is the measure of concreteness." Miriam Hansen has shown how this somatic anthropology has an aesthetic edge in the essay, reflecting Benjamin's concern with the effects of material changes – economic, technological, historical – on the human sensorium understood as a historically mutable perceptual system.[14]

Therefore even as he avoids making *völkisch* or ethnic-genetic distinc-tions *within* the anthropological domain, Benjamin does not shy away from claims about human nature as such. To wit: "it is another nature that speaks to the camera as to the eye."[15] "Technical reproduction captures images that completely escape natural optics."[16] Following from this divergence between the optical capacities of humans and machines – between the respective natures that speak to the eye and to the camera – different political possibilities emerge when politics is based on perception: "mass movements are presented more clearly to the camera than to the glance [*Blick*]." Or in French: "Les mouvements de masse se présentent plus nettement aux appareils enregisteurs qu'à l'œil nu."[17] For Aristotle the naked eye circumscribed the *polis* according to the laws of natural optics. Technology inaugurates an anthropological revolution, whereby the natural glance cedes its definitional power to the apparatus, which mechanizes and therefore modernizes eusynoptos.

Neither a conglomeration of individuals defined by sheer quantity (Arendt), nor a natural species constituted through an ideal type (Kant), the Benjaminian fascist mass coheres into a unified political entity in the moment it sees itself onscreen – the moment of its becoming eusynoptic. But have we solved the problem of scale posed at the outset? Do images of mass spectacle allow for an expansion of the film audience, numbered in the dozens, so that it approaches the size of those conventional units of fascist politics, *ethnoi* such as the nation or the *Volksgemeinschaft*? Or, rather more feebly, does the eusynoptic mass onscreen function as a mere synecdoche for larger constellations of collectivity, a representative part that suggests a larger ethnic whole but only by inference? On this point, we arrive at the very heart of a Benjaminian conception of collective life in modernity: mechanical reproduction.

When the cinematic audience sees its avatar in the crowds or cadres marching before their leader, the mass that appears onscreen is not a unique collection of individuals like the Aristotelian *polis*, where each citizen hears the singular call of the herald. By the time the eusynoptic mass reaches the screen, it has already been shorn of its auratic singularity through a mechanical procedure, the technical process of replication, that has transformed the original image into positive prints for exhibition. It is the copy, not the original, that is shown to viewers. It is the copy, not the unique image, that meets the eyes of the audience. Those viewers, knowing full well that other audiences are watching the same images elsewhere, take in the mechanically reproduced mass at a glance. Therefore the eusynoptic mass onscreen is not a part of some greater whole. It is that greater whole: a mechanized body capable of reproducing on a scale that has, in principle, no upper bound. Unconstrained by laws of breeding or merely natural imperatives, the modern eusynoptic mass is limited only by the power of the apparatus itself.

This is the perceptual regime underlying the claim that fascism aestheticizes political life. When the cinematic audience views the eusynoptic mass projected in the theater, the face of modern mechanized politics stares back. And this regime entails specific practical consequences: "all efforts to aestheticize politics culminate in one point. That one point is war. War, and only war, makes it possible to give mass movements of the largest scale a goal while preserving traditional property relations."[18] War is the ultimate *telos* for the aesthetic mass. War gives the utmost expression to sensations and popular sentiments while keeping the real, material relations that organize society in place. Therefore when he proceeds to cite a long passage on martial beauty by Marinetti, a writer whom Benn praised as the "creative power" behind modern literary style, Benjamin reinscribes the aestheticizing impulse of fascism within a teleological framework. The final end and aim of the eusynoptic mass is the sheer expression of the senses in war, which is represented in Marinetti's apocalyptic vision of "blooming meadows" lit up by the "fiery orchids of machine guns."[19] Aristotle, too, alludes to war in his aesthetic definition of the *polis*. He entertains the possibility of a city that lacks an aesthetic limit, asking, as we have seen, "who will be the general (στρατηγòς) of such an excessive multitude, and who will be herald if not Stentor?" Benjamin imagines just such a large-scale eusynoptic entity. Unbounded by the natural eye and ear yet comprehended by a mechanical *optos*, the fascist mass expresses the total fury of modern life unchecked by a general's order or the voice of a Stentor. Instead those sensations are administered by a *Führer*.

I

In December 1939 W. H. Auden visited a German-language cinema on Manhattan's upper-east side after reading a review in the *New York Post* that described a jingoistic outburst among the cinema's German patrons. In Edward Mendelson's telling, Auden traveled "to see the audience as much as the film," but for our purposes, the reaction of the audience is inextricable from the character of the film itself: *Feldzug in Polen* was a newsreel documentary about the Nazi invasion of Poland.[20] Here is an excerpt of the review by Archer Winsten that caught Auden's attention:

> At last there was a picture of Hitler reviewing the troops. As the solid blocks of soldiers marched past, goose-stepping almost off the ground and making

an enormously effective picture of mechanized drill, the 86th [*sic*] Street Garden theatre burst into sudden and violent applause.[21]

When Auden went to see the film it sparked an even more ferocious response: "quite ordinary, supposedly harmless Germans in the audience were shouting 'Kill the Poles,'" Auden later recalled.[22] Here we have something of a primal scene of the eusynoptic mass: two descriptions of an audience reacting to a fascist newsreel; two versions of a collective body seeing itself onscreen.

These reports by Auden and Winsten raise a key question for an aesthetic theory of collective human essence: If the eusynoptic mass becomes politicized in the moment it sees itself as an aesthetic object, then how are we to explain the divergence between the behavior of the audience in the theater and the cinematic image? Winsten describes the audience observing soldiers marching in rank, those "solid blocks" joined for the purpose of war. Why, then, does the audience erupt in applause and murderous cries instead of imitating that mechanical precision? Whence the *anti*-mimetic effects produced by the cinematic image on the audience?

Up to this point in our analysis the eusynoptic mass seems to be defined solely by its outer extent, a monolithic block of undifferentiated content – "in the great festival parades, the monster assemblies, in mass sporting events and in war that are all supplied by the camera today, the mass looks itself in the face." That is to say, the fascist groups recorded in film reflect the external aspect of the modern mass, its face or countenance. This account leaves unexplained how, if at all, eusynoptos might define, or at the very least inform, the *inner* constitution of collective life. Consider the Expressionism Debate. In *Das Wort,* theorists distinguished between distinct kinds of human collectivity: the mass as quantity of matter and a *Volk* motivated by a collective purpose. While the qualitative characteristics of a mass remained underdetermined – indeed, their underdetermination is the defining feature of a mass for a later theorist like Arendt – the *Volk* in left theories of popular culture has a coherent political identity and pursues practical, indeed revolutionary goals. Activating and enhancing the latent potential of the "progressive part of the *Volk*," in Brecht's formulation, implies, then, a need to identify and discriminate between various parts of the *Volk* – progressive ones, to be sure, but also those less progressive or reactionary elements targeted by the *völkisch* populism of a writer like Börries von Münchhausen.[23] Hence the qualitative distinctions between mass and *Volk*, as well as subdistinctions of parts within the *Volk* as a whole, refer not to the external dimensions of a collective body, their shape or appearance, but to internal qualities that define its nature as lifeless or living, inert or purposive, revolutionary or reactionary.

Like his *Volksfront* contemporaries, Benjamin makes a sharp distinction between two kinds of collectivity, not mass and *Volk*, but petit-bourgeoisie and class-conscious proletariat. In a passage from the *Zweite Fassung* that Hansen describes as the most detailed account of mass politics in Benjamin's *oeuvre*, the petit-bourgeoisie "is not a class; it is in fact only a mass"; and more specifically "a mass as impenetrable and compact."[24] Even while denying the mass a place in an economic classification, Benjamin ascribes material attributes to the petit-bourgeoisie, namely compactness and impenetrability. On the other hand the class-conscious proletariat "forms a compact mass only from the outside, in the imagination of its oppressors."[25] Crucially, though, such external features belie the true nature of the revolutionary working class since "in the moment the class-conscious proletariat takes up its battle for liberation, its apparently compact mass has in truth already loosened."[26] Therefore the distinction between external and internal is paramount for the respective constellations of petit-bourgeoisie and class-conscious proletariat. The petit-bourgeoisie is a compact mass through and through while the class-conscious proletariat, external appearances to the contrary, possesses an internal looseness that permits freedom of movement and a capacity for resistance. And should the mechanism operating in support of that inner flexibility need spelling out, Benjamin clarifies that a specific form of action, namely collective action, enables the struggle for liberation: "the loosening of the proletarian masses is the work of solidarity."

Benjamin draws a distinction between two forms of modern collectivity by describing the physical constitution of two different material bodies – the one compact and impenetrable, the other loose, pliant and labile. Unlike the reductionist physicalism of *Volksfront* critics, who characterized the mass as a mere quantity of matter, Benjamin offers finer grained descriptions of the physical nature of collective bodies, and he does not stop there. He correlates those physical characteristics with a series of philosophically, and politically, potent internal qualities such as reason, emotion and collective agency. For the petit-bourgeoisie, compactness means that "in truth, the reactive moment is definitive." Furthermore, Benjamin points out in a parallel formulation, "the emotional moment is definitive." Compactness entails rigidity and emotional reactivity for Benjamin, attributes that may bind individuals into a collective whole but only through an emotive and thus debased form of pseudo-solidarity.

Hence the petit-bourgeoisie can only respond to antecedent impulses; it is contingent upon another agent to initiate action. So construed, the petit-bourgeois mass operates as the thesis to the antithesis of the class-conscious proletariat, which "ceases to stand under the rule of mere reactions [*unter der Herrschaft bloßer Reaktionen*]" and instead "proceeds to action" directed by "a collective *ratio*." United in the practice of a genuine, deliberate solidarity, the proletariat is not bound by the iron law of reaction. It determines its own actions through collective reason.

Thus Benjaminian collectivity pivots on a conceptual dyad familiar from the analysis of Du Bois and Schiller: heteronomy and autonomy. The petit-bourgeoisie reacts, ruled by a law external to itself, whereas the class-conscious proletariat determines its *own law* (auto-nomos). Du Bois, working in a Boasian vein, contested the heteronomy of racial types and championed autonomous collective bodies "striving together for the accomplishment of certain more or less vividly conceived ideals of life."[27] *Volksfront* theorists distanced themselves from the lifeless masses – heteronomous in their brute, inert physicality – by theorizing a vital *Volk* animated by progressive ends. For his part, Benjamin goes further. He understands the revolutionary subject of history not as a mere political *bios*, a living *Volk* or an organic proletariat, but as a collective *anthropos*: a conscious social body that may determine its own ends through reason.

II

One significant omission in Benjamin's discussion of petit-bourgeoisie and class-conscious proletariat is an explication of the collective *ratio* that supposedly governs group action. Does collective reason arise from the sum of rational decisions taken independently by individual members of a class? Might collective reason be deliberative, a matter of consensus and debate? Does Benjamin tacitly invoke intuitive access to some sort of general will? Facing a similar dilemma, Lukács notoriously claimed that "rationally appropriate reaction [*rationell angemessene Reaktion*]" must be "imputed" to the class-conscious proletariat, which in turn requires a revolutionary vanguard to derive ideological content from its ostensibly superior insight in order then to impute it to the working class.[28]

Though he refrains from elaborating on the nature of collective reason as such, Benjamin does reflect on the mental life of the masses shortly after his discussion of the petit-bourgeoisie and class-conscious proletariat in the *Zweite Fassung*. Analyzing mass psychology and collective *un*-reason,

Benjamin describes a communal aesthetic practice, namely, laughter at the film image, that acts as an antidote to mass psychoses:

> If one looks into what are the dangerous tensions that technology and its consequences have produced in the great masses – tensions that at critical stages assume a psychotic character – one comes to the realization that this same technization has created the possibility of psychic immunization against such mass psychoses through certain films, in which a forced development of sadistic fantasies or masochistic delusions can prevent their natural and dangerous maturation in the masses. Collective laughter represents the preemptive and healing outbreak of such mass psychoses.[29]

If left to its own devices, pent-up psychic energy would erupt in outbreaks of violent delusion. Such symptoms of mass psychosis, which are a familiar feature of fascism, are in fact enumerated by Benjamin in his discussion of the petit-bourgeoisie and proletariat: "the manifestations of the compact mass carry an exclusively panicked aspect, whether they give expression to enthusiasm for war, the hatred of the Jews, or the instinct for self-preservation."[30] In keeping with the emotional reactivity of the compact mass, sadomasochistic and psychotic reactions are expressed through regressive behaviors like war fever and primary narcissism, which constitute a "natural and dangerous maturation" of a dysregulated mass mind. Collective laughter, however, is "a forced development" that offers an alternative to that natural process, channeling instinctual drives into a safe outlet within a controlled environment – the movie theater as therapeutic container.

By bringing collective psychic content before the eyes of viewers, moving images precipitate an affective-behavioral response, collective laughter, that resolves aggressive instincts and immunizes the mass mind against future outbreaks. Therapeutic responses are due in part to the character of certain films; Benjamin singles out Chaplin and Disney's Mickey Mouse films for their healing qualities. But the salutary effects of cinema also result from the power of the apparatus itself:

> And so those processes of the camera are so many procedures by means of which collective perception is able to make the individual perceptions of the psychotic or the dreamer its own. The old truth of Heraclitus – those who are awake have their world in common, those who sleep have each a world unto themselves – has been broken by film.[31]

The camera collectivizes psychic life and projects it before an audience assembled in the theater. What were the solitary sensations of the dreamer or the psychotic become sensations held in common, replacing

Heraclitus's old truth with a new optical reality and a new communal world. Through the revelatory power of the apparatus, then, the collective unconscious is rendered visually conscious. The mental life of a large-scale mass, which would otherwise have been hidden or repressed, is presented as an aesthetic image onscreen. In other words, for the film audience, the mass psyche becomes eusynoptic. Collective mental life *is easily taken in at a glance.* So if the bird's-eye view captures the external dimensions of modern collectivity, allowing the mass to look itself in the face as an aesthetic image onscreen and thereby understand itself as a modern political entity, then the camera also peers into the internal reaches of the collective mind, unveiling for the audience its own psyche before its eyes.

This brings us back to the problem of collective *ratio.* Presented with images of its unconscious self, a collective body discharges pent-up pathological content in the moment it sees its mental life onscreen. Therefore instead of finding its ultimate expression in war or in outbreaks of anti-semitism and reflexive acts of self-preservation – sheer blazes of pathos and perception that fail to penetrate the reality of material relations – a therapeutic counter-expression, collective laughter, serves as an alternative *telos* for the modern mass. Cinema permits a collective body to become aware of its unconscious desires instead of suffering a compulsion to repeat, which is, by definition, a reactionary response inasmuch as repetition lets the past determine the present while blocking potential for growth. On this model, however, psychic tensions are defused rather than being dictated by "the rule of mere reactions." With the reality principle thus activated through a collective aesthetic practice, the film audience works through its psychotic symptoms, which disposes it to claim its political essence as a self-conscious, rational and revolutionary collective as opposed to a merely reactive or reactionary emotional body.

Such an account of the internal dynamics of the eusynoptic mass helps resolve the problems posed by the film audiences of Auden and Winsten. Recall the review by Winsten in the *Post*: "As the solid blocks of soldiers marched past, goose-stepping almost off the ground and making an enormously effective picture of mechanized drill, the 86th Street Garden theatre burst into sudden and violent applause." The cinematic image described by Archer is a quintessential compact mass: ranks of soldiers marching before the *Führer*. At first glance it might seem that this image generates anti-mimetic effects in the audience – the sudden applause, the unrestrained cries at odds with the mechanical obedience of the troops – but in truth those reactions are entirely consistent with the behavior of the compact mass, whose external rigidity encourages emotional reactivity.

Further: the images of soldiers in rank activate the collective psyche of the film audience, touching their "sadistic fantasies" and "masochistic delusions" – a fantasy of domination, in this case over the Poles, though it could just as easily be the Jews; a masochistic yearning to be dominated by a *Führer* who casts his gaze over the troops and, by extension, the rows of patrons seated in the cinema. Thus the outburst of the audience is by no means anti-mimetic. On the contrary the viewers see their most primal urges projected onscreen, which elicits their expressive cries – "Kill the Poles!" What makes Benjamin's exposition of the aesthetic mass radical – and a progressive response to the mass ornament, which Kracauer diagnoses as a product of capitalist rationalization – is that he opens up the possibility that the audience will refuse this desire to "burst into sudden and violent applause," as Winsten puts it, and instead burst into laughter, a laughter that loosens the mass and therein promotes genuine solidarity as a necessary concomitant, rather than an antithesis, of collective rational action. Benjamin restores to the mass the reason that capitalism and fascism had robbed it of.

This form of collective reason has less to do with models of rationality developed by later Frankfurt School theorists, which tended to stress the Marxist side of the Marx-Freud synthesis, than with a recuperation of a reality principle conceived in broadly psychoanalytic terms. One thing is for certain: the eusynoptic mass is not a proxy for a public sphere. The fascist outbreaks imagined by Benjamin and recounted by Auden lay bare a *pre*-communicative domain populated by subjects shattered utterly by the total administration of society. Having regressed well beyond the point where intersubjective communication is possible, these psyches are impelled by drives that manifest along classic sadomasochistic lines. Incapable of speech with another, they make noises and hope their cries will be heard. Little wonder, then, that the pre-communicative masses find the non-communicative or even anti-communicative appeals of a *Führer* so attractive. A charismatic leader who flouts the claims of language is well suited to an audience whose capacity for communication has atrophied into unviability.

But the descent into unreason does not entail the forfeiture of claims to rationality as such. Far from it. In providing a mechanism for loosening the masses, Benjamin furnishes a necessary antecedent to communication that is consistent with reason conceived as a means for achieving liberatory ends: that is, for achieving self-determination of individuals or groups on terms of mutuality instead of subordination and domination. On this model a task for criticism is to develop cathartic strategies where purgation and positive affect are not ends in themselves, which would short-circuit repair by channeling affects toward narcissistic gratification or a moralism that affords sadomasochistic satisfaction – in either case, activations of the pleasure principle whose comforting regressions only harden the reactivity of the bourgeoisie. Rational catharsis, if it is to qualify as a form of reason, must prepare for and eventually cross over into communicative faculties that permit a return to intersubjective reality.

Nor does Benjaminian reason prefigure the critical rationality developed by Adorno, where the dyadic relationship between reader and text offers an escape from instrumental reason. For Adorno, avant-garde works of art, which hold open generative contradictions as parts of intentional and integrated totalities, negate the heteronomy of an administered society that suppresses conflict, levels out difference, and renders subjects as objects through processes of reification. When placed alongside the Benjaminian model of a collective body working through its primal urges together, Adornian critical rationality begins to look more like a symptom than a solution: a retreat into a private world of projective fantasy that shuts out the reality of society and the presence of others. Compared to the collective reason of the cinematic audience, Adornian critical rationality is revealed as having a weak account of alterity overinvested in the power of artworks to act as proxies for other humans as well as for the collective bodies they combine to form, including society as a whole.

Insofar as Adorno developed his conception of high modernist critical rationality through an intense engagement with Benjamin, especially the Work of Art essay, the thesis that fascism and the culture industry constitute forms of "psychoanalysis in reverse" – a phrase Adorno adopted from his Frankfurt School colleague Leo Lowenthal – can be interpreted, at least in part, as a commentary on the psychoanalytic elements in Benjamin's discussion of the eusynoptic mass. If, contrary to the desired analytic trajectory, capitalism and fascism dissolve ego into id, then Benjamin reverses this reversal. He moves from primal drives of the mass to an autonomous and hence more flexible collective. In other words he endows the masses with an ego. This is the force of Benjaminian reason: the provision of a reality principle less committed to a particular model – the totality of capitalism, for example – than to a principle whose vector points toward productive engagement with others – a preliminary, perhaps, but nonetheless essential step in recognizing the true material basis of political reality.

At historical junctures, not least the present one, when claims to a shared reality have lost their purchase and common facts have devolved into irreconcilable alternatives, when communicative reason is no longer viable and mere conviction becomes the ultimate criterion of truth, a Benjaminian reality principle coupled with techniques of rational catharsis would be a way of reclaiming a practical remit for art and aesthetics. Discharging and then analyzing pathological symptoms in a controlled setting – the theater, the concert hall, the seminar room – would constitute a modernized aesthetic education that prepares a collective to determine its own ends through reason – a determination that means choosing what kind of humans we ought to be in a world where *anthropos* is by nature an aesthetic animal.

Notes

Introduction

1 Boas, "The Study of Geography," 9–16.
2 Ibid., 13.
3 Ibid., 14.
4 Kant, *Kritik der Urteilskraft*, 5:185, 5:183; 20:209. All translations in this introduction are my own. Pages are cited according to the Academy edition.
5 Ibid., 5:183.
6 Zumwalt, *Franz Boas*, 35; Boas, "The Study of Geography," 11.
7 Kant, *Kritik der Urteilskraft*, 20:214–215.
8 Zammito, *Kant, Herder, and the Birth of Anthropology*.
9 Bourdieu, *Distinction*; Eagleton, *The Ideology of the Aesthetic*; Rose, "The Fear of Aesthetics in Art and Literary Theory," 223–244.
10 Armstrong, *The Radical Aesthetic*; Ferry, *Homo Aestheticus*; Loesberg, *A Return to Aesthetics*; Scarry, *On Beauty and Being Just*.
11 Ngai, *Our Aesthetic Categories*, 38–48.
12 Clune, *A Defense of Judgment*.
13 Kant, *Kritik der Urteilskraft*, 5:187.
14 Ibid., 5:227, emphasis original; see also 20:240.
15 Weheliye, *Habeas Viscus*, 5, 4.
16 Ibid., 32.
17 Wilderson, *Afropessimism*, 209. Emphasis original.
18 Ibid., 167, emphasis original.
19 Fanon, *Les damnés de la terre*, 5.
20 Ibid., 9.
21 Levine, *Forms*.
22 Fanon, *Les damnés de la terre*, 7.
23 Rancière, *La mésentente*, 20, 48.
24 Honneth, "Bemerkungen zum philosophischen Ansatz von Jacques Rancière," 79.
25 Fanon, *Les damnés de la terre*, 62.
26 Ibid., 233.
27 Ibid., 148–149.

28 Boas, "The Study of Geography," 13, 14.
29 Ibid., 15.
30 Ibid., 16.
31 Warren, *What Was African American Literature?*, 44–55.

Chapter 1

1 Kant, *Anthropology from a Pragmatic Point of View*, 7:119. Hereafter *APPV*. For ease of reference, quotations from Kant in this chapter are from the Cambridge editions and refer to the Academy pagination. Interpolations from the German are from the Academy edition, Kant, *Kants gesammelte Schriften*.
2 Zammito, *Kant, Herder, and the Birth of Anthropology*.
3 Bernasconi, "Who Invented the Concept of Race?," 11–36.
4 Bernasconi, "Kant as an Unfamiliar Source of Racism," 145–166; Boxill and Hill Jr., "Kant and Race," 448–471; Eigen and Larrimore, eds. *The German Invention of Race*; Eze, "The Color of Reason," 103–140; Larrimore, "Antinomies of Race," 341–363; Mikkelsen, "Translator's Introduction," 1–40; Serequeberhan, "The Critique of Eurocentrism," 141–161.
5 Gikandi, *Slavery and the Culture of Taste*, 4–7, 26–27.
6 Kant, "Observations on the Feeling of the Beautiful and Sublime," 2:253.
7 Zammito, *Kant, Herder, and the Birth of Anthropology*, 155–160, 245–246.
8 Although the Cambridge edition has opted for a more literal translation of *Kritik der Urteilskraft* as *The Critique of the Power of Judgment*, I prefer the older and more elegant rendering here and elsewhere in this chapter.
9 Kleingeld, "Kant's Second Thoughts on Colonialism," 43–67; Kleingeld, "Kant's Second Thoughts on Race," 573–592.
10 Kleingeld, "Kant's Second Thoughts on Colonialism," 49, 64; Kleingeld, "Kant's Second Thoughts on Race," 592.
11 Beiser, *Diotima's Children*, 158–195; Bindman, *Ape to Apollo*, 81–92; Potts, *Flesh and the Ideal*, 145–181.
12 Kant, *Critique of the Power of Judgment*, 5:338. Hereafter *CJ*.
13 Ibid., 5:204.
14 Ibid., 5:227.
15 Beck, *Early German Philosophy*, 278–279.
16 See Schiller, *Kallias*, 163–164.
17 Kant, *CJ*, 5:227.
18 Ibid.
19 Allison, *Kant's Theory of Taste*, 143; Guyer, *Kant and the Claims of Taste*, 225–226; Guyer, *Kant and the Experience of Freedom*, 41–44; Zammito, *The Genesis*, 128; Zuckert, *Kant on Beauty and Biology*.
20 Kant, *CJ*, 5:232. Unless otherwise noted, all emphasis is Kant's.
21 Ibid.
22 Kant, *Blomberg Logic*, 24:50–51.
23 Reynolds, "To the Idler."
24 Kant, *Anthropology Mrongovius*, 25.2:1331.

25 Kant, *CJ*, 5:231–232.
26 Ibid., 5:235.
27 Ibid., 5:233.
28 Kant, "Of the Different Races," 2:429.
29 Kant, *CJ*, 5:234.
30 Ibid.
31 Ibid.
32 Zuckert, "Boring Beauty," 121.
33 Guyer, *Kant and the Experience of Freedom*, 42.
34 Bindman, *Ape to Apollo*, 187–189.
35 Kant, "Determination," 8:100.
36 Ibid.
37 Kant, *CJ*, 5:233.
38 Ibid., 5:232.
39 Makkreel, *Imagination and Interpretation in Kant*, 115.
40 Bindman, *Ape to Apollo*, 163–181; Gray, "Kant's Race Theory," 393–406.
41 Herder, *Outlines of a Philosophy of the History of Man*, 166.
42 Forster, "Something More about the Human Races," 152.
43 Kant, "Determination," 8:99–100.
44 Kant, "On the Use of Teleological Principles in Philosophy," 8:182.
45 Kant, *CJ*, 5:417–418.
46 Ibid., 5:234–235.
47 Kant, "*Anthropology Mrongovius*," 25.2:1330
48 Kant, "Of the Different Races," 2:431.
49 Kant, *CJ*, 5:233.
50 Mikkelsen, "Translator's Introduction," 27.
51 Kant, "On the Use of Teleological Principles," 8:166–167.
52 Kant, "Determination," 8:95–96.
53 Ibid., 8:97.
54 Zammito, *The Genesis*, 206.
55 Ibid.
56 Kleingeld, "Kant's Second Thoughts on Colonialism," 50–52; Kleingeld, "Kant's Second Thoughts on Race," 591; see also Bernasconi, "Kant's Third Thoughts on Race," 291–296; Kleingeld, "Kant's Second Thoughts on Colonialism," 60–65.
57 Kant, *APPV*, 7:320.
58 Kant, *CJ*, 5:235.
59 Kant, "On the Use of Teleological Principles," 8:174.
60 Ibid., 8:166ff.
61 Gray, "Kant's Race Theory," 393–408; Louden, *Kant's Impure Ethics*, 99; Mikkelsen, "Translator's Introduction," 24; Tucker, *The Moment of Racial Sight*, 15–74.
62 Kant, "Determination," 8:101.
63 Kant, "On the Use of Teleological Principles," 8:165, 8:168, 8:175.
64 Cf. Kant, "*Anthropology Mrongovius*," 25.2:1330–1331.

Chapter 2

1 Förster, *The Twenty-Five Years of Philosophy*; Huneman, "Introduction," 1–36; Lenoir, "Kant, Blumenbach, and Vital Materialism," 77–108; Lenoir, *The Strategy of Life*; Richards, *The Romantic Conception of Life*.

2 Förster calls this process "intuitive understanding," which he adopts from Kant. For the relationship between real and ideal in Goethe, see especially Förster, *The Twenty-Five Years*, 250–276.

3 See Huneman, "Introduction," 7; Russell, *Form and Function*, 25–26.

4 Rehbock, *The Philosophical Naturalists*, 75–87; Richards, *The Romantic Conception*, 407–508, 491–502, 527–533; Sloan, "Whewell's Philosophy of Discovery," 53–59.

5 Kaplan, "The Miscegenation Issue in the Election of 1864," 219–265; Lemire, *"Miscegenation,"* 115–144; Wood, *Black Scare*, 53–103.

6 Walker, *Beauty*, viii.

7 Goethe, *Versuch die Metamorphose der Pflanzen zu erklären*, 149–150. My translations from Goethe.

8 Goethe, "Vorträge," 279–280.

9 Goethe, *Versuch die Metamorphose*, 112.

10 Ibid., 119.

11 Richards, *The Romantic Conception*, 413–419.

12 Goethe, "Weitere Versuche," 155; Kuhn, "Kommentar zu 'Weitere Versuche,'" 952.

13 Goethe, "Einwirkung der neueren Philosophie," 444.

14 Goethe, "Botanik als Wissenschaft," 93.

15 Goethe, *Die Metamorphose der Pflanzen*, 745.

16 Goethe, "Versuch über die Gestalt," 164.

17 Ibid., 168.

18 Goethe, "Zur Vergleichungslehre," 213.

19 Goethe, "Vorträge," 280. The complete title is: "Lectures on the First Three Chapters of the Development of a General Theory of Anatomy, Based on Osteology."

20 Goethe, "Vorträge," 271.

21 Goethe, "Erster Entwurf," 244.

22 Goethe, "Vorträge," 268.

23 Goethe, "Vorträge," 270; Goethe, "Versuch über die Gestalt," 175.

24 Goethe, "In wiefern die Idee," 219.

25 Ibid., 221, emphasis original.

26 Ibid., 221–222.

27 Appel, *The Cuvier-Geoffroy Debate*, 138, 154; see also Huneman, "Naturalising Purpose," 649–674; Ospovat, "Perfect Adaptation and Teleological Explanation, 33–56; Theunissen, "The Relevance of Cuvier's *Lois Zoologiques*," 543–556.

28 Russell, *Form and Function*, 35.

29 Goethe, "Principes de Philosophie Zoologique," 810–842.

30 Walker, "Report on a Memoir," 119–179.
31 Willich, *Elements*. Willich's primer on Kant contains summaries of the three *Critiques* and the political writings of the 1790s.
32 Walker, "Refutation of the Ideal System," 11, 17; Walker, "Refutation of the Sceptical System," 48; see also Sloan, "Kant and British Bioscience," 149–170.
33 For the Garve-Feder review, see Guyer and Wood, "Introduction," 67–68.
34 King, s.v. "Walker, Alexander," 130n.14; Rehbock, *The Philosophical Naturalists*; Richards, "The 'Moral Anatomy' of Robert Knox," 392n.56.
35 John Struthers, qtd. in Cranefield, "Introduction," v; Lawrence, "The Power and the Glory," 213–227; Ruston, "Natural Enemies in Science," 70–83.
36 Cooper, "Definition and Control," 342; Cooper, "Victorian Discourses on Women and Beauty," 34–55; Cranefield, "Introduction," iii–vi; King, "Walker, Alexander," 128–131.
37 Walker, "Plan of the Natural System," xxxi–xxxii.
38 Walker, "Outlines of a Natural System of Science," 77; Walker, "Preliminary Discourse," iv.
39 Walker, "Critique on the Antique Statues," 224, emphasis original.
40 Ibid., 226–227.
41 Ibid., 229.
42 Walker, *Beauty*, xi–xii.
43 Walker, *Beauty*, 187, 193.
44 Walker, *Beauty*, 5.
45 See Walker, *Beauty*, chs. 6–7, 11–14; for a useful summary, see Walker, *Beauty*, 125–127.
46 Ibid., 125.
47 Ibid., 88–89.
48 Ibid., 4.
49 Ibid., 199–200.
50 Ibid., 125.
51 See, for example, Walker, "Outlines," 82; Walker, "Plan of the Natural System," xxxiii–xxxiv.
52 Walker, "An Attempt to Systematize," 283–292.
53 The usual attributions of *Kalygnomia* to the Edinburgh physician John Robertson do not acknowledge passages taken from Walker's writings. See Bates, *The Anatomy of Robert Knox*, 147; McGrath, *Seeing Her Sex*, 47; White, "Medical Police," 418. For the congruity, see, for example, Bell, *Kalygnomia*, 10–11; Walker, "Plan of the Natural System," xxxiii–xxxiv. The repurposing of Walker's writings suggest he was somehow involved in the composition of *Kalygnomia*.
54 Bell, *Kalygnomia*, 8; Geoffroy Saint-Hilaire [Walker], "Anatomical Report," 580; Walker, "An Attempt," 287; Walker, *Beauty*, 151. Though attributed to Geoffroy, the "Anatomical Report" contains excerpts of Walker's earlier writings and must have been written at least in part by him.
55 Walker, "An Attempt to Systematize," 287–288.
56 Cooper, "Definition and Control," 351–354.

57 Walker, *Beauty*, 208.
58 Ibid., 249.
59 Ibid., 12.
60 Qtd. in Richards, "The 'Moral Anatomy,'" 392n.56.
61 Croly and Wakeman, *Miscegenation*, 2.
62 Ibid., 14, 29.
63 Ibid., 11–14; Walker, *Intermarriage*, 221–225.
64 Walker, *Beauty*, 184.
65 Croly and Wakeman, *Miscegenation*, 4, 6, 11, 17; Stocking, *Victorian Anthropology*, 46–77.
66 Croly and Wakeman, *Miscegenation*, 24.
67 Ibid., 3.
68 Ibid., 25.
69 Ibid.
70 Ibid., 27.
71 Curran, *The Anatomy of Blackness*.
72 Smith, *Nature, Human Nature, and Human Difference*.
73 Linné, "The God-Given Order of Nature," 13; Romain, "Entries in the *Encyclopédie*," 91.
74 Croly and Wakeman, *Miscegenation*, 36.
75 Ibid.
76 Ibid., 25.
77 Ibid., 36.
78 Ibid.
79 Ibid.
80 Ibid.
81 Ibid.
82 Ibid., 37.
83 Ibid., 25.

Chapter 3

1 Du Bois, *Dusk of Dawn*, 71.
2 Ibid., 72.
3 Croly and Wakeman, *Miscegenation*, 36.
4 Du Bois, *Black Folk: Then and Now*.
5 Posnock, *Color and Culture*, 111–145; Thompson, "Aesthetic Hygiene," 243–253; Watts, *Hearing the Hurt*, 25–49.
6 Du Bois, "Criteria of Negro Art," in Du Bois, *Writings: The Suppression of the African Slave-Trade*, 1000.
7 Gooding-Williams, "Evading Narrative Myth," 517–542; Gooding-Williams, "Philosophy of History and Social Critique in *The Souls of Black Folk*," 99–114.
8 Gooding-Williams, *In the Shadow of Du Bois*, 13–15.

9 Shaw, *W. E. B. Du Bois and The Souls of Black Folk*; Watts, *Hearing the Hurt*, 25–49; Zamir, *Dark Voices*, 13–14, 113–168, 248–249.

10 Reed Jr., *W. E. B. Du Bois and American Political Thought*, 4.

11 Baker, *From Savage to Negro*, 98–126; Liss, "Diasporic Identities," 127–166.

12 Du Bois, *Black Folk: Then and Now*, preface; Du Bois, *Health and Physique of the Negro American*; Liss, "Diasporic Identities," 156n.12.

13 Du Bois, *Dusk of Dawn*, 160–161; Levering-Lewis, *W. E. B. Du Bois*, 612.

14 Boas, "The Real Race Problem," 23.

15 Du Bois, "The First Universal Race Congress," in Du Bois, *Writings by W. E. B. Du Bois*, 2.48–49. For Evans, see fn. 100.

16 Stocking, "The Critique of Racial Formalism," 161–194.

17 Boas, *The Mind of Primitive Man*, 35–51.

18 Allen, "Franz Boas's Physical Anthropology," 79–84.

19 Boas, *The Mind*, 3.

20 Boas, *Anthropology and Modern Life*, 62.

21 Du Bois, "The Conservation of Races," in Du Bois, *Writings: The Suppression of the African Slave-Trade*, 818.

22 Baker, *From Savage to Negro*, 113.

23 Du Bois, "The Study of the Negro Problems," in Du Bois, *Writings by W. E. B. Du Bois*, 1.50.

24 Du Bois, *The Souls of Black Folk*, 1.

25 Du Bois, *The Autobiography*, 143; Du Bois, *Dusk of Dawn*, 19.

26 Du Bois to Herbert Aptheker in Aptheker, *The Correspondence of W. E. B. Du Bois*, 3.395.

27 Du Bois, *Dusk of Dawn*, 14.

28 Ibid.

29 Du Bois, "Conservation," 821.

30 Appiah, "The Uncompleted Argument," 21–37; Gooding-Williams, *In the Shadow of Du Bois*, 13–15, 19–65; Outlaw, "'Conserve' Races?," 15–37; Sundquist, *To Wake the Nations*, 461–463.

31 Du Bois, "Conservation," 817.

32 Ibid., 816.

33 See Stocking, *Race, Culture, and Evolution*, 214.

34 Du Bois, "Conservation," 820.

35 Ibid.

36 Stocking, "Matthew Arnold," 69–90.

37 Darwin, *The Origin of Species*, 360; Harris, *The Rise of Anthropological Theory*, 116–118, 124–125.

38 Du Bois, *Souls*, 79.

39 Du Bois, "The Acquittal," in Du Bois, *Writings: The Suppression of the African Slave-Trade*, 1108; Du Bois, "Results of the Investigation," 4; see also Du Bois, *Dusk of Dawn*, 110; Du Bois, *Souls*, 3; Du Bois, "Two Negro Conventions," 61.

40 Moses, "W. E. B. Du Bois's 'The Conservation of Races,'" 275–294.

41 Washington, *Up from Slavery*, 173–174.

42 Du Bois, *The College-Bred Negro*, 10.

43 Du Bois, *Souls*, 39.

44 Du Bois, *Dusk of Dawn*, 71.

45 Du Bois, *Souls*, 38.

46 Ibid., 39.

47 Byerman, *Seizing the Word*, 21.

48 Du Bois, *Souls*, 40.

49 Ibid.

50 Ibid.

51 Ibid., 39.

52 Ibid.

53 Du Bois, "On *The Souls of Black Folk*," in Sundquist, *The Oxford W. E. B. Du Bois Reader*, 304–305.

54 Du Bois, *Dusk of Dawn*, xxxiii.

55 Cain, "From Liberalism to Communism," 456–473; Du Bois, "On Stalin."

56 Du Bois, *Darkwater*, 119.

57 Ibid., 119–120.

58 Schiller, *Kallias*, 152.

59 Ibid., 151.

60 Schiller, *On the Aesthetic Education of Man*, 56–57, emphasis original.

61 Du Bois, "Does Education Pay?," in Du Bois, *Writings by W. E. B. Du Bois*, 1.13.

62 For Scherer, see Johns Hopkins Circular, July 1895, Vol. XIV, No. 120, 96.

63 Buckley, "The Bostonian Cult of Classicism," 27–40; Spuler, *"Germanistik" in America*, 47–48, 161–162.

64 Scherer, *Geschichte der Deutschen Literatur*, 586.

65 Du Bois, *Darkwater*, 120.

66 Ibid.

67 Ibid.

68 Ibid., 115.

69 Ibid., 116.

70 Claborn, "W. E. B. Du Bois at the Grand Canyon," 122–128.

71 Du Bois, *Darkwater*, 116.

72 Ibid., 110.

73 Wordsworth, *The Major Works*, 385. Wordsworth's name is misspelled in the curriculum.

74 Du Bois, *Darkwater*, 110.

75 Ibid., 111.

76 Ibid., 110–111.

77 Du Bois, "Criteria of Negro Art," in Du Bois, *Writings: The Suppression of the African Slave-Trade*, 993.

78 Ibid., 994.

79 Ibid., 1000.

80 Ibid., 995.

81 Stocking, *Race, Culture, and Evolution*, 145–146.
82 Du Bois, "Race Friction between Black and White," in Du Bois, *Writings by W. E. B. Du Bois*, 1.389–390.
83 Du Bois, "A Lunatic or a Traitor," in Du Bois, *Writings: The Suppression of the African Slave-Trade*, 990; Du Bois, "Marcus Garvey," in ibid., 977.
84 Du Bois, "My Evolving Program for Negro Freedom," in Du Bois, *Writings in Non-Periodical Literature*, 228.
85 Du Bois, *Dusk of Dawn*, 106.
86 See Levering-Lewis, *W. E. B. Du Bois*, 570–572.
87 See Du Bois, "Counsels of Despair," in Du Bois, *Writings: The Suppression of the African Slave-Trade*, 1254–1259.
88 Du Bois, *Dusk of Dawn*, 100.
89 Ibid., 110.
90 Ibid., 107.
91 Du Bois, "The Negro College," in Du Bois, *Writings: The Suppression of the African Slave-Trade*, 1010, 1012–1013.
92 Ibid., 1012.
93 Ibid., 1018.
94 Du Bois, *Dusk of Dawn*, 101.
95 Ibid., 108.
96 Du Bois, "The Revelation of Saint Orgne the Damned," in Du Bois, *Writings: The Suppression of the African Slave-Trade*, 1060.
97 Ibid., 1061.
98 Du Bois, *Dusk of Dawn*, 100–101; Du Bois, "The Right to Work," in Du Bois, *Writings: The Suppression of the African Slave-Trade*, 1238.
99 Darnell, *Invisible Genealogies*; Young, *Ruth Benedict*.
100 Evans, *Before Cultures*, 160.
101 Hegeman, *Patterns for America*, 50.
102 Herskovits, "Negro History," 55; see Levering-Lewis, *W. E. B. Du Bois*, 625–627.
103 Du Bois, "Review of *The Myth of the Negro Past*," 226–227.
104 Mead, "Patterns of Culture," 207–208.
105 Ibid., 202.
106 Du Bois to Ruth K. Williams. September 10, 1946 in Aptheker, *The Correspondence of W. E. B. Du Bois*, 3.55.
107 Benedict, *Race*, 83.
108 Ibid., 86.
109 Ibid.
110 See Rigdon, *The Culture Facade*, 11–15.
111 Qtd. in ibid., 51. Ibid., 11–15, 30, 32.
112 See ibid., 87–134.
113 Lewis, "Wealth Differences in a Mexican Village," 270.
114 See Levering-Lewis, *W. E. B. Du Bois*, 642–643.
115 Du Bois, "My Evolving Program," 227.

116 Ibid., 237.
117 Ibid., 238.
118 Benedict, "They Dance for Rain at Zuñi," 225.
119 Benedict, "Psychological Types in the Cultures of the Southwest," 248.
120 Ibid., 261.
121 Benedict, "An Introduction to Zuñi Mythology," 231.
122 Ibid., 231–232, 242–244.
123 Harris, *The Rise of Anthropological Theory,* 398–400.
124 Manganaro, "Textual Play, Power, and Cultural Critique," 5, 10.
125 Bennett, "Cultural Studies and the Culture Concept," 550–553.
126 Benedict, *Patterns of Culture,* 46; see Harris, *The Rise of Anthropological Theory,* 398; Mead, "Patterns of Culture," 208.
127 Benedict, "Primitive Freedom," 386–398.
128 Ibid., 391.

Chapter 4

1 Eliot, "The Perfect Critic," 57–58.
2 Ibid., 51.
3 Symons, "Impressionistic Writing," 343–344.
4 Markert, *Arthur Symons,* 17, 26; Symons, "The Decadent Movement in Literature," 170.
5 Symons, "The Decadent Movement," 169.
6 Ibid., 170; Pater, "The School of Giorgione," 135.
7 Sherry, *Modernism and the Reinvention of Decadence,* 1–14, 29–36.
8 Fried, *What Was Literary Impressionism?*; Matz, *Literary Impressionism and Modernist Aesthetics.*
9 Cullingford, *Yeats, Ireland and Fascism*; Foster, "Fascism," 213–223; North, *The Political Aesthetic of Yeats, Eliot, and Pound,* 21–73.
10 Howes, *Yeats's Nations,* 2–3; Kiberd, *Inventing Ireland,* 1–2, 326; Moses, "Irish Modernist Imaginaries," 208; Preston, *Learning to Kneel,* 67; Said, "Yeats and Decolonization," 69–98.
11 Yeats, "Introduction," in *Later Essays,* 215–216.
12 Dowling, *The Vulgarization of Art,* 1–24; Kelly, "The Fifth Bell," 109–175; Rosenthal, *Good Form,* 10–41.
13 Shaftesbury, "Sensus communis," 59.
14 Ibid., 52
15 Ibid., 48, 55.
16 Klein, *Shaftesbury and the Culture of Politeness,* 33.
17 "Those who do not ask this, whether it is without due regard or at an improper time that they act"; ἀναισθητῶς is then rendered in the standard edition as "without feeling, judgment." Shaftesbury, "Sensus Communis," I.IV, 276.
18 Liddell and Scott, *A Greek-English Lexicon,* s. v. ὑπόληψις.

19 Shaftesbury, "Sensus communis," 51.
20 Ibid., 52–53.
21 Ibid., 52.
22 Ibid., 36.
23 Ibid., 52.
24 The *sensus communis* should not to be confused with the Shaftesburian "moral sense." The former is an instinct for sociability satisfied by sensory contact with others, the latter a single faculty underlying both aesthetic and ethical judgment. See Bodway, "The Matter of the Moral Sense," 533–548; Irwin, "Shaftesbury's Place in the History of Moral Realism," 865–882; Raphael, *The Moral Sense*, 1–17; cf. Pater, *Marius the Epicurean*, II.4.
25 Zammito, *Kant, Herder*, 108, 241, 474n.20.
26 Kant, *CJ*, 5:294.
27 Herder, *Viertes*, 420.
28 Ibid. Translations from Herder are my own.
29 Zammito, *Kant, Herder*, 160–161.
30 Herder, *Viertes*, 280.
31 Herder, *Ideen*, 255.
32 Ibid., 1210.
33 Ibid., 272, 273.
34 Ibid., 271.
35 Sikka, *Herder on Humanity and Cultural Difference*, 126–159. Löchte, *Johann Gottfried Herder*, 13–18, 75–89.
36 Herder, *Ideen*, 266.
37 Ibid., 265.
38 Adler, "Herder Ästhetik als Rationalitätstyp," 135–136; Fugate, *The Psychological Basis of Herder's Aesthetics*, 16–70; Gaukroger, "The Role of Aesthetics in Herder's Anthropology," 94–105.
39 Sikka, *Herder on Humanity*, 167.
40 Ibid., 162, emphasis original.
41 Herder, *Ideen*, 289.
42 Ibid., 291.
43 Ibid., 294.
44 Herder, *Viertes*, 279–280.
45 Ibid., 287.
46 Bunzl, "Franz Boas and the Humboldtian Tradition, 17–52.
47 Ibid., 43–52.
48 Tylor, *Primitive Culture*, vii, 15, 2.
49 Ibid., 163, 305–306.
50 Ibid., 247–248; Stocking, *Victorian Anthropology*, 161.
51 Castle, *Modernism and the Celtic Revival*, 40–97; Etherington, *Literary Primitivism*; Gould, "Frazer, Yeats and the Reconsecration of Folklore," 121–153; Mattar, *Primitivism*, 41–129.
52 Sheils, "Dark Cognition," 299–321.
53 Tylor, *Primitive Culture*, 70–71.

54 Ibid., 88–94.
55 Ibid., 124.
56 Ibid., 125.
57 Ibid., 129.
58 Yeats, "Introduction," in *Later Essays*, 210.
59 Yeats, "The Irish Censorship," in *Uncollected Prose by W. B. Yeats*, II.484.
60 Mattar, *Primitivism*, 42, 65.
61 Ibid., 71; Stocking, *Victorian Anthropology*, 260.
62 O'Shea, *A Descriptive Catalog of W. B. Yeats's Library*, 149, 289.
63 Yeats, "My Friend's Book," in *Later Essays*, 114.
64 Yeats, "Bishop Berkeley," in *Later Essays*, 354n.35
65 Lang, *The Making of Religion*, 31.
66 Ibid., 32.
67 Hume, *An Enquiry Concerning Human Understanding*, 16.
68 Lang, *The Making of Religion*, 32.
69 Ibid., 35.
70 de Man, "Image and Emblem in Yeats," 148–151.
71 Yeats, "Religious Belief Necessary to Religious Art," in *Early Essays*, 213.
72 Yeats, "The Thinking of the Body," in *Early Essays*, 212.
73 A common dating is 1914 and the publication of *Responsibilities*.
74 Yeats, "The Message of the Folk-Lorist," in *Early Articles and Reviews*, 210.
75 Yeats, "Four Years," in *Autobiographies*, 148.
76 Hallam, "On Some of the Characteristics of Modern Poetry," 87–139.
77 Yeats, "A Bundle of Poets" (1893), 200–202; "Young Ireland" (1897), 327; "Mr. Lionel Johnson's Poems" (1898), 387; "John Eglinton and Spiritual Art" (1898), 420. All included in *Early Articles and Reviews*.
78 Dwan, "Important Nonsense" 230; Foster, *W. B. Yeats*, I.159; Thatcher, *Nietzsche in England*, 100, 139.
79 Yeats, "Magic," 34.
80 Ibid., 36.
81 Yeats, *On the Boiler*, in *Later Essays*, 246.
82 Yeats, "Hopes and Fears for Irish Literature," in *Early Articles and Reviews*, 188.
83 Yeats, "Nationality and Literature," in *Uncollected Prose by W. B. Yeats*, I.269.
84 Yeats, "Modern Irish Poetry," in *Prefaces and Introduction*, 109.
85 Yeats, *The Irish Dramatic Movement*, 109.
86 Yeats, "The Child and the State," in *Uncollected Prose*, II.458.
87 Yeats, [Alternate ending for 'If I were Four-and-Twenty'], in *Later Essays*, 255.
88 Childs, "Class and Eugenics," 169–178; Howes, *Yeats's Nations*, 168; Kelly, "The Fifth Bell," 109–175.
89 Yeats, "Magic," 34.
90 Ibid., 35.
91 Ibid., 25.
92 Yeats, *Per Amica Silentia Lunae*, in *Later Essays*, 18, 21–22.
93 Yeats, "Magic," 35.

94 Yeats, "Hodos Chameliontos," in *Autobiographies*, 210.

95 Ibid.

96 Anderson, *Imagined Communities*, 6.

97 Yeats, *The Celtic Twilight*, in *Mythologies*, 83.

98 Yeats, "Ireland and the Arts," in *Early Essays*, 152.

99 Yeats, "The Celt in Ireland," in *Letters to the New Island*, 53.

100 Yeats, "The Galway Plains," in *Early Essays*, 158.

101 Yeats, "*Samhain:* 1904 – First Principles," in *The Irish Dramatic Movement*, 57.

102 Yeats, "*Samhain:* 1903 – The Reform of the Theatre," in *The Irish Dramatic Movement*, 27.

103 Yeats, "The Galway Plains," in *Early Essays*, 158.

104 Yeats, "The De-Anglicising of Ireland," in *Uncollected Prose*, I.254–256.

105 Hyde, "The Necessity for De-Anglicising Ireland," 140, 118.

106 Ibid., 118, 161.

107 Ibid., 129, 154.

108 See Moses, "Irish Modernist Imaginaries," 207–210.

109 Hyde, "The Necessity," 128–129; Hyde adapts the latter passage from the French philologist Henri d'Arbois de Jubainville. Hyde, "The Necessity," 135.

110 Ibid., 156.

111 Ibid., 160.

112 Ibid., 161.

113 Ibid., 132.

114 Yeats, *The Irish Dramatic Movement*, 59.

115 Yeats, "*Samhain:* 1904 – First Principles," in *The Irish Dramatic Movement*, 59.

116 Yeats, "J. M. Synge and the Ireland of His Time," in *Early Essays*, 245.

117 Foster, *W. B. Yeats*, II.658.

118 Yeats, "Swedenborg, Mediums, and the Desolate Places," in *Later Essays*, 55.

119 Yeats, "Le Movement Celtique," in *Early Articles and Reviews*, 409. In their introductory note, Frayne and Marchaterre note the article was anonymously translated.

120 Yeats, "The Tragic Theatre," in *Early Essays*, 178.

121 Ibid., 177.

122 Pater, "Conclusion," 118, 178.

123 Pater, *Plato and Platonism*, 14; Plato, *Cratylus*, 402a.

124 The English, German and French translations may be found in Liddell and Scott, Frisk, and Boisacq respectively (s. v. χῶρος). Boisacq, *Dictionnaire étymologique*; Frisk, *Griechisches Etymologisches Wörterbuch*; Liddell and Scott, *A Greek–English Lexicon*, s. v. χωρέω.

125 Boedeker, "χῶρος and χορός," 85–91; Chantraine, *La formation des noms en grec ancien*, 12. Incidentally, χορός is cognate with the Old Irish *gort*, "field," which is the name of the town near Coole Park and Thoor Ballylee, where Yeats spent many productive summers. See Curtius, *Grundzüge der griechischen Etymologie*, fifth edition, 200; Byrne, *Dictionary of the Irish Language*, s.v. *gort*.

126 Curtius, *Grundzüge der griechischen Etymologie*, 1858 edition, 168.

127 Pater, "Conclusion," 119.

128 Ibid.

129 Ibid.

130 Symons, "To Rhoda," n.p.

131 Symons, "The World as Ballet," 245.

132 Ibid., 245–246.

133 Beckson, *Arthur Symons*, 82, 100.

134 Ellman, *Yeats*, 38, 45.

135 Yeats, *The Death of Cuchulain*, 1052.

136 Ellis, *The Plays of W. B. Yeats*; Kermode, *Romantic Image*, 89; Jones, *Literature, Modernism, and Dance*, 29–42, 59–62; Mester, *Movement and Modernism*, 27–65; John Clinton Vickers, *Image into Symbol: The Evolution of the Dance in the Poetry and Drama of W.B. Yeats* (PhD dissertation, University of Massachusetts, 1974).

137 Kermode, *Romantic Image*, 75.

138 Nye, *Mime, Music and Drama on the Eighteenth-Century Stage*, 40–41; see also Homans, *Apollo's Angels*; Winter, *The Pre-Romantic Ballet*.

139 Jones, *Literature, Modernism, and Dance*, 51–56.

140 Mester, *Movement and Modernism*, 30–31.

141 Ibid., 58–62.

142 Yeats, *The Collected Poems of W. B. Yeats*, 601.

143 Jones, *Literature, Modernism, and Dance*, 61.

144 Homans, *Apollo's Angels*, 19; Winter, *Pre-Romantic Ballet*, 152.

145 Yeats, "The Celtic Element in Literature," in *Early Essays*, 135.

146 Ibid., 132.

147 Mattar, *Primitivism*, 72, 75.

148 Foster, *W. B. Yeats*, II.131.

149 Moses, "The Rebirth of Tragedy," 563; Preston, *Learning to Kneel*, 66–70.

150 Yeats, "Certain Noble Plays of Japan," in *Early Essays*, 165.

151 Foster, *W. B. Yeats*, II.644.

152 Yeats, *The Death of Cuchulain*, 1051–1052.

Chapter 5

1 Raabe, *Der Ausgang des Expressionismus*; McBride, "Berlin Dada and the Time of Revolution," 491–507; Sheppard, "Dada and Expressionism," 45–83.

2 Gray, "Metaphysical Mimesis," 39–65.

3 Sokel, *Der literarische Expressionismus*, 181–188, 201ff; Riedel, *Der neue Mensch*, 3–4; Taylor, *Left-Wing Nietzscheans*, 4.

4 Vietta and Kemper, *Expressionismus*, 189; Sokel, *Der literarische Expressionismus*, 201.

5 Sokel, *Der literarische Expressionismus*; Vietta and Kemper, *Expressionismus*, 14, 17–18; Anz, *Literatur des Expressionismus*, 18–23.

6 Vietta and Kemper, *Expressionismus,* 191, 192; Sokel, *Der literarische Expressionismus,* 175–282; Vietta and Kemper, *Expressionismus,* 17–18, 186–213; Anz, *Literatur des Expressionismus,* 44–49.

7 Anz, *Literatur des Expressionismus,* 44–45.

8 For a "spatial turn" in the field of modernist studies, see Friedman, "Periodizing Modernism," 425–443; Mao and Walkowitz, "The New Modernist Studies," 737–748.

9 Benjamin, "Das Kunstwerk," I.II.506, emphasis original.

10 See Skolnik, *Jewish Pasts, German Fictions,* 128.

11 Quoted in Bauschinger, *Else Lasker-Schüler: Ihr Werk und Ihre Zeit,* 256.

12 All quotations from Lasker-Schüler are cited by volume and page from the Jüdischer Verlag critical edition. Lasker-Schüler, *Gedichte,* I.I.62. My translations.

13 "The wind, the wind,/The heavenly child." Rölleke, *Kinder- und Hausmärchen,* 90. Thanks to Katrin Pahl for bringing this allusion to my attention.

14 Martens, *Vitalismus und Expressionismus,* 116–126.

15 Ibid., 120.

16 Lasker-Schüler, *Das Peter Hille-Buch,* III.I.47.

17 Ibid., 31.

18 See Bauschinger, *Else Lasker-Schüler: Ihr Werk und Ihre Zeit,* 63.

19 Bab, *Die Berliner Bohème,* 78.

20 Bauschinger, *Else Lasker-Schüler: Biographie,* 109.

21 Dick, "Anmerkungen zu 'Das Peter Hille-Buch' (1906)," 67; Bauschinger, *Else Lasker-Schüler: Biographie,* 112, 117.

22 Anger, *Four Metaphors of Modernism,* 18–19; Bauschinger, *Else Lasker-Schüler: Biographie,* 116–117.

23 For an exception, see Else Lasker-Schüler to Anna Lindwurm-Lindner, February 17, 1897, in Lasker-Schüler, *Briefe,* VI.11.

24 Lasker-Schüler, *Briefe nach Norwegen,* III.I.209; Dick, "Anmerkungen zu 'Briefe nach Norwegen' (1911/1912)," 210.

25 Bauschinger, *Else Lasker-Schüler: Biographie,* 118; Goldscheider, "Wo ich bin, ist es grün," 51.

26 Lasker-Schüler, *Das Peter Hille-Buch,* III.I.50.

27 Sokel, "The Prose of German Expressionism," 77–78.

28 Lasker-Schüler, *Das Peter Hille-Buch,* 34.

29 Lasker-Schüler, "Max Brod," III.I.161–162.

30 cf. Bauschinger, *Else Lasker-Schüler: Biographie,* 112.

31 Lasker-Schüler, *Das Peter Hille-Buch,* III.I.59

32 Adams, "Der Expressionismus und die Krise der deutschen Frauenbewegung," 115.

33 Bauschinger, *Else Lasker-Schüler: Ihr Werk und Ihre Zeit,* 79.

34 Taylor, *Left-Wing Nietzscheans,* 3–7.

35 Bauschinger, *Else Lasker-Schüler: Biographie,* 54.

36 Lasker-Schüler, *Das Peter Hille-Buch,* III.I.49.

37 Hart, "Die Neue Gemeinschaft," 10.
38 Ibid., 8, emphasis original.
39 Ibid., 13.
40 Julius Hart, "Der Neue Mensch," 24.
41 Ibid., 27; Heinrich Hart, "Die Neue Gemeinschaft," 11, 12.
42 Hart, "Der Neue Mensch," 25.
43 Ibid., 28.
44 Ibid., 17.
45 Ibid., 19.
46 Ibid., 24.
47 Kant, *Kritik der praktischen Vernunft*, in *Gesammelte Schriften*, 5:161.
48 Ibid., 26.
49 Lasker-Schüler, "Der Derwisch," *Prosa: 1903–1920*, III.I.116; Lasker-Schüler, "Apollotheater," in *Prosa: 1903–1920*, III.I.122.
50 Lasker-Schüler, *Die Nächte Tino von Bagdads*, III.I.78.
51 Ibid., 79.
52 Hille, "Else Lasker-Schüler," 565.
53 Benn, "Rede auf Else Lasker-Schüler," in *Gesammelte Werke*, I.539.
54 Else Lasker-Schüler to Julius Hart, August 23, 1900, in *Briefe*, VI.20.
55 Paret, *The Berlin Secession*, 50–54.
56 Schutte and Sprengel, "Einleitung," 66–75.
57 Paret, *Die Berliner Sezession*, 48–49.
58 Lasker-Schüler, "Oskar Kokoschka," III.I.147–148.
59 Bauschinger, *Else Lasker-Schüler: Biographie*, 49.
60 Lasker-Schüler, "Der achtzigjährige Maler Simson Goldberg," in *Prosa: 1921–1945*, IV.I.282.
61 Ibid., 281.
62 Paret, *Die Berliner Secession*, 196; Else Lasker-Schüler to Harry Graf Kessler, November 30, 1905, in *Briefe*, VI.68–69.
63 Lasker-Schüler, *Briefe nach Norwegen*, III.I.200, 212.
64 Arnold, *Die Literatur des Expressionismus*, 9–15.
65 Ibid., 12; Anz, *Literatur des Expressionismus*, 3–4.
66 Arnold, *Literatur des Expressionismus*, 13.
67 Williams, "Prosaic Intensities," 97.
68 Hiller, "Die Jüngst-Berliner," 234.
69 Manheim, "*Im Kampf um die Kunst*," 10–11.
70 Vinnen, "Quosque tandem," 8.
71 See Paret, *German Encounters with Modernism*, 60–91.
72 Marc, "Untitled," 75.
73 See Lasker-Schüler, "Der Antisemitismus," in *Prosa: 1921–1945*, IV.I.493.
74 Anonymous, "Die Tochter eines Beduinenscheichs erhält den Kleistpreis!"
75 Qtd. in Bauschinger, *Else Lasker-Schüler: Biographie*, 247.
76 Lasker-Schüler, "Im neopathetischen Cabaret," in *Prosa: 1903–1920*, 157.
77 Hiller, "Zur neuen Lyrik," 25.
78 Pinthus, "Jakob van Hoddis," 349.

79 Hoddis, "Weltende," 39.
80 Anz, *Literature des Expressionismus*, 46.
81 Hiller qtd. in Skrodzki and Oellers, *Gedichte: Anmerkungen*, I.II.119.
82 Bauschinger, *Else Lasker-Schüler: Biographie*, 183.
83 Wright, "Intimate Strangers," 287–319; for the *Neue Gemeinschaft*, see Bauschinger, *Else Lasker-Schüler: Ihr Werk und Ihre Zeit*, 60; Ankum, *Women in the Metropolis*, 1–11; Meskimmon, *We Weren't Modern Enough*, 1–20.
84 Adams, "Der Expressionismus," 115.
85 Miller, *Cultures of Modernism*, 62.
86 Lasker-Schüler, "Rundfrage," in *Prosa: 1903–1920*, IV.I.225.
87 Miller, *Cultures of Modernism*, 80–89.
88 Bauschinger, *Else Lasker-Schüler: Biographie*, 407; Müller-Urban and Urban, *Starke Frauen im Bergischen Land*, n.p.
89 Benn, "Rede auf Else Lasker-Schüler," I.538.
90 Qtd. in Bauschinger, *Else Lasker-Schüler: Ihr Werk und Ihre Zeit*, 36.
91 Ibid., 111.
92 Schmidt-Bergmann, "Zur Geschichte des italienischen Futurismus," 56.
93 Bauschinger, *Else Lasker-Schüler: Ihr Werk und Ihre Zeit*, 170; Liska, *When Kafka Says We*, 65–78.
94 Donahue, "Introduction," 20.
95 Said, *Orientalism*, 17–19.
96 Marchand, *German Orientalism in the Age of Empire*, xvii–xxxiv.
97 Arnold, *Prosa des Expressionismus*, 21–23, 34–43; Arnold, *Literatur des Expressionismus*, 80–93; Sander and Solbach, "Nachwort," 660–670; Dollenmayer, "The Advent of Döblinism," 56–57.
98 Schmidt-Bergmann, "Zur Geschichte," 114.
99 Arnold, *Prosa des Expressionismus*, 33; Schmidt-Bergmann, "Zur Geschichte," 125, 139; Schäfer, "The Physiology of Charisma," 79–93.
100 Lasker-Schüler, *Der Wunderrabbiner von Barcelona*, IV.I.9.
101 Ibid., 11.
102 Lasker-Schüler, *Ich räume auf! Meine Anklage gegen meine Verleger*, 66.
103 Qtd. in Bauschinger, *Else Lasker-Schüler: Biographie*, 400; Lasker-Schüler, "Ein Brief an die Redaktion der *Neuen Zürcher Zeitung*," III.45; Miller, "Reading the Politics of Else Lasker-Schüler's 1914 *Hebrew Ballads*," 135–159; Lasker-Schüler to Max Gaffner, August 1, 1937 in Lasker-Schüler, *Briefe*; Bauschinger, *Else Lasker-Schüler: Ihr Werk und Ihre Zeit*, 237–238.
104 Miller, "Reading the Politics," 137.
105 Lasker-Schüler, *Der Wunderrabbiner*, 14.
106 Ibid., 14–15.
107 Arnold, *Die Literatur des Expressionismus*, 84–85; Dollenmayer, "The Advent of Döblinism," 58.
108 Lasker-Schüler, *Der Wunderrabbiner*, 14.
109 Ibid., 15.
110 Skolnik, *Jewish Pasts*, 105–146.
111 Schachter, *Diasporic Modernisms*, 4–5.

112 Liddel and Scott, *A Greek–English Lexicon*, s.v. διασπορά, σπείρω.
113 Lasker-Schüler, *Der Wunderrabbiner*, 10.
114 Ibid., 10–11.
115 Ibid., 16.
116 See Skrodzki and Shedletzky, "Die kreisende Weltfabrik," IV.II.37.
117 Lasker-Schüler, "Die kreisende Weltfabrik," IV.II.25.
118 Ibid., 24.
119 Ibid., 25.
120 Ibid.

Chapter 6

1 Lukács, *Die Theorie des Romans*, 22. My translation.
2 Editors of *Das Wort* [Fritz Erpenbeck, Willi Bredel and Bertolt Brecht], "Einige Bemerkungen zum Abschluss unserer Expressionismus-Diskussion," 131.
3 Eysteinsson, *The Concept of Modernism*, 22–24; Jameson, "Reflections in Conclusion," 197 passim.
4 Erpenbeck, "Volkstümlichkeit," 122–128; Berghahn, "Volkstümlichkeit und Realismus," 7–37; Lunn, *Marxism and Modernism*, 82, 88–89.
5 See Benjamin, "Conversations with Brecht," 94–95, 97–98.
6 Benjamin, "Das Kunstwerk," I.II.506, emphasis original.
7 See Lukács, "Größe und Verfall," 254–273.
8 Benjamin, "Das Kunstwerk," 506, 508.
9 Emmerich, *Gottfried Benn*, 33; Leeder, "Nihilismus und Musik," 23–37.
10 Benn, "Lebensweg eines Intellektualisten," in *Gesammelte Werke*, IV.28.
11 Ibid.
12 Friedrich, "Aus einer Sammelrezension über Lyrik," 97; Lasker-Schüler, "Doktor Benn," II.228.
13 See Lasker-Schüler, *Briefe und Bilder*, III.I.311; Dick, *Anmerkungen*, III.II.273.
14 Emmerich, *Gottfried Benn*, 49, 42–43.
15 Benn, "Das Moderne Ich," in *Gesammelte Werke*, I.17
16 Benn, "Antwort," in *Gesammelte Werke*, IV.240; Benn, "Das Moderne Ich," in *Gesammelte Werke*, I.601.
17 Benn, "Zur Problematik," in *Gesammelte Werke*, I.76.
18 Ibid., 82.
19 Benn, "Lyrik," in *Gesammelte Werke*, IV.383; Berwald, "Unfreundliche Übernahme," 51–61.
20 Nietzsche, *Die Geburt der Tragödie oder Griechentum und Pessimismus*, 24.
21 Ibid., 55.
22 Benn, "Nach dem Nihilismus," in *Gesammelte Werke*, I.152.
23 See Kapraun, "O gieb in Giftempfängnis das Ich, dem ich vorbei," 79–83; Dittrich, "Recolonizing the Mind," 37–58.

24 Benn, "Der Aufbau der Persönlichkeit," in *Gesammelte Werke*, I.99.
25 Benn, "Zur Problematik," in *Gesammelte Werke*, I.81–82.
26 Ibid., 79; see Winchester, "Nietzsche's Racial Profiling," 255–256.
27 Mann, "Gottfried Benn," 42.
28 Dittrich, "Recolonizing the Mind," 37–58.
29 Emmerich, *Gottfried Benn*, 81–92; Lethen, *Der Sound der Väter*, 165–180; Alter, *Gottfried Benn*, 86–144.
30 Kisch, "Antwort auf Gerhart Pohls Brief," 136.
31 See Dyck, *Gottfried Benn*, 84–87.
32 Ibid., 94–95.
33 Münchhausen, "Die neue Dichtung," 230.
34 Benn, "Der neue Staat," in *Gesammelte Werke*, I.442.
35 Dennis, "On the Role of Maxims," III.251–272.
36 Benn, "Der neue Staat," in *Gesammelte Werke*, I.443–444.
37 Benn, "Zucht und Zukunft," *Gesammelte Werke*, I.460.
38 Benn, "Der neue Staat," in *Gesammelte Werke*, IV.394.
39 Benn, "Zucht und Zukunft," in *Gesammelte Werke*, I.461; see also Gann, *Gehirn und Züchtung*, 157–160.
40 Benn, "Geist und Seele," in *Gesammelte Werke*, I.234.
41 Ibid., I.239.
42 Nietzsche, *Die Geburt der Tragödie*, 24–25; Benn, "Rede auf Stefan George," in *Gesammelte Werke*, I.476.
43 Lacoue-Labarthe, *Heidegger, Art and Politics*, 58.
44 Benn, "Rede auf Stefan George," in *Gesammelte Werke*, 481.
45 Benn, "Geist und Seele," in *Gesammelte Werke*, I.235–236.
46 Benn, "Dorische Welt," in *Gesammelte Werke*, I.262–294.
47 Benn, "Die Eigengesetzlichkeit der Kunst," in *Gesammelte Werke*, I.213.
48 Hoffmann, "Totalität und totalitär," 37–50.
49 Mann, "Gottfried Benn," 45.
50 Qtd. in Raabe, *Expressionismus*, 228.
51 See Schiller, *Die Expressionismus-Debatte 1937–1939*, 10.
52 Bloch, "Diskussionen über Expressionismus," 180–181; Walden, "Vulgär-Expressionismus," 80.
53 Lukács, "Es Geht um den Realismus," 212; Kurella, "Nun ist dies Erbe zuende ...," 57; Hitler, "Adolf Hitler zur Eröffnung der Ausstellung 'Entartete Kunst,'" 203.
54 Schiller, *Die Expressionismus-Debatte 1937–1939*.
55 Schmidt, *Wenn die Partei das Volk entdeckt*, 10–11, 19–20, 62–63.
56 Qtd. in Braun, *The Theatre of Meyerhold*, 264.
57 Balász, "Meyerhold und Stanislawsky," 125.
58 *Neue Deutsche Biographie*, s.v. "Alfred Kurella"; Kurella, "Nun ist dies Erbe zuende ...," 56.
59 Ibid., 57.
60 Mittenzwei, "Marxismus und Realismus," 20–26.
61 Eliot, "Ulysses, Order, and Myth," 177.

62 Kurella, "Nun ist dies Erbe zuende . . .," 60; Leonhard, "Eine Epoche," 178; Kurella, "Schlußwort," 256.
63 Balász, "Meyerhold und Stanislawsky," 124.
64 *Etymologisches Wörterbuch des Deutsche*, s.v. "Volk."
65 Ibid., "Volkstum."
66 Jahn, *Deutsches Volksthum*, 9; Venters, "Would You Die for the Fatherland?," 41–51.
67 Vondung, *Völkisch-nationale und nationalsozialistische Literaturtheorie*, 113–114.
68 Qtd. in Ibid., 114.
69 Kurella, "Nun ist dies Erbe zuende . . .," 56.
70 Kurella, "Schlußwort," 257.
71 Berghahn, "Volkstümlichkeit und Realismus," 9.
72 Lukács, "Es geht um den Realismus," 228.
73 Ibid., 223–224.
74 Ibid., 224, emphasis original.
75 Ibid.
76 Ibid., 227.
77 Ibid.
78 de Man, "Georg Lukács's 'Theory of the Novel,'" 58; Eagleton, *Marxism and Literary Criticism*, 34; Kinney, "Metaphor and Method," 175–184; Burkett, "Lukács on Science," 3–15.
79 Lukács, *Blum-Thesen*, 699–722.
80 Lukács, *Geschichte und Klassenbewußtsein*, 328.
81 Hohendahl, "The Theory of the Novel and the Concept of Realism in Lukács and Adorno," 75–98; Shneyder, "On the Hegelian Roots of Lukács's Theory of Realism," 259–269.
82 Adorno, *Minima Moralia*, §145, 256. My translation.
83 Ibid.
84 *Meyers Lexikon*, s.v. "Asphaltkultur." Eighth Edition [achte Auflage]. s.v. "Asphaltkultur."
85 Münchhausen, "Die neue Dichtung," 233.
86 Bloch, "Diskussionen," 190.
87 Walden, "Vulgär-Expressionismus," 87.
88 Ibid., 86.
89 Kersten, "Strömungen der expressionistischen Periode," 101.
90 Arendt, *The Origins of Totalitarianism*, 311.
91 Ibid., 308.
92 Leonhard, "Eine Epoche," 178.
93 Brecht, "Volkstümlichkeit und Realismus," 331.
94 Lukács, "Es geht um den Realismus," 228.

Coda

1 Schiller, *Über die ästhetische Erziehung des Menschen*, 109.
2 Aristotelis, *Politica*, 1326b23–4. My translation.

3 Shaftesbury, "Sensus communis," 52.
4 Aristotelis, *Politica*, 1327b18, 1326a33–35, 1326b3–7.
5 Hall, *Ethnic Identity in Greek Antiquity*, 34–40.
6 Shaftesbury, "Sensus communis," 52.
7 Tiedemann and Schweppenhäuser, "Anmerkungen der Herausgeber," VII.II.661–663; Hansen, *Cinema and Experience*, 83–85.
8 Benjamin, *Gesammelte Schriften*, I.II.506.
9 Ibid., I.II.466.
10 Benjamin, "Conversations with Brecht," 94–95, 97–98.
11 Benjamin, *Gesammelte Schriften*, I.II:467.
12 Ibid., I.II:737.
13 "Assemblies of hundreds of thousands of men let themselves be embraced best from the bird's eye view." Benjamin, *Gesammelte Schriften*, I.II:737.
14 Hansen, *Cinema and Experience*, 191; Bolz and van Reijen, *Walter Benjamin*, 87–106.
15 Benjamin, *Gesammelte Schriften*, I.II.500.
16 Ibid., I.II:476.
17 Ibid., I.II:737.
18 Ibid., I.II.467–468.
19 Benn, "Rede auf Marinetti," in *Gesammelte Werke*, I.479; qtd. in Benjamin, *Gesammelte Schriften*, I.II:468.
20 Mendelson, *Early Auden, Later Auden*, 419.
21 Qtd. in ibid., 419.
22 Ibid., 418.
23 Brecht, "Volkstümlichkeit und Realismus," 331.
24 Benjamin, *Gesammelte Schriften*, VII.I.370; see Hansen, *Cinema and Experience*, 97.
25 Benjamin, *Gesammelte Schriften*, VII.I.370.
26 Ibid.
27 Du Bois, "The Conservation of Races," in Du Bois, *Writings: The Suppression of the African Slave Trade*, 816.
28 Lukács, "Klassenbewußtsein," 223.
29 Benjamin, *Gesammelte Schriften*, VII.I:377, emphasis original.
30 Ibid., VII.I:370.
31 Ibid., VII.I:377.

Bibliography

Adams, Marion. "Der Expressionismus und die Krise der deutschen Frauenbewegung." In *Expressionismus und Kulturkrise*, edited by Bernd Hüppauf, 105–130. Heidelberg: Carl Winter, 1983.

Adler, Hans. "Herder Ästhetik als Rationalitätstyp." In *Johann Gottfried Herder: Geschichte und Kultur*, edited by Martin Bollacher, 131–140. Würzburg: Königshausen and Neumann, 1994.

Adorno, Theodor W. *Minima Moralia: Reflexionen aus dem beschädigten Leben*. Frankfurt: Suhrkamp, 1980.

Adorno, Theodor, Walter Benjamin, Ernst Bloch, Bertolt Brecht and Georg Lukács. *Aesthetics and Politics*. London: New Left Books, 1977.

Allen, John S. "Franz Boas's Physical Anthropology: The Critique of Racial Formalism Revisited." *Current Anthropology* 30.1 (1989): 79–84.

Allison, Henry. *Kant's Theory of Taste: A Reading of the Critique of Aesthetic Judgment*. Cambridge: Cambridge University Press, 2001.

Alter, Reinhard. *Gottfried Benn: The Artist and Politics (1910–1934)*. Bern: Herbert Lang, 1976.

Anderson, Benedict. *Imagined Communities: Reflections on the Origin and Spread of Nationalism*. Revised edition. London: Verso, 2006.

Anger, Jenny. *Four Metaphors of Modernism: From Der Sturm to the Societé Anonyme*. Minneapolis: University of Minnesota Press, 2018.

Ankum, Katharina von, ed. *Women in the Metropolis: Gender and Modernity in Weimar Culture*. Berkeley: University of California Press, 1997.

Anonymous, "Die Tochter eines Beduinenscheichs erhält den Kleistpreis!" *Völkischer Beobachter*, November 18, 1932.

Anz, Thomas. *Literatur des Expressionismus*. Stuttgart: J. B. Metzler, 2002.

Appel, Toby A. *The Cuvier-Geoffroy Debate: French Biology in the Decades before Darwin*. Oxford: Oxford University Press, 1987.

Appiah, Anthony. "The Uncompleted Argument: Du Bois and the Illusion of Race." *Critical Inquiry* 12.1 (1985): 21–37.

Aptheker, Herbert. *The Correspondence of W. E. B. Du Bois*. Vol. 3. Amherst: University of Massachusetts Press, 1978.

Arendt, Hannah. *The Origins of Totalitarianism*. New York: Harcourt, Brace & World, 1966.

Aristotelis. *Politica*. Oxford: Clarendon Press, 1957.

Armstrong, Isobel. *The Radical Aesthetic*. Oxford: Blackwell, 2000.

Arnold, Arnim. *Die Literatur des Expressionismus: Sprachliche und thematische Quellen*. Stuttgart: W. Kohlhammer, 1966.

Prosa des Expressionismus. Stuttgart: W. Kohlhammer, 1972.

Bab, Julius. *Die Berliner Bohème*. Igel: Paderborn, 1994 [originally published 1904].

Baker, Lee D. *From Savage to Negro: Anthropology and the Construction of Race, 1896–1954*. Berkeley: University of California Press, 1998.

Balász, Béla. "Meyerhold und Stanislawsky." In *Die Expressionismusdebatte: Materialien zu einer marxistischen Realismuskonzeption*, edited by Hans-Jürgen Schmitt, 121–130. Frankfurt: Suhrkamp, 1973.

Bates, A. W. *The Anatomy of Robert Knox: Murder, Mad Science and Medical Regulation in Nineteenth-Century Edinburgh*. Brighton: Sussex Academic Press, 2010.

Bauschinger, Sigrid. *Else Lasker-Schüler: Biographie*. Göttingen: Wallstein Verlag, 2004.

Else Lasker-Schüler: Ihr Werk und Ihre Zeit. Heidelberg: Lothar Stiehm Verlag, 1980.

Beck, Lewis White. *Early German Philosophy: Kant and His Predecessors*. Cambridge, MA: Belknap Press of Harvard University Press, 1969.

Beckson, Karl. *Arthur Symons: A Life*. Oxford: Clarendon Press, 1987.

Beiser, Frederick. *Diotima's Children: German Aesthetic Rationalism from Leibniz to Lessing*. Oxford: Oxford University Press, 2009.

Bell, T. *Kalygnomia; or, The Laws of Female Beauty*. London: Walpole Press, 1899.

Benedict, Ruth. "An Introduction to Zuñi Mythology." In *An Anthropologist at Work*, edited by Margaret Mead, 226–245. New York: Atherton Press, 1966.

Patterns of Culture. Boston: Houghton Mifflin, 2005.

"Primitive Freedom." In *An Anthropologist at Work*, edited by Margaret Mead, 386–398. New York: Atherton Press, 1959.

"Psychological Types in the Cultures of the Southwest." In *An Anthropologist at Work*, edited by Margaret Mead, 248–261. New York: Atherton Press, 1966.

Race: Science and Politics. New York: Viking Press, 1968.

"They Dance for Rain at Zuñi." In *An Anthropologist at Work*, edited by Margaret Mead, 222–225. New York: Atherton Press, 1966.

Benjamin, Walter. "Conversations with Brecht." In Theodor Adorno, Walter Benjamin, Ernst Bloch, Bertolt Brecht and Georg Lukács, *Aesthetics and Politics*, 86–99. London: New Left Books, 1977.

Gesammelte Schriften, edited by Rolf Tiedemeann and Hermann Schweppenhäuser. 7 vols. Frankfurt: Suhrkamp, 1974–1989.

"Das Kunstwerk im Zeitalter seiner technischen Reproduzierbarkeit." In *Gesammelte Schriften*, edited by Rolf Tiedemann and Hermann Schweppenhäuser, 431–508. Vol. 1.2. Frankfurt: Suhrkamp Verlag, 1991.

Bennett, Tony. "Cultural Studies and the Culture Concept." *Cultural Studies* 29.4 (2015): 546–568.

Berghahn, Klaus L. "Volkstümlichkeit und Realismus: Nochmals zur Brecht-Lukács-Debatte." *Basis* 4 (1973): 387–398.

Bernasconi, Robert. "Kant as an Unfamiliar Source of Racism." In *Philosophers on Race*, edited by Julie K. Ward and Tommy L. Lott. Oxford: Blackwell, 2002.

"Kant's Third Thoughts on Race." In *Reading Kant's Geography*, edited by Stuart Elden and Eduardo Mendieta. Albany, NY: State University of New York Press, 2011.

"Who Invented the Concept of Race? Kant's Role in the Enlightenment Construction of Race." In *Race*, edited by Robert Bernasconi, 11–36. Oxford: Blackwell, 2001.

Berwald, Olaf. "Unfreundliche Übernahme: Benns Nietzscherezeption." In *Gottfried Benn (1886–1956): Studien zum Werk*, edited by Walter Delabar and Ursula Kocher, 51–62. Bielefeld: Aisthesis Verlag, 2007.

Bindman, David. *Ape to Apollo: Race and Aesthetics in the Eighteenth Century.* Ithaca, NY: Cornell University Press, 2002.

Bloch, Ernst. "Diskussionen über Expressionismus." In *Die Expressionismusdebatte: Materialien zu einer marxistischen Realismuskonzeption*, edited by Hans-Jürgen Schmitt, 180–181. Frankfurt: Suhrkamp, 1973.

Boas, Franz. *Anthropology and Modern Life.* New York: Dover, 1986.

The Mind of Primitive Man. New York: Macmillan, 1938.

"The Real Race Problem." *The Crisis* 1.2 (1910): 22–25.

"The Study of Geography." In *Volksgeist as Method and Ethic: Essays on Boasian Ethnography and the German Anthropological Tradition*, edited by George W. Stocking, Jr., 9–16. Madison: University of Wisconsin Press, 1996.

Bodway, Jacob. "The Matter of the Moral Sense: Shaftesbury and the Rhetoric of Tact." *Modern Philology* 111.3 (2014): 533–548.

Boedeker, Deborah Dickmann. "χῶρος and χορός." In *Aphrodite's Entry into Greek Epic*, 85–91. Leiden: Brill, 1974.

Boisacq, Émile. *Dictionnaire étymologique de la langue grecque: étudiée dans ses rapports avec les autres langues indo-européennes.* Heidelberg: Carl Winter, 1916.

Bolz, Norbert, and Willem van Reijen. *Walter Benjamin.* Frankfurt: Campus Verlag, 1991.

Bourdieu, Pierre. *Distinction: A Social Critique of the Judgment of Taste.* Cambridge, MA: Harvard University Press, 1984.

Boxill, Bernard, and Thomas E. Hill Jr. "Kant and Race." In *Race and Racism*, edited by Bernard Boxill, 448–471. Oxford: Oxford University Press, 2001.

Braun, Edward. *The Theatre of Meyerhold: Revolution and the Modern Stage.* London: Methuen, 1986.

Brecht, Bertolt. "Volkstümlichkeit und Realismus." In *Die Expressionismusdebatte: Materialien zu einer marxistischen Realismuskonzeption*, edited by Hans-Jürgen Schmitt, 329–336. Frankfurt: Suhrkamp, 1973.

Buckley, Thomas L. "The Bostonian Cult of Classicism: The Reception of Goethe and Schiller in the Literary Reviews of the *North American Review, Christian Examiner*, and the *Dial*, 1817–1865." In *The Fortunes of German Writers in America: Studies in Literary Reception*, edited by Wolfgang Elfe, James Hardin and Gunther Holst, 27–40. Columbia: South Carolina University Press, 1992.

Bunzl, Matti. "Franz Boas and the Humboldtian Tradition: From *Volksgeist* and *Nationalcharakter* to an Anthropological Concept of Culture." In *Volksgeist as Method and Ethic: Essays on Boasian Ethnography and the German Anthropological Tradition*, edited by George W. Stocking Jr., 17–78. Madison: University of Wisconsin Press, 1996.

Burkett, Paul. "Lukács on Science: A New Act in the Tragedy." *Historical Materialism* 21.3 (2013): 3–15.

Byerman, Keith E. *Seizing the Word: History, Art, and Self in the Work of W. E. B. Du Bois*. Atlanta, GA: University of Georgia Press, 1994.

Byrne, Mary E. *Dictionary of the Irish Language: Based Mainly on Old and Middle Irish Materials*. Dublin: Royal Irish Academy; Hodges, Figgis and Co., 1955.

Cain, William E. "From Liberalism to Communism: The Political Thought of W. E. B. Du Bois." In *Cultures of United States Imperialism*, edited by Amy Kaplan and Donald E. Pease, 456–473. Durham, NC: Duke University Press, 1993.

Castle, Gregory. *Modernism and the Celtic Revival*. Cambridge, Cambridge University Press, 2001.

Chantraine, Pierre. *La formation des noms en grec ancien*. Paris: Libraire ancienne Honoré Champion, 1933.

Childs, Donald J. "Class and Eugenics." In *W. B. Yeats in Context*, edited by David Holdeman and Ben Levitas, 169–178. Cambridge, Cambridge University Press, 2010.

Claborn, John. "W. E. B. Du Bois at the Grand Canyon: Nature, History, and Race in Darkwater." In *The Oxford Handbook of Ecocriticism*, edited by Greg Garrard, 118–131. Oxford: Oxford University Press, 2014.

Clune, Michael W. *A Defense of Judgment*. Chicago: University of Chicago Press, 2021.

Cooper, Robyn. "Definition and Control: Alexander Walker's Trilogy on Woman." *Journal of the History of Sexuality* 2.3 (1992): 341–364.

"Victorian Discourses on Women and Beauty: The Alexander Walker Texts." *Gender & History* 5.1 (1993).

Cranefield, Paul. "Introduction." In *Documents and Dates of Modern Discoveries in the Nervous System*, iii–vi. Metuchen, NJ: Scarecrow Reprint Corp., 1973.

Croly, David Goodman, and George Wakeman. *Miscegenation: The Theory of the Blending of the Races, Applied to the American White Man and Negro*. New York: Dexter, Hamilton, and Company, 1864.

Cullingford, Elizabeth. *Yeats, Ireland and Fascism*. London: Macmillan, 1981.

Curran, Andrew. *The Anatomy of Blackness: Science & Slavery in an Age of Enlightenment*. Baltimore: Johns Hopkins University Press, 2011.

Curtius, Georg. *Grundzüge der griechischen Etymologie*. Leipzig: B. G. Teubner, 1858.

Grundzüge der griechischen Etymologie. Fifth edition. Leipzig: B. G. Teubner, 1879.

Darnell, Regna. *Invisible Genealogies: A History of Americanist Anthropology*. Lincoln: University of Nebraska Press, 2001.

Darwin, Charles. *The Origin of Species*. Oxford: Oxford University Press, 2008.

de Man, Paul. "Georg Lukács's 'Theory of the Novel.'" In *Blindness and Insight: Essays in the Rhetoric of Contemporary Criticism*, 51–59. Minneapolis: University of Minnesota Press, 1983.

"Image and Emblem in Yeats." In *The Rhetoric of Romanticism*, 145–238. New York: Columbia University Press, 1984.

Dennis, Matthew. "On the Role of Maxims: Nietzsche's Critique of Kant's Philosophical Anthropology." In *Nietzsche and Kant on Aesthetics and Anthropology. Vol. 3, Nietzsche's Engagements with Kant and the Kantian Legacy*, edited by Maria Branco and Katia Hay, 251–272. New York: Bloomsbury Academic, 2017.

Dick, Ricarda. "Anmerkungen zu 'Briefe nach Norwegen' (1911/1912)." In *Else Lasker-Schüler Prosa: 1903–1920 Anmerkungen*, edited by Ricarda Dick, 177–236. Frankfurt: Jüdischer Verlag, 2008.

"Anmerkungen zu 'Das Peter Hille-Buch' (1906)." In *Else Lasker-Schüler Prosa: 1903–1920 Anmerkungen*, edited by Ricarda Dick, 49–80. Frankfurt: Jüdischer Verlag, 2008.

Dittrich, Joshua. "Recolonizing the Mind: Gottfried Benn's Primitivism." *New German Critique* 43.1 (February 2016): 37–58.

Dollenmayer, David. "The Advent of Döblinism: *Die drei Sprünge des Wang-lun* and *Wadzeks Kampf mit der Dampfturbine*." In *A Companion to the Works of Alfred Döblin*, edited by Roland Dollinger, Wunf Koepke and Heidi Thomann Tewarson, 55–74. Rochester, NY: Camden House, 2003.

Donahue, Neil H. "Introduction." In *A Companion to the Literature of German Expressionism*, edited by Neil H. Donahue. Rochester, NY: Camden House, 2005.

Dowling, Linda. *The Vulgarization of Art*. Charlottesville: University Press of Virginia, 1996.

Du Bois, W. E. B. *The Autobiography of W. E. B. Du Bois: A Soliloquy on Viewing My Life from the Last Decade of Its First Century*. New York: International Publishers, 1968.

Black Folk: Then and Now. Oxford: Oxford University Press, 2007.

ed. *The College-Bred Negro*. Atlanta, GA: Atlanta University Press, 1900.

Darkwater: Voices from within the Veil. Oxford: Oxford University Press, 2007.

Dusk of Dawn: An Essay toward and Autobiography of a Race Concept. Oxford: Oxford University Press, 2007.

ed. *Health and Physique of the Negro American*. Atlanta, GA: Atlanta University Press, 1906.

"My Evolving Program for Negro Freedom." In *Writings in Non-Periodical Literature*, edited by Herbert Aptheker, 216–241. Millwood, NY: Kraus-Thomson Organization Ltd., 1982.

"Results of the Investigation." In *Some Efforts of American Negroes for Their Own Social Betterment: Report of an Investigation under the Direction of Atlanta University; Together with the Proceedings of the Third Conference for the Study of the Negro Problems, Held at Atlanta University, May 25–26, 1898*, edited by W. E. B. Du Bois, 4–44. Atlanta, GA: Atlanta University Press, 1898.

"Review of *The Myth of the Negro Past*." *The Annals of the American Academy of Political and Social Science* 222 (1942): 226–227.

The Souls of Black Folk. Oxford: Oxford University Press, 2007.

"On Stalin." National Guardian, March 16, 1953. In *Newspaper Columns*, edited by Herbert Aptheker. Vol. 2. White Plains, NY: Kraus-Thomson Organization Ltd., 1986.

"Two Negro Conventions." In *The Complete Published Works of W. E. B. Du Bois*, edited by Herbert Aptheker. Vol. 1. Millwood, NY: Kraus-Thomson Organization Limited, 1982.

Writings: The Suppression of the African Slave-Trade; The Souls of Black Folk; Dusk of Dawn; Essays and Articles from the Crisis, edited by Nathan Huggins. New York: The Library of America, 1986.

Writings by W. E. B. Du Bois in Periodicals Edited by Others, edited by Herbert Aptheker. 2 vols. Millwood, NY: Kraus-Thomson Organization Ltd., 1982.

Durkheim, Émile. *Les formes élémentaires de la vie religieuse*. Paris: Presses Universitaires de France, 1968.

Dwan, David. "Important Nonsense: Yeats and Symbolism." *New Literary History* 50.2 (Spring 2019): 219–243.

Dyck, Joachim. *Gottfried Benn: Einführung in Leben und Werk*. Berlin: Walter de Gruyter, 2009.

Eagleton, Terry. *The Ideology of the Aesthetic*. Oxford: Basil Blackwell, 1990.

Marxism and Literary Criticism. London: Methuen & Co. Ltd., 1976.

Editors of *Das Wort* [Fritz Erpenbeck, Willi Bredel and Bertolt Brecht]. "Einige Bemerkungen zum Abschluss unserer Expressionismus-Diskussion." In *Die Expressionismusdebatte: Materialien zu einer marxistischen Realismuskonzeption*, edited by Hans-Jürgen Schmitt, 131–132. Frankfurt: Suhrkamp, 1973.

Eigen, Sarah, and Mark Larrimore, eds. *The German Invention of Race*. Albany, NY: State University of New York Press, 2006.

Eliot, T. S. "The Perfect Critic." In *Selected Prose of T. S. Eliot*, edited by Frank Kermode, 50–58. London: Faber and Faber, 1975.

"Ulysses, Order, and Myth." In *Selected Prose of T. S. Eliot*, edited by Frank Kermode. London: Faber and Faber, 1975.

Ellis, Sylvia C. *The Plays of W. B. Yeats: Yeats and the Dancer*. New York: St. Martin's Press, 1995.

Ellman, Richard. *Yeats: The Man and the Masks*. London: Macmillan, 1949.

Emmerich, Wolfgang. *Gottfried Benn*. Reinbek bei Hamburg: Rowohlt Taschenbuch Verlag, 2006.

Erpenbeck, Fritz. "Volkstümlichkeit." *Das Wort* 7 (1938): 122–128.

Etherington, Ben. *Literary Primitivism*. Stanford, CA: Stanford University Press, 2017.

Etymologisches Wörterbuch des Deutsche Q-Z, s.v. "Volk." Berlin: Akademie-Verlag, 1989.

Evans, Brad. *Before Cultures: The Ethnographic Imagination in American Literature, 1865–1920*. Chicago: University of Chicago Press, 2005.

Eysteinsson, Astradur. *The Concept of Modernism*. Ithaca, NY: Cornell University Press, 1990.

Eze, Emmanuel Chukwudi. "The Color of Reason: The Idea of 'Race' in Kant's Anthropology." In *Postcolonial African Philosophy*, edited by Emmanuel Chukwudi Eze, 103–140. Cambridge: Blackwell, 1997.

Fanon, Frantz. *Les damnés de la terre*. Paris: François Maspero, 1968.

Ferry, Luc. *Homo Aestheticus: The Invention of Taste in the Democratic Age*. Chicago: University of Chicago Press, 1993.

Förster, Eckart. *The Twenty-Five Years of Philosophy: A Systematic Reconstruction*, translated by Brady Bowman. Cambridge, MA: Harvard University Press, 2012.

Forster, Georg. "Something More about the Human Races." In *Kant and the Concept of Race: Late Eighteenth-Century Writings*, edited by Jon Mikkelsen, 143–167. Albany, NY: State University of New York Press, 2013.

Foster, R. F. "Fascism." In *W. B. Yeats in Context*, edited by David Holdeman and Ben Levitas, 213–223. Cambridge: Cambridge University Press, 2010.

  W. B. Yeats: A Life. Volume 1: The Apprentice Mage, 1865–1914. Oxford: Oxford University Press, 1997.

  W. B. Yeats: A Life. Volume 2: The Arch-Poet, 1915–1939. Oxford: Oxford University Press, 2003.

Fried, Michael. *What Was Literary Impressionism?* Cambridge, MA: Belknap Press of Harvard University Press, 2018.

Friedman, Susan Stanford. "Periodizing Modernism: Postcolonial Modernities and the Space/Time Borders of Modernist Studies." *Modernism/Modernity* 13.3 (September 2006): 425–443.

Friedrich, Hans. "Aus einer Sammelrezension über Lyrik." In *Benn – Wirkung wider Willen: Dokumente zur Wirkungsgeschichte Benns*, edited by Peter Uwe Hohendahl, 96–97. Frankfurt: Athenäum Verlag, 1971.

Frisk, Hjalmar. *Griechisches Etymologisches Wörterbuch*. Heidelberg: Carl Winter, 1970.

Fugate, Joe K. *The Psychological Basis of Herder's Aesthetics*. The Hague: Mouton, 1966.

Gann, Thomas. *Gehirn und Züchtung*. Bielefeld: transcript Verlag, 2007.

Gaukroger, Stepher. "The Role of Aesthetics in Herder's Anthropology." In *Herder: Philosophy and Anthropology*, edited by Anik Waldow and Nigel DeSouza, 94–105. Oxford: Oxford University Press, 2017.

Geoffroy Saint-Hilaire, Etienne [Walker, Alexander]. "Anatomical Report." *The European Review* (September 1824): 580–583.

Gikandi, Simon. *Slavery and the Culture of Taste.* Princeton, NJ: Princeton University Press, 2011.

Goethe, Johann Wolfgang. "Botanik als Wissenschaft." In *Sämtliche Werke. Briefe, Tagebücher und Gespräche. Vol. 24 Schriften zur Morphologie*, edited by Dorothea Kuhn. Frankfurt: Deutscher Klassiker Verlag, 1987.

"Einwirkung der neueren Philosophie." In *Sämtliche Werke. Briefe, Tagebücher und Gespräche. Vol. 24 Schriften zur Morphologie*, edited by Dorothea Kuhn. Frankfurt: Deutscher Klassiker Verlag, 1987.

"Erster Entwurf einer allgemeinen Einleitung in die vergleichende Anatomie, ausgehend von der Osteologie." In *Sämtliche Werke. Briefe, Tagebücher und Gespräche. Vol. 24 Schriften zur Morphologie*, edited by Dorothea Kuhn. Frankfurt: Deutscher Klassiker Verlag, 1987.

Die Metamorphose der Pflanzen. In *Sämtliche Werke. Briefe, Tagebücher und Gespräche. Vol. 24 Schriften zur Morphologie*, edited by Dorothea Kuhn. Frankfurt: Deutscher Klassiker Verlag, 1987.

"Principes de Philosophie Zoologique discutés en Mars 1830 au sein de l'Académie Royal des Sciences par Mr. Geoffroy de Saint-Hilaire." In *Sämtliche Werke. Briefe, Tagebücher und Gespräche. Vol. 24 Schriften zur Morphologie*, edited by Dorothea Kuhn. Frankfurt: Deutscher Klassiker Verlag, 1987.

"Zur Vergleichungslehre." In *Sämtliche Werke. Briefe, Tagebücher und Gespräche. Vol. 24 Schriften zur Morphologie*, edited by Dorothea Kuhn. Frankfurt: Deutscher Klassiker Verlag, 1987.

Versuch die Metamorphose der Pflanzen zu erklären. In *Sämtliche Werke. Briefe, Tagebücher und Gespräche. Vol. 24 Schriften zur Morphologie*, edited by Dorothea Kuhn. Frankfurt: Deutscher Klassiker Verlag, 1987.

"Versuch über die Gestalt der Tiere." In *Sämtliche Werke. Briefe, Tagebücher und Gespräche. Vol. 24 Schriften zur Morphologie*, edited by Dorothea Kuhn. Frankfurt: Deutscher Klassiker Verlag, 1987.

"Vorträge, über die drei ersten Kapitel des Entwurfs einer allgemeinen Einleitung in die vergleichende Anatomie, ausgehend von der Osteologie." In *Sämtliche Werke. Briefe, Tagebücher und Gespräche. Vol. 24 Schriften zur Morphologie*, edited by Dorothea Kuhn. Frankfurt: Deutscher Klassiker Verlag, 1987.

"Weitere Versuche zur Pflanzenmetamorphose." In *Sämtliche Werke. Briefe, Tagebücher und Gespräche. Vol. 24 Schriften zur Morphologie*, edited by Dorothea Kuhn. Frankfurt: Deutscher Klassiker Verlag, 1987.

"In wiefern die Idee: Schönheit sei Vollkommenheit mit Freiheit, auf organische Naturen angewendet werden könne." In *Sämtliche Werke. Briefe, Tagebücher und Gespräche. Vol. 24 Schriften zur Morphologie*, edited by Dorothea Kuhn. Frankfurt: Deutscher Klassiker Verlag, 1987.

Goldscheider, Paul. "Wo ich bin, ist es grün." In *Lasker-Schüler: Ein Buch zum 100. Geburtstag der Dichterin*, edited by Michael Schmid, 50–54. Wuppertal: Peter Hammer, 1969.

Gooding-Williams, Robert. "Evading Narrative Myth, Evading Prophetic Pragmatism: Cornel West's *The American Evasion of Philosophy*." *The Massachusetts Review* 32.4 (Winter 1991): 517–542.

"Philosophy of History and Social Critique in *The Souls of Black Folk*." *Social Science Information* 26.1 (1987): 99–114.

In the Shadow of Du Bois: Afro-Modern Political Thought in America. Cambridge, MA: Harvard University Press, 2009.

Gould, Warwick. "Frazer, Yeats and the Reconsecration of Folklore." In *Sir James Frazer and the Literary Imagination*, edited by Robert Fraser, 121–153. London: Macmillan, 1990.

Gray, Richard T. "Metaphysical Mimesis: Nietzsche's Geburt der Tragödie and the Aesthetics of Literary Expressionism." In *A Companion to the Literature of German Expressionism*, edited by Neil H. Donahue, 39–65. Rochester, NY: Camden House, 2005.

Gray, Sally Hatch. "Kant's Race Theory, Forster's Counter, and the Metaphysics of Color." *The Eighteenth Century* 53.4 (2012): 393–412.

Guyer, Paul. *Kant and the Claims of Taste*. Cambridge, MA: Harvard University Press, 1979.

Kant and the Experience of Freedom. Cambridge: Cambridge University Press, 1996.

Guyer, Paul, and Allen Wood. *Introduction to the Critique of Pure Reason*. Cambridge: Cambridge University Press, 1998.

Hall, Jonathan M. *Ethnic Identity in Greek Antiquity*. Cambridge: Cambridge University Press, 1997.

Hallam, Arthur Henry. "On Some of the Characteristics of Modern Poetry, and on the Lyrical Poems of Alfred Tennyson." In *The Poems of Arthur Henry Hallam, together with His Essay on the Lyrical Poems of Alfred Tennyson*, edited by Richard Le Gallienne, 87–139. London: E. Mathews and J. Lane, 1893.

Hansen, Miriam. *Cinema and Experience*. Berkeley: University of California Press, 2012.

Harris, Marvin. *The Rise of Anthropological Theory: A History of Theories of Culture.* Walnut Creek, CA: AltaMira Press, 2001.

Hart, Heinrich. "Die Neue Gemeinschaft." In *Das Reich der Erfüllung: Flugschriften zur Begründung einer neuen Weltanschauung*, edited by Heinrich Hart and Julius Hart, 8–13. Vol. 2. Leipzig: Eugen Diedrichs, 1901.

Hart, Julius. "Der Neue Mensch." In *Das Reich der Erfüllung: Flugschriften zur Begründung einer neuen Weltanschauung*, edited by Heinrich Hart and Julius Hart. Vol. 2. Leipzig: Eugen Diedrichs, 1901.

Hegeman, Susan. *Patterns for America: Modernism and the Concept of Culture.* Princeton, NJ: Princeton University Press, 1999.

Herder, Johann Gottfried. *Ideen zur Philosophie der Geschichte der Menschheit.* Frankfurt: Deutscher Klassiker Verlag, 1989.

Outlines of a Philosophy of the History of Man, translated by T. Churchill. New York: Bergman, 1966.

Viertes Kritisches Wäldchen. In *Johann Gottfried Herder Schriften zur Ästhetik und Literatur 1767–1781,* edited by Gunter E. Grimm, 247–442. Frankfurt: Deutscher Klassiker Verlag, 1993.

Herskovits, Melville. "Negro History: *Black Folk – Then and Now,* by W. E. B. Du Bois." *The New Republic* (August 16, 1939).

Hille, Peter. "Else Lasker-Schüler." In *Else Lasker-Schüler: Dichtungen und Dokumente,* edited by Ernst Ginsberg, 565. Munich: Kösel Verlag, 1951.

Hiller, Kurt. "Die Jüngst-Berliner." In *Die Berliner Moderne: 1885–1914,* edited by Jürgen Schutte and Peter Sprengel, 230–236. Stuttgart: Philipp Reclam Jun., 1987.

"Zur neuen Lyrik." In *Expressionismus: der Kampf um eine literarische Bewegung,* edited by Paul Raabe, 25–34. Zurich: Arche Verlag, 1987.

Hitler, Adolf. "Adolf Hitler zur Eröffnung der Ausstellung 'Entartete Kunst.'" In *Die Kunstpolitik des Nationalsozialismus,* edited by Hildegard Brenner, 203–204. Reinbek bei Hamburg: Rohwolt Taschenbuch Verlag, 1963.

Hoddis, Jakob van. "Weltende." In *Menschheitsdämmerung,* edited by Kurt Pinthus. Reinbek bei Hamburg: Rowohlt Taschenbuch Verlag, 1959.

Hoffmann, Dieter. "Totalität und totalitär: Gottfried Benn und die Expressionismusdebatte." In *Gottfried Benn (1886–1956): Studien zum Werk,* edited by Walter Delabar and Ursula Kocher, 37–50. Bielefeld: Aisthesis Verlag, 2007.

Hohendahl, Peter Uwe. "The Theory of the Novel and the Concept of Realism in Lukács and Adorno." In *Georg Lukács Reconsidered: Critical Essays in Politics, Philosophy and Aesthetics,* edited by Michael J. Thompson, 75–98. London: Continuum, 2011.

Homans, Jennifer. *Apollo's Angels: A History of Ballet.* New York: Random House, 2010.

Honneth, Axel. "Bemerkungen zum philosophischen Ansatz von Jacques Rancière." In *Anerkennung oder Unvernehmen?: Eine Debatte,* edited by Katia Genel and Jean-Philippe Deranty, 73–88. Frankfurt: Suhrkamp, 2021.

Howes, Marjorie Elizabeth. *Yeats's Nations: Gender, Class, and Irishness.* Cambridge: Cambridge University Press, 1996.

Hume, David. *An Enquiry Concerning Human Understanding.* Oxford: Clarendon Press, 2000.

Huneman, Phillipe. "Introduction." In *Understanding Purpose: Kant and the Philosophy of Biology,* edited by Philippe Huneman, 1–36. Rochester, NY: University of Rochester Press, 2007.

"Naturalising Purpose: From Comparative Anatomy to the 'Adventure of Reason.'" *Studies in History and Philosophy of Biological and Biomedical Sciences* 37 (2006): 649–674.

Hyde, Douglas. "The Necessity for De-Anglicising Ireland." In *The Revival of Irish Literature,* 115–161. London: T. Fisher Unwin, 1894.

Irwin, T. H. "Shaftesbury's Place in the History of Moral Realism." *Philosophical Studies* 170.4 (2015): 865–882.

Jahn, Friedrich Ludwig. *Deutsches Volksthum*. Lübeck: Niemann und Comp, 1810.

Jameson, Fredric. "Reflections in Conclusion." In Theodor Adorno, Walter Benjamin, Ernst Bloch, Bertolt Brecht and Georg Lukács, *Aesthetics and Politics*, 196–213. London: New Left Books, 1977.

Johns Hopkins Circular, July 1895, Vol. XIV, No. 120. https://jscholarship .library.jhu.edu/handle/1774.2/32953.

Jones, Susan. *Literature, Modernism, and Dance*. Oxford: Oxford University Press, 2013.

Kant, Immanuel. *"Anthropology Mrongovius."* In *Lectures on Anthropology*, edited by Allen W. Wood and Robert Louden, 335–509. Cambridge: Cambridge University Press, 2012.

Anthropology from a Pragmatic Point of View. In *Anthropology, History, and, Education*, edited by Robert B. Louden, 231–429. Cambridge: Cambridge University Press, 2007.

Blomberg Logic. In *Lectures on Logic*, edited and translated by J. Michael Young, 5–246. Cambridge: Cambridge University Press, 1992.

Critique of the Power of Judgment, edited by Paul Guyer, translated by Paul Guyer and Eric Matthews. Cambridge: Cambridge University Press, 2000.

"Determination of the Concept of a Human Race." In *Anthropology, History, and, Education*, edited by Robert B. Louden, 143–162. Cambridge: Cambridge University Press, 2007.

"Of the Different Races of Human Beings." In *Anthropology, History, and Education*, edited by Robert B. Louden, 82–97. Cambridge: Cambridge University Press, 2007.

Kants gesammelte Schriften. Königlich Preussischen Akademie der Wissenschaften Auflage. Berlin: G. Reimer, 1902 (vol. 1, 1910).

Kritik der Urteilskraft. Hamburg: Felix Meiner Verlag, 2009.

"Observations on the Feeling of the Beautiful and Sublime." In *Anthropology, History, and, Education*, edited by Robert B. Louden, 18–62. Cambridge: Cambridge University Press, 2007.

"On the Use of Teleological Principles in Philosophy." In *Anthropology, History, and Education*, edited by Robert B. Louden, 192–218. Cambridge: Cambridge University Press, 2007.

Kaplan, Sidney. "The Miscegenation Issue in the Election of 1864." In *Interracialism: Black-White Intermarriage in American History, Literature, and Law*, edited by Werner Sollors, 219–265. Oxford: Oxford University Press, 2000.

Kapraun, Carolina. "'O gieb in Giftempfängnis das Ich, dem ich vorbei': Das poetologische Konzept des 'Rausches' bei Gottfried Benn." In *Gottfried Benn (1886–1956): Studien zum Werk*, edited by Walter Delabar and Ursula Kocher, 63–84. Bielefeld: Aisthesis Verlag, 2007.

Kelly, John S. "The Fifth Bell: Race and Class in Yeats's Political Thought." In *Irish Writers and Politics*, edited by Okifumi Komesu and Masaru Sekine, 109–175. Savage, MD: Barnes & Noble Books, 1990.

Kermode, Frank. *Romantic Image*. London: Routledge and Paul, 1957.

Kersten, Kurt. "Strömungen der expressionistischen Periode." In *Die Expressionismusdebatte: Materialien zu einer marxistischen Realismuskonzeption*, edited by Hans-Jürgen Schmitt, 95–103. Frankfurt: Suhrkamp, 1973.

Kiberd, Declan. *Inventing Ireland: The Literature of the Modern Nation*. London: Jonathan Cape, 1995.

King, Lawrence J. "Walker, Alexander." In *Complete Dictionary of Scientific Biography*, 128–131. Vol. 14. Detroit: Charles Scribner's Sons, 2009.

Kinney, John. "Metaphor and Method: Georg Lukács's Debt to Organic Theory." *Journal of Aesthetics and Art Criticism* 39.2 (1980): 175–184.

Kisch, Egon Erwin. "Antwort auf Gerhart Pohls Brief." In *Benn – Wirkung wider Willen: Dokumente zur Wirkungsgeschichte Benns*, edited by Peter Uwe Hohendahl, 136–137. Frankfurt: Athenäum Verlag, 1971.

Klein, Lawrence E. *Shaftesbury and the Culture of Politeness: Moral Discourse and Cultural Politics in Early Eighteenth-Century England*. Cambridge: Cambridge University Press, 1994.

Kleingeld, Pauline. "Kant's Second Thoughts on Colonialism." In *Kant and Colonialism*, edited by Katrin Flikschuh and Lea Ypi, 43–67. Oxford: Oxford University Press, 2014.

"Kant's Second Thoughts on Race." *The Philosophical Quarterly* 57.229 (2007): 573–592.

Kuhn, Dorothea. "Kommentar zu 'Weitere Versuche.'" In *Sämtliche Werke. Briefe, Tagebücher und Gespräche. Vol. 24 Schriften zur Morphologie*, edited by Dorothea Kuhn. Frankfurt: Deutscher Klassiker Verlag, 1987.

Kurella, Alfred. "Nun ist dies Erbe zuende …" In *Die Expressionismusdebatte: Materialien zu einer marxistischen Realismuskonzeption*, edited by Hans-Jürgen Schmitt, 50–60. Frankfurt: Suhrkamp, 1973.

"Schußwort." In Die *Die Expressionismusdebatte: Materialien zu einer marxistischen Realismuskonzeption*, edited by Hans-Jürgen Schmitt, 231–257. Frankfurt: Suhrkamp, 1973.

Lacoue-Labarthe, Philippe. *Heidegger, Art and Politics: The Fiction of the Political*, translated by Chris Turner. Oxford: Basil Blackwell, 1990.

Lang, Andrew. *The Making of Religion*. Second edition. London: Longmans, Green, and Co. 1900.

Larrimore, Mark. "Antinomies of Race: Diversity and Destiny in Kant." *Patterns of Prejudice* 42.4–5 (2008): 341–363.

"Sublime Waste: Kant on the Destiny of the 'Races.'" *Canadian Journal of Philosophy* 29 (1999): 99–125.

Lasker-Schüler, Else. "Ein Brief an die Redaktion der *Neuen Zürcher Zeitung*." In *Else Lasker- Schüler: Gesammelte Werke in Drei Bände*, edited by Werner Kraft. Vol. 3. Munich: Kösel Verlag, 1961.

Briefe, edited by Ulrike Marquardt. Frankfurt: Jüdischer Verlag, 2003.

Briefe nach Norwegen. In *Prosa: 1903–1920*, edited by Ricarda Dick, 177–261. Frankfurt: Jüdischer Verlag, 1998.

Gedichte, edited by Karl Jürgen Skodzki with assistance from Norbert Oellers. Frankfurt: Jüdischer Verlag, 1996.

Die Nächte Tino von Bagdads. In *Prosa: 1903–1920*, edited by Ricarda Dick, 67–97. Frankfurt: Jüdischer Verlag, 1998.

Das Peter Hille-Buch. In *Prosa: 1903–1920*, edited by Ricarda Dick, 29–66. Frankfurt: Jüdischer Verlag, 1998.

Prosa: 1903–1920, edited by Ricarda Dick. Frankfurt: Jüdischer Verlag, 1998.

Prosa: 1921–1945, Nachgelassene Schriften, edited by Karl Jürgen Skrodzki and Itta Sheletzky. Frankfurt: Jüdischer Verlag, 2001.

Lawrence, Christopher. "The Power and the Glory: Humphry Davy and Romanticism." In *Romanticism and the Sciences*, edited by Andrew Cunningham and Nicholas Jardine, 213–227. Cambridge: Cambridge University Press, 1990.

Leeder, Karen. "'Nihilismus und Musik': Gottfried Benn (1886–1956) – The Unlikely Expressionist." *Oxford German Studies* 42.1 (2013): 23–37.

Lemire, Elise. *"Miscegenation": Making Race in America*. Philadelphia: University of Pennsylvania Press, 2002.

Lenoir, Timothy. "Kant, Blumenbach, and Vital Materialism in German Biology." *Isis* 71.1 (March 1980): 77–108.

The Strategy of Life: Teleology and Mechanism in Nineteenth-Century German Biology. Dordrecht: Reidel, 1982.

Leonhard, Rudolf. "Eine Epoche." In *Die Expressionismusdebatte: Materialien zu einer marxistischen Realismuskonzeption*, edited by Hans-Jürgen Schmitt, 172–179. Frankfurt: Suhrkamp, 1973.

Lethen, Helmut. *Der Sound der Väter: Gottfried Benn und seine Zeit*. Berlin: Rowohlt, 2006.

Levering-Lewis, David. *W. E. B. Du Bois: A Biography*. New York: Henry Holt and Company, 2009.

Levine, Caroline. *Forms: Whole, Rhythm, Hierarchy, Network*. Princeton, NJ: Princeton University Press, 2017.

Lewis, Oscar. "Wealth Differences in a Mexican Village." In *Anthropological Essays*, 269–276. New York: Random House, 1970.

Liddell, Henry Georg and Robert Scott, eds. *A Greek–English Lexicon*. Oxford: Clarendon Press, 1996.

Linné, Carl von. "The God-Given Order of Nature." In *Race and the Enlightenment: A Reader*, edited by Emmanuel Chukwudi Eze, 10–14. Cambridge: Blackwell, 1997.

Liska, Vivian. *When Kafka Says We: Uncommon Communities in German-Jewish Literature*. Bloomington: Indiana University Press, 2009.

Liss, Julia E. "Diasporic Identities: The Science and Politics of Race in the Work of Franz Boas and W. E. B. Du Bois, 1894–1919." *Cultural Anthropology* 13.2 (May 1998): 127–166.

Löchte, Anne. *Johann Gottfried Herder: Kulturtheorie und Humanitätsidee der Ideen, Humanitätsbriefe und Adrastea*. Würzburg: Königshausen and Neumann, 2005.

Loesberg, Jonathan. *A Return to Aesthetics: Autonomy, Indifference, and Postmodernism*. Stanford, CA: Stanford University Press, 2005.

Lott, Tommy L. "Du Bois on the Invention of Race." *The Philosophical Forum* 24.1–3 (1993): 166–187.

Louden, Robert. *Kant's Impure Ethics*. Oxford: Oxford University Press, 2000.

Lukács, Georg. *Blum-Thesen (Auszüge)*. In *Georg Lukács Werke, Band 2, Frühschriften*, 697–722. Neuwied und Berlin: Hermann Luchterhand Verlag, 1968.

"Es Geht um den Realismus." In *Die Expressionismusdebatte: Materialien zu einer marxistischen Realismuskonzeption*, edited by Hans-Jürgen Schmitt, 192–230. Frankfurt: Suhrkamp, 1973.

Geschichte und Klassenbewußtsein. Darmstadt und Neuwied: Hermann Luchterhand Verlag, 1977.

"'Größe und Verfall' des Expressionismus." In *Expressionismus: Der Kampf um eine literarische Bewegung*, edited by Paul Raabe, 254–273. Zurich: Arche Verlag, 1987.

"Klassenbewußtsein." In *Geschichte und Klassenbewußtsein*, 218–256. Darmstadt und Neuwied: Hermann Luchterhand Verlag, 1977.

Die Theorie des Romans. Neuwied und Berlin: Hermann Luchterhand, 1963.

Lunn, Eugene. *Marxism and Modernism: An Historical Study of Lukács, Brecht, Benjamin, and Adorno*. Berkeley: University of California Press, 1982.

Makkreel, Rudolf. *Imagination and Interpretation in Kant: The Hermeneutical Import of the Critique of Judgment*. Chicago: University of Chicago Press, 1990.

Manganaro, Marc. "Textual Play, Power, and Cultural Critique: An Orientation to Modernist Anthropology." In *Modernist Anthropology: From Fieldwork to Text*, edited by Marc Manganaro, 3–50. Princeton, NJ: Princeton University Press, 1990.

Manheim, Ron. *"Im Kampf um die Kunst": die Diskussion von 1911 über zeitgenössische Kunst in Deutschland*. Hamburg: Verlag der Buchhandlung Sautter + Lackmann, 1987.

Mann, Klaus. "Gottfried Benn: Die Geschichte einer Verirrung." In *Die Expressionismusdebatte: Materialien zu einer marxistischen Realismuskonzeption*, edited by Hans-Jürgen Schmitt, 39–49. Frankfurt: Suhrkamp, 1973.

Mao, Douglas, and Rebecca L. Walkowitz. "The New Modernist Studies." *PMLA* 123.3 (May 2008): 737–748.

Marc, Franz. "Untitled." In *Im Kampf um die Kunst*, 75–78. Munich: R. Piper & Co., 1911.

Marchand, Susan. *German Orientalism in the Age of Empire*. Cambridge: Cambridge University Press, 2009.

Markert, Lawrence W. *Arthur Symons: Critic of the Seven Arts*. Ann Arbor: UMI Research Press, 1988.

Martens, Gunter. *Vitalismus und Expressionismus*. Stuttgart: W. Kohlhammer, 1971.

Martin, Stewart. "Capitalist Life in Lukács." In *Georg Lukács: The Fundamental Dissonance of Existence; Aesthetics, Politics, Literature*, edited by Timothy Bewes and Timothy Hall, 138–156. London: Continuum, 2011.

Mattar, Sinéad Garrigan. *Primitivism, Science, and the Irish Revival*. Oxford: Clarendon Press, 2004.

Matz, Jesse. *Literary Impressionism and Modernist Aesthetics*. Cambridge: Cambridge University Press, 2001.

McBride, Patrizia C. "Berlin Dada and the Time of Revolution." *PMLA* 133.3 (May 2018): 491–507.

McGrath, Roberta. *Seeing Her Sex: Medical Archives and the Female Body*. Manchester: Manchester University Press, 2002.

Mead, Margaret. "Patterns of Culture: 1922–1934." In *An Anthropologist at Work*, edited by Margaret Mead, 201–212. Boston: Houghton Mifflin, 1959.

Mendelson, Edward. *Early Auden, Later Auden: A Critical Biography*. Princeton, NJ: Princeton University Press, 2017.

Meskimmon, Marsha. *We Weren't Modern Enough: Women Artists and the Limits of German Modernism*. Berkeley: University of California Press, 1999.

Mester, Terri A. *Movement and Modernism: Yeats, Eliot, Lawrence, Williams, and Early Twentieth-Century Dance*. Fayetteville: University of Arkansas Press, 1997.

Meyers Lexikon, s.v. "Asphaltkultur." Eighth edition. Leipzig: Bibliographisches Institut, 1936.

Mikkelsen, Jon M. "Translator's Introduction." In *Kant and the Concept of Race: Late Eighteenth-Century Writings*, edited by Jon M. Mikkelsen, 1–40. Albany: State University of New York Press, 2013.

Miller, Cristanne. *Cultures of Modernism: Marianne Moore, Mina Loy, & Else Lasker-Schüler; Gender and Literary Community in New York and Berlin*. Ann Arbor: University of Michigan Press, 2005.

"Reading the Politics of Else Lasker-Schüler's 1914 Hebrew Ballads." *Modernism/Modernity* 6.2 (April 1999): 135–159.

Mittenzwei, Werner. "Marxismus und Realismus: Die Brecht-Lukács Debatte." *Das Argument* 46 (1968): 12–43.

Moses, Michael Valdez. "Irish Modernist Imaginaries." In *The Cambridge Companion to Irish Modernism*, edited by Joe Cleary, 206–220. Cambridge: Cambridge University Press, 2014.

"The Rebirth of Tragedy: Yeats, Nietzsche, the Irish National Theatre, and the Anti-Modern Cult of Cuchulain." *Modernism/Modernity* 11.3 (2004): 561–579.

Moses, Wilson J. "W. E. B. Du Bois's 'The Conservation of Races' and Its Context: Idealism, Conservatism and Hero Worship." *Massachusetts Review* 34.2 (Summer 1993): 275–294.

Müller-Urban, Kristiane, and Eberhard Urban, eds. *Starke Frauen im Bergischen Land: 30 Porträts*. Düsseldorf: Droste Verlag, 2016.

Münchhausen, Börries von. "Die neue Dichtung." In *Expressionismus: Der Kampf um eine literarische Bewegung*, edited by Paul Raabe, 229–234. Zurich: Arche Verlag, 1987.

Neue Deutsche Biographie, s.v. "Alfred Kurella." Edited by die historische Kommission bei der Bayerischen Akademie der Wissenschaft. Berlin: Duncker & Humboldt, 1982.

Ngai, Sianne. *Our Aesthetic Categories: Zany, Cute, Interesting.* Cambridge, MA: Harvard University Press, 2012.

Nietzsche, Friedrich. *Der Antichrist.* In *Werke,* edited by Giorgio Colli and Mazzino Montinari. Berlin: Walter de Gruyter & Co., 1969.

Die Geburt der Tragödie oder Griechentum und Pessimismus. In *Werke in drei Bänden,* edited by Rolf Toman. Cologne: Könemann, 1994.

North, Michael. *The Political Aesthetic of Yeats, Eliot, and Pound.* Cambridge: Cambridge University Press, 1991.

Nye, Edward. *Mime, Music and Drama on the Eighteenth-Century Stage.* Cambridge: Cambridge University Press, 2011.

O'Shea, Edward. *A Descriptive Catalog of W. B. Yeats's Library.* London: Garland, 1985.

Ospovat, Dov. "Perfect Adaptation and Teleological Explanation: Approaches to the Problem of the History of Life in the Mid-nineteenth Century." *Studies in History of Biology* 2 (1978): 33–56.

Outlaw, Lucius. "'Conserve' Races?: In Defense of W. E. B. Du Bois." In *W. E. B. Du Bois: On Race and Culture,* edited by Bernard Bell, Emily Grosholz and James Steward, 15–37. New York: Routledge, 1996.

Paret, Peter. *Die Berliner Sezession: Moderne Kunst und ihre Feinde im Kaiserlichen Deutschland.* Berlin: Severin und Siedler, 1981.

The Berlin Secession: Modernism and Its Enemies in Imperial Germany. Cambridge, MA: Belknap Press of Harvard University Press, 1980.

German Encounters with Modernism, 1840–1945. Cambridge: Cambridge University Press, 2001.

Pater, Walter. "Conclusion." In *Studies in the History of the Renaissance,* edited by Matthew Beaumont. Oxford: Oxford University Press, 2010.

Marius the Epicurean: His Sensations and Ideas. London: Macmillan and Co., 1910.

Plato and Platonism. London: Macmillan and Co., 1910.

"The School of Giorgione." In *Studies in the History of the Renaissance,* edited by Matthew Beaumont. Oxford: Oxford University Press, 2010.

Pinthus, Kurt. "Jakob van Hoddis." In *Menschheitsdämmerung,* edited by Kurt Pinthus, 350–351. Reinbek bei Hamburg: Rowohlt Taschenbuch Verlag, 1959.

Plato, *Cratylus.* In *The Dialogues of Plato,* translated by B. Jowett, 41–106. Vol. 3. Oxford: The Clarendon Press, 1953.

Posnock, Ross. *Color and Culture: Black Writers and the Making of the Modern Intellectual.* Cambridge, MA: Harvard University Press, 1998.

Potts, Alex. *Flesh and the Ideal: Winckelmann and the Origins of Art History.* New Haven, CT: Yale University Press, 1994.

Preston, Carrie. J. *Learning to Kneel: Noh, Modernism, and Journeys in Teaching.* New York: Columbia University Press, 2016.

Raabe, Paul. *Der Ausgang des Expressionismus*. Biberach an der Riss: Wege und Gestalten, 1966.

ed. *Expressionismus: der Kampf um eine literarische Bewegung*. Zurich: Arche Verlag, 1987.

Rancière, Jacques. *La mésentente: politique et philosophie*. Paris: Galilée, 1995.

Raphael, D. Daiches. *The Moral Sense*. London: Oxford University Press, 1947.

Reed Jr., Adolph. *W. E. B. Du Bois and American Political Thought: Fabianism and the Color Line*. Oxford: Oxford University Press, 1997.

Rehbock, Philip F. *The Philosophical Naturalists: Themes in Early Nineteenth-Century British Biology*. Madison: University of Wisconsin Press, 1983.

Reynolds, Sir Joshua. "To the Idler." The Idler 82, November 10, 1759.

Richards, Evelleen. "The 'Moral Anatomy' of Robert Knox: The Interplay between Biological and Social Thought in Victorian Scientific Naturalism." *Journal of the History of Biology* 22.3 (Fall 1989): 373–436.

Richards, Robert J. *The Romantic Conception of Life: Science and Philosophy in the Age of Goethe*. Chicago: University of Chicago Press, 2002.

Riedel, Walter. *Der neue Mensch: Mythos und Wirklichkeit*. Bonn: H. Bouvier und Co., 1970.

Rigdon, Susan M. *The Culture Facade: Art, Science, and Politics in the Work of Oscar Lewis*. Urbana: University of Illinois Press, 1988.

Rölleke, Heinz ed. *Kinder- und Hausmärchen*. Stuttgart: Reclam, 1984.

Romain, M. le. "Entries in the *Encyclopédie* and the *Encyclopedia Brittanica*." In *Race and the Enlightenment: A Reader*, edited by Emmanuel Chukwudi Eze, 91–93. Cambridge: Blackwell, 1997.

Rose, Sam. "The Fear of Aesthetics in Art and Literary Theory." *New Literary History* 48.2 (Spring 2017): 223–244.

Rosenthal, Jesse. *Good Form: The Ethical Experience of the Victorian Novel*. Princeton, NJ: Princeton University Press, 2017.

Russell, E. S. *Form and Function: A Contribution to the History of Animal Morphology*. London: John Murray, 1916.

Ruston, Sharon. "Natural Enemies in Science." *Romanticism* 11.1 (January 2008): 70–83.

Said, Edward W. *Orientalism*. New York: Penguin, 2003.

"Yeats and Decolonization." In *Nationalism, Colonialism, and Literature*, edited by Terry Eagleton, Fredric Jameson and Edward W. Said, 69–95. Minneapolis: University of Minnesota Press, 1990.

Sander, Gabriele, and Andreas Solbach, eds. "Nachwort." In *Die drei Sprünge des Wang-lun*, 638–670. Düsseldorf: Walter Verlag, 2007.

Scarry, Elaine. *On Beauty and Being Just*. Princeton, NJ: Princeton University Press, 1999.

Schachter, Allison. *Diasporic Modernisms: Hebrew and Yiddish Literature in the Twentieth Century*. Oxford: Oxford University Press, 2012.

Schäfer, Armin. "The Physiology of Charisma: Alfred Döblin's Novel *The Three Leaps of Wang Lun*." *New German Critique* 38.3 (2011): 79–93.

Scherer, Wilhelm. *Geschichte der Deutschen Literatur*. Ninth edition. Berlin: Weidmannsche Buchhandlung, 1902.

Schiller, Dieter. *Die Expressionismus-Debatte 1937–1939: Aus dem redaktionellen Briefwechsel der Zeitschrift "Das Wort."* Berlin: Helle Panke, 2002.

Schiller, Friedrich. *On the Aesthetic Education of Man*, edited by Alexander Schmidt. London: Penguin Books, 2016.

Kallias or Concerning Beauty: Letters to Gottfried Körner. In *Classic and Romantic German Aesthetics*, edited by J. M. Bernstein, 145–183. Cambridge: Cambridge University Press, 2003.

Über die ästhetische Erziehung des Menschen in einer Reihe von Briefen. Munich: Carl Hanser Verlag, 1981.

Schmidt, Birgit. *Wenn die Partei das Volk entdeckt: Anna Seghers, Bodo Uhse, Ludwig Renn u.a; ein kritischer Beitrag zur Volksfrontideologie und ihrer Literatur*. Münster: Unrast, 2002.

Schmidt-Bergmann, Hansgeorg. "Zur Geschichte des italienischen Futurismus." In *Futurismus: Geschichte, Ästhetik, Dokumente*, edited by Hansgeorg Schmidt-Bergmann, 27–72. Hamburg: Rowohlt Verlag, 2009.

Schutte, Jürgen, and Peter Sprengel. "Einleitung." In *Die Berliner Moderne: 1885–1914*, edited by Jürgen Schutte and Peter Sprengel, 13–94. Stuttgart: Philipp Reclam Jun., 1987.

Serequeberhan, Tsenay. "The Critique of Eurocentrism and the Practice of African Philosophy." In *Postcolonial African Philosophy*, edited by Emmanuel Chukwudi Eze, 141–161. Cambridge: Blackwell, 1997.

Shaftesbury, "Sensus Communis." In *Anthony Ashley Cooper, Third Earl of Shaftesbury: Standard Edition: sämtliche Werke, ausgewählte Briefe und nachgelassene Schriften*, edited by Wolfram Benda, Wolfgang Lottes, Friedrich A. Uehlein and Erwin Wolff, 14–129. Stuttgart: frommann-holzboog, 1709.

[Anthony Ashley Cooper, Third Earl of Shaftesbury]. "Sensus communis, an essay on the freedom of wit and humour in a letter to a friend." In *Characteristics of Men, Manners, Opinions, Times*, edited by Lawrence E. Klein, 29–69. Cambridge: Cambridge University Press, 1999.

Shaw, Stephanie B. *W. E. B. Du Bois and The Souls of Black Folk*. Chapel Hill: University of North Carolina Press, 2013.

Sheils, Barry. "'Dark Cognition': W. B., J. G. Herder and the Imperfection of Tradition." *Irish Studies Review* 20.3 (August 2012): 299–321.

Sheppard, Richard. "Dada and Expressionism." In *Publications of the English Goethe Society*, edited by Frank M. Fowler, Brian A. Rowley and Ann C. Weaver. Leeds: W. S. Maney & Son Ltd., 1979.

Sherry, Vincent. *Modernism and the Reinvention of Decadence*. Cambridge: Cambridge University Press, 2015.

Shneyder, Vadim. "On the Hegelian Roots of Lukács's Theory of Realism." *Studies in Eastern European Thought* 65 (2013): 259–269.

Sikka, Sonia, *Herder on Humanity and Cultural Difference: Enlightened Relativism*. Cambridge: Cambridge University Press, 2011.

Skolnik, Jonathan. *Jewish Pasts, German Fictions: History, Memory, and Minority Culture in Germany, 1824–1955*. Stanford, CA: Stanford University Press, 2014.

Skrodzki, Karl Jürgen, and Norbert Oellers, eds. *Gedichte: Anmerkungen*. Frankfurt: Jüdischer Verlag, 1996.

Skrodzki, Karl Jürgen, and Itta Shedletzky. "Die kreisende Weltfabrik." In *Anmerkungen zur Prosa 1921–1945*, edited by Karl Jürgen Skrodzki and Itta Shedletzky, 35–38. Frankfurt: Jüdischer Verlag, 2001.

Sloan, Phillip R. "Kant and British Bioscience." In *Understanding Purpose: Kant and the Philosophy of Biology*, edited by Philippe Huneman, 149–170. Rochester, NY: University of Rochester Press, 2007.

"Whewell's Philosophy of Discovery and the Archetype of the Vertebrate Skeleton: The Role of German Philosophy of Science in Richard Owen's Biology." *Annals of Science*, 60.1 (2003): 39–61.

Smith, Justin. *Nature, Human Nature, and Human Difference: Race in Early Modern Philosophy*. Princeton, NJ: Princeton University Press, 2017.

Sokel, Walter. *Der literarische Expressionismus: der Expressionismus in der deutschen Literatur des zwanzigsten Jahrhunderts*. Munich: Albert Langen and Georg Müller, 1960.

"The Prose of German Expressionism." In *A Companion to the Literature of German Expressionism*, edited by Neil H. Donahue, 69–88. Rochester, NY: Camden House, 2005.

Spuler, Richard. *"Germanistik" in America: The Reception of German Classicism, 1870-1905*. Stuttgart: Akademischer Verlag, 1982.

Stocking, George W. "The Critique of Racial Formalism." In *Race, Culture, and Evolution: Essays in the History of Anthropology*, 161–194. Chicago: University of Chicago Press, 1968.

"Matthew Arnold, E. B. Taylor, and the Uses of Invention." In *Race, Culture, and Evolution: Essays in the History of Anthropology*, 69–90. Chicago: University of Chicago Press, 1968.

Race, Culture, and Evolution: Essays in the History of Anthropology. Chicago: University of Chicago Press, 1968.

Victorian Anthropology. New York: The Free Press, 1987.

Sundquist, Eric, ed. *The Oxford W. E. B. Du Bois Reader*. Oxford: Oxford University Press, 1996.

To Wake the Nations: Race in the Making of American Literature. Cambridge, MA: Harvard University Press, 1993.

Symons, Arthur. "The Decadent Movement in Literature." In *The Symbolist Movement in Literature*, edited by Matthew Creasy, 169–183. Manchester: Carcanet Press, 2014.

"Impressionistic Writing." In *Dramatis Personae*, 343–350. Indianapolis: The Bobbs- Merrill Company, 1923.

"To Rhoda." In *Studies in Seven Arts*. London: Martin Secker, 1924.

"The World as Ballet." In *Studies in Seven Arts*, 244–246. London: Martin Secker, 1924.

Taylor, Seth. *Left-Wing Nietzscheans: The Politics of German Expressionism*. Berlin: Walter de Gruyter, 1990.

Thatcher, D. S. *Nietzsche in England, 1890–1914: The Growth of a Reputation*. Toronto: University of Toronto Press, 1970.

Theunissen, Bert. "The Relevance of Cuvier's *Lois Zoologiques* for His Paleontological Work." *Annals of Science* 43 (1986).

Thompson, Mark Christian. "Aesthetic Hygiene: Marcus Garvey, W. E. B. Du Bois, and the Work of Art." In *A Companion to African American Literature*, edited by Gene Andrew Jarret, 243–253. Chichester: Wiley-Blackwell, 2013.

Tiedemann, Rolf, and Hermann Schweppenhäuser. "Anmerkungen der Herausgeber." In *Walter Benjamin: Gesammelte Schriften*, edited by Rolf Tiedemann and Hermann Schweppenhäuser, 523–726. Vol. VII.2. Frankfurt: Surhkamp Verlag, 1989.

Tucker, Irene. *The Moment of Racial Sight*. Chicago: University of Chicago Press, 2012.

Tylor, E. B. *Primitive Culture: Researches into the Development of Mythology, Philosophy, Religion, Art, and Custom*. Vol. 1. Cambridge: Cambridge University Press, 2010.

Venters, Scott. "'Would You Die for the Fatherland?': Disciplining the German Commemorative Body." *Theatre History Studies* 35 (2016): 41–51.

Vietta, Silvio and Hans-Georg Kemper. *Expressionismus*. Fifth edition. Munich: Wilhelf Fink Verlag, 1994.

Vinnen, Carl. "Quosque tandem." In *Ein Protest deutscher Künstler*, 2–16. Eugen Dietrichs: Jena, 1911.

Vondung, Klaus. *Völkisch-nationale und nationalsozialistische Literaturtheorie*. Munich: Paul List Verlag, 1973.

Walden, Herwarth. "Vulgär-Expressionismus." In *Die Expressionismusdebatte: Materialien zu einer marxistischen Realismuskonzeption*, edited by Hans-Jürgen Schmitt, 75–90. Frankfurt: Suhrkamp, 1973.

Walker, Alexander. "An Attempt to Systematize Anatomy, Physiology, and Pathology." *Annals of Philosophy* 6 (1815): 283–292.

Beauty: Illustrated Chiefly by an Analysis and Classification of Beauty in Woman. Second revised edition. London: Henry G. Bohn, 1846.

"Critique on the Antique Statues and Those of Michael Angelo; in Which Not Only the Defects of Their Attitudes, but Also the Errors Which They Present with Regard to the Particular Muscles Brought into Action Are Pointed Out." *Archives of Universal Science* (1809): 224–232.

Intermarriage: or How and Why Beauty, Health, and Intellect Result from Certain Marriages, and Deformity, Disease, and Insanity from Others. Birmingham: Edward Baker, 1897.

"Outlines of a Natural System of Science." In *The European Review, or, Mind and Its Productions, in Britain, France, Italy, &c*, edited by Alexander Walker, 76–86. Vol. 1 (June). Edinburgh: Walker & Greig, 1824.

"Plan of the Natural System." *Archives of Universal Science* 1 (January 1809): xxvii–xxxvii.

"Preliminary Discourse." *Archives of Universal Science* 1 (1809): i–xxxvii.

"Refutation of the Ideal System of Berkeley, Bishop of Cloyne."*Archives of Universal Science* 1 (January 1809): 1–30.

"Refutation of the Sceptical System of Hume." *Archives of Universal Science* 2 (1809): 29–76.

"Report on a Memoir of DRS Gall and Spurzheim, Relative to the Anatomy of the Brain. By M. M. Tenon, Portal, Sabatier, Pinel and Cuvier; With Critical Observations. By the Editor." *Archives of Universal Science* 3 (July 1809): 119–179.

Warren, Kenneth W. *What Was African American Literature?* Cambridge, MA: Harvard University Press, 2011.

Washington, Booker T. *Up from Slavery*. Oxford: Oxford University Press, 2009.

Watts, Eric King. *Hearing the Hurt: Rhetoric, Aesthetics, and Politics of the New Negro Movement*. Tuscaloosa: University of Alabama Press, 2012.

Weheliye, Alexander G. *Habeas Viscus: Racializing Assemblages, Biopolitics, and Black Feminist Theories of the Human*. Durham, NC: Duke University Press, 2014.

White, Brenda M. "Medical Police. Politics and Police: The Fate of John Robertson." *Medical History* 27 (1983): 407–422.

Wilderson, Frank B. *Afropessimism*. New York: Liveright, 2021.

Williams, Rhys W. "Prosaic Intensities: The Short Prose of German Expressionism." In *A Companion to the Literature of German Expressionism*, edited by Neil H. Donahue, 89–110. Rochester, NY: Camden House, 2005.

Willich, A. F. M. *Elements of the Critical Philosophy: Containing a Concise Account of Its Origin and Tendency; a View of all the Works Published by Its Founder, Professor Immanuel Kant; and a Glossary for the Explanation of Terms and Phrases*. London: T. N. Longman, 1798.

Winchester, James. "Nietzsche's Racial Profiling." In *Race and Racism in Modern Philosophy*, edited by Andrew Valls, 255–276. Ithaca, NY: Cornell University Press, 2005.

Winter, Marian Hannah. *The Pre-Romantic Ballet*. Brooklyn, NY: Dance Horizons, 1974.

Wood, Forrest. *Black Scare: The Racist Response to Emancipation and Reconstruction*. Berkeley: University of California Press, 1968.

Wordsworth, William. *The Major Works*. Oxford: Oxford University Press, 2008.

Wright, Barbara D. "Intimate Strangers: Women in German Expressionism." In *A Companion to the Literature of German Expressionism*, edited by Neil H. Donahue, 287–320. Rochester, NY: Camden House, 2005.

Yeats, W. B. "The Arrow: 20 October 1906 – The Season's Work." In *The Irish Dramatic Movement*, edited by Mary FitzGerald and Richard J. Finneran. New York: Scribner, 2003.

Autobiographies, edited by William H. O'Donnell and Douglas N. Archibald. New York: Scribner, 1999.

The Collected Poems of W. B. Yeats, edited by Richard J. Finneran. New York: Scribner, 1996.

The Death of Cuchulain. In *The Variorum Edition of the Plays of W. B. Yeats*, edited by Russel K. Alspach, 1051–1063. London: Macmillan, 1966.

Early Articles and Reviews: Uncollected Articles and Reviews Written between 1886 and 1900, edited by John P. Frayne and Madeleine Marchaterre. New York: Scribner, 2004.

Early Essays, edited by Richard J. Finneran and George Bornstein. New York: Scribner, 2007.

The Irish Dramatic Movement, edited by Mary FitzGerald and Richard J. Finneran. New York: Scribner, 2003.

Later Essays, edited by William H. O'Donnell. New York: Scribner, 1994.

Letters to the New Island, edited by George Bornstein and Hugh Witemeyer. New York: Macmillan, 1989.

Mythologies, edited by Warwick Gould and Deirdre Toomey. London: Palgrave Macmillan, 2005.

On the Boiler. In *Later Essays*, edited by William H. O'Donnell, 220–251. New York: Scribner, 1994.

Per Amica Silentia Lunae. In *Later Essays*, edited by William H. O'Donnell, 1–33. New York: Scribner, 1994.

Prefaces and Introduction, edited by William H. O'Donnell. New York: Macmillan, 2008.

"Samhain 1904 – First Principles." In *The Irish Dramatic Movement*, edited by Mary FitzGerald and Richard J. Finneran. New York: Scribner, 2003.

Uncollected Prose by W. B. Yeats. Collected by John P. Frayne. Volume 1: First Reviews and Articles, 1886–1896. New York: Columbia University Press, 1970.

Uncollected Prose by W. B. Yeats. Volume 2: Reviews, Articles and Other Miscellaneous Prose, 1897–1939, edited by John P. Frayne and Colton Johnson. New York: Columbia University Press, 1976.

"The Withering of the Boughs." In *The Variorum Edition of the Poems of W. B. Yeats*, edited by Peter Allt and Russell K. Alspach. New York: Macmillan, 1957.

Young, Virginia Heyer. *Ruth Benedict: Beyond Relativity, beyond Pattern*. Lincoln: University of Nebraska Press, 2005.

Zamir, Shamoon. *Dark Voices: W. E. B. Du Bois and American Thought, 1888–1903*. Chicago: University of Chicago Press, 1995.

Zammito, John. *The Genesis of Kant's Critique of Judgment*. Chicago: University of Chicago Press, 1992.

Kant, Herder, and the Birth of Anthropology. Chicago: University of Chicago Press, 2002.

Zuckert, Rachel. "Boring Beauty and Universal Morality: Kant on the Ideal of Beauty." *Inquiry: An Interdisciplinary Journal of Philosophy* 48.2 (2005): 107–130.

Kant on Beauty and Biology: An Interpretation of the Critique of Judgment. Cambridge: Cambridge University Press, 2007.

Zumwalt, Rosemary Lévy. *Franz Boas: The Emergence of the Anthropologist.* Lincoln: University of Nebraska Press, 2019.

Index

For EU product safety concerns, contact us at Calle de José Abascal, 56–1°,
28003 Madrid, Spain or eugpsr@cambridge.org.